LIBRARY OF NEW TESTAMENT STUDIES

421

formerly the Journal for the Study of the New Testament Supplement series

Editor

Mark Goodacre

THE SOCIAL SIGNIFICANCE OF RECONCILIATION IN PAUL'S THEOLOGY

Narrative Readings in Romans

Corneliu Constantineanu

t&t clark

Published by T&T Clark International
A Continuum imprint
The Tower Building, 11 York Road, London SE1 7NX
80 Maiden Lane, Suite 704, New York, NY 10038

www.continuumbooks.com

British Library Cataloguing-in-Publication Data
A catalogue record for this book is available from the British Library

ISBN: 978-0-567-58198-3 (hardback)

Typeset by Pindar NZ, Auckland, New Zealand
Printed in Great Britain by the MPG Books Group, Bodmin and King's Lynn

To my wife, *Ioana,*

and my daughters, *Anamaria* and *Carmen,*

who have graciously supported and encouraged me throughout the
years of my research. I have always been inspired and humbled by
their unconditional love, great understanding and an amazing patience
with my long hours of research and writing. To them this book is
dedicated with the assurance of my utmost gratitude and love.

CONTENTS

ACKNOWLEDGEMENTS

It is with a deep sense of gratitude that I acknowledge, first of all, the great privilege and grace that God has granted me to take this most wonderful journey of study and reflection. In a world in which millions of people cannot even read, and many more millions of gifted people do not have the chance for advanced study, I take the grace I have been given with all humility and responsibility.

As is always the case, everything we accomplish both in our personal and academic life is due to many people who teach, mentor, encourage, support, guide and help us in our endeavours. It is impossible to mention everyone who deserves to be mentioned here, but I would still want to acknowledge at least several special people who made this project become reality.

The greatest appreciation goes to Langham Partnership International, especially to the leadership team – John R. W. Stott, Christopher Wright, Paul Berg and Howard Peskett – for the scholarship they have given me and without which none of this would have been possible. Not only was Langham totally dedicated in its financial commitment but it has also created a wonderful network of support and fellowship among fellow Langham scholars and, most significantly, has inspired a vision for theological education that shaped a new generation of what I call *believing and practising scholars*. Uncle John (Stott) deserves special mention not only as the founder of Langham, but also as the greatest example of a life radically renewed by the gospel and as a living illustration of the reality of God's grace and of the power of the gospel of reconciliation and love. It is also here that I would like to thank the Overseas Council International (OCI) for supporting me financially through the first period of research. Similarly, I am grateful to the Free University of Amsterdam for the 'Bridging Gap' scholarship.

I then wish to express my gratitude to my *Doktorvater*, Professor Haddon Willmer, professor emeritus of Leeds University. He has provided me with invaluable guidance, constant encouragement, and an example of academic excellence. He has opened my eyes to the social and political dimensions of the gospel and has continuously challenged and encouraged me towards 'hard thinking'. I also thank Dr Rollin Grams, whose insights as a New Testament scholar have significantly shaped my thinking and writing.

Special thanks go to the Evandeoski Teoloski Fakultet (ETF), Osijek, Croatia, for their support and encouragement over the years. Particularly, I would like to thank Professor Peter Kuzmič, the Rector of ETF, for being the most persistent positive influence in my life. He has taught me, among many other things, to do nothing less than Barth did: to hold the Bible in one hand and the newspaper in the other! And it is precisely because he taught me not only in the classroom but by his own life and example, that I have captured a holistic vision of the Kingdom of God, a passion for God, His world, and His people. And it was his life that has constantly challenged me to devote my own life to profound study, prayer, and authentic Christian living: and, of course, to start walking the long and thorny, but rewarding and joyful, journey of becoming a 'task theologian'. Thanks also go to all staff members and several generations of my assistants in the Graduate Department, Daniel Darko, Yordan Zhekov, Vasile Marchis, Daniel Copil and Marino Mojtić for filling in as necessary when my research took me away from my duties in the school.

Three other people deserve special thanks as they have significantly shaped my thinking on the subject of reconciliation: Myron Augsburger, Robert Schreiter and, especially, Miroslav Volf whom I have had the great privilege to have as a professor, mentor and friend for more than 15 years now. No one has challenged me more profoundly in my theology and Christian praxis than Volf has, and I will never forget his most serious admonition for a student of theology: 'If you do not do theology out of devotion to Jesus, pack your things and go home!'

The community of the Oxford Centre for Mission Studies – Vinay Samuel, Chris Sugden, Bernard Far, Dave Adams, Ben Knighton, Hilary Guest, Carol Seward, Blanche Marslin, and fellow research students – has provided an environment of academic excellence, spiritual nourishment and warm friendship during the long months of intensive research that I spent in Oxford away from my family.

I would like to thank members of my family and friends who helped me financially at the beginning of the project. These are my brother, Ion Constantineanu, and my dear friends Emil and Lidia Bogdan, Mihaela and Gabriela Creinicean, Gelu and Rodica Anheliuc. And those who sustained me morally and spiritually – my entire extended family; Susan Sutter, my friend and faithful prayer partner; and Sue Dryer who has greatly helped me with proofreading and indexing the book.

My 'Oxford family' has made my research visits in Oxford a great delight and to them I am very grateful: Carl and Betsy Armerding, Marcel and Mirela Macelaru, Cristi and Oana Romocea, Razvan and Madalina Novacovski, and the Mansha brothers. Daniel and Mirela Martin I thank for their help, great friendship and genuine love. I will never forget the wonderful weekend 'retreats to London' and especially the food I brought with me back to Oxford!

I would like to thank the current editors of the Library of New Testament Studies of T&T Clark/Continuum for considering the book for publication and for all their editorial help.

Finally and unquestionably I owe a great debt of gratitude to Ioana, my wife, and to my daughters, Anamaria and Carmen, for their gracious understanding, amazing love and noble efforts to help me in every single way through all these years. To them this work is dedicated with the assurance of my utmost gratitude and love.

ABBREVIATIONS

ABD	*The Anchor Bible Dictionary*
Ant.	*Antiquities of the Jews*
BAGD	*W. Bauer, W. F. Arndt, F. W. Gingrich and F. W. Danker, Greek-English Lexicon of the New Testament*
BS	*Biblioteca Sacra*
BTB	*Biblical Theology Bulletin*
CBQ	*Catholic Biblical Quarterly*
CR	*Currents in Research: Biblical Studies*
CTM	*Concordia Theological Monthly*
CUP	Cambridge University Press
DBI	*Dictionary of Biblical Imagery*
DNTB	*Dictionary of New Testament Background*
DPL	*Dictionary of Paul and His Letters*
EC	Evangelical churches
ERT	*Evangelical Review of Theology*
IVP	InterVarsity Press
JBL	*Journal of Biblical Literature*
JES	*Journal of Ecumenical Studies*
JETS	*Journal of the Evangelical Theological Society*
JosAs	*Joseph and Aseneth*
JSNT	*Journal for the Study of the New Testament*
JSNTS	*Journal for the Study of the New Testament Supplement Series*
JSOT	*Journal for the Study of the Old Testament*
JSOTS	*Journal for the Study of the Old Testament Supplement Series*
JTSA	*Journal of Theology for Southern Africa*
LNTS	Library of New Testament Studies
MT	*Modern Theology*
NICNT	*New International Commentary on the New Testament*
NIDNTT	*The New International Dictionary of New Testament Theology*
NIDOTTE	*New International Dictionary of Old Testament Theology and Exegesis*
NIV	New International Version
NJB	*New Jerusalem Bible*
NovT	*Novum Testamentum*
NRV	*New Revised Version*

NT	New Testament
NTPG	*New Testament and the People of God*
NTS	*New Testament Studies*
OCI	Overseas Council International
OT	Old Testament
OUP	Oxford University Press
RE	*Review and Expositor*
ROC	Romanian Orthodox Church
RSS	*Religion, State & Society*
RSV	Revised Standard Version
SBL	Society of Biblical Literature
SBLDS	Society of Biblical Literature Dissertation Series
SNTSMS	Society for New Testament Studies Monograph Series
SPCK	Society for Promoting Christian Knowledge
TB	*Tyndale Bulletin*
TDNT	*Theological Dictionary of the New Testament*
TS	*Theological Studies*
Vit. Mos.	*De Vita Mosis*
VT	*Vetus Testamentum*
W&W	*Word & World*
WBC	*Word Biblical Commentary*
WMANT	Wissenschaftliche Monographien zum AT & NT
WUNT	Wissenschaftliche Untersuchungen zum Neuen Testament
ZNW	*Zeitschrift für Neutestamentliche Wissenschaft*

PREFACE

This book is a revised version of a doctoral thesis submitted to the Oxford Centre for Mission Studies and the University of Leeds, UK, in 2006. The starting point of this work is the observation that traditional exegetical scholarship has treated Paul's presentation of reconciliation as referring to reconciliation between people and God, and has primarily focused its attention on key καταλλάσσω/καταλλαγή passages in the Pauline corpus (Rom. 5.10–11; 2 Cor. 5.14–21; Col. 1.20–21; Eph. 2.11–22). The present study challenges this view and argues that Paul has a more complex understanding of the concept and uses a rich symbolism to describe reconciliation as a multifaceted reality that encompasses reconciliation with God and reconciliation between human beings, forming together an inseparable reality. The discussion is placed within Paul's overall religious, social and political contexts, showing that an analysis of the social dimension of reconciliation in his thought is both plausible and necessary. I argue that the social meaning of reconciliation is to be understood within Paul's comprehensive vision of reconciliation: a vision grounded in the story of Christ and Paul's own reconciliation experience, substantiated by the Isaianic vision of cosmic peace, and given form and expression in a rich symbolism of reconciliation.

Having established this framework of reference, the study offers an analysis of two major sections of Romans, respectively Chapters 5–8 and Chapters 12–15, using primarily insights from a narrative reading of Paul. A special emphasis is placed on Paul's use of the story of Jesus Christ for community formation, for the shaping of identity, values and practices of the community. In Romans 5–8 I find that Paul shows the inseparability of the horizontal and the vertical dimensions of reconciliation. By describing the complex dynamic of the incorporation of the believer 'in Christ', through baptism, Paul draws his readers into the same story of Christ, thus reminding them that they are an integral part of, and active participants in, the ongoing story of God's reconciling the world through Christ. In this way, God's reconciling initiative, shown in the very act of Christ's death on the cross, is not only the pronouncement of God's reconciling the world, but also the ground and model for reconciliation among people. Similarly, in Romans 12–15 I find that Paul expresses the social dimension of reconciliation in various ways: as genuine love for one another and for enemies; as welcoming the weak and powerless; as affirming the other; as blessing one's persecutors; as overcoming evil with good and living at peace with all. These, I argue, are practices of reconciliation which are anchored in, and presuppose, the story of Christ as both the ground and paradigm for a reconciling way of life. Thus, by placing these practices within the larger horizon of God's reconciliation of the world in Christ, Paul provides an unshakable foundation for both the possibility and the actuality of social reconciliation. So then, Paul's ultimate vision of the reconciliation of all things in Christ gives assurance and hope, and an irresistible impetus to the believer's ministry of reconciliation in all its forms and manifestations.

I conclude with several suggestions for how the churches in Romania can build on a Pauline understanding of reconciliation as presented in this research. It is suggested that communities of believers could make a contribution to the public arena by offering and maintaining a sense of fundamental values for human life in the world; by discerning, unmasking and resisting any form of totalitarianism and absolutism; and by offering a framework of hope, and a vision of life, that will enable people not only to cope with 'otherness' and 'difference', but also to promote a culture of peace and justice, of freedom and love, of forgiveness and reconciliation, i.e., a culture of life.

Timisoara, October 2009
Corneliu Constantineanu

1

INTRODUCTION

1.1 *The subject matter: setting out the problem*

There are several major factors which justify a study on the social significance of reconciliation. First, the tragic realities of the recent years in the Balkans in a context of worldwide increasing tendencies towards radical nationalism, escalating racial, ethnic and religious conflicts, as well as an amplification of various forms of intolerance and exclusion, are all pointing to an immediate need for reconciliation. More specifically, the post-communist religious, political, social, and economic situation of Romania has created a specific social unrest manifested particularly in a tense relationship between different religious groups, and in a slow process of reciprocal 'estrangement' between different ethnic groups, especially between the Hungarian minority and the Romanians in Transylvania. In such circumstances the churches need to consider more seriously and without delay their task and possibilities for a real contribution to a ministry of reconciliation. This gives us, in short, the *urgency* of reconciliation.

Second, such a study seems necessary also because of the *primacy* of reconciliation in Christian theology and the biblical tradition. It is a truism to affirm that throughout the history of Christian thinking, 'reconciliation' has been regarded as fundamental for Christian faith and theology, a central theological category expressing the very heart of the gospel. Probably no one illustrates this fact better than Karl Barth, whose comprehensive doctrine of reconciliation is indeed 'unsurpassed in the history of Protestant theology and perhaps in the entire history of the Church universal'.[1] Barth brings together Christology, soteriology, anthropology, and ecclesiology under an all-encompassing analysis of 'The Doctrine of Reconciliation', thus placing 'reconciliation' at the very centre of his *Church Dogmatics*, precisely because reconciliation represents the 'centre of Christian knowledge' and 'to fail here is to fail everywhere, while to be on the right track here makes it impossible to be completely mistaken in the whole'.[2] Among the New Testament (NT) writers Paul is the one who makes extensive

---

1. David L. Müller, *Foundations of Karl Barth's Doctrine of Reconciliation: Jesus Christ Crucified and Risen* (Mampeter: Mellen, 1990), p. 251.
2. Karl Barth, *Church Dogmatics* IV.1 (Edinburgh: T&T Clark, 1956), p. ix.

use of the concept as a key aspect of his proclamation.[3] His insistence has resulted in an abundance of literature on reconciliation from the pens of biblical scholars.[4]

Given the urgency of reconciliation on the one hand, and its importance for Christian theology and faith on the other hand, one would think that the churches would have reflected on the social implications of reconciliation for their concrete historical circumstances. This is, however, not the case. It is with sadness that we note the failure of the various Christian communities, in many different instances, to enact reconciliation in their context. Not only have they failed to act as agents of peace as they watched helplessly from a distance the tragedies taking place around them, but at times they have found themselves participating actively in the conflict, even intensifying it! In this regard, Baum remarks that even though '*the Christian gospel summons the church to exercise the ministry of reconciliation in situations defined by strife and hostility . . . churches have rarely exercised the ministry of reconciliation*'; even where present, such ministry is still '*a pioneering activity*'.[5] This state of affairs constrains us to reflect seriously on the inability of Christian communities to incarnate the message of reconciliation as well as to look for adequate resources that will enable them in their ministry of reconciliation.

The observations above bring us to the third reason for undertaking such a project, namely the absence of reflection on the *social meaning of reconciliation*. Exploring the theological literature on reconciliation, Miroslav Volf discovers 'a deeply disturbing absence of sustained attempts to relate the core beliefs about reconciliation to the shape of churches' social responsibility'.[6] He also draws attention to the misconceptions regarding the 'ministry of reconciliation', and how the social agenda of the church has been isolated from the message of reconciliation. On the one hand, the doctrine of reconciliation is reduced to the reconciliation of the soul with God, and so it 'has a theological and personal meaning, but no wider social meaning'. On the other hand, there are those who criticise such withdrawal from the society and take up the notion of 'liberation', the pursuit of freedom and justice, 'as the only appropriate response to social problems'.[7] These two extremes have contributed substantially

---

3.   Ralph Martin went so far as to argue that 'reconciliation' represents the centre or the organizing principle of Paul's entire theology. (R. Martin, *Reconciliation: A Study of Paul's Theology* (rev. edn; Grand Rapids: Zondervan, 1989).) There is a wide spectrum of publications on the subject and we will analyse this in the next chapter.

4.   The next chapter, a review of the related literature, will illustrate this aspect.

5.   Gregory Baum and Harold Wells (eds.), *The Reconciliation of Peoples: Challenges to the Churches* (Geneva: WCC Publications, 1997), pp. 184–92 (italics in the original).

6.   'The Social Meaning of Reconciliation', in *Transformation* 16(1) (1999), pp. 7–12 (8) (italics added).

7.   Ibid., p. 9. Among contemporary theologians, Miroslav Volf is one who has written extensively on, and probably made the most significant contribution to, the topic of reconciliation. Not only does Volf address the question of social meaning of reconciliation from various angles, but he also offers strong, biblical grounds for his theology. Even though the nature of the present research does not require extensive review of his writings, at significant points in the study I will interact with his work. His major works in this area include: *The End of Memory: Remembering Rightly in a Violent World* (Grand Rapids:

to the inefficiency of churches in situations of conflict. Furthermore, as we shall see in detail in the next chapter, an overview of Pauline exegetical scholarship on reconciliation reveals a similar situation; i.e., an absence of reflection on the social significance of reconciliation in that body of literature. Traditional scholarship has treated Paul's presentation of reconciliation as referring to reconciliation between people and God and has primarily focused its attention on key καταλλάσσω/καταλλαγή ('reconcile'/'reconciliation') passages in the Pauline corpus.

All these factors have contributed to making evident the necessity for a study in which the social meaning of reconciliation in Paul's theology is *explored* and *explicated*.

1.2 *The scope and nature of the inquiry*

The present study is an inquiry into the social significance of reconciliation in Paul's theology, an attempt to explore and explicate the relationship between theology (in this case, the doctrine of reconciliation) and practice. We will undertake a study of Paul's concept of reconciliation as he presents it in his letters in response to various historical, social, cultural, religious and theological factors, by asking a number of essential questions such as: Is there a social dimension of reconciliation in Paul? Is reconciliation in Paul limited to a particular word or is it given expression in a variety of symbols and metaphors? What is the christological foundation of reconciliation? How does Paul bring together Jews and Gentiles, of different origin, background, and identity, to live in peace and unity with one another and transcend the boundaries of their differences by forming a single, united community? More significantly, is Paul presenting God's reconciliation of the world through Christ's death and resurrection as the ground and model for reconciliation among people? These and similar questions will guide us in the present work.

One more note on the purpose of this study is in order here. Even though the primary concern of this book is with the social dimension of reconciliation in Paul's theology, its overall purpose includes an interpretation of Paul's understanding of God's reconciliation of the world in Christ in such a way as to be both exegetically sound and relevant to the social and political needs for reconciliation in concrete,

Eerdmans, 2006); *Free of Charge: Giving and Forgiving in a Culture Stripped of Grace* (Grand Rapids: Zondervan, 2005); 'Forgiveness, Reconciliation, and Justice: A Theological Contribution to a More Peaceful Social Environment', *Millennium: Journal of International Studies* 29(3) (2000), pp. 861–77; 'The Final Reconciliation: Reflections on a Social Dimension of the Eschatological Transition', *Modern Theology* 16(1) (2000a), pp. 91–113; 'Love Your Heavenly Enemy: How are We Going to Live Eternally with Those We Can't Stand Now?' *Christianity Today* (23 October 2000b); 'The Trinity is our Social Program: The Doctrine of the Trinity and the Shape of Social Engagement', *Modern Theology* 14(3) (1998b); 'When Gospel and Culture Intersect: Notes on the Nature of Christian Difference', *Evangelical Review of Theology* 22(3) (1998), pp. 196–207; 'A Theology of Embrace in an Age of Exclusion', *The 1997 Washington Forum* (World Vision, 1997); *Exclusion and Embrace. A Theological Exploration of Identity, Otherness and Reconciliation* (Nashville, TN: Abingdon, 1996).

historical contexts. I believe that a new understanding and explication of the social meaning of reconciliation in Paul will represent an important resource for churches in their efforts to find a solid biblical basis and model for their social engagement and responsibility in the world and ultimately to enable churches in Romania and elsewhere to act as reconciling agents in carrying out the ministry of reconciliation. The next section on methodological considerations will place all the above questions in the context of recent developments in Pauline scholarship and point out the concrete steps we will follow for the present inquiry.

1.3 *Methodological considerations*

When the author of 2 Peter wrote in his epistle that 'There are some things in Paul's letters hard to understand . . .' (2 Pet. 3.16) he might not have had any idea that the statement he made then would still be true twenty centuries on! Indeed, throughout the history of biblical scholarship, Pauline students have struggled again and again to uncover the complex architecture of Paul's theology. What are the most important themes of Paul's theology? Is there a centre to his thought? What are the crucial factors that influenced his theology? How are we to understand and interpret Paul in fresh ways? What is the significance of his theology for the life of the church in the world today? These, and similar questions, have been asked by those who tirelessly labour in the field of Pauline studies in their search for new and more adequate answers.

1.3.1 *(Re)constructing Paul's theology*
Important and relevant insights for the present research come into play as we consider some of the recent developments in biblical studies in general and in Pauline studies in particular, which contribute to a growing awareness of, and appreciation for, the social dimensions of Paul's gospel.

The quest for the centre of Paul's theology
In the last century or so, from Albert Schweitzer's 'mystical union with Christ', to J. Christiaan Beker's 'triumph of God', Paul's thought has been approached from a systematic perspective, and has been interpreted in light of a consistent centre and structured around major doctrinal categories. 'Justification by faith' was by far the favourite doctrine around which Paul's thought was organized. But there have been some other viable options presented, such as 'in Christ', 'God', 'gospel', 'mission', 'reconciliation', etc. Admittedly, systematising Paul's theology in this way has some merit in as much as it offers a simple and clear structure to some of the most common topics found in his writings. Yet, the quest for *the centre* of Paul's theology has proven problematic for different reasons,[8] and has given way to other approaches, which take better into consideration the dynamic and complex nature of Paul's theologising.

---

8.   Indeed, as the members of the Pauline Theology Group of the SBL note, it became evident that

The new perspective on Paul

During the several centuries of interpretation that concentrated on 'justification by faith' as the hermeneutical key to Paul's thought, an individualistic reading of Paul was implicitly encouraged. Nevertheless, with the 'new perspective on Paul', initiated by E. P. Sanders in the 1970s, a new dimension of Paul's gospel came into focus as a fresh understanding of the Judaism of Paul's days became clear. Thus, it was argued that Paul's main interest was not necessarily, or ultimately, with the salvation of individuals 'by faith' as opposed to salvation by observing 'the law'. Rather, Paul's main concern was to defend the right and the privilege of the Gentiles to become members of God's people, solely on the basis of faith in Christ, without other pre-requisites, such as becoming observers of Jewish law and traditions. It was thus the relationship between Jews and Gentiles in his churches and their life together as one people of God that Paul had to struggle with, both at a theological and at a practical/ethical level. This is, of course, a simplistic way of summing up the new perspective on Paul, but it does illustrate the shift in emphasis from an individualistic to a more relational, social reading of Paul. Conversely, reconsidering Paul's theology in light of this new understanding also became necessary.[9]

Paul's theologising

An important issue being discussed in recent times by the students of Paul is the actual locus of 'theology' within the letters: where exactly is theology located, and how can it be retrieved from Paul's letters? Is the theology of a letter in its *argument*, in the *tension* between the letter's argument and the position of the congregation to which it was sent, or in the theological *event* evoked by the letter? In an excellent article dealing with these questions, Jouette Bassler argues that Paul's theology is to be understood not as something static, as a synthesis of theological propositions and presuppositions, but rather as a complex and dynamic activity.[10] Thus, when studying Paul we ought to ask how and to what extent has Paul *transformed, redefined*, and *reshaped* his beliefs, and *why* has he done so, while at the same time paying considerable attention to the ever-changing situations and contexts of the churches to which he wrote.[11] It follows then that Pauline theology should be construed as 'a more

'the various presentations of Paul's theology tended to reflect the theological perspectives of Paul's interpreters more clearly than the theological emphases of the apostle himself'. (Jouette M. Bassler (ed.), *Pauline Theology Volume I: Thessalonians, Philippians, Galatians, Philemon* (Minneapolis: Fortress, 1991), p. ix.)

9.   James Dunn remarks that, in the light of the new perspective on Paul, 'A fresh attempt at a full restatement of Paul's theology is made all the more necessary . . . not to mention all the considerable consequences which were bound to follow for our contemporary understanding of his theology.' (J. Dunn, *The Theology of Paul the Apostle* (Grand Rapids: Eerdmans, 1998), p. 5.)

10.   Jouette M. Bassler, 'Paul's Theology: Whence and Whither?' in David M. Hay (ed.) *Pauline Theology Volume II: 1 & 2 Corinthians* (Minneapolis: Fortress, 1993).

11.   The SBL symposium on Pauline theology published in the first volume of *Pauline Theology* series also raises similar questions. (Bassler (ed.) *Pauline Theology Volume I.*)

complex series of activities, *all of which contribute* to Paul's theology and none of which in isolation *is* Paul's theology'.[12] Bassler offers a working definition of Paul's theology as both 'his critical appropriation and application of the Christian witness', thus taking into consideration 'not only Paul's thought world, his thoughts, and his targeted communication of them, but also the process of movement from one to the other'. She offers the following model:

> The *raw material of Paul's theology* (the kerygmatic story, scripture, traditions, etc.) passed through *the lens of Paul's experience* (his common Christian experience as well as his unique experience as one 'set apart by God for the gospel') and generated a *coherent (and characteristic) set of convictions*. These convictions, then, were refracted through a prism, Paul's *perception of the situations that obtained in various communities*, where they were resolved into specific *words on target for those communities*.[13]

The benefits of such a model are threefold: it helps locate the various aspects that constitute Paul's theology, it views theology as a complex and dynamic activity, and it is sensitive to the different situations each epistle addresses. By paying careful attention to these elements, one can avoid the temptation of artificially imposing a system on Paul's theology.

Seeing Paul's thought from this perspective renders the older quest for *the centre* of his theology obsolete, its place taken by the more complex question: How did Paul theologise, how did he argue theologically? In other words, it is no longer sufficient to uncover Paul's doctrines, beliefs, or even the narrative behind his argumentations, but it is necessary to also explore what were the resources Paul used, what exactly he did with them, what particular influences shaped Paul's argumentation, and what he wanted to accomplish through them.

Intertextuality: Paul and the Old Testament

Probably the most important aspect of Paul's preaching and theologising is the fact that the gospel he proclaimed was not an innovation of his own. On the contrary, throughout his letters Paul states in various ways that his *gospel*, the subject matter of his preaching – the son of God, Jesus Christ, the Messiah, the Lord – was promised by the God of Israel as recorded in the OT. In explicating his understanding of the gospel, as well as its implications for the everyday life of Christians in their particular contexts, the OT was foundational for Paul's preaching and ministry. Indeed, what God was and is still doing through his son, Jesus Christ, is nothing else than a culmination of God's deeds done in the past and promised to his people. To understand what God is doing now, and will be doing in the future, is to understand what he has begun to do already, and this was recorded in the sacred Scriptures.

---

12. Bassler, 'Paul's Theology', p. 11.
13. Ibid., (italics in original).

Biblical scholars have highlighted the crucial role of the OT in the writings of the NT.[14] The language of the OT, the great stories of the people of God, and the mighty deeds of the God of Israel greatly influenced and shaped Paul's mind and thinking: they represent the reservoir from which Paul drew in his reflections and formulations of his theology, the symbolic universe that determined his understanding of reality and of God's dealing with the world. That is why the field of Pauline studies has developed significantly through the growing interest in the complex phenomenon of *intertextuality* – the dynamics of the presence/influence of an older literary fragment into/upon a later text. In intertextuality the later authors are seen not simply as rigidly transposing an older fragment into the new text but rather as dynamic *interpreters* of those texts. In this regard, Hays argues persuasively that a study of intertextuality in Paul 'is both possible and fruitful because Paul repeatedly situates his discourse within the symbolic field created by a single great textual precursor: Israel's Scripture'.[15] The OT not only shaped Paul's life fundamentally but it was a determinant factor for his theologising, for the way in which he expressed his faith. Of course, the task of identifying, testing, and interpreting Paul's concrete allusions to, or echoes[16] of, particular OT texts is not necessarily an easy or simple undertaking. However, although the task has inevitably a subjective character and requires a great deal of sensitivity and imagination, there are also rules which govern such endeavours.[17]

In a recent study Watson makes a significant contribution to the understanding of Paul as an interpreter of the OT.[18] From this perspective, Paul's theology is not simply 'illustrated' with texts from the OT. Rather the Scripture of Israel forms substantially Paul's thinking and thus represents the very core out of which Paul's theology grows and is developed. Watson argues that there is a three-way conversation to observe: the text, the interpretation of the text in Jewish literature, and Paul's interpretation of the text in conversation, as it were, with Jewish literature. The point is that there is a theological dialogue already going on when Paul jumps into the discussions, and that this dialogue is thoroughly text-based. So, what we need to do is to investigate not

---

14. C. H. Dodd argues that the [Israel's] Scripture had a profound influence upon the NT writers, that it functioned as a 'substructure' to their thinking. (C. H. Dodd, *According to the Scriptures: The Substructure of NT Theology* (London: Fontana, 1965)), p. 15.

15. Richard Hays, *Echoes of Scriptures in the Letters of Paul* (New Haven: Yale University Press, 1989), p. 15.

16. Given the difficulty of a systematic differentiation between these categories, Richard Hays uses the terms flexibly. However, as a general rule '*allusion* is used of obvious intertextual references, *echo* of subtler ones'. (Hays, *Echoes*, p. 29.)

17. Richard Hays proposes seven criteria 'for testing claims about the presence and meaning of scriptural echoes in Paul' (ibid., pp. 29–32): availability, volume, recurrence, thematic coherence, historical plausibility, history of interpretation, and satisfaction.

18. Francis Watson, *Paul and the Hermeneutics of Faith* (London: T&T Clark International, 2004). Also here we should include Richard Hays' most recent book *The Conversion of the Imagination: Paul as Interpreter of Israel's Scripture* (Grand Rapids: Eerdmans, 2005) in which the author shows not only that Paul was an interpreter of Israel's Scripture but also how his reading of that Scripture reshaped the theological vision and the life of his churches.

just Paul's theological statements but Paul's theological reading of the OT as well as his 'answers' to a theological-textual dialogue within Judaism.

We will see in Chapter 4 that the OT, particularly Isaiah, would enable Paul to substantiate his vision of reconciliation consequently to his Damascus road experience.

Theology and ethics in Paul

One of the reasons that reconciliation has been treated exclusively in its vertical dimension is that theology and ethics in Paul have been studied separately, as two distinct bodies of teaching. As such, as long as one paid exclusive attention to the theology of reconciliation, the ethical aspect of it – that is, its social meaning or significance – was neglected. Therefore, for a proper treatment of Paul's understanding of reconciliation, especially in its social dimension, one has to pay considerable attention to the close relationship between theology and ethics in Paul's thought.

In his significant study, *Theology and Ethics in Paul*,[19] Victor Paul Furnish puts forward the thesis that 'ethical concerns are not secondary but radically integral to his [Paul's] basic theological convictions'.[20] He argues persuasively that, for Paul, theology and ethics are intrinsically related, and that we cannot understand properly one without the other: '. . . the relationship between proclamation and exhortation is not just formal, or only accidental, but thoroughly integral and vital to the apostle's whole understanding of the gospel. Just as his ethical teaching has significant theological dimensions, so do the major themes of his preaching have significant ethical dimensions'.[21]

Thus, according to Furnish, in order to understand Paul's ethics one must see its theological presuppositions and, vice versa, for an understanding of his theology one must see its ethical implications. In his words, '. . . the relation of indicative and imperative, the relation of "theological" proclamation and "moral" exhortation, is *the* crucial problem in interpreting the Pauline ethic'.[22] This implies that for an adequate treatment of the Pauline concept of reconciliation one should pay considerable attention not only to the explicit theological statements but also to its ethical implications within the teaching of Paul. And yet, these two aspects should not be considered separately, as one resulting from the other. If the indicative and imperative are indeed in such a close connection, we should keep them somehow together. Again Furnish is to the point:

> Paul understands these two dimensions of the gospel in such a way that, though they are not
> absolutely identified, they are closely and necessarily associated. God's *claim* is regarded by
> the apostle as a constitutive part of God's *gift*. The Pauline concept of grace is *inclusive* of

19. V. P. Furnish, *Theology and Ethics in Paul* (Nashville, TN: Abingdon, 1968).
20. Ibid., p. 13.
21. Ibid., p. 112.
22. Ibid., p. 9. This was also the conclusion he reached after his survey of the nineteenth- and twentieth-century interpretation of Paul's ethics.

the Pauline concept of obedience. For this reason it is not quite right to say that, for Paul, the imperative is 'based upon' or 'proceeds out of' the indicative. This suggests that the imperative is designed somehow to 'realise' or 'actualise' what God has given only as a 'possibility' ... The Pauline imperative is not just the result of the indicative but fully integral to it.[23]

The precise and complex nature of the relationship between indicative and imperative,[24] particularly as it relates to the question of reconciliation, needs to be carefully considered. As the present study will show, a narrative reading of Paul's letter offers an excellent way to understand the dynamic and intrinsic relationship between indicative and imperative, an understanding which holds together theology and ethics in Paul.

1.3.2 *Narrative approaches to Paul*

A number of scholars who have pointed out the limits of the long-debated search for the 'centre' of Paul's theology have rightly insisted that there are other aspects of vital importance one needs to consider for an adequate assessment of Paul's thought, such as his apocalyptic matrix, gospel, mission, ethics, his own self-understanding and experience – all these 'bind together' in a very promising narrative approach to Pauline letters.

For the last three decades narrative analysis has provided a stimulating avenue for biblical studies as it was extensively used in the analysis of the historical books of the OT and of the gospels in the NT. But narrative study has not very often been applied to Paul's letters. The dominant view in Pauline study has been that expressed by Christiaan Beker: 'Paul is not a storyteller . . . [he] is a man of the proposition, the argument, and the dialogue, not a man of the parable or story'.[25] In recent years, however, this situation has changed and there is now a growing interest in studying Paul in terms of the narrative (sub)structures of his theological formulations, in terms

---

23. Ibid., pp. 224–25. In a subsequent book, *The Love Command in the New Testament*, Furnish summarizes the issue in this way: 'No better title for Paul's "theology" can be devised than his own formulation in Gal. 5.6: "faith active in love". Love is both the context and the content of faith; *God's* love makes faith possible and *man's* love gives it visibility and effect in the world' (V. P. Furnish, *The Love Command in the New Testament* (Nashville, TN: Abingdon, 1972), p. 94).

24. Beginning with Bultmann's 'The Problem of Ethics in Paul' (in Brian S. Rosner (ed.), *Understanding Paul's Ethics* (Grand Rapids: Eerdmans, 1995)), many other New Testament scholars came to understand the relationship between indicative and imperative as being essential not only for Paul's ethic but for the understanding of his thought in general. We mention only a few here: W. Schrage, *The Ethics of the New Testament* (Edinburgh: T&T Clark, 1988); A. Verhey, *The Great Reversal* (Grand Rapids: Eerdmans, 1984); W. Dennison, 'Indicative and Imperative: The Basic Structure of Pauline Ethics', *Calvin Theological Journal* 14(1) (1979), pp. 55–78; and Michael Parsons, 'Being Precedes Act: Indicative and Imperative in Paul's Writings' (in Rosner, *Understanding Paul's Ethics*).

25. Christiaan J. Beker, *Paul the Apostle: The Triumph of God in Life and Thought* (Philadelphia: Fortress, 1984) p. 353. Similarly, Francis Watson concludes his assessment of the narrative dynamics in Paul with a clear statement that Paul's gospel is 'an essentially nonnarratable gospel'. (F. Watson, 'Is There a Story in these Texts?' in Bruce W. Longenecker (ed.), *Narrative Dynamics in Paul: A Critical Assessment* (Louisville, KY: Westminster John Knox, 2002), p. 239.)

of the 'story' or 'stories' he told. It is claimed by those who employ such analysis that Paul's theological discourse and arguments are fundamentally determined and shaped by an underlying narrative. Paul's discourse is thus sustained, given coherence and controlled by such a narrative substructure. This direction of inquiry has proved very helpful and has shed new light on many aspects of Paul's letters and theology. Consequently, in the last two decades, several significant studies have emerged which have pointed out various narrative elements in the writings of Paul. Among the authors who made particular contributions in this field I would refer briefly to Richard Hays, Norman Petersen, N. T. Wright, Ben Witherington, Stephen Fowl, Sylvia Keesmaat, Katherine Grieb and Douglas Campbell.[26]

Richard B. Hays is considered to be the one who made the first and the strongest case for a narrative analysis of Paul's letters. Indeed, though there are now several slightly different methodologies being employed in narrative analysis, most scholars agree that Hays provided 'much of the impetus for the contemporary study of narrative ingredients in Paul's thought . . . [and] methodological foundations for and suggestive insights into narratological features of Paul's theology'.[27]

In his groundbreaking study *The Faith of Jesus Christ*, Hays has argued convincingly that the narrative structure of the gospel is integral to Paul's way of thinking. Paul's argumentation, notes Hays, is constructed upon 'the story of Jesus Christ' which provides both the foundational substructure of Paul's discourse and the contours of its logic. In his search for 'the constant elements of the gospel', Hays

---

26. Richard Hays, *The Faith of Jesus Christ* (Chico, CA: Scholars Press, 1983); idem, 'Is Paul's Gospel Narratable?' *JSNT* 27(2) (2004a), pp. 217–39; Norman Petersen, *Rediscovering Paul* (Philadelphia: Fortress, 1985); N. T. Wright, *The Climax of the Covenant* (Edinburgh: T&T Clark); idem, *The New Testament and the People of God* (London: SPCK, 1992) *(NTPG)*; idem, 'New Exodus, New Inheritance: the Narrative Substructure of Romans 3–8' in Sven K. Soderlund and N. T. Wright (eds), *Romans and the People of God* (Grand Rapids: Eerdmans, 1999); Stephen Fowl, *The Story of Jesus in the Letters of Paul* (JSNTS, 36; Sheffield: Sheffield Academic, 1990); Ben Witherington III, *Paul's Narrative Thought World* (Louisville, KY: Westminster/John Knox Press, 1994); Sylvia C. Keesmaat, *Paul and his Story* (JSNTS, 181; Sheffield: Sheffield Academic, 1999); A. Katherine Grieb, *The Story of Romans: A Narrative Defense of God's Righteousness* (Louisville, KY: Westminster John Knox Press, 2002); Douglas A. Campbell, 'The Story of Jesus in Romans and Galatians' in B. W. Longenecker (ed.), *Narrative Dynamics in Paul: A Critical Assessment* (Louisville, KY: Westminster John Knox, 2002). Mention should also be made of several other authors who studied Paul in terms of the larger category of story even if I may not have the space to interact in detail with their writings: Rollin Grams, *Gospel and Mission in Paul's Ethics* (Ph.D. Dissertation presented to Duke University, 1989. Printed by University Microfilms International, Ann Arbor, MI, 1990), and his 'Paul and Missions: The Narrative of Israel and the Mission of the Church' (unpublished paper presented at OCMS Lectures, Oxford, on 1 August 2000). Similarly, Michael J. Gorman's study *Cruciformity: Paul's Narrative Spirituality of the Cross* (Grand Rapids: Eerdmans, 2001), among other recent studies, has also advanced the narrative approach to Paul. Lastly, but significantly, a very special mention should be made of the important volume edited by Bruce W. Longenecker, *Narrative Dynamics in Paul: A Critical Assessment* in which leading British NT scholars make an in-depth assessment of the strengths and weaknesses of a narrative approach applied to Paul's letters and illustrate the extent to which such an approach is becoming commonplace in Pauline scholarship.

27. Bruce W. Longenecker, 'Narrative Interest in the Study of Paul: Retrospective and Prospective', in B. Longenecker (ed.) *Narrative Dynamics in Paul*, p. 5.

contends that neither Paul's personal subjective religious experience, nor existential categories provide an adequate explanation of these elements and one should look for an account 'which would be more faithful to the forms in which Paul actually thought'.[28] Theological propositions cannot be the basis out of which Paul worked. To determine that, one should pay careful attention to both the *nature* and *method* of Paul's discourse. By a close examination of Gal. 3.1–4.11, Hays shows that

> the framework of Paul's thought is constituted neither by a system of doctrines nor by his personal religious experience but by a 'sacred story', a narrative structure. In these texts, Paul 'theologizes' by reflecting upon this story as an ordering pattern for thought and experience; he deals with the 'variable elements' of the concrete situation (for instance, the challenge of his opponents in Galatia) by interpreting them within the framework of his 'sacred story', which is a story about Jesus Christ.[29]

Admittedly, we do not find narratives on the surface of Paul's letters. This is simply because Paul's readers already know the gospel story and so he does not need to retell it. But his frequent allusions, for example, to 'Jesus Christ crucified' represent a shorthand of the gospel through which Paul intends 'to recall and evoke a more comprehensive narrative pattern' and 'to draw out the implications of this story for shaping the belief and practice of his infant churches'.[30] From such allusions, continues Hays, one can discern the basic form of a story of Christ and 'examine the way in which this story operates as a constraint governing the logic of Paul's argumentation'.[31]

Hays is, of course, aware of the major problem faced by a narrative analysis in Paul and he rightly asks: 'in the case of Paul, where we encounter texts discursive in form, how is it possible to discern the shape of the narrative structure which, as we have proposed, underlies the argumentation? What does it mean to claim that a discourse has a "narrative substructure"? Does it make sense to say that a *story* can function as a constraint on the logic of an *argument*?'[32] Drawing on other works of various proponents of narrative studies (Northrop Frye, Paul Ricoeur, and Robert Funk), Hays demonstrated the possibility of an 'organic relationship' between the language of story and reflective discourse.

As for the concrete steps for a narrative inquiry, Hays suggests two phases: 'we may first identify within the discourse allusions to the story and seek to discern its general outlines; then, in a second phase of inquiry we may ask how this story shapes the logic of argumentation in the discourse'.[33] While Hays' first study

28. Hays, *The Faith of Jesus Christ*, p. 5.
29. Ibid.
30. Ibid.
31. Ibid., p. 6.
32. Ibid., p. 20.
33. Ibid.

focused on the narrative substructure of Galatians 3.1–4.11 and represented the first solid methodological foundations for a particular narrative approach to Paul, in his subsequent works Hays extends the scope of his inquiry to include other letters and passages with clear narrative substructures, particularly Romans 5.[34] As we will see, Hays offers a springboard for the present study in our attempt not simply to identify the general outline of the story of Christ in Romans but particularly to see how Paul draws on the story of Christ in his argument for reconciliation.

The second influential work on 'the sociology of Paul's narrative world' is **Norman Petersen**'s *Rediscovering Paul*.[35] Starting from the premise that '[l]etters have stories and it is from these stories that we construct the narrative worlds of both the letters and their stories', Petersen uses Paul's letter to Philemon 'to establish methods for moving from letter to their stories, but also for moving back to the letters from the stories, since the whole point of the project is to see what the stories can tell us about the letters'.[36] Using insights from both literary criticism and social anthropology, Petersen is interested in Paul's theologizing in order to identify the symbolic universe that his theology presupposes. Thus, like Richard Hays before him, he works with a twofold distinction between (1) a generative 'symbolic world' and (2) a subsequent theological discourse. However, as Longenecker rightly notes, despite their similarity in the bipartite structure of Paul's thought, Petersen locates the 'narrative' component within the theological reflective discourse while for Hays this is to be found within the primary 'substructures' of the epistemic processes.[37]

Ben Witherington's *Paul's Narrative Thought World* offers another excellent argument for understanding Paul's theology as arising out of a 'grand Story' and places Paul's theology in the larger framework of 'Paul's narrative thought world'.[38] Not only do we discover in Paul's letters narratives about Christ, Israel, the world, Christians, etc., but Witherington is convinced that '*all* Paul's ideas, all his arguments, all his practical advice, all his social arrangements are ultimately grounded in a story . . . Paul's thought, including both theology and ethics, is grounded in a grand narrative and in a story that has continued to develop out of that narrative'.[39] Thus, Witherington maintains that for Paul there is an overarching macro-story of God's dealing with humankind and that it is from this 'fundamental story . . . [that] all his discourse arises'. He further distinguishes within this larger drama of Paul's narrative thought world, four smaller but interrelated stories:

---

34. Richard Hays 'Christ Died for the Ungodly: Narrative Soteriology in Paul?', *Horizons in Biblical Theology* 26 (2004b): pp. 48–68. Hays had already hinted in the conclusion of his first major study to other passages that are suitable for a narrative analysis: 1 Cor. 15; Phil. 2.5–11; Rom. 3.21–26; and Rom. 5.12–21.

35. Petersen, N., *Rediscovering Paul*, p. ix.

36. Ibid., p. 43.

37. Bruce Longenecker, 'The Narrative Approach to Paul: an Early Retrospective', *Currents in Biblical Research* 1(1) (2002b), pp. 88–111 (92).

38. Witherington, *Paul's Narrative*.

39. Ibid., p. 2.

(1) the story of a world gone wrong; (2) the story of Israel in that world; (3) the story of Christ, which arises out of the story of Israel and humankind on the human side of things, but in a larger sense arises out of the very story of God as creator and redeemer; and (4) the story of Christians, including Paul himself, which arises out of all three of these previous stories and is the first full installment of the story of a world set right again.[40]

Even though together these stories form the tapestry of Paul's thought world, it is the story of Christ that represents 'the hinge, crucial turning point, and climax of the entire larger drama, which more than anything else affects how *the* Story will ultimately turn out'.[41] Witherington is not the only one to remark that 'the story of Christ' takes a central place in Paul's thought and in his theologising. Most of the authors who employ a narrative approach to Paul give an essential role to the story of Jesus.[42]

Witherington differs from the previous two authors in his understanding of how narrative operates in that he sees not a twofold but a threefold scheme of Paul's theologising: 'symbolic universe', 'narrative thought world' and 'theological articulation'. Here is how Witherington distinguishes them:

(1) Paul's symbolic universe, which entails those things that Paul takes to be inherently true and real, the fixed stars in Paul's mental sky; (2) Paul's narrative thought world, which is Paul's reflections on his symbolic universe in terms of the grand Story. This undergirds (3) Paul's articulation of his theology, ethics, and so forth, in response to the situations he must address.[43]

Not only does Witherington provide evidence for the importance of narrative/story in interpreting Paul but he also shows that many of the arguments Paul makes throughout his letters could be easily misread unless they are seen in the light of Paul's larger story. Particularly relevant for our purposes is Witherington's last story, the story of Christians, in which he emphasizes the formative role of the story of Christ for the life of the believer, not simply as something from afar but, in fact, as a story into which they have entered and to which they are conforming. Very appropriately, Witherington entitles that chapter, 'The Christening of the Believer' stating that:

---

40. Ibid., p. 5.
41. Ibid.
42. We have seen that for Hays, 'the story of Jesus Christ' is the basis upon which Paul's entire argumentation is constructed, providing the foundational substructure of Paul's discourse and the contours of its logic. Douglas Campbell also suggests that 'the story of Jesus . . . is an *irreducible* element in Paul's theological description . . . as well as a highly integrative approach that illuminates and strengthen connections in his thinking with other significant themes and issues' (Campbell, D. 'The Story of Jesus', p. 98).
43. Witherington, *Paul's Narrative*, p. 6.

'the aim of the Christian life is conformity to the image of Christ – in mind, heart, will, and emotions'.[44]

N. T. Wright has also employed a narrative analysis of a particular passage in Paul;[45] also in his *New Testament and the People of God* he has advocated a much broader use of such methodology based on an analysis of the complex process of human cognition.[46] For Wright, human writing in general should not be conceived of either simply as a "neutral" description of the world', or merely as 'a collection of subjective feelings'; rather, he suggests, we should understand it 'as the articulation of worldviews, or, better still, *the telling of stories which bring worldviews into articulation*'.[47] Therefore, part of the task of those who approach a text is 'to lay bare, and explicate, what the writer has achieved at this level of implied narrative, and ultimately implied worldview, and how' (p. 65). Wright places the narrative at the heart of human cognition: the narrative gives expression to a 'worldview' which, in turn, represents 'the presuppositional, pre-cognitive stage . . . the ultimate concerns of human beings' (p. 122).

Worldviews are not necessarily something 'in the open', visible for the observer to see and analyse. Rather, they are 'like the foundations of a house: vital, but invisible. They are that *through* which, not *at* which, a society or an individual normally looks; they form the grid according to which humans organize reality, not bits of reality that offer themselves for organization' (p. 125). The way worldviews come to expression at the surface in everyday life is through '*basic beliefs and aims*' – which could also be conceived as 'shorthand forms of the stories which those who hold them are telling themselves and one another about the way the world is' (p. 126). These beliefs and aims, in turn, give rise to '*consequent beliefs* and *intentions* about the world, oneself, one's society, one's god' which are variously manifested 'into opinions held and motivations acted upon with varying degrees of conviction' (p. 126).

Wright's understanding of 'story' provides an excellent way into a narrative approach to reflective discourses such as Paul's letters. For him, stories are not simply instruments which enable us to connect and make sense of random events in our life. They are 'one of the most basic modes of human life' providing 'a vital framework for experiencing the world'. Human life in itself 'can be seen as grounded in, and constituted by, the implicit or explicit stories which humans tell themselves and one another' (p. 38). Stories are one of the key elements which make up a worldview and they do not simply illustrate one's beliefs but rather generate and shape them.

44. Ibid., p. 338.

45. Wright, 'The Vindication of the Law: Narrative Analysis and Romans 8.1–11', in his *The Climax of the Covenant*.

46. Wright, *NTPG*. Especially relevant are: 'Stories, Worldviews and Knowledge' (pp. 38–46), his discussion of the nature of stories (pp. 69–80) and 'worldviews' (pp. 122–26), and his hints as to how a narrative approach might apply to Paul's letters (pp. 403–09).

47. Wright, *NTPG*, p. 65. All immediate subsequent references to Wright in this section refer to this book, and the page numbers are indicated in brackets at the end of the quote.

If beliefs and aims are expressions of a worldview, 'stories which characterize the worldview itself are thus located, on the map of human knowing at a more fundamental level than explicitly formulated beliefs, including theological beliefs' (p. 38).

If that is the case, then we may be right to assume with Petersen that 'letters have stories', and that beneath Paul's theological discourse is a story, or several stories, to which he gives expression in various ways in his letters and which also shape(s) his argumentations and theology. Indeed, Wright claims that an implicit narrative structure can be identified in Paul's letters:

> Within all his letters . . . we discover a larger implicit narrative, which stands out clearly as the true referential sequence behind the poetic sequence demanded by the different rhetorical needs of the various letters. Like his own story, this larger narrative is the Jewish story . . . Paul presupposes this story even when he does not expound it directly, and it is arguable that we can only understand the more limited narrative worlds of the different letters if we locate them at their appropriate points within this overall story-world, and indeed within the symbolic universe that accompanies it (p. 405).

1.3.3 *The significance of a narrative reading*
Our brief overview has highlighted indeed various narrative elements of Paul's theology, different authors identifying different stories, thus placing the 'narrative structure' of Paul's letter at different levels.

Narrative substructure of Paul's theology
One result of the new narrative impetus in the Pauline scholarship is the acknowledgment that Paul's theology presupposes a narrative substructure or 'symbolic universe', a larger story of God's saving purposes for humanity, a story that reached its climax in the life-story of Jesus Christ. Observing the multilayered character of Paul's theology, James Dunn is representative of those who see the benefit of conceiving Paul's theology as emerging from a complex interplay between several stories, even though he prefers to use a model of 'dialogue' for Paul's theologising. He writes:

> [W]e could readily speak of the substructure of Paul's theology as the story of God and creation, with the story of Israel superimposed upon it. On top of that again we have the story of Jesus, and then Paul's own story, with the initial intertwining of these last two stories as the decisive turning point in Paul's life and theology. Finally, there are the complex interactions of Paul's own story with the stories of those who had believed before him and of those who came to form the churches founded by them.[48]

Douglas Campbell also observes that 'the story of Jesus, properly understood . . . is an *irreducible* element in Paul's theological description . . . as well as a highly

---

48. Dunn, *The Theology of Paul*, p. 18.

integrative approach that illuminates and strengthens connections in his thinking with other significant themes and issues'.[49] Similarly, Wayne Meeks provides another illustration of the fact that the language about 'story' and 'narrative' became a normal part of the discourse in Pauline studies. In the chapter on 'Moral Story' he presents a remarkable argument about Paul's main concern in using the narrative to shape a specific moral community, 'to suggest, cajole, argue, threaten, shame, and encourage those communities into behaving, in their specific situations, in ways somehow homologous to that fundamental story'.[50] Paul's theologising was thus not a matter of simply repeating the story of Christ for his readers. He made a conscious effort to articulate the ways in which his readers are included in the story, to show how they share in the same story of Christ. In our analysis of Romans 5–8 in Chapter 5 we will see how Paul describes in detail the incorporation of believers 'in Christ' and his story and the privileges and responsibilities for the believers' lives following from this new reality of being participants in the story of God's reconciling the world in Christ.

Story and ethics

Another relevant feature that emerges from the literature surveyed above is that one of the major thrusts in the narrative approaches in both biblical and theological studies is ethics. For the proponents of a narrative reading of Paul, the major consequence of such a reading is an enhanced account of Pauline ethics.[51] After Meeks, who has stressed this issue very much, more recently David Horrell concludes his essay 'Paul's Narrative or Narrative Substructure?' with this statement: 'in a world conscious of the power of stories to form identity, values, and practice, the rediscovery of Paul's gospel *as story* is of critical value'.[52] And indeed, it seems that the importance of narrative for moral formation is not a recent invention. Paul's contemporary, the Jewish theologian Philo of Alexandria, considered Moses to have been a superior legislator exactly because he established the laws in a narrative framework.[53] It is thus very plausible to consider that Paul shared Philo's view not simply with regard

---

49. Campbell, 'Story of Jesus', p. 98.

50. Wayne A. Meeks, *The Origin of Christian Morality: The First Two Centuries* (New Haven: Yale University Press, 1993), pp. 196–97.

51. See Alexandra Brown, 'Response to Sylvia Keesmaat and Richard Hays', *Horizons in Biblical Theology*, 26(2) (December 2004), pp. 115–22 (115). Among theologians and ethicists, Stanley Hauerwas and Alistair MacIntyre have emphasized the formative place of narrative in the shaping of moral identity, and even more, the indispensable role of narrative in moral instruction and development. For them, it is narrative that shapes identity and community, forms character and informs conduct. Especially relevant are S. Hauerwas, *A Community of Character: Toward a Constructive Christian Social Ethic, Vision and Virtue* (Notre Dame: University of Notre Name Press, 1981); idem, *Character and Christian Life* (San Antonio: Trinity University Press, 1975); and A. MacIntyre, *After Virtue* (Notre Dame: University of Notre Name Press, 1984).

52. David Horrell, 'Paul's Narrative or Narrative Substructure?' in Longenecker (ed.), *Narrative Dynamics in Paul*, p. 170 (italics in original).

53. Philo of Alexandria, *On the Creation of the World*, 3 and *Life of Moses*, 2.47–51. See Meeks, *The Origin of Christian Morality*, p. 189.

to Moses but also in respect of the importance of narrative. In his latest study on Pauline ethics, Horrell pursues the issues further and offers a more nuanced and complex dynamic between narrative, theology and ethics as a conceptual framework for reading Paul's texts. He writes:

> Paul's letters are to be seen as reflecting, and contributing to, a narrative myth which constructs a particular symbolic universe, giving meaning and order to the lives of those who inhabit it. This myth, enacted in ritual, is an identity- and community-forming narrative which shapes both the world-view (the 'is') and the ethos (the 'ought') of its adherents . . . This broad framework of interpretation suggests that, at least at a general level, everything in Paul's letters is potentially relevant to a consideration of his 'ethics'. If the myth itself – the central story and its symbols and ideas – shapes the ethos and social practice of the community, then our inquiry cannot be limited only to certain explicitly paraenetic sections of the texts.[54]

This is indeed significant. It shows the intrinsic relationship between theology and ethics in Paul and that we simply cannot study one without the other without the risk of misreading Paul. This is one of the arguments I put forward in this book, namely that one cannot have an adequate understanding of Paul's treatment of reconciliation by examining the theological (vertical) dimension while leaving out the social (horizontal) dimension of reconciliation. In other words, to reduce the concept of reconciliation in Paul's theology exclusively to the reconciliation of human beings with God (which most of the exegetical Pauline scholarship did) means not only to leave the church with no resources to deal with complex social processes, but also to misread Paul's letters. Theology and ethics are so intertwined in Paul's argumentations that we have to keep them together. For Paul, reconciliation is at one and the same time vertical and horizontal. Thus, in the light of the discussion above, I hope to show that a narrative reading of reconciliation alongside the story of Christ will make it possible to bring together these two dimensions of reconciliation in a more holistic, integrative understanding.

1.3.4 *Definitions, narrative features and shorthand references in Paul*
A few words are necessary as to the nature/definition of story. If one agrees that it is plausible to think of Paul's theological articulations as being generated by his larger narrative thought world, the immediate questions which arise are: how does Paul evoke such stories, and how can we identify narrative patterns in his discourse? Given the letter form of the Pauline texts, these are particularly important questions. I take the position that for a narrative analysis in Paul there is no need to adopt either a strict and fixed definition of 'story' or a particular narrative theory. In fact, there is a danger in imposing a universally established type of story form and then trying to

---

54. David G. Horrell, *Solidarity and Difference: A Contemporary Reading of Paul's Ethics* (London: T&T Clark, 2005), pp. 97–8.

make Paul's stories fit into all the details of that form.[55] Indeed, one justified criticism made against the narrative approach is that the category of 'narrative' is extremely fluid and vague and that it can mean different things to different people.[56] Therefore, instead of imposing an essential definition of 'story' and searching for recognizable narrative elements that will fit in an already established structure or formula, we should rather look for various 'narrative features' through which stories are identified and recognized by the readers. This position vis-à-vis a narrative approach to Paul's theology is presented by Campbell in an essay in which he lists the overlapping narrative features of stories:

> [I]t seems wise to sit loosely to any notion of definition and to speak of various narrative features, the possession of a sufficient number of which allows us to recognise narrative elements, or even relatively complete stories, in the broader texture of Paul's thought as revealed in Romans and Galatians. Among those features that suggest narrative is *a striking personal dimension* conveyed largely by *the activity of personal actors*, who usually undertake *actions*, often *in relation to one another*, and *to whom events occur*. These actions and events often then unfold to create a *plot*, the latter often also exhibiting *a problem-solution structure*. Hence stories are especially useful types of texts for giving an account of the *behaviour, actions, history*, and/or *accomplishments, of people* (or, more strictly, of personal actors).[57]

These narrative features will be helpful in our attempt to identify within Paul's discourse the story to which he refers (or aspects of it) and its basic outline. Campbell points out that these key narrative features will be identifiable in a variety of formulations and that 'once an element has been recognised, the rest of the story – or at least part of it – will be implicit in this recognition'.[58] However, he cautiously adds that the 'allusions to key narrative elements must be genuine, and the further implied elements plausible and relevant'.[59] Once the genuine narrative features have been identified, I will proceed with the exegetical analysis of the story of Christ and reconciliation, attempting to establish what the role/function of the story (or of a particular feature of the story) is within the logic of the argument and, specifically, its role/function in the rhetoric of reconciliation in the letter. One more important point needs to be made here regarding the importance of a particular rhetorical technique that Paul is using in his argumentation, namely his shorthand references and/or allusions to

55. This real danger is identified by James Dunn who rightly states: 'The danger in all these cases is of postulating an established form and deducing *from the postulated form* the function and significance of various particulars within the letter, sometimes even despite the internal logic of the letter itself. The application of a too-idealised form of "story" to Paul's theology raises the same unease' (J. Dunn, 'The Narrative Approach to Paul: Whose Story?', in Longenecker (ed.), *Narrative Dynamics in Paul*, p. 221).

56. Alexandra Brown makes such a point in her response to the narrative approach of Keesmaat and Hays, 'Response to Sylvia Keesmaat and Richard Hays', pp. 115–16.

57. Campbell, 'The Story of Jesus', p. 99 (italics added).

58. Ibid., p. 100.

59. Ibid., p. 101.

various narratives. Because in most of the cases Paul's readers knew the larger story/ stories to which he referred, there was no need for Paul to restate it/them in full in his letters. Thus, he knew that even brief phrases or allusory references to some parts of a particular story would bring to the mind of the readers the larger narrative, the entire story.

In an important study on 'Rhetorical Shorthand in Pauline Argumentation' in the Corinthian correspondence, Margaret Mitchell demonstrates, with the help of ancient Graeco-Roman shorthand rhetorical techniques, that Paul's various brief references to 'the gospel', 'the proclamation' and 'the word', were effective ways to abbreviate the entire narrative sequence of God's unique intervention in human history, in Jesus Christ, for the salvation of the world.[60] Such shorthand forms (brevity of expression, synecdoche, and metaphor) pointed to the whole underlying narrative and served to describe and interpret its meaning. An allusion or short reference to any particular event in the story brought to the readers' minds the whole story because it is only within the larger narrative structure that the parts had their meaning. Mitchell illustrates it by giving the example of 'the gospel' functioning as such a shorthand for a larger narrative:

> the very phrase τὸ εὐαγγέλιον . . . serves as a 'superabbreviation' of the whole, functioning as a title which both characterizes its full contents and interprets its meaning for the hearer. The logic of the gospel title is unitary: no single event in the narrative stands apart from or uninterpreted by the rest. In usage the single phrase τὸ εὐαγγέλιον allows Paul, with great economy and elegance, to insert the entire long narrative of God's plan 'according to the Scriptures' into an argument without repeating the whole.[61]

In our efforts to interpret Paul's understanding and presentation of reconciliation in his theology, it is important to realize that his arguments were firmly grounded on under-lying narratives given expression through various shorthand formulations. A careful study of such shorthand expressions and narrative features is therefore mandatory for a proper understanding of Paul's specific argumentations in different contexts. This will allow us to have a better understanding of the function of the respective narratives in the logic of Paul's arguments. By employing such techniques, Paul is able to call to mind an entire narrative just by a brief allusion to one of its component parts or features and this enables him to give a deeper meaning to what he actually writes. And

---

60. Margaret M. Mitchell, 'Rhetorical Shorthand in Pauline Argumentation: the Functions of "the Gospel" in the Corinthian Correspondence', in L. Ann Jervis and Peter Richardson (eds), *Gospel in Paul: Studies on Corinthians, Galatians and Romans for Richard N. Longenecker* (JSNTS, 108; Sheffield: Sheffield Academic, 1994), pp. 63–88. Rollin Grams had earlier argued for a similar point in his dissertation 'Gospel and Mission'.

61. Mitchell, 'Rhetorical Shorthand', p. 64. Both Wright (*NTPG*, pp. 403–09) and Richard Hays (*The Faith of Jesus Christ*) have also shown how even Paul's short references to 'Christ' in his letters function not simply as a proper name but as allusions and appeals to the whole story of the gospel, of God's story of redemption accomplished in and through Jesus Christ.

this is an important aspect, since Paul does not write narratives but letters in which he addresses various and complex issues in his churches and engages in dynamic argumentation. By direct reference only to *some* narrative features which suggest the whole story, 'Paul is able to construct new texts which incorporate the authority of the underlying gospel narrative through pointed, carefully chosen shorthand references to it.'[62] As we will see, Paul's allusions and brief references to particular narratives are not arbitrary. Rather they are carefully and sensibly employed to serve his specific theological and rhetorical purposes in specific contexts.

Concrete steps into the inquiry

In our narrative analysis in Romans 5–8, we will proceed in basically two major steps. First, by using the key 'narrative features' described above, I will try to identify allusions/references to the story Paul is employing. Secondly, I will explore how the story is used by Paul to shape the logic of his argument and will ask the kind of questions I have suggested above: How does this particular story shape the identity, values and practices of the community? How does it shape their understanding of reconciliation? The crucial question, of course, will be: what is the social significance of reconciliation in Paul?

1.3.5 *Objectives, Paul's theologising, and methodology*

Our interest in this study is not necessarily with the theoretical framework of a narrative theory applied to the study of Paul but rather, following Paul's own central concern, to explore his use of the story of Jesus Christ for community formation, as a way to shape a particular sort of community with specific practices – that is, to inspire the forming of a reconciling community 'in Christ' which exists to illustrate and to proclaim the reconciliation of the world. I propose that when we read what Paul has to say about reconciliation alongside the story of Christ, we get a larger, more comprehensive understanding of reconciliation, not least an excellent highlight of the social dimension of Paul's complex concept.

Thus, acknowledging that there is indeed a narrative dimension to Paul's thought, and that stories shape identity, values and practices, as we have seen, the objective of this research is to explore the way in which the stories that shaped Paul's life, with a special attention to the central story of Jesus Christ, function to shape the identity, values and practices of the Christian believers. How do these stories transform their perception of reality, and how do they open new possibilities for action; i.e., for a reconciling life? How does the particular narrative Paul alludes to help restructure the believers' personal and corporate experience vis-à-vis reconciliation?

We will be asking concretely: how does Paul use the story of Christ, or particular features of that story, and how does he relate it to reconciliation? How is he using it in order to shape a reconciling community? What are the implications for the believers,

---

62. Mitchell, 'Rhetorical Shorthand', p. 68.

in terms of beliefs and practices, of the fact that that they are 'in Christ' and therefore part of the story of Christ? One crucial question that we will attempt to answer is this: is there a way in which God's reconciliation in Christ becomes the *ground* and *model* for reconciliation between human enemies? How does Paul relate the complex and multifaceted metaphor of reconciliation to other key theological concepts, to the life and practice of the community?

However, as we have seen above, because theology for Paul was a very complex activity we need also to pay close attention to his dynamic theologising – as he employs different tactics and methods in order to reach his ends, which, in most cases, had to do with affecting the lives of his congregations, to spur the early Christians to employ a distinctive way of being and acting in the world. Thus, we will consider carefully the texts within which *different aspects* of Paul's theologising are present, and identify properly whether there is evidence of *narratives, intertextuality, focal lenses, beliefs, practices* or something else. In the light of Paul's dynamic theologising, the following questions become not only relevant but very important: are there *narratives of reconciliation* in Romans? How does Paul relate some of his *basic beliefs* to reconciliation? How does the rich *symbolism of reconciliation* in Paul highlight the social aspects of reconciliation? What are some concrete *practices of reconciliation* that Paul promotes?

Given the nature of the present inquiry as well as Paul's complex and dynamic theologising, it is evident that in addition to the narrative approach to Paul we will make use of insights from several other approaches including social criticism and cultural anthropology. These approaches are helpful for a more adequate understanding of Paul in his own terms – especially as they facilitate an analysis of Paul and his world through lenses appropriate for a study of a culture totally removed and different from our own, thus enabling us to resist our tendencies for ethnocentric and anachronistic readings of Paul.

1.4 *Establishing the parameters of research*

Studies on reconciliation in Paul have generally concentrated on four classical passages where the καταλλάσσω/καταλλαγή terminology appears, namely Rom. 5.1–11; 2 Cor. 5.11–21; Eph. 2.11–22, and Col. 1.15–23. The present study, however, departs from a 'word-study' approach and argues for the need to consider the larger symbolism of reconciliation that Paul is employing and by which he gives expression to a more complex concept of reconciliation than is usually acknowledged in the exegetical literature. Thus, in our study of reconciliation in Paul we will consider also such concepts as 'peace', 'love', 'welcome', 'unity', 'acceptance', and 'friendship', and therefore extend the inquiry to include other texts than the four passages usually examined. This is also required, as we have seen, by Paul's dynamic theologising as well as by the contextual nature of his writings. In the light of these considerations and given our concrete research question on the social significance of reconciliation, we have deliberately decided to focus our exegesis on Paul's letter to the Romans, more specifically on Romans 5–8 and 12–15. We thus hope to show that Paul's discussion of reconciliation is not limited to Rom. 5.1–11 but is present throughout Romans, particularly chapters 5–8 and 12–15, and further that it is not limited to reconciliation with God but comprises *also* an intrinsic, social or horizontal dimension. Moreover, by selecting two textual units in Romans which traditionally are considered to belong to the 'theological' and 'ethical' sections of the letter, we hope to show that there is no such delimitation for Paul and that theology and ethics are present and inseparable in both texts in Romans. To be sure, we will place our entire discussion within Paul's overall Jewish and Graeco-Roman underlying framework of reference as well as his larger vision of reconciliation, and therefore references will be made to Paul's key reconciliation motifs and texts elsewhere in his letters, such as 2 Cor. 5–6 and Romans 9–11. However, we hope to show that by setting the exegetical focus within the parameters of the two large sections of Romans, we will be able to ensure an in-depth exploration of our specific research question.

1.5 *The structure of the argument*

We begin (in Chapter 2) with a review of the Pauline scholarship on reconciliation which will reveal the lack of concern for the social significance of reconciliation in Paul's theology and consequently will locate our study within the relevant literature, showing how it depends upon, differs from or builds further on the previous works. Chapter 3 offers the underlying religious, social, and political framework of Paul's life and thought, within which to interpret the social meaning of reconciliation in his writings. It will show that an analysis of the social dimension of reconciliation is not only plausible but, indeed, necessary.

In Chapter 4 we will build on the premise that Paul's life, mission, and writings, indeed his theology, were informed and supported from beneath by a narrative framework, a unifying worldview and redemptive vision of reality which determined a particular way of being and living in the world. His gospel was fundamentally related to his vision of final, cosmic reconciliation and peace. We will thus argue that the social dimension of reconciliation in Paul can be properly understood within his larger vision of reconciliation of all things in Christ, the vision which inspired him throughout his life and ministry and gave him the impetus to be permanently engaged in *reconciling practices* – between Jews and Gentiles, between various individuals and groups within the churches, and between Christians and 'outsiders'. More specifically, the argument put forward in this chapter is that, beginning with his own radical experience of conversion and reconciliation on the Damascus road, a particular vision of reality started to emerge for Paul brought by the death and resurrection of Christ. Paul's vision of reconciliation is thus radically shaped by, and grounded on the story of Christ: a world of new possibilities and radical innovations is opened up now 'in Christ', with serious implications for all those living within this new reality. It then became clear for Paul that the great vision of restoration and peace found in Isaiah was being fulfilled in his days. And so it was there that Paul found important material elements which solidly substantiated his further understanding and vision of reconciliation. However, to give expression to such a profound and complex phenomenon of reconciliation, Paul uses many symbols and concepts from his Hellenistic, Graeco-Roman context; particularly καταλλάσσω/καταλλαγή used in the Hellenistic context primarily for interpersonal relationships, in the sociological and political spheres of life. Given his own personal experience of reconciliation and the Isaianic vision of peace, Paul gives expression to a complex concept of reconciliation which has personal, social, political, and cosmological dimensions.

In Chapter 5 we offer an exegetical analysis of Romans 5–8, using insights from a narrative reading of Paul, with a special emphasis on the function of the story of Christ in the argument of the letter. We will argue that reconciliation was an integral part of the gospel and that Paul presented it as a complex, multifaceted reality encompassing a vertical reconciliation with God as well as a horizontal, social dimension of reconciliation between people. For Paul the believers' reconciliation with God is inseparable from their reconciliation with others; he wanted to communicate a very clear message, namely that unity, reconciliation, harmony, and acceptance among the believers in Rome were an intrinsic part of the very gospel of reconciliation they professed. In the light of Paul's argument for the complex dynamic of the incorporation of the believers 'in Christ' through baptism, signifying a real sharing and participation in the same story of Christ, we will point to the fact that Paul included his readers into the larger story of God's decisive reconciliation in Christ whereby they become themselves an integral part of the ongoing story of God's reconciliation of the world. The reality of believers' reconciliation with God, and their new identity and status 'in Christ', carry with them the responsibility of engaging in reconciling practices grounded in, and modelled by, Christ's work of reconciliation. Finally, we will examine how Paul's ultimate vision of the reconciliation of all things in Christ gives assurance and hope, and an irresistible impetus to the believer's ministry of reconciliation in all its forms and manifestations.

In Chapter 6 we will argue that Paul's exhortations in Romans 12–15 are concrete elaborations of the theme of reconciliation which he has so thoroughly grounded in the story of Christ in Romans 5–8. I will show that the overwhelming emphasis on 'unity', 'acceptance', 'love', 'peace', and 'welcome' illustrates Paul's rich symbolism of reconciliation which is now given expression in the form of 'reconciling practices'. Paul urges his readers to live out these practices that are integral to the nature of the gospel and to their being 'in Christ'. We will argue that the practices of reconciliation Paul presents are also anchored in and presuppose the story of Christ as both the ground and the paradigm for their reconciling way of life. We will show that by placing these practices within the larger horizon of God's reconciliation of the world in Christ, Paul provides an unshakable foundation for both the possibility and the actuality of social reconciliation.

In the last chapter we attempt to offer some cogent, exegetically based and informed reflections on the social significance of reconciliation in Paul and the contribution it could make to an ongoing dialogue on the role of churches in the public arena in the contemporary Romanian context. The discussion will be placed within the framework of the re-emerging of religious phenomena as an important element in the social arena. We will then look at two ways in which Pauline reconciliation is understood and practised by the Romanian Orthodox Church and by the evangelical churches, and will compare these with the findings from our study. Finally, we will also consider the specific issue of ethnic minorities in Romania and see how a Pauline understanding of reconciliation might be relevant to the issue.

2

PAULINE SCHOLARSHIP ON RECONCILIATION: A
REVIEW OF THE RELATED LITERATURE

2.1 *Introduction*

This chapter offers a survey of various treatments of the question of reconciliation in the Pauline exegetical scholarship. I will try to show where the present study fits within the relevant literature and how this depends upon, differs from or builds further on the previous works. Ultimately, the discussion will reveal the lack of concern for the social significance of reconciliation in Paul's theology and therefore the need for the present research.

From a purely linguistic and statistical standpoint, 'reconciliation' terminology is rare in the NT and it is used almost entirely in the Pauline letters.[1] It has, however, received special attention from scholars and commentators on Paul as being one of the major themes in Pauline theology. As the bibliography illustrates, there are many monographs on reconciliation, and a very large number of specialised articles in scholarly journals, not to mention the extended space that biblical commentaries give to the topic of reconciliation. It would be an extremely difficult task to attempt a detailed history of the doctrine of reconciliation, and it is beyond the purpose of the present research to do so. Rather, our intention here is to offer a brief overview and assessment of the recent exegetical NT scholarship on reconciliation. We will follow the basic questions that were being asked regarding reconciliation in Paul, identify the different angles from which the concept has been approached, and attempt to answer the question of why the doctrine of reconciliation has been restricted mostly to the human-divine relations and is not read socio-politically in the exegetical scholarship.

Pauline exegetical scholarship on reconciliation has focused primarily on three areas of inquiry. The first group of studies has attempted to identify the origin of the concept of reconciliation in Paul, emphasising either the Jewish or Graeco-Roman

---

1. Two Greek verbs and one noun are used for the idea of reconciliation: καταλλάσσω and ἀποκαταλλάσσω ('to reconcile'); and καταλλαγή ('reconciliation'). These appear 12 times, exclusively in Paul. There are only two other verbs used outside Paul: διαλλάσσω ('become reconciled', in Matthew 5.24) which refers to reconciliation with one's brother before an altar offering is made, and συναλλάσσω ('reconcile', in Acts 7.26), which refers to solving a dispute between two brothers.

background of the concept. A second group of studies has sought to determine the place or the significance of reconciliation in Paul's theology as a whole. The third group has endeavoured to define the nature of reconciliation, in its various aspects, looking more closely to specific reconciliation passages, while trying to identify particular elements of the doctrine. In addition to these categories there are some recent studies that emphasise the rhetorical function of Paul's use of reconciliation.

2.2 *The origin of the concept of reconciliation*

Since reconciliation language appears exclusively in the Pauline corpus, scholars have long debated the exact origin of the concept in Paul. An early attempt was to locate the source or the background of Paul's concept in the Hellenistic diplomatic context and the Jewish Hellenistic tradition, particularly the Jewish martyr tradition.

The word translated 'reconciliation' comes from the Greek verbs καταλλάσσω (with the noun καταλλάγη), and ἀποκαταλλάσσω, and all these three forms are used exclusively in the Pauline corpus. Καταλλάσσω is derived from another word, ἀλλάσσώ meaning 'to change', 'to alter', 'to renew', 'to be or to become other', 'to exchange one condition for another', indeed 'to become another in the inner, deepest sense, to change our self or identity'.[2] It was used by the Greek writers with two major senses referring to the exchanging of things, and eliminating enmity and creating friendship. What is commonly acknowledged by biblical scholars is the fact that the word group καταλλάσσω – καταλλαγή was used in the Hellenistic literature in interpersonal relationships, especially in the politico-military context for peace treaties, but not in a religious context for referring to the reconciliation between God and people.[3] But they notice an important transition to the Hellenistic Jewish writers who adopted the terminology and used it with reference to God as being reconciled to his people. Such a usage is present particularly in 2 Macc. 1.5, 5.20, 7.33, 8.29.[4] Howard Marshall captures well the general view on reconciliation presented here.

> [W]hen people fall into sin and apostasy they arouse the wrath of Yahweh. He proceeds
> to punish them, and on the completion of the punishment his anger is satisfied and he is
> reconciled to the people. But the experience of punishment may lead the people to pray to

2.   Buchsel, Friedrich, 'ἀλλάσσώ κτλ', in Kittel, Gerhard (ed.), *Theological Dictionary of the New Testament, Vol. 1.* (Geoffrey Bromiley (trans.); Grand Rapids: Eerdmans, 1964), pp. 251–58; Stanley E. Porter, Καταλλάσσω *in Ancient Greek Literature, with Reference to the Pauline Writings* (Cordoba: Ediciones El Almendro, 1994), p. 13.

3.   So, for example, Porter, Καταλλάσσω, pp. 39–76.

4.   2 Macc. 1.5 'May he hear your prayers and be reconciled to you, and may he not forsake you in time of evil'; 2 Macc. 5.20 '. . . and what was forsaken in the wrath of the Almighty was restored again in all its glory when the great Lord became reconciled'; 2 Macc. 7.33 'And if our living Lord is angry for a little while, to rebuke and discipline us, he will again be reconciled with his own servants'; 2 Macc. 8.29 'When they had done this, they made common supplication and implored the merciful Lord to be wholly reconciled with his servants'.

Yahweh to be reconciled to them and to give up his anger, and Yahweh may respond to such prayers. Even more powerful is the action of the martyrs who, while recognising that their suffering and death are primarily for their own sins, beseech God to accept their suffering as being on behalf of the nation and to be reconciled to the nation as a whole. In short, God is reconciled, i.e., abandons his anger, as a result of the prayer of the people and their endurance (in themselves or their representatives) of the punishment which he inflicts upon them. Men act in such a way as to induce God to be favourable to them.[5]

Based on this precedent, Marshall concludes, '. . . there is a high degree of prob-ability that the Jewish martyr tradition, which surfaces in this particular form in 2 Maccabees, has provided the catalyst to the development of Paul's use of the category of reconciliation'.[6] Against this view, Cilliers Breytenbach offers in his significant study, *Versöhnung: Eine Studie zur paulinischen Soteriology*, a thorough argument for the origin of reconciliation in the Hellenistic diplomatic sphere where it was used for making peace between enemies.[7] According to Breytenbach, the Jewish religious tradition of atonement and the Hellenistic secular notion of reconciliation were different in origin and belonged to two different semantic fields. However, it was Paul who brought these two notions together and interpreted both in the light of Jesus' death 'for us'. It is thus to Breytenbach's credit to have shown both the significance of the notion of 'reconciliation' in ancient politics and that Paul, by making use of such political concepts,[8] shows that he understood Graeco-Roman political life and used it as a source for his writings.

There is no question that Paul's usage of the word reflects both the secular Hellenistic and Jewish Hellenistic usages. However, this alone cannot fully explain Paul's innovative and multifaceted way of using the metaphor of reconciliation. This is most clearly evident in his insistence that it is always God who is the subject of reconciliation and people who are the object of that reconciliation. So, while reflect-ing both Hellenistic and Judaic ideas, reconciliation in Paul has still more nuances of meaning.

Another suggestion for the origin of Paul's concept of reconciliation is the OT background, particularly the concept of 'peace' and 'new creation' in Deutero-Isaiah. G. K. Beale[9] is representative of those who have argued for an OT matrix of Paul's

---

5.   I. Howard Marshall, 'The Meaning of "Reconciliation"', in Robert A. Guelich (ed.), *Unity and Diversity in New Testament Theology* (Grand Rapids: Eerdmans, 1978), p. 121. Breytenbach points out that the same kind of usage is found in Philo (*Vit. Mos.* 2.166; *JosAs.* 11.18) and Josephus (*Ant.* 7.153), where David's or Israel's prayers of repentance cause God to be reconciled to them (Cilliers Breytenbach, *Versöhnung: Eine Studie zur paulinischen Soteriologie* (WMANT, 60; Neukirchen-Vluyn: Neukirchener, 1989), pp. 70–81.

6.   Marshall, I. H., 'The Meaning', p. 130.

7.   Breytenbach, *Versöhnung*, pp. 40–83.

8.   See next chapter ('3.4.3 Paul's political terms') for a list of such terms used by Paul.

9.   'The Old Testament Background of Reconciliation in 2 Corinthians 5–7 and Its Bearing on the

development of a 'reconciliation' motif.[10] Giving a fresh analysis of 2 Cor. 5.17–7.6 and paying special attention to the fact that Paul seems to link very closely the ideas of reconciliation and new creation, Beale proposes Isaiah 40–66 as the specific OT background for Paul's concept of reconciliation. Particularly, he shows that 'Paul understands both "new creation" in Christ as well as "reconciliation" in Christ (2 Cor. 5.17–21) as the inaugurated fulfilment of Isaiah's and the prophets' promise of a new creation in which Israel would be restored into a peaceful relationship with God . . .'[11]

The argument is solidly built on the close parallelism between the complex of ideas found in 2 Cor. 5.14–21 and those in Isaiah 40–66. God's anger over Israel's sin, manifested in Israel's exile and separation from her God, will cease, and he will take the initiative to restore his people through a redemptive act of new creation – when people will return to their homeland – and so peace will be re-established between Israel and her God through the vicarious suffering and death of his Servant. Thus Beale concludes that in 2 Cor. 5.14–21,

> 'reconciliation' in Christ is Paul's way of explaining that Isaiah's promises of 'restoration' from the alienation of exile have begun to be fulfilled by the atonement and forgiveness of sins in Christ. The believer's separation and alienation from God because of sin have been overcome through the divine grace expressed in Christ, who has restored the believer into a reconciled relationship of peace with God.[12]

This proposal for the origin of Paul's concept of reconciliation brings valuable insights into Paul's reflection on, and usage of, particular OT texts and is helpful in illustrating the broad conceptual background. This is especially relevant as recent scholarship on Paul emphasizes the centrality of Israel's story in the formulation of his theology. However, some authors argue that this attempt may not adequately explain the exact origin of the terms καταλλάσσω/καταλλαγή.[13]

Following on an assertion advanced but not substantiated by Hofius, Seyoon Kim

Literary Problem of 2 Corinthians 6:14–7:1', in G. K. Beale (ed.) *The Right Doctrines from the Wrong Text?* (Grand Rapids: Baker, 1994), pp. 217–47.

10. See especially Otfried Hofius, 'Erwägungen zur Gestalt und Herkunft des paulinischen Versöhnungsgedankens', in O. Hofius (ed.), *Paulusstudien* (Tubingen: J. C. B. Mohr-Siebeck, 1989), pp. 1–14 who argues that the background of 2 Cor. 5.18–21 is Isaiah 52–53; Otto Betz, 'Fleischliche und "geistiche" Christuserkenntnis nach 2 Korinther 5:16', in O. Betz (ed.), *Jesus – der Herr der Kirche* (Tubingen: Mohr-Siebeck, 1990), pp. 114–28; Peter Stuhlmacher, 'Das Evangelium von der Versöhnung in Christus', in Peter Stuhlmacher and Helmut Class (eds), *Das Evangelium von der Versohnung in Christus* (Stuttgart: Calwer Verlag, 1979), pp. 44–49.

11. Beale, 'Old Testament Background', p. 219.

12. Ibid., p. 223.

13. See especially Seyoon Kim, who stresses that simply pointing to the concept of 'peace' in Isaiah fails 'to explain how Paul could have come to designate God's saving act in Christ's death and his apostolic ministry in terms of his καταλλάσσειν/καταλλαγή while interpreting them in the light of Isa. 52–53, when the terminology is lacking in the Isaianic passage'. (Seyoon Kim, '2 Cor. 5:11–21 and the Origin of

proposes yet another thesis, namely 'that "reconciliation", the unique Pauline meta-phor for God's saving act in Christ, originated from Paul's personal experience of God's reconciliation of him to himself on the Damascus road'.[14] His starting point is represented by the three facts commonly accepted by the biblical commentators and which he considers in mutual connection: (1) 'reconciliation' terminology is uniquely Pauline in the NT; (2) in his use of 'reconciliation' language Paul reflects both the Hellenistic and Jewish Hellenistic background, and yet he makes a fundamental innovation by his insistence that it is God who reconciles human beings to himself and not vice versa; (3) in one of the earliest Pauline passages where the reconciliation language appears, 2 Cor. 5.11–21, Paul makes several allusions to his Damascus experience of divine reconciliation and call.[15]

By a careful exegesis of the passage in 2 Corinthians Kim argues convincingly that Paul talks there about his own Damascus-road experience of reconciliation to God, his commission to the ministry of reconciliation, grounding his statement on God's reconciliation effected in Christ's death.[16] The reason why Paul needed to recall and defend that particular experience as genuine was that his opponents seem to have attacked and discredited him exactly at that very point. They might have criticised Paul for grounding his gospel and apostleship on a 'doubtful' ecstatic visionary experience rather than on the proper apostolic teaching and authority. Moreover, Paul's construction of his *apologia*, especially his double insistence that his 'fleshly' perception of Christ has radically changed after the Damascus experience, and that, accordingly, he has been made a 'new creature', 'reconciled' to God and entrusted with the 'ministry of reconciliation', may be an indication that another major charge of his opponents had to do with his past as a fierce persecutor of the church and, implicitly, an enemy of Jesus Christ and God.[17] In his reply, continues Kim, Paul acknowledges his past hostility to Jesus as well as his persecution of the church. At the moment of his encounter with the risen Christ, however, God revealed to him that the crucified Jesus was in fact the Messiah of Israel, the Lord. And that experi-ence had caused Paul to come to a correct knowledge about Jesus Christ and his vicarious death on behalf of humankind, finding himself forgiven and being made a 'new creature'. The point Paul wanted to make was 'to underscore his having been liberated from the burden of his past hostility to Christ and his church through God's

Paul's Concept of "Reconciliation"', *Novum Testamentum* 34 (1997), pp. 360–84 (364). [Henceforth as 'The Origin']).

14. Ibid., p. 360. Kim points out two earlier commentators who had indicated that probability: A. Klöpper, *Kommentar über das zweite Sendschreiben des Apostles Paulus und die Gemeinde zu Korinth* (Berlin: Reimer, 1874), p. 302; A. Menzies, *The Second Epistle of the Apostle Paul to the Corinthians* (London: Macmillan, 1912), p. 43.

15. See Kim 'The Origin', especially pp. 360–66 and pp. 382–84.

16. Ibid., p. 368. C. Wolff makes a similar point in his article 'True Apostolic Knowledge of Christ: Exegetical Reflections on 2 Corinthians 5:14ff', in A. J. M. Wedderburn (ed.), *Paul and Jesus* (JSNTS, 37; Sheffield: Sheffield Academic, 1989), pp. 81–98.

17. Kim, 'The Origin', pp. 378–79.

forgiveness and to indicate that his opponents' insinuation about his past is therefore quite futile'.[18] It is at this point in his argument in 2 Corinthians that Paul introduces the term 'reconciliation' to highlight the extraordinary miracles of God's grace: not only was Paul, the 'enemy' of Christ (and God), 'reconciled' to God, but he was appointed as his 'ambassador of reconciliation' and entrusted with the 'message of reconciliation'. Paul's own experience and message was nothing less than a perfect illustration of the gospel, 'the message of God's work of reconciling the world to himself through Christ's atoning death'.[19] Kim concludes his study on the origin of Paul's unique formulation of the concept of reconciliation as follows:

> Paul developed his soteriological metaphor 'reconciliation' . . . out of his theological reflection on his personal experience on the Damascus road. In our judgement, it is this supposition rather than anything else that can explain convincingly the fundamental innovation he wrought in the Jewish idea of reconciliation: it is not human beings who reconcile an angry God to themselves through their prayer, repentance or good works; but rather it is God who has reconciled human beings to himself and still brings them to reconciliation to himself through the atoning death of Jesus Christ. For on the Damascus road Paul himself experienced God's reconciling him, a hostile enemy, to himself, forgiving his sins and making him a new creature by his grace.[20]

If Kim's proposal is right, there may be important implications for an understanding of the Pauline doctrine of reconciliation, especially in its social significance.[21] First is the relationship between justice and love. Paul's insistence that he experienced God's reconciling grace when he was an enemy of God (cf. Rom. 5.10 'For if *while we were enemies*, we were reconciled to God'), seems to suggest that the initiative for reconciliation may be taken by the 'offended' party, before the 'justice' is done to it by the offending party. It does not mean that justice becomes less important. But by the very initiation of the process of reconciliation the possibility of doing justice is opened. Paul had to 'give account' in a sense for his past, and by his subsequent life he proved to have 'corrected' his behaviour.

A second implication has to do with the intrinsic relationship between the reconciliation of human beings to God and reconciliation between human beings. When the resurrected Christ told Paul that persecuting the church meant, in fact, persecuting him, he may have understood that enmity toward human beings was enmity toward

---

18. Ibid., p. 380. Indeed, Paul's allusion to Isa. 43.18f. ('Do not remember the former things, and do not discuss *the old things. Behold* I make *new things*'), seems to strengthen Kim's reading. Like the original exhortation for Israel 'to forget their past sin and judgement but look to God's work of restoration/new creation', Paul himself was admonished by God 'to forget his past sin of acting in hostility to Christ and persecuting his church and rejoice in God's new creation of him in Christ' (ibid.).

19. Ibid., p. 382.

20. Ibid., pp. 382–83.

21. For an excellent theological treatment of this point see Volf, 'The Social Meaning of Reconciliation'.

God and vice versa. And in the same manner, reconciliation with God meant reconciliation with those he had persecuted, which Paul proved in his life. We will take
up these points in a later chapter of the present work and see whether there is a good
exegetical and theological foundation to sustain them.

2.3 *The significance of reconciliation in Paul's theology*

A number of other studies on reconciliation have concentrated on the significance of
the doctrine and its place in Paul's theology and, in what follows, we will look at the
most significant authors in this regard.

2.3.1 *Vincent Taylor: reconciliation as an essential element of atonement*

A major work on the subject, written from a NT theology perspective, is *Forgiveness
and Reconciliation: A Study in New Testament Theology*, by Vincent Taylor.[22] The
basic thrust of the book is to show that the NT teaching about forgiveness, justification, reconciliation, fellowship, and sanctification, are interrelated and they are all
components of the larger, more comprehensive, doctrine of atonement. We should
probably note as significant the fact that Taylor gives a very extensive treatment of
reconciliation which includes the congruous themes such as peace, freedom, sonship,
and fellowship, and he rightly insists that for an extensive treatment of reconciliation
in the NT one should consider all instances 'wherever reconciliation is described,
even though the Pauline terminology is not employed'[23] (p. 70). A major concern of
Taylor in his search for a definition of reconciliation[24] is to determine how much of
the reconciliation material in the NT illustrates the content of reconciliation and how
much its fruits or effects. And consequently, how exactly do forgiveness, justification, reconciliation, and fellowship relate to one another as essential components of
atonement? This is how Taylor presents this complex interrelationship:

> Reconciliation . . . as the restoration of the soul to fellowship with God already includes within
> itself the remission of sins and *justification* and is at one and the same time *fellowship* with

---

22. V. Taylor, *Forgiveness and Reconciliation* (2nd edn; London: Macmillan, 1946). Since in this
section I refer only to this study of Taylor, I indicate the exact location of the quotes by placing the page
number in brackets immediately at the end of quote, in the main text.

23. Unfortunately, Taylor does not elaborate on this particular point, but as we will see in subsequent
chapters, he hints strongly at what Gerd Theissen will later call Paul's 'symbolism of reconciliation' being
larger than the specific word, a point we will interact with and substantiate in this work.

24. After analysing the four 'classical passages', he summarises in six points the Pauline teaching on
reconciliation: (1) it is the restoration of men to fellowship with God; (2) it is only reconciliation of men to
God not vice versa; (3) reconciliation is an act accomplished by God; (4) men cannot contribute anything
to their reconciliation to God except their consent and readiness to be reconciled; (5) their condition from
which men are reconciled is one of enmity and estrangement; (6) reconciliation is brought through Christ,
by his sacrificial death (pp. 71–84, especially p. 84).

God and the introduction to fellowship. *Sanctification* . . . is the fruition and the climax of
this fellowship with God and men; it is perfect love, beatitude, and the final gift of the vision
of God [pp. 141–42] . . . it is the goal and consummation of reconciliation and fellowship
[p. 144].

Taylor's work has highlighted several relevant and important matters. First, it
emphasises the fact that any adequate inquiry into the theme of reconciliation in
Paul's theology cannot in any way be limited to a single word study since 'there is
every reason to think that [Paul] . . . describes reconciliation in cases where he does
not use the word' (p. 84). Second, it shows that Paul's teaching and understanding
of reconciliation is larger in its scope than the reconciliation of men with God, and
includes further social implications. Taylor states: 'it is neither possible nor desir-
able to limit the theme to forgiveness and reconciliation with God, for all kinds of
human relationships, personal, religious, social, and international are suggested by
it' (p. xiii). Unfortunately, even though Taylor has constantly in mind the further
social implications of reconciliation, he does not explore them in any detail, 'partly
because, in themselves, they are far-reaching enough to warrant independent study,
but mainly because, in the writer's view, for purposes both of understanding and
of practical treatment, they depend upon the primary question of forgiveness and
reconciliation with God' (p. xiii).

2.3.2 *Ralph Martin: reconciliation as the centre of Pauline theology*
Among NT scholars Ralph Martin has probably written more extensively on the
Pauline concept of reconciliation than anyone else.[25] His treatment of reconciliation is part of his search for a 'centre' that will unite all the books of the NT, 'an
underlying common thread that binds them together into the church's authoritative
canon'.[26] Identifying reconciliation elements of pre-Pauline Christianity, Paul's own
redaction and additions,[27] as well as the development of the theme in the school
of Paul, Martin constructs a 'trajectory of reconciliation' and proposes that the
single term 'reconciliation', 'broadly conceived and applied' represents the *centrum*

25. He started with 'Reconciliation and Forgiveness in the Letter to the Colossians', in Robert
Banks (ed.), *Reconciliation and Hope* (Exeter: Paternoster Press, 1974), pp. 104–24, followed by two
programmatic essays in 1980, 'New Testament Theology: Impasse and Exit', *Expository Times*, 91 (1980),
pp. 264–69 and 'New Testament Theology: A Proposal. The Theme of Reconciliation', *Expository Times*
91 (1980), pp. 364–68. Out of the last two, Martin later on developed his monograph, *Reconciliation: A
Study of Paul's Theology* (rev. edn; Grand Rapids: Zondervan, 1989) as well as 'Reconciliation: Romans
5:1–11', in Soderlund and Wright (eds), *Romans and the People of God*, pp. 36–48.
26. Martin, 'New Testament Theology: Impasse and Exit', p. 267.
27. In his earliest article on the topic, 'Reconciliation and Forgiveness', Martin distinguishes pre-
Pauline traditional composition in the two christological hymns in Colossians, Col. 1.12–23 'Christian
Experience and the Hymn to Christ', and Col. 2.13–15 'New Life in Christ and the Hymn to the Saviour'.
But, as we will see later in our evaluation, the idea of a pre-Pauline formulation of the concept of reconciliation finds less support among biblical scholars today.

Paulinum, the overarching core of his soteriology – indeed, 'the organising principle of NT theology'.[28] But it was only in his subsequent book, *Reconciliation: a Study of Paul's Theology*, that he developed in detail the thesis that 'reconciliation is a term sufficiently broad as an "umbrella idea" to accommodate the leading aspects of Paul's main thinking'.[29] I will, therefore, concentrate on this last work for an evaluation of Martin's treatment of the significance of reconciliation in Paul's theology.

Beginning with the formative factors of Paul's theology – background influences, Paul's conversion or call, his leading themes, and his view of the human condition – Martin sets forth his thesis that 'reconciliation' can be taken as an interpretative key to Paul's thought. He highlights the significance of Paul's own experience on the Damascus road, and that Paul's theology was *'fashioned and shaped as a reflective transcript of his own experience'* (p. 31, italics in the original). And it is the theme of reconciliation, contends Martin, rather than justification, salvation, or communion with Christ, which can encompass the major dimensions of Paul's thought, because it is 'reconciliation' which best accounts for the three necessary criteria: (1) the cosmic predicament of disorder and alienation; (2) God's restoration through Jesus Christ; and (3) Paul's own experience of grace.

Having set the stage for his thesis, Martin then does a very careful exegesis of the key texts where the term appears in 2 Corinthians 5, Colossians 1, and Romans 5 and 11, using linguistic, form-critical, and historical methods. He notes that even though it is not a frequent word in the NT, the importance of 'reconciliation' as a concept far exceeds the limited appearance of specific words. One way in which Martin proves the importance of the concept is by the evidence he brings to sustain the 'trajectory of reconciliation' – the development of the tradition from pre-Pauline times, then Paul's own redaction and contribution, to the later Pauline school of thought. The main reason for Paul adopting and using reconciliation language as a key category for his gospel was the very fact that he had to proclaim this gospel in a Gentile environment where the OT and Judaic tradition of convenantal nomism was incomprehensible. And so, he made perfect use of a terminology related to the universal need of forgiveness and personal relationships. Martin summarises Paul's exposition of reconciliation in the following five points (pp. 151–53): (1) God is the provider of the new relationship he freely offers; (2) at great cost, epitomised in Christ's blood or death on the cross, God has moved to deal with a situation only he could resolve; (3) human need is the dark canvas against which the divine love shines brightly; (4) above all, reconciliation moves always on the plane of personal relationships; (5) reconciliation is the way Paul formulated his gospel in communicating it to the Gentiles.

The argument continues with a comparative survey of Paul and Jesus, where Martin shows that 'Paul's gospel of reconciliation stood in continuity with the

---

28. 'New Testament Theology: A Proposal', pp. 364–68.

29. In the Preface. All immediate subsequent references to Martin in this section refer to this book, and the page numbers are indicated in brackets at the end of the quote.

ministry and message of Jesus of Nazareth' and that 'Paul is expressing in a fresh idiom what is implicit in Jesus' life and achievement' (p. 223). The conclusion of the study is obvious: 'reconciliation' meets the criteria that justify it as Paul's theological core and 'provides a suitable umbrella under which the main features of Paul's kerygma and its practical outworking may be set' (p. 239).

A positive aspect emphasized in Martin's book is that the vertical dimension of reconciliation with God should flow into the horizontal aspect of reconciliation, with all its social implications, for in Paul's understanding, 'the dimension of reconciliation is as much horizontal as vertical' (p. 229). Paul's insistence to the Philippians that they should 'shine as light in the world holding forth the word of life' (Phil. 2.15–16), demonstrating thus their true experience as reconciled people,[30] is a clear suggestion that, 'Reconciliation is more than a theological code-word for God's work of restoring men and women to himself. It marks the way of life to which those people are summoned by the fact that they are reconciled and share in God's continuing ministry of reconcilement in the world' (p. 130).

In light of these remarks, and particularly after he initially acknowledges 'the present relevance of reconciliation to social and racial issues . . . to ecological matters, to the vexed geopolitical challenges such as world peace and justice' (p. 6), it is somewhat disappointing that Martin does not explore these aspects of Paul's teaching and that, given the different focus of his argument, he 'wisely resisted' the temptation to comment on such matters!

Despite its detailed and careful analysis, Martin's thesis and conclusion are not generally accepted by biblical scholars.[31] The main difficulty of this approach, in their opinion, is its reductionist tendencies of imposing a rather artificial demand that the texts should be systematically organised. Karl Donfried is representative of those who critique this position: 'Martin has not only failed to demonstrate that reconciliation is the *centrum Paulinum*, he has also failed to take seriously some of the major advances made in the last two decades in our understanding of Paul.'[32] Similarly, Martin's theory that Paul took over a pre-Pauline conception of reconcili-

30. Martin had earlier pointed out that even though reconciliation with God is an indispensable foundation in the process, 'there must be a personal dimension, otherwise the profound teaching remains *in abstracto* and detached from human experience' (p. 98).

31. In reviewing his work a number of commentators are critical of the whole search for a 'centre' in New Testament theology and think that Martin fails to demonstrate that reconciliation is such a centre in Paul's theology. Among them we mention Charles H. Giblin, Beverly Roberts Gaventa, James M. Reese, Jeffrey W. Gillette, John Drane, James Davis, Gregory Allen, and W. Hulitt Gloer.

32. In his review of Martin's book, in *Interpretation* 37 (1983), p. 84. On the other hand, there are some scholars who argue along the same line as Martin. Peter Stuhlmacher, for example, argues that it is possible to provide a summary description of the whole New Testament thought, and proposes that 'the gospel of reconciliation of God with his creation through the sending of the messiah Jesus Christ is the heartbeat of the New Testament'. (P. Stuhlmacher, 'The Gospel of Reconciliation in Christ – Basic Features and Issues of a Biblical Theology of the New Testament', *Horizons in Biblical Theology* 1 (1979), pp. 161–90 (180).

ation is hardly supported today.[33] These two remarks alone raise sufficient doubt for the argument as a whole. However, this should not hinder us from appreciating the significance and the strength of Martin's work, especially the forceful way in which he brings to our attention a new understanding of reconciliation and its importance in Paul's theology. We might not be convinced that reconciliation represents 'the centre' of Paul's theology, but Martin's analysis has established that reconciliation is, at least, a major theme in Pauline theology.

2.3.3 *Ernst Käsemann: reconciliation as a marginal concept in Paul*

At the opposite end of the spectrum as to the significance of reconciliation in Paul's theology is Ernst Käsemann who argues in his article 'Some Thoughts on the Theme "The Doctrine of Reconciliation in the NT"'[34] that the motif of reconciliation 'appears only in the general realm of Paulinism, *though without having any significant meaning for Pauline theology as a whole*'.[35] It is just one of the many ways in which the Christ-event may be interpreted, and, more concretely, statements about reconciliation are important just to highlight the doctrine of justification which is 'the heart of the Christian message'.[36] There are basically two sets of arguments that Käsemann brings to support his thesis: the paucity of direct references to reconciliation in the NT, and the fact that, even when they are used, they reflect hymnic and liturgical materials originally used by the primitive Hellenistic Jewish communities. Following Käsemann, Rudolf Pesch, pointing out the rarity of the appearance of the concept throughout Paul's letters, agrees that reconciliation cannot assume a leading role in Paul's theology.[37]

The main difficulty with such an approach is its tendency to measure the significance of a concept based on the frequency of its explicit occurrences and the fact that is does not also consider, for example, the whole range of terms and synonyms which describe the 'idea' of reconciliation in Pauline arguments, as well as the occasional nature of the letters. This kind of 'concordance' study is, in most of the cases, misleading.[38] And then, ironically, in his attempt to dismiss the idea of a centre in

---

33. As we have seen in the previous sections, there are better alternative explanations for the origin of the concept of reconciliation. For further and more detailed argumentation against a pre-Pauline tradition see Jan Lambrecht, —'"Reconcile Yourselves . . .", A Reading of 2 Corinthians 5, 11–21', in Bieringer, R. and J. Lambrecht (eds), *Studies on 2 Corinthians* (Leuven: University Press, 1994b), pp. 389–90; Marshall, I. H. 'The Meaning', pp. 129–30; Margaret E. Thrall, 'Salvation Proclaimed, 2 Corinthians 5:18–21: Reconciliation with God', *Expository Times* 93 (1981), pp. 227–32 (229).

34. In James M. Robinson (ed.), *The Future of Our Religious Past: Essays in Honour of Rudolf Bultmann* (London: SCM Press, 1971), pp. 49–64.

35. Ibid., p. 51.

36. Ibid., p. 63.

37. Rudolf Pesch, 'Reconciliation: New Testament', in Johannes Bauer (ed.), *Bauer Encyclopaedia of Biblical Theology, Vol. 2* (3rd edn; London: Sheed and Ward, 1970), pp. 735–38.

38. As an illustration we may consider, for example, Paul's use of 'forgiveness'. Although the verb 'forgive' appears 72 times in the NT, mostly in the gospels, Paul uses it only 4 times! The same with 'forgiven' and 'forgiveness': out of a total of 46 and 22 occurrences in the NT respectively, in Paul these words

Paul's theology, and with it the place of reconciliation, it seems that Käsemann ends up establishing another centre, that of 'justification'.[39] Finally, as we have mentioned earlier, the idea of a pre-Pauline tradition of reconciliation is not adequately grounded and it is seriously challenged today.

2.3.4 *Reconciliation as a major Pauline concept*

Another group of studies on the Pauline understanding of reconciliation stresses the centrality and importance of the concept in Paul's thought. Thus, in a representative study Fitzmyer reconsiders the topic precisely because 'the role of the reconciliation in his [Paul's] theology has been called in question'.[40] Arguing against Käsemann, he shows that reconciliation was a figure as significant as all the other figures that Paul used to interpret the effects of the Christ-event. And since one of Paul's dominant interests was exactly in what Christ, by his death and resurrection, has accomplished for human beings, he made good use of various figures derived from his Jewish and Hellenistic background which enabled him to express best the various aspects of Christ's work in response to the manifold concrete challenges of his day. Similar points are made by other scholars among whom are Herman Ridderbos,[41] Peter Stuhlmacher,[42] and W. Hulitt Gloer.[43]

---

appear only 4 and 2 times, with the last two in Ephesians and Colossians! Can we conclude, based on these simple facts, that 'forgiveness' is not an important category in Paul's theology? On the contrary, I think the opposite is rather the case even if Paul expressed it in a different way from that of the evangelists. William Hulitt Gloer rightly points out the shortcomings of such an approach, and offers another example: 'Does the fact that Paul mentions the Lord's Supper only once in his letters indicate that it had little significance for him? Certainly not! It does, however, indicate that Paul felt no need to discuss it in his other letters, and, therefore, reminds us of the *occasional* nature of Paul's writings, and that they are addressed to particular situations and issues.' (W. H. Gloer, *An Exegetical and Theological Study of Paul's Understanding of New Creation and Reconciliation in 2 Cor. 5:14–21* (Lewiston: The Edwin Mellen Press, 1996), p. 190.

39.   There is, of course, more to be said on Käsemann's serious and detailed treatment of the doctrine of justification, especially as it relates to the doctrine of reconciliation, and the brevity of our comments here should not be taken as a complete statement of his understanding and treatment of the doctrine of reconciliation. We will certainly continue to engage with Käsemann's thought, as we develop our argument in subsequent chapters.

40.   Joseph Fitzmyer, 'Reconciliation in Pauline Theology', in James Flanagan and Anita Robinson (eds), *No Famine in the Land: Studies in Honor of John L McKenzie* (Missoula, MT: Scholars Press, 1975), pp. 155–78. Fitzmyer is referring, of course, to the study by Käsemann, with whom he is constantly in dialogue (p. 155).

41.   'The Biblical Message of Reconciliation', in H. Ridderbos, *Studies in Scripture and Its Authority* (Grand Rapids: Eerdmans, 1978), pp. 72–90; see also 'Reconciliation' in his book *Paul: An Outline of His Theology* (John Richard De Witt (trans.); Grand Rapids: Eerdmans, 1975), pp. 182–204.

42.   'The Gospel of Reconciliation in Christ'. See note 45.

43.   *An Exegetical and Theological Study.* See note 54. Gloer refers also to Rudolf Schnackenburg's *New Testament Theology Today* (David Askew (trans.); London: Geoffrey Chapman, 1963), and F. Stagg's *New Testament Theology* (Nashville, TN, 1962), both of whom maintain the significant place of reconciliation in Paul's theology and in the whole New Testament.

2.4 *The nature of reconciliation*

So far, we have discussed and/or referred to more comprehensive studies which focus on reconciliation as a whole. The most numerous studies, however, concentrate on specific passages in the Pauline corpus highlighting one or more particular aspects or elements of the concept of reconciliation. They focus on one of the various questions related to the concept: the extent of reconciliation, whether it is only human beings who are reconciled to God or is it God also who is being reconciled, or whether there is more to that;[44] the means of reconciliation and how it is effected;[45] the effects or the consequences of reconciliation;[46] the objective vs. subjective nature of reconciliation;[47] the ministry of reconciliation;[48] and the relationship between reconciliation and atonement/justification/expiation.[49] Some studies concentrate on several of these or related issues,[50] while some may not necessarily fit in any of these categories.[51] I do not

---

44. John Murray, 'The Reconciliation', *The Westminster Theological Journal* 29 (1966), pp. 1–23; Leon Morris, 'Reconciliation', *Christianity Today* 13(8) (1969), pp. 331–32; Thrall, 'Salvation Proclaimed', pp. 227–32; C. J. Burdon, 'Paul and the Crucified Church', *Expository Times* 95(5) (1984), pp. 137–41; P. T. O'Brien, 'Col. 1:20 and the Reconciliation of all Things', *The Reformed Theological Review* 33(1) (1974), pp. 45–53; Thomas Talbott, 'The New Testament and Universal Reconciliation', *Christian Scholar's Review* 21(4) (1992), pp. 376–94; John F. Walvoord, 'Reconciliation', *BS* 120(77) (1963), pp. 3–12; F. F. Bruce, 'Christ as Conqueror and Reconciler', *BS* 141(564) (1984), pp. 291–302.

45. William Hulitt Gloer, '2 Corinthians 5,14–21', *RE* 86 (1989), pp. 397–405; Herman Binder, 'Versöhnung Als Die Grosse Wende' (Reconciliation as the Great Turning Point), *Theologische Zeitschrift* 29 (1973), pp. 305–12.

46. J. H. Roberts, 'Some Biblical Foundations for a Mission of Reconciliation', in *Missionalia* 7(1) (1979), pp. 3–17.

47. M. Aldrich Willard, 'The Objective Nature of Reconciliation', *BS* 118(469) (1961), pp. 18–21.

48. Reimund Bieringer, 'Paul's Understanding of Diakonia in 2 Corinthians 5:18', in R. Bieringer and J. Lambrecht (eds) *Studies in 2 Corinthians* (Leuven: University Press, 1994), pp. 413–28; Victor Paul Furnish, 'The Ministry of Reconciliation', *Currents in Theology and Mission* 4(4) (1977), pp. 204–18; Clark Hyde, 'The Ministry of Reconciliation', *St Luke's Journal of Theology* 31(2) (1988), pp. 111–25; John De Gruchy, 'The Struggle for Justice and Ministry of Reconciliation', in *JTSA* 62 (1988), pp. 43–52; David L. Turner, 'Paul and the Ministry of Reconciliation in 2 Cor. 5:11–6:2', *Criswell Theological Review* 4(1) (1989), pp. 77–95; J. I. H. McDonald, 'Paul and the Preaching Ministry: A Reconsideration of 2 Cor. 2:14–17 in its Context', *JSNT* 17 (1983), pp. 35–50.

49. Lambrecht, '"Reconcile Yourselves . . ."', pp. 363–412; Adolf Koeberle, 'Reconciliation and Justification', *CTM* 21(9) (1950), pp. 641–58; Vincent Brummer, 'Atonement and Reconciliation', *Religious Studies* 28 (1992), pp. 435–52; Martin H. Franzmann, 'Reconciliation and Justification', *CTM* 21(2) (1950), pp. 81–93.

50. Charles B. Cousar, 'II Corinthians 5:17–21', *Interpretation* 35 (1981), pp. 180–83; Bruce W. Fong, 'Addressing the Issue of Racial Reconciliation According to the Principles of Eph 2: 11–22', *JETS* 38(4) (1995), pp. 565–80; F. Forster, '"Reconcile", 2 Cor. 5:18–20', *CTM* 21(3) (1950), pp. 296–98; M. Aldrich Willard, 'The Objective Nature of Reconciliation', *BS* 118(469) (1961), pp. 18–21; W. R. Domeris, 'Biblical Perspectives on Reconciliation', *JTSA* 60 (1987), pp. 77–80; Cilliers Breytenbach, 'On Reconciliation: An Exegetical Response', *JTSA* 70 (1990), pp. 64–68; Jack P. Lewis, *Interpreting 2 Corinthians 5:14–21. An Exercise in Hermeneutics* (Studies in the Bible and Early Christianity, 17; Lewiston, NY: The Edwin Mellen Press, 1989). See also Buchsel, 'ἀλλάσσω'; H. Vorlander and C. Brown, 'καταλλάσσω' in *NIDNTT* Vol. 3, pp. 166–74.

51. Christoph Stenschke, 'The Death of Jesus and the New Testament Doctrine of Reconciliation in

consider it necessary to interact in detail here with these last studies given both the different focus of the present research, namely the social meaning of reconciliation in Pauline theology, and the fact that most of the above-mentioned studies focus almost exclusively on the vertical dimension of reconciliation, between God and human beings. However, we will be in critical dialogue with them at significant points throughout the work, build on various aspects which have emerged from these studies, and, when appropriate, will interact fully and adequately with them at that point.

Three general observations could be made regarding the basic questions being addressed in the Pauline treatment of reconciliation in the studies mentioned above. First, whatever their exact concern or question on Paul's concept of reconciliation, the above studies have focused their attention exclusively on the four passages where Paul uses καταλλάσσω/καταλλαγή terminology: Rom. 5.10–11; 2 Cor. 5.14–21; Col. 1.20–21; Eph. 2.11–22.[52]

Second, based on these passages, the basic teaching on reconciliation is usually presented, with insignificant variations, in the following five major points: 1) God is always the subject of reconciliation; he is the reconciler who reconciles the world to himself; God is not reconciled and he does not reconcile himself to human beings or to the world; it is always humans that are reconciled to God and are urged to reconcile themselves to him (2 Cor. 5.20); God took the initiative in bringing about reconciliation, while man was still at enmity towards God; 2) Reconciliation has been effected by the death of Christ (Rom. 5.10); 3) Reconciliation denotes a real change and transformation in the relationship between God and human beings, a restoration

---

Recent Discussion', *The European Journal of Theology* 9 (2000), pp. 131–58; C. D. Stanley, '"Neither Jew nor Greek": Ethnic Conflict in Graeco-Roman Society', *JSNT* 64 (1996), pp. 101–24; W. Rader, *The Church and Racial Hostility: A History of Interpretation of Ephesians 2:11–22*; R. G. Tanner, 'St. Paul's View of Militia and Contemporary Social Values', in E. A. Livingstone (ed.), *Studia Biblica 1978: III. Papers on Paul and Other New Testament Papers* (Sheffield: Sheffield University Press, 1980), pp. 377–382; Krister Stendahl, 'Hate, Nonretaliation, and Love: Coals of Fire', in G. Stassen *et al.* (eds), *Meanings: The Bible as Documents and as Guide* (Philadelphia: Fortress, 1984), pp. 137–49; Michel Desjardins, *Peace, Violence and the New Testament* (Sheffield; Sheffield Academic, 1997); Margaret M. Mitchell, *Paul and the Rhetoric of Reconciliation* (Tubingen: Mohr, 1991); Gregory J. Allen, *Reconciliation in the Pauline Tradition: Its Occasions, Meanings, and Functions* (Th.D. dissertation, Boston University, School of Theology, 1995; UMI: Ann Arbor, 1998); W. Hulitt Gloer, 'Ambassadors of Reconciliation: Paul's Genius In Applying the Gospel in a Multi-Cultural World: 2 Corinthians 5:14–21', *RE* 104 (2007), pp. 589–604; James R. A. Merrick, 'Justice, Forgiveness, and Reconciliation: The Reconciliatory Cross as Forgiving Justice', *Evangelical Review of Theology* 30(3) (2006), pp. 292–308; Teresa Okure, 'The Ministry of Reconciliation (2 Cor 5:14–21): Paul's Key to the Problem of "the Other" in Corinth', *Mission Studies* 23(1) (2006), pp. 105–21; David Tombs and Joseph Liechty (eds), *Explorations in Reconciliation: New Directions in Theology* (Aldershot: Ashgate, 2006); Max Turner, 'Human Reconciliation in the New Testament with Special Reference to Philemon, Colossians and Ephesians', *European Journal of Theology* 16(1) (2006), pp. 37–47; Ivar Vegge, *2 Corinthians: A Letter about Reconciliation* (WUNT, 239; Tubingen: Mohr Siebeck, 2008). In addition we should mention the discussions of specific texts on reconciliation in the commentaries.

52. Some authors eliminate Ephesians and Colossians from the study of Paul's reconciliation on the grounds that they are not Pauline while others notice the similarity and continuity of Paul's teaching with his authentic letters.

of fellowship with God (2 Cor. 5.18; Rom. 5.10); the change refers to the human side and affects the whole state of life (the language of 'new creation' is used); 4) To become effective, reconciliation needs to be appropriated; 5) There is a ministry of reconciliation to be carried out into the world by those who have been reconciled (2 Cor. 5.18–19).

Finally, most of the studies address issues that have to do in one way or another with the vertical dimension of reconciliation, between God and human beings, at a personal, religious level and do not investigate the social significance of the concept in Paul's theology.

2.5 *Conclusion: implications for the present research*

Several preliminary conclusions emerge from our survey of the Pauline exegetical scholarship on reconciliation. First, the focus of research has been shaped basically by three major sets of questions: what is the origin of Paul's usage of the concept of reconciliation? What is the place of the concept in Paul's theology? What is the exact nature of reconciliation? Second, though a very prominent concept in Paul, reconciliation has been treated, methodologically, in a very limited way, in two respects. On the one hand, it has been textually limited to the four passages in Paul's letters where the word itself appears. On the other hand, as a theological category, Paul's concept has been limited almost exclusively to its vertical dimension, of reconciliation between individuals and God, and given a narrow, religious interpretation. Even though some authors point also to a social dimension of reconciliation in Paul's theology it does not receive more than a marginal note in their studies.

A third important insight that comes out in our survey is the recognition that an adequate treatment of reconciliation in Paul needs to go beyond a mere word study. Many scholars agree that reconciliation is an important concept in Pauline theology, larger than the language used per se, and it is present even where the word is not used. And this leads us to the fourth concluding remark, namely, that reconciliation – a concept derived from interpersonal relationships – does have further social and political implications. Unfortunately, as our survey has also revealed, there have been no attempts to explore concretely these dimensions of Paul's theology. It is indeed striking that reconciliation, a figure derived from the socio-political spheres of life,[53] came to be interpreted in a narrow, individualistic, religious way. To my knowledge, there is not any study which has tried to deal particularly with the social meaning of reconciliation in Pauline theology. However, Paul's concept of reconciliation can

---

53. Fitzmyer reminds us that in our treatment of reconciliation we should always bear in mind that 'The notions of enmity, hostility, estrangement, and alienation, as well as their counterparts, reconciliation, atonement, friendship, and intimacy are derived from social intercourse of human persons or from the relations of ethnic and national groups, such as Jews and Greeks, Palestinians and Romans' (J. Fitzmyer, *Pauline Theology* (Englewood Cliffs, NJ: Prentice-Hall, 1967), p. 162). A similar point is made also in Beker's *Paul the Apostle* regarding metaphors/symbols for salvation.

offer much help today as we face the challenges of a complex and divided world. Indeed, as Fitzmyer notes, for Christians, the motivation to struggle for peace and unity, and against hatred and racism 'is found in Paul's idea of reconciliation, in the breaking down of the barriers between men (and by implication, between nations)'.[54] There is, definitely, a need for further reflection on these aspects of reconciliation.[55]

With all this in mind, it comes as a surprise that studies on reconciliation have not paid attention to the social dimension of the concept in Paul. Various reasons have been given for such a limitation. As we have seen, some authors openly acknowledge that reconciliation has further social implications, yet they 'resist' the temptation even to comment on them, let alone explore in detail their significance (e.g. Taylor, Martin). This is due to both their different focus of research and a sensitive awareness that any engagement with the far-reaching social dimensions of reconciliation in Paul would require a totally different study. In part, the present work is an attempt to fill in that particular gap.

Our survey illustrates yet another more important reason why the horizontal dimension of reconciliation has been neglected in the NT scholarship. It is a rather common assumption that a proper understanding of the social meaning of reconciliation as well as a practical treatment of the subject are dependent upon the primary question of reconciliation with God which should thus receive adequate attention. While this basic presupposition may prove to be correct, it does not justify a neglect of the other aspect. The fact that reconciliation with God has primacy has meant, in practice, a surprisingly great absence of studies offering social explications of the message of reconciliation. Conversely, very detailed, if at times irrelevant, treatments of reconciliation with God are abundant.

A further explanation for not giving a more social and political exegesis of the concept is offered by pointing to Paul's own limitation. Paul was not a social engineer, it is said, and so he was not concerned with the wider relevance and impact his churches might have exercised upon the surrounding societies. Rather, it is argued, Paul's only concern was the establishment and consolidation of new Christian communities. Again, while there are elements of truth in these statements, recent studies have shown that, in fact, the two concerns do not exclude each other but are closely interrelated. There are many instances in Paul's letters that prove not only his interest but also his constant concern to remind his listeners to behave in an appropriate way towards 'the other' be they from within or outside the Christian community.[56]

---

54. Fitzmyer, *Pauline Theology*, p. 167.

55. Fitzmyer concludes: 'But on another level of dealings between groups and individuals within a given national or ethnic society there is still further need for reflection on the Pauline message of reconciliation', ibid., p. 167.

56. Mark G. Brett (ed.), *Ethnicity and the Bible* (Leiden: Brill, 1996); William S. Campbell, *Paul's Gospel in an Intercultural Context* (Berlin: Peter Lang, 1992); Fong, 'Addressing the Issue of Racial Reconciliation'; Grams, 'Paul and Missions'; R. Jewett, *Christian Tolerance: Paul's Message to the Modern Church* (Philadelphia: Westminster Press, 1982); Abraham J. Malherbe, *Social Aspects of Early Christianity* (Philadelphia, PA: Fortress, 1983), and *Paul and the Thessalonians* (Philadelphia,

In addition, we might also refer to another reality which may explain the lack of reflection on the social and political issues, particularly in Paul. Even though it does not come directly from the survey of our literature, it is, somehow, presupposed throughout. Paul has been invoked, throughout the history of Christianity, to justify all kinds of oppression: from slavery to submissiveness of women to men or wives to their husbands, to anti-Semitism and unconditional compliance to the state. These long traditions of (mis)interpretation which made Paul 'responsible' for all these issues have caused great misunderstandings of his theology, and have caused scholars to look in other places and sources for a social and political application of the gospel. Coupled with a post-Reformation, individualistic appropriation of Paul it was natural that the other dimensions of his gospel would be lost. It is in response to these 'misinterpretations' of Paul that recent studies try to react and offer new ways of understanding Paul. Neil Elliott's *Liberating Paul: The Justice of God and the Politics of the Apostle*,[57] offers an excellent example. Showing first how Paul has been misinterpreted and appropriated by the powerful and privileged in order to maintain their own privileges at the expense of their victims, Elliott then provides an illuminating and challenging approach towards recovering the political dimensions of Paul's theology. We will comment further on his work later in the book.

Finally, we should refer indeed to the limitations of the classical historical-critical methodology of biblical studies, especially in the traditional 'word-study' approaches, as many scholars have pointed out.[58] Our survey has revealed the results of such a method and the need to overcome it for an adequate treatment of reconciliation in Paul. We have, we believe, provided a reasonable argument for both the need and the appropriateness of an inquiry into the social meaning of reconciliation in Pauline theology.

PA: Fortress, 1987); E. Earle Ellis, *Pauline Theology: Ministry and Society* (Grand Rapids: Eerdmans, 1989).

57. N. Elliott, *Liberating Paul: The Justice of God and the Politics of the Apostle* (Maryknoll, NY: Orbis, 1999).

58. For example, Mark G. Brett, *Biblical Criticism in Crisis* (Cambridge: CUP, 1991); Francis Watson (ed.), *The Open Text: New Directions for Biblical Studies?* (London: SCM Press, 1993).

3

FROM CREATION TO NEW CREATION: THE UNDERLYING FRAMEWORK OF PAUL'S UNDERSTANDING OF RECONCILIATION

3.1 *Introduction*

One of the major conclusions of the review chapter was that the Pauline concept of reconciliation has been restricted to a treatment of its vertical dimension; i.e., the reconciliation of individuals to God. This concentration on the individualistic, theological and religious aspects of reconciliation diverted scholars from discussing the social and political implications of the concept for the complex realities of everyday life. There have been virtually no such considerations in the exegetical scholarship. One of the main reasons invoked for this restriction was the claim that Paul was not concerned with the social, political realities of the world, but rather with solely preaching the gospel of salvation. Further, the claim goes, Paul expected the imminent end of the world and so he did not care much about what happened with the wider world. We hope that our discussion in this chapter will invalidate such a view.

Far from an escapist mentality, we will argue, Paul's creational theology – i.e., his understanding of God's relation to, and sovereignty over creation, over nations and over history, and the way this reality was irreversibly affected by God's intervention in Christ – gave him a positive view of the world and of the place and role of the larger structures of society. Furthermore, the way he formulated his gospel shows that Paul was well acquainted with the religious, cultural, social, and political matrix of the Graeco-Roman world with which he thoroughly engaged. As we hope to argue in this chapter, within this larger framework of reference it is plausible, indeed necessary, to enquire about the social meaning of reconciliation in Paul, since his theology, like much of the theological discourse of the NT, was meant not simply to 'offer salvation' in a narrow spiritual sense, but also to affect moral dispositions, to shape particular communities, to determine specific behaviour and a particular way of being in and for the world.

In this chapter, therefore, I intend to offer the underlying framework of Paul's life and thought within which one is to interpret the social meaning of reconciliation in his writings. I will first address Paul's theological/religious background which informed his social and political ideas and praxis. Then I will discuss the social and political context within which Paul lived, thought, and wrote, and within which his congregations had to embody the reality of the gospel. Special emphasis is placed on the close integration of religion and politics in the ancient world. We will conclude with a short note on Paul's political terms.

3.2 *The Jewish context: Paul's storied worldview*

It is increasingly acknowledged today that Paul's upbringing as a Jew fundamentally conditioned the way in which he perceived the world and the reality around him, even after his conversion. While his Christian theology shows some discontinuity with the Jewish theology, there was also significant continuity, and contemporary authors attempt to bring this aspect to light in various ways.[1] Paul's autobiographical statements in Phil. 3.4–7, 2 Cor. 11.22, 1 Cor. 15.9, and Gal. 1.13–14 show clearly his Jewish credentials, his zeal for the traditions of his ancestors, his unique advances in Judaism – which, probably, few Jews or Jewish Christians would have equalled – and his sophisticated education in Judaism. A particularly significant element which appears in all these accounts is his 'zeal' as a Pharisee which prompted him to persecute the church.[2] Paul's early life might have been modelled by Elijah's example – both in his zeal as persecutor of those he saw as compromised Jews, and in his reaction to the encounter with God (1 Kings 18–19).[3] However, it is most probably Isaiah who profoundly influenced Paul in his apostolic endeavours, as several scholars have pointed out.[4] Gal. 1.13–16 (especially v. 16b) is an indication that Paul came to an understanding that this particular form of 'zeal' was wrong and that he changed his 'mission', from bringing persecution to being a light to the nations. And it was the role of the servant that pointed the way forward.

    While Paul redefined some aspects of his Jewish past it is evident that he continued

---

1.   J. Neyrey, for example, employs insights from cultural anthropology to show that Paul maintained a passionate concern for his inherited Jewish categories as order, hierarchy, purity, etc. (J. Neyrey, *Paul In Other Words: A Cultural Reading of His Letters* (Louisville, KY: Westminster/John Knox, 1990.)) More broadly, Wright demonstrates in his various writings on Paul that Paul's symbolic universe or worldview was fundamentally Jewish and that Paul understood his own Christian ministry as a climax or the culmination of the story shared by all Jewish people. His gospel represented the fulfilment of God's promises to Israel. Of course, Paul redefines the basic elements of the Jewish worldview in the light of Christ and the Spirit, but his work and mission could only be understood fully within the worldview of the second Temple Judaism. See also W. R. Stegner, 'Jew, Paul the' in G. F. Hawthorne *et al.* (eds), *Dictionary of Paul and His Letters* (Logos Library, electronic edn; Downers Grove, IL: IVP, 1997). Stegner discusses the continuity of Paul's thought with his Jewish past.

2.   Paul's Jewish worldview, as we will see, gave Paul not only a particular understanding of reality but also reasons to *persecute* the nascent Christian movement. The fact that his encounter with the risen Christ happened while Paul was persecuting the early Christians is significant. Central among the reasons for Paul's persecuting activity was the message of the early Christians that the new community of the 'people of God' was defined neither by ethnic identity nor by adherence to Torah but by allegiance to Christ. To be 'in Christ' was a sufficient mark of the membership into God's people, thus replacing the claims of the Torah. We will look more carefully into this issue in the next chapter.

3.   See N. T. Wright, 'Paul, Arabia and Elijah (Galatians 1:17)', *JBL* 115(4) (1996), pp. 683–92.

4.   Richard Hays (*Echoes*, pp. 165–73, 225–6), for example, argued that Isa. 49.1–6 set out Paul's apostolic agenda.

to see himself a part of Israel, as Rom. 11.1 clearly indicates: 'I ask, then, has God rejected his people? By no means! I myself am an Israelite, a descendant of Abraham, a member of the tribe of Benjamin.' It is significant to note that even years after his conversion he still claims his Jewish heritage[5] (2 Cor. 11.12). And it could not be otherwise since his Christian faith could make sense only as the continuation, indeed as the culmination, of the Jewish story, of the story of the God of Abraham fulfilling all his promises in Christ. Paul was (and remained) first and foremost a Jewish thinker however much his Jewish beliefs had been rethought in the light of the gospel of Christ and however much his Graeco-Roman environment influenced and shaped his writings. That is why in order to understand Paul and his gospel, it is vitally important to understand well the essentials of his Jewish religious framework,[6] the basic features of Judaism of the first century that Paul carries with him in his Christian life.

Obviously, there is neither space nor need here to go into an exposition of Judaism since significant work has been done in this area.[7] We will simply point out the three fundamental aspects of Jewish theology of the first century, i.e., monotheism, election, and eschatology, and their significance for a better understanding of the social meaning of reconciliation in Paul. More specifically, if Paul's 'political sensibilities were driven by his theological ones, and not vice-versa,'[8] it is essential that we should consider the theological Jewish story-shaped worldview of Paul with its stories, symbols, beliefs, and practices. These were not simply theoretical convictions for Paul but rather foundational for his existence, representing the grid through which the entire reality was perceived. It is against such a background that we can properly understand and assess Paul's life and thought.[9] Naturally, as we will see in the next chapter, the Damascus experience forced Paul to reassess/redefine key elements of

---

5.   One unanimously accepted fact about Paul is that he was a Jew. However, a wide spectrum of opinions appears as soon as one inquires about the kind of Jew he was, and about the degree of continuity and/or discontinuity with Judaism he showed after his Damascus experience. The views range from those who see him more as a 'Hellenized Jew' to those who see him as a 'Palestinian Jew' though it is now commonly acknowledged that these are rather inappropriate dichotomies to describe Judaism since there was not so clear-cut a distinction between the two, and Palestine was also pervaded with Hellenism. Similarly, some authors emphasize more the continuity with his Jewish heritage while others a more radical discontinuity.

6.   The majority of Pauline scholars today acknowledge this fact. However, because too much stress is put on the fact that Paul's Jewish heritage became 'obsolete' with his conversion, the tendency exists among many to treat his Jewish background only superficially and not at a foundational level.

7.   E. P. Sanders' monumental work *Paul and Palestinian Judaism* (London: SCM Press, 1977), which both redefines Judaism and anchors Paul firmly in first-century Judaism, and W. D. Davies' *Paul and Rabbinic Judaism* (London: SPCK, 1948) represent key texts in this area. For excellent summaries of the basic features of the first-century Judaism see in particular Wright, *NTPG*, pp. 145–338; J. Ziesler, *Pauline Christianity* (rev. edn; Oxford: OUP, 1990), pp. 8–12; Dunn, *The Theology of Paul*, pp. 28–50, 82–84; Witherington, *Paul's Narrative*, pp. 9–75; and idem, *The Paul Quest: The Renewed Search for the Jew of Tarsus* (Leicester: IVP, 1998), pp. 53–69.

8.   Wright, 'Paul's Gospel and Caesar's Empire', in Richard A. Horsley (ed.), *Paul and Politics: Ekklesia, Israel, Imperium, Interpretatio* (Harrisburg, PA: Trinity, 2000), p. 164.

9.   By considering the overall picture of the Jewish worldview in the time of Paul, we hope to be in

his Jewish worldview, but it did not replace it as the overall framework of reference. Paul's controlling narrative contains both the sense of his own call and mission and the very foundational story, expressed in several closely interrelated stories that he was trying to live out and proclaim.[10] It is through an adequate understanding and elucidation of Paul's Jewish narrative world that we may be able to integrate best the various aspects of Paul's theology. Inevitably, because they are the stories of the true and only God, they will challenge other stories of so-called gods, as we will see later in this chapter.

3.3 *The social context of Paul*

The purpose of this section is to offer a brief description of the social context within which Paul and his congregations lived, and to assess Paul's awareness of and attitudes toward the larger social environment (society at large, outsiders, institutions, etc.). It is hoped that this will make a solid argument for the possibility and necessity of addressing the question of the social meaning of reconciliation in Paul.

Paul's writings have not been generally used as a resource for dealing with contemporary social and political issues. It is often assumed that although the earthly life and ministry of Jesus was dominated by his concern for the poor and the oppressed, Paul, on the contrary, transformed Jesus' original message and intention into a purely spiritual religion – a message of eternal salvation for the sinners. Paul, it is argued, had little, if any, interest for the affairs of 'this world'. And a glance through some of the statements Paul makes might seem to give just such a preliminary view:

> Let each of you remain in the condition in which you were called. Were you a slave when called? Do not be concerned about it. Even if you can gain your freedom, make use of your present condition now more than ever. For whoever was called in the Lord as a slave is a freed person belonging to the Lord, just as whoever was free when called is a slave of Christ. (1 Cor. 7.20–22)

> Set your minds on things that are above, not on things that are on earth. (Col. 3.2)

> . . . and those who deal with the world as though they had no dealings with it. For the present form of this world is passing away, (1 Cor. 7.31)

a better position to inquire and assess 'why Paul wrote the way he did and why people behaved the way they did' (Wright, *NTPG*, pp. 245–46).

10. The underlying story is that of God, the creator of the world, who has acted decisively in Jesus Christ to redeem the world. But this larger narrative finds expression in several other interrelated stories which Paul tells in all of his writings and in the letter to the Romans. See N. T. Wright, 'Paul and Caesar: A New Reading of Romans', in Craig Bartholomew *et al.* (eds), *A Royal Priesthood? The Use of the Bible Ethically and Politically* (Carlisle: Paternoster Press, 2002), pp. 182–85 for an excellent summary of these stories.

These and similar passages have caused commentators to look in other places for guidance for a 'biblical foundation' for Christian social involvement – particularly to the OT prophets and the Gospels. There are several reasons for this situation. First, interpreters were unable to see any concern for the 'secular' matters in the letters of Paul because they operated with a modern presupposition of a dichotomy between 'sacred' and 'profane' aspects of reality. However, for Paul and for all first-century Christians there was *one realm of reality* in which body and soul, religion and politics, private and public, individual and social aspects of reality were intermingled in a complex unified vision of life. It was primarily by our own presuppositional 'assignment' of Paul to the 'sacred' or 'spiritual/religious' realm that we were unable to perceive him as being interested in social and political issues as well. Once we become aware of the unified worldview of Paul and attempt to read him on his own terms, we may discover a new facet of Paul.

Another reason for the individualistic, narrowly religious and spiritual reading of Paul was that throughout most of Christian history we have read Paul through Augustinian and Lutheran eyes, so that Paul was 'reduced' more or less to an abstract principle of 'justification by faith' understood in a very narrow sense. Thus it was argued there is nothing that Paul could contribute to our questions regarding the social realities in which Christians live. Further, there were some aspects of Pauline teaching ('submission', 'slavery', etc.) that – when 'misinterpreted' in a particular way – had enhanced the propensity of church leadership to 'domesticate' Paul's teaching for their own interests and advantages.[11] Finally, a wrong understanding of Paul's eschatology represented another major reason, if not the most important indeed, for discharging Paul of any social relevance. It was, namely, the belief, widely held even today by many, according to which Paul expected the end of the world to happen very soon, even in his lifetime, and so he had no reason to concern himself with the world that was to 'pass away' anyhow. But this is not what Paul meant by his eschatological language. As our study will show at various points, his understanding of the 'new age' as already breaking did not prevent him from engaging with the wider world.

Sociology of knowledge and NT studies

One of the main contributions of the sociology of knowledge to the study of the NT is to draw attention to the fact that the documents of the NT provide strong evidence for the complex interrelationships that exist between gospel and culture, between church and society. Philip Esler, for example, correctly points out that the writings of the NT reveal 'a pervasive relationship between *kerygma* and context, that is, between the religious affirmations of the early Christian communities and the social realities which affected them.'[12] Even such a profound religious experience as conversion, which

---

11. This was extensively shown by Neil Elliott (*Liberating Paul*) and Mark Strom, *Reframing Paul: Conversations in Grace & Community* (Downers Grove, IL: IVP, 2000).

12. Philip F. Esler, *The First Christians in their Social World: Social-Scientific Approaches to New Testament Interpretation* (London: Routledge, 1994), p. ix.

has tended to be understood in purely individual and religious terms, is increasingly recognized to be 'a social process as well as an individual transformation.'[13] It is, therefore, mandatory that for a proper understanding and interpretation of much of the NT text, one has to make a thorough analysis of the context, of the social realities within which the authors wrote and the social dimensions of human existence as a whole.[14]

There is no question that the essence of the gospel was the same for the early church, whether it was preached by Paul to the Gentiles or by Peter to a Jewish audience. It consisted in the proclamation of Jesus of Nazareth – especially his death and resurrection – as God's revelation of his love for the world and, at the same time, of his judgement of the sins of the world. However, the fact that there appeared with Paul a fundamental shift in the communication of the gospel for the Gentile audience (the language, arguments, models, and categories were different) is a clear and basic indication that Paul was very much aware of a different social and cultural environment, one which required these changes. In other words, Paul did not ignore but rather considered carefully each new context in which he and the new Christians found themselves and presented the gospel in appropriate language and categories for his various audiences. Moreover, changes occurred not only in the way the gospel was presented but also in the ethical implications of that gospel, as Tidball correctly notes:

> what Paul was doing was to apply the ethics of the gospel to a new social environment. Gone are the concerns of a Jewish religious society; uppermost now are the concerns of a pagan Gentile society. The dominant concerns therefore become those of moral and sexual ethics (I Cor. 5 & 6; especially 6.9-11; Eph. 4.28 etc.); family relationships (Eph. 5.21–6:4; Col. 3.18-21); relationships at work (Eph. 6.5-9; Col. 3.22-25) and attitudes to the state (Rom. 13.1-7; 1 Tim. 2:1-3). A further area which now becomes prominent is the topic of relationships within the Christian community itself (Gal. 6.1-6; Eph. 4.1–5.2; Col. 3.12–17).[15]

Addressing the issues of Paul's ethics in practice, James Dunn also remarks that Paul's concern was not solely with personal issues but rather 'his concern at every turn was with social interaction'. He continues:

> In asking how Paul's ethical principles worked in practice, therefore, it is important to recall the reality of Paul's social world and that/those of his churches . . . The interface between

---

13. Nicholas H. Taylor, 'The Social Nature of Conversion in the Early Christian World', in P. F. Esler, (ed.), *Modelling Early Christianity: Social-scientific Studies of the New Testament in its Context* (London: Routledge, 1995), p. 128.

14. Robin Scroggs, 'The Sociological Interpretation of the New Testament: The Present State of Research', in Robin Gill (ed.), *Theology and Sociology* (London: Cassell, 1996), pp. 255–61.

15. Derek Tidball, *The Social Context of the New Testament* (Carlisle: Paternoster Press, 1997a), pp. 74–75.

the churches and their social context, the movement across the boundaries (out and in), and the tensions within the churches themselves are all factors to be borne in mind when talking about Paul's ethics in practice.[16]

Similarly, Wayne Meeks argues persuasively that the 'new kind of morality' that Christians manifested had profound social implications.[17] This not only marked them out from the multiplicity of sects and religious movements of the first century, but also contributed substantially to their becoming, in the subsequent centuries, a dominant political and cultural force in the Roman Empire. The same author reminds us that the ultimate concern of the writings of the NT was to determine a particular way of life for their recipients, especially at the community level. This new morality that the gospel affects is also an integral part of the larger context within which the community lives; i.e., its culture.

These brief statements have illustrated that there is a social dimension to Paul's theology and that his theology was meant to affect the life of the believers in their particular historical situation. If this is true then it follows that an adequate discussion of the *social meaning* of reconciliation in Paul cannot be limited to a simple description of the theological aspect of reconciliation and how it bears on the social ethics, or even only on the structure of Paul's ethical argument. Rather it has to describe also the cultural milieu, the social matrix within which such ethics have meaning. Many times we treat Paul's letters as if they were simply theological treatises ignoring that, in fact, Paul wrote to real communities of people living in the midst of complex social environments.[18]

Social dimension of beliefs: social factors and the formation of beliefs

Given the diverse social and religious backgrounds of the Christians before their conversion, many beliefs were constructed in various ways by the believers which led potentially to different social implications of a particular belief.[19] More fundamentally, the very explication of the meaning of a particular belief was a complex process in which the social world of the believers played a major role. Meeks points out the dialectical process in which the meaning of a particular belief is shaped and he rightly emphasizes that the social dimension of belief is an integral part of its meaning: 'what we may crudely call its social consequences were an integral part of that process'.[20] If 'the force of a belief-statement is determined by the whole matrix of social patterns

---

16. Dunn, *Theology of Paul*, pp. 672–73.

17. Meeks, *The Origin of Christian Morality*.

18. See further D. J. Tidball, 'Social Setting of Mission Churches', in G. F. Hawthorne *et al.* (eds), *Dictionary of Paul and his Letters* (Logos Library, electronic edn; Downers Grove, IL: IVP, 1997b).

19. Wayne A. Meeks, 'The Social Context of Pauline Theology', *Interpretation* 36 (1982), pp. 266–77 (275).

20. Ibid., p. 275.

within which it is uttered,'[21] the neglect of the social context in Pauline studies leads inevitably to distortions of doctrine.

Apocalypticism

Paul strongly believed that with the coming of Christ, world history had already entered into a 'new age' even though the culmination of the 'age to come' would only be realized at the end of time, with Christ's second coming. As they live already in the final, eschatological age, the believers experience even now, though not in fullness, its great promises. A particularly relevant expectation that we find throughout Paul's letters and/or in those of his close associates, is that in the eschatological kingdom of God, the present social order will be transformed (Rom. 8.18–23; 1 Cor. 7.29–31; Gal. 6.14; Eph. 1.10; 1 Thess. 1.10; 1 Thess. 4.16; 2 Thess. 1.6–10; Tit. 2.12–14). As we will see in the next chapter, given his particular understanding of the overlap between the ages, Paul believed that the believers already experience the signs of the 'new creation' of God in this world and encouraged his congregations to live out their personal transformation and also to participate in the transformation of the world (2 Cor. 5.14–6.10).

Church, society and boundaries: ambivalence and dialectical relationship to the world

Paul's language of 'belonging' and 'separation' offers a view into the way in which the identity of those who 'belong to Christ' was maintained and positioned vis-à-vis the outside world. There is ambivalence and a dialectical relationship manifested by the first Christians with regard to 'the world'.[22] On the one hand, the insider/outsider terminology implies a negative perception of society and the 'qualitative difference' between outsiders and insiders. On the other hand, however, Christians are not to withdraw from society. As a diaspora Jew himself, Paul knew that despite the various purity codes and boundary markers that differentiated the Jewish communities from the larger society, the Jews did relate in various ways to the wider society in which they lived.[23] Now, as an apostle to the Gentiles, Paul encouraged his congregations

21. Idem, *The First Urban Christians: The Social World of the Apostle Paul* (New Haven and London: Yale University Press, 1983), p. 164.

22. Ibid., pp. 85–107. See also Meeks' *Origin of Christian Morality*, pp. 61–65.

23. John M. G. Barclay has documented this aspect in his book, *The Jews in the Mediterranean Diaspora: From Alexander to Trajan* (Edinburgh: T&T Clark, 1996). He brings together and analyses new evidence from archaeology, inscriptions and diaspora literature about the life of a great variety of diaspora Jewish communities living in such places as Egypt, Syria, Cyrenaica, Rome, and Asia. While there were clear antagonisms between Jews and non-Jews in these areas, Barclay also describes many instances of varying degrees of social integration and interaction between these communities, especially given the existence of a great diversity of 'Judaisms' with different specificities in each of their own local environments. Barclay reserves a whole chapter (Chapter 13) for his treatment of Paul as an 'anomalous' diaspora Jew, and shows that he was highly assimilated and more acculturated compared with many other Jews in diaspora, though he was much less accommodated to the Hellenistic culture than, for example, Philo and Josephus. Also relevant for the question of interaction of diaspora Jews in the wider society, is

not only to continue to participate, as good citizens, in the life of the city, but also to behave in a manner that would bring approval from the outsiders. Thus, for example, the strong work ethic of the believers in Thessalonika was intended to 'earn the respect of outsiders' (1 Thess. 4.12), while the exercise of the spiritual gifts in the Corinthian congregation were to be amended not to give the wrong impression to the outsiders (1 Cor. 14.23).

It is important that we have a good grasp of this dialectical relationship of early Christianity to the world. Far too many times in the history of Christianity and of scholarship, Paul was easily categorized as either an 'antagonist' to the larger society around him, or a 'conformist'. This was done by taking unilaterally just some of his explicit statements and then forming definite conclusions based on them. However, it is misleading to treat Paul in this way and it might lead to further distortions of his theology. Paul did not have a uniform, either-or position vis-à-vis the world, but rather he showed a more complex dialectical view. His attitude to the state is such an example. He clearly and unambiguously refuses to conform to its expectations and demands – for example, to conform to the emperor cult. At the same time, however, Paul legitimizes the state as 'God's servant for good' (Rom. 13.4) without blindly and unquestionably accepting its authority. We find similar tensions in Paul's view of slaves and women. On the one hand, 'in Christ' there was no difference anymore, all were equal (Gal. 3.28). On the other hand, slaves were still to submit to their masters, and fulfil their duties even better than before, while women were exhorted to be submissive. We will come back to this in the course of this study and show in more detail how and why Paul was able to hold together these views. Suffice it here to say that the attitude and relation of early Christians to the outside world was complex and that it should be given careful consideration. The tension should not be removed: the world is God's good creation and yet is now in a present state of corruption and the 'god of this world' is active in it; Christians were 'resident aliens' in this world and had their 'citizenship in heaven' (Phil. 3.20), and yet they were encouraged neither to withdraw from the world (1 Cor. 5.10) nor to totally deny or reject its realities and values. In fact, as we will see in detail in Chapter 6 below, it was precisely because of their new identity and status that they were able to work towards the transformation of this world.

1 Thessalonians, one of Paul's earliest letters, is an excellent example of how Paul was, from the very beginning of his ministry, concerned with both the internal cohesion and growth of the Christians communities, but also with the Thessalonians' social conduct and positive attitude and behaviour towards outsiders. It was of greatest importance for Paul that Christians should not 'repay evil for evil but always seek

---

the study by Leonard V. Rutgers, *The Jews in Late Ancient Rome: Evidence of Cultural Interaction in the Roman Diaspora* (Leiden: Koninklijke Brill, 2000), in which the author, against the prevalent view that Jews lived in isolation from their surroundings, offers a more nuanced picture of social integration and cultural interaction and shows that, by borrowing and adopting some Roman cultural elements, the Jews of the diaspora did not have to renounce their own particular identity.

to do good to one another and *to all*' (1 Thess. 5.15); that they should 'increase and
abound in love for one another and *for all*' (1 Thess. 3.12); that they should 'aspire
to live quietly, to mind [their] own affairs, and to work with [their] hands . . . so that
[they] *may behave properly toward outsiders*' (1 Thess. 4.11–12). Whether or not
Paul was influenced by, or in conversation with the philosophical teachings of the
day,[24] it is clear that while his primary interest was with the internal dynamics of the
Christian community, he was nevertheless very much interested in the Christians'
relationship to the larger society and wanted them to act as responsible members
in it.

This section has illustrated that in order to get an accurate picture of the significance of any of Paul's doctrines we need to set it within the larger context of the
social dimensions of his communities in their environment. Neglecting the social
context leads inevitably to distortions of doctrine. That is why it is mandatory to
understand, first, the complex social matrix within which Paul's communities lived,
and only then attempt to sketch the contours of the meaning of a particular teaching
in Paul's writing.

3.4 *The political context of Paul*

3.4.1 *Recent developments in Pauline studies: the political dimension*
Conventional interpretations of Paul have generally either evaded political and social
issues in Paul's theology, or understood him as simply endorsing the existing political
powers in a conservative attitude of maintaining the social and political status quo.
Several recent trends in Pauline studies, however, seem to challenge this view and to
argue instead that Paul was more profoundly political than is usually perceived and
that the gospel he preached had significant social and political dimensions.[25] It is true,
the extent of such concerns and the basic orientation of Paul's political thought are
matters of debate in recent scholarship and there is a wide spectrum of views among
scholars regarding Paul's attitude to and reflection on social and political issues.[26]

---

24. Abraham J. Malherbe (*Paul and the Thessalonians*, pp. 95–107) argues that in order for Paul to
be relevant and intelligible in that context, he shaped his ethical discourse using terms common to the
contemporary Stoic, Cynic and Epicurean philosophical discussions of social and political conduct.
    25. The most recent and significant studies include two excellent books edited by Richard Horsley:
Paul and Politics: Ekklesia, Israel, Imperium, Interpretation (Harrisburg, PA: Trinity, 2000), and *Paul
and Empire: Religion and Power in Roman Imperial Society* (Harrisburg, PA: Trinity, 1997). There are
also several very significant monographs: Bruno Blumenfeld, *The Political Paul: Justice, Democracy and
Kingship in a Hellenistic Framework* (JSNTS, 210; Sheffield: Sheffield Academic, 2001); Neil Elliott,
Liberating Paul; Mark Strom, *Reframing Paul*; R. A. Horsley and M. A. Silberman, *The Message and the
Kingdom: How Jesus and Paul Ignited a Revolution and Transformed the Ancient World* (Minneapolis:
Fortress, 1997); Elsa Tamez, *The Amnesty of Grace: Justification by Faith from a Latin American
Perspective* (Nashville, TN: Abingdon, 1993); Robert Grant, *Paul in the Roman World: The Conflict at
Corinth* (Louisville, KY: Westminster John Knox Press, 2001).
    26. On the one hand, there are those who interpret Paul as having a basic conservative attitude (among

What is becoming clearer, however, is the fact that the gospel Paul proclaimed was not in any way detached from everyday reality and that it had also a political message at its heart. Further still, some studies show that the political dimension of the gospel was not secondary or accidental to Paul's writings but rather an integral and fundamental element of it. The gospel of the crucified and resurrected Christ, it is claimed, not only has few 'social and political implications' but is rather political at its core.[27]

But is this new 'political emphasis' in reading Scripture as new as it appears? Tim Gorringe shows that such readings are not necessarily a recent innovation in the history of biblical interpretations and that Christian churches were always aware of the political message of the Scriptures, the Bible being constantly used in defence of various political positions.[28] What can be said to be new in the more recent political readings of Scripture, Gorringe explains, are the insights from the sociology of knowledge, namely that all knowledge is socially situated. In the realm of biblical studies this insight determines new kinds of questions to be asked of both the text and the reader, since they are both profoundly influenced by their own society. Thus, these questions that the new exegesis poses (about the type of society, social location, social class, social conflicts, social interests), cause a 'political' reading of biblical texts and make it possible for the Bible to become an instrument of social and political change. Gorringe writes: 'The perceptions generated by the sociology of knowledge, therefore, whilst not political in the sense of inculcating a political programme, always situate exegesis in its political context and as such can be profoundly illuminating.'[29]

Any attempt to highlight and deal with the importance of the social and political dimensions for a proper understanding of Paul's thought must start by acknowledging that such aspects are not necessarily obvious, available at a glance to a reader of his letters twenty centuries afar from the initial context. That is why it is legitimate to ask, with many commentators, whether we can really talk of political aspects of

whom are R. Grant, E. E. Ellis, D. Tidball and B. Blumenfeld). On the other hand, there are those who argue that Paul's letters reflected a more profound political thought (T. Gorringe, W. Wink, D. Georgi, N. Elliott, M. Strom, R. Horsley, N. T. Wright and others).

27. These are the initial findings of two research groups, one in the USA, 'Paul and Political Group' led by Richard Horsley (published in the two volumes *Paul and Politics* and *Paul and Empire*), and the other in the UK, 'Scripture and Hermeneutics Group' led by Craig Bartholomew, particularly the third volume, *A Royal Priesthood?*

28. Tim Gorringe, 'Political Reading of Scripture' in John Barton (ed.), *The Cambridge Companion to Biblical Interpretation* (Cambridge: CUP, 1998), pp. 67–80. Gorringe shows that it was eventually with Luther's two-kingdom doctrine that a divide started to emerge between religious/spiritual and political realms. The split increased even further with the scientific approaches to religion and the German universities' insistence on the academic detachment in biblical studies, and so a 'non-political' reading of the NT became prevalent. Bernard McGrane also shows in his *Beyond Anthropology: Society and the Other* that it was in the Western European culture, starting with the eighteenth century, that a clear distinction emerged between 'religion' and 'politics' as two distinct spheres of life.

29. Gorringe, 'Political Reading', pp. 70–71.

Paul's thought. How can we realistically talk about the social and political aspects of Paul's thought when we know that his primary concern was *not* with society at large but with Christian communities, their formation, maintenance, dynamics and life? Did he have a solid understanding of politics, of society at large, and had he reflected on the social/political realities of his day? Was Paul concerned with the way in which Christians were perceived by their non-Christian neighbours and citizens? What about the generally accepted view that he maintained a 'socially conservative' position and encouraged a 'status quo' vis-à-vis such issues as authority/state, women, and slaves?

These are all extremely important questions and in the following pages none will be ignored while maintaining and arguing for the political dimensions of Paul's gospel. We will see that Paul's immediate or primary concern with the Christian communities does not mean that he was not also preoccupied with issues of society at large or, especially, with aspects of Christian living in the world. As we will see in the present work, there is no dichotomy in Paul's mind regarding the life of Christians inside and outside Christian community; that is, there are not two different sets of morals for the believers – one for life within the church and another for their life in the world. As we have already seen, for Paul it is absolutely clear that the beliefs of Christians are not (cannot be) separated from the life of the Christians in their own contexts but are, in fact, deeply integrated into one comprehensive worldview and way of life. We will see that in many cases where commentators of Paul regard him as a-social and a-political, it is because of a long history of domesticating Paul to the power interests of Christians and their own purposes. It is for the same reason that we find ourselves, at times, unable to see beyond what we are accustomed to seeing and hearing regarding Paul's attitudes to social and political issues. One could hardly disagree with Käsemann's powerful assertion that 'the history of Pauline interpretation is the history of the apostle's ecclesiastical domestication'.[30]

3.4.2 *Religion and politics in the first-century Mediterranean world*

Contrary to what our modern pervasive assumptions and cultural background teach us, religion and politics were *not* two separate areas of life in the ancient world but rather were very closely connected and integrated into a large, holistic picture of reality. This fact is very well illustrated by the dynamics of the widespread first-century Roman imperial cult – especially in the relationship between the divine nature of the Emperor and his political power. Religion, politics, and power were closely inter-related issues in the Roman world. Any attempt to analyse and discuss the social and political dimensions of Paul's gospel has to pay close attention to this important fact. Before looking more closely into the cult of the Emperor, a very important note is in order here. By taking the imperial cult as an illustration of the interconnectedness

---

30. Used as the motto by Neil Elliott for his chapter entitled 'Paul in the service of Death', *Liberating Paul*, p. 1.

and integration between religion and politics in the ancient world, I do not imply that the emperor cult replaced other forms of religion. We know that throughout the Roman Empire alongside a rich cultural and ethnic pluralism, flourished also a rich diversity of religious practices with some having a very local representation. Paul himself gives examples of this rich religious life, for instance in 1 Cor. 8–10, where he challenges various pagan religious practices incompatible with the gospel he preached. Thus, we are aware that given the widespread forms of religion and the very local nature of religious life in the Empire, there was an increased probability for religious conflicts and that Paul has confronted various forms of such conflicts. However, the limited space in the present book allows for only one particular religious form to be highlighted, namely the cult of the emperor, and to this we now turn for a more detailed exploration.

The Roman imperial cult

An abundance of archaeological discoveries of Roman imperial temples, coins and statues of emperors, and many texts inscribed on stones from the first-century Mediterranean world, especially in Asia Minor, offer a clear picture of the cult of the Roman emperor in all the details of actual practices, its purposes and its theoretical framework. The cult of Caesar represented a rather developed way by which the new Roman provinces were controlled and governed. The imperial cult was primarily 'an important expression of loyalty and gratitude toward the emperor . . . The cult both articulated the position of the emperor in the world and provided provincial elites with a language for diplomacy and strategy for developing relations with this power-ful figure.'[31] In the Mediterranean Hellenistic world the cult of the Roman emperor was created on the basis and forms of traditional Greek religion with the purpose of promoting and conveying piety towards the emperor – who was counted among the gods and for whom temples and shrines were erected and honours and sacrifices offered as to a 'god'.[32]

In Paul's days the imperial cult and its corresponding ceremonies were not irregular, private and temporary events but institutionalized public rituals performed regularly for the emperor in local communities through public celebrations, especially in big cities such as Corinth and Ephesus. The cult was present everywhere and was manifested in varied forms from place to place – sanctuaries, imperial temples and statues, coins, public ceremonies, sacrifices, processions, donations, honours, etc. –

31. D. A. deSilva, 'Ruler Cult', in Craig A. Evans and Stanley E. Porter (eds), *Dictionary of New Testament Background* (Downers Grove: InterVarsity Press, 2000): (CD-ROM, electronic edn; Libronix Digital Library, 2000).

32. S. R. F. Price, 'Rituals and Powers', in Horsley (ed.), *Paul and Empire*, pp. 47–71. Two other essays in the same collection are extremely insightful and offer excellent illustrations and supported documentation of the proportions and extent of the spread of the Roman imperial cult: P. A. Brunt, '*Laus Imperii*', pp. 25–35, and Paul Zanker, 'The Power of Images', pp. 72–86.

as shown in the text of this inscription illustrating the benevolence of an individual toward the imperial family:

> In the magistracy of Gaius Caesar, son of Augustus, leader of the youth, he sacrificed again at [the festivals of] the Nedameia and Sebasta and offered sweet-meats to the citizens and Romans and foreigners. In the magistracy of Apollonodotus, when news came of the safety and victory of Augustus he sacrificed at *the good news* [gospel] to all the gods and goddesses and feasted at the sacrifice the citizens, the Romans and the foreigners and gave to those mentioned a bottle of wine and three pounds of bread. He also dedicated to the sons of Augustus a sanctuary and temple from his own money in the most prominent part of the square, on which his name was also inscribed, wanting to show his gratitude and piety to the whole [imperial] house . . . He also founded at the harbour of the market a temple to Augustus god Caesar, so that no table place should lack his goodwill and piety to the god [Augustus].[33]

It is remarkable to observe that all the essential elements of honours, temples, festivals, sacrifices, goodwill, and piety offered to the traditional gods are now also offered to the emperor – whose actions are explicitly compared with those of the gods. Paul's near contemporary, Philo of Alexandria, writes highlighting the same truth:

> The whole inhabited world voted him honors usually accorded the Olympian gods. These are so well attested by temples, gateways, vestibules, and colonnades that every city which contains magnificent works new and old is surpassed in these by the beauty and magnitude of those appropriated to Caesar.'[34]

Augustus was perceived more and more as a benefactor of the whole world and the imperial rule as providing an overarching umbrella under which all people could live.[35] And, as Price argues, all these rituals are not simply 'honours' offered to the emperor but they represent rather a cognitive system which defines the nature of the king and of the state, 'a way of conceptualizing the world'; all the temples, sacrifices, processions and images are 'crucially important collective constructs to which the individual reacts'.[36]

33. 'A Catalogue of Imperial Temples and Shrines in Asia Minor', quoted in Price, ibid., pp. 48–49.
34. Philo of Alexandria, *Embassy to Gaius* (Logos Library Systems, electronic edn; Nashville, TN: Thomas Nelson, 1997).
35. This is how Nikolas of Damascus, a contemporary of Augustus, described the reaction of the Greeks towards Augustus: 'The whole of humanity turns to the *Sebastos* (i.e., Augustus) filled with reverence. Cities and provincial councils honor him with temples and sacrifices, for this is his due. In this way do they give thanks to him everywhere for his benevolence.' As quoted by Zanker in 'Power of Images', p. 72.
36. Price, 'Rituals and Powers', pp. 50–51. Price further contends that even though politics and religion were so closely connected in antiquity, starting with Origen in the third century, a distinction has been made between religious and political honours and so the imperial cult was subsequently inadequately interpreted simply as an expression of political loyalty (pp. 51–52).

The essential framework of the imperial cult was given by the regular imperial festivals. And it was during these festivals and their rituals that 'the vague and elusive ideas concerning the emperor, the "collective representations", were focused in action and made powerful',[37] The incorporation of the imperial cult in the public life of the cities is illustrated by the location of the imperial temples and sanctuaries in the most prominent and prestigious places within the city. In addition to temples and altars erected for the emperor in the civic centres, there was also a special imperial space provided in the main squares of the cities, which further illustrates the impact of the emperor on the city and the desire to give him the greatest possible prominence. The birthday and various anniversaries of the emperor became important dates in the calendar of Greek cities and were publicly celebrated with various ceremonies, while the imperial image became ubiquitous and started to be venerated.

The fact that both diplomacy and the imperial cult – which were ways of representing the emperor and were both concerned with power – used religious language, is a clear indication that politics (diplomacy) and religion (the imperial cult) were not separate but closely interconnected spheres.[38] As Price points out, Roman ambassadors served often as the priests in the imperial cult and there were instructions given by the city officials as to the way they should address the emperor: 'they were to address Augustus as one who had attained the eminence and power of the gods, and were to promise further divine honours which would "deify him even more".'[39] It was not unusual, then, that some ambassadors addressed the emperor as 'unconquered hero' while others presented divine honours to him. This is another expression of the fact that 'the political-religious institutions in which power relations were constituted were virtually inseparable from the local social-economic networks of imperial society'.[40]

Thus, in the first-century world, religion was not perceived primarily as a search for the 'salvation of the soul' into eternal life – though there are evidences that some forms of religion, especially the 'mystery cults', did focus on the inwardness and privacy of worship, on the salvation of the individual through initiation of specific mysteries.[41] Similarly, politics did not simply mean the exercise of power by a complex of military and administrative apparatus of the 'state officials'. This dichotomy

37. Ibid., p. 57.
38. Hafeman points out that the spectacular parades of the conqueror emperor entering Rome through the *Porta Triumphalis* after a great military victory, had become, by the time of the New Testament, 'the most important and well-known *political-religious* institution of the period' (italics added). (S. J Hafeman, 'Roman Triumph', in Craig A. Evans and Stanley E. Porter (eds), *Dictionary of New Testament Background* (Logos Library, electronic edn; Downers Grove, IL: IVP, 2000).) See also D. W. J. Gill, 'Roman Political System', in Evans and Porter (eds), *DNTB*.
39. Price, 'Rituals and Power', p. 69.
40. Richard Horsley, 'The Gospel of Imperial Salvation – Introduction', in *Paul and Empire*, p. 11. Cicero also indicated the intimate relationship of religion and politics in his time: 'There is really no human activity in which human *virtus* approaches more closely the divine power of the gods than the founding of new states or the preservation of those already founded.' Quoted by Horsley, ibid., p. 14.
41. Marvin W. Meyer, 'Mystery Religions', in D. N. Freedman (ed.), *The Anchor Bible Dictionary* (electronic edn; New York: Doubleday, 1996).

between religion and politics is a modern conventional imposition on two spheres of life which had, at that time, a fundamental correspondence. The cult of the emperor represented an integral part of Roman imperial society, provided the means for cohesion and unity among different cities and provinces in the Roman Empire, and generated social order. From our discussion above, it is possible to think that Paul might have formulated his gospel also in reaction to the widespread claims of the emperor cult and the broader imperial ideology.

Paul's missionary concerns within the framework of Roman imperial ideology

A significant element that is relevant for our study in Romans is Paul's missionary concern in the framework of Roman imperial ideology. The letter to the Romans stands out not simply as Paul's mature thinking and reflection but also as an illustration of his major concern with a unique message and ministry: to preach the gospel of the Lord Jesus Christ to the whole world. His distinctive call was driven by a vision of a united community 'in Christ', made up of Jews and Gentiles, transcending barriers of ethnicity, nationality, gender and social class. But equally significant, the larger framework within which Paul conducted most of his ministry was the Roman Empire with its ideology and rhetoric of 'peace and security', of 'justice', of 'salvation' that were radically different from the message of the gospel of Christ. Inevitably, in the process of relating the gospel to the world of his day, Paul challenged and critically engaged with the dominant cultural values of his day from the unwavering principle of his total surrender and obedience to Christ (2 Cor. 10.4). From this perspective we are probably right to say that whatever else Paul is doing in his letter to the Romans, he is also formulating the gospel as an implicit and sometimes explicit response to the dominant culture with its widespread cult of the emperor, challenging but also engaging it from the perspective of God's intervention in the world in Jesus Christ.[42] Wright states that '[Paul] engaged with the wider Hellenistic culture of his day, both in *partial affirmation* and in *substantial critique*, operating on the principle . . . of taking every thought captive to obey the Messiah.'[43]

This perspective is relevant and important for our argument in Chapters 5 and 6 in our analysis of Romans. As we will see, Paul argues forcefully that those who are 'in Christ' have the possibility and responsibility to leave behind their sinful past and live a new life of peace and reconciliation on the basis of their being a 'new'

---

42. Particularly relevant for this discussion and argument are several studies by N. T. Wright: 'Paul and Caesar: A New Reading of Romans' in Bartholomew *et al.* (eds) *A Royal Priesthood?*; 'Paul's Gospel and Caesar's Empire'; 'God and Caesar, Then and Now' in Martyn Percy and Stephen Lowe (eds) *The Character of Wisdom* (Festschrift Wesley Carr; Aldershot: Ashgate, 2004), pp. 157–72; and his 'Gospel and Empire' chapter in his latest book *Paul: Fresh Perspectives* (London, SPCK, 2005), pp. 59–79. Also the books edited by Richard Horsley, *Paul and Empire; Paul and Politics*, and his latest *Paul and the Roman Imperial Order* (Harrisburg/London: Trinity, 2004).

43. Wright, *Paul*, p. 59 (italics added).

community guided by a new system of values and principles (Romans 5–6). This alternative way of perceiving the world and living out such convictions in the midst of it has, no doubt, determined strong reactions from the world, which led to various forms of suffering for the new community. That is why one of the parallel points in Paul's argument in Romans 5–8 was exactly how to deal with suffering, how the believers should react to persecution and hostility. Romans 9–11 tells the story of God's dealing with the world via Israel reaching its climax in Jesus, with the main purpose to give the Gentile Christians a proper attitude to the Jews and give up any feeling of superiority over them. However, this same story may also be viewed as a 'counter-story to the standard imperial narrative of Roman history reaching its climax in Augustus Caesar'.[44] Romans 12–15 is primarily about the new transformed life of the community of those gathered 'in Christ', a life lived in front of a watching and hostile world. But what transpires also is that this new life of total allegiance to Christ and not to Caesar is not to be confused with a life of anarchy and rebellion against the powers that be, as we will see in Romans 13. On the contrary, guided by the life and example of Jesus' death on the cross, the proper response to the powers is a life of discernment, engagement and of self-giving love as worship to the only Lord, Jesus Christ, worship expressed in genuine love shown in concrete manifestations towards the other. The very living together of Jews and Gentiles and their overcoming of traditional barriers and separations to join as one family in the new community in Christ, represents a strong and undeniable sign of the working power of God in their midst and a powerful message to the powers that the ultimate purpose of life is accomplished by other means than those propagated by the imperial ideology.

3.4.3 *Paul's political terms*

Against the background of Roman Empire, on the one hand, and of a Hellenistic popular philosophy on the other, many of Paul's terms and concepts like εὐαγγὲ λιον, δικαιοσουνη, ἐκκλησια, κοινωνία, πίστις, ἐιρηνη, πόλις/πολιτέια/πολιτεῦμα, καταλλάσω/καταλλαγή, etc., can be seen in a completely different light – not as simply religious and spiritual concepts but also as having a very concrete social and political dimension. This is, for example, one of the major conclusions of a thoroughly documented study by Bruno Blumenfeld, *The Political Paul: Justice, Democracy and Kingship in a Hellenistic Framework*, which analyses and places Paul within the tradition of political reflection of Hellenistic Pythagoreans.[45] In a similar fashion, Margaret Mitchell discusses the 'political' nature of 1 Corinthians and argues

---

44. Ibid., p. 78.

45. Blumenfeld argues that Paul's views in general, and especially in Romans and Philippians, 'are structurally, argumentatively and conceptually coherent with Classical and Hellenistic political thought' (*The Political Paul*, p. 12). Even though, as I hope to show later on, Blumenfeld leaves out other important dimensions of Paul's thought (particularly his theology) and takes a rather questionable approach which leads him to similar conclusions (especially about Paul's attitude and stance vis-à-vis Roman Empire), his study is important as it highlights the pervasive political aspect in Paul's theology.

persuasively that Paul responds to the evident factionalism in Corinth (σχίσματα – an inherently political problem entangled with religious aspects and motivations) with a strong, deliberative rhetoric of reconciliation by drawing on contemporary political terms.[46] These studies show that to neglect the political dimension of Paul's thought means that his theology cannot be fully understood or appreciated, and also that a simply apolitical reading de-contextualizes him and gives us a false impression regarding his thought.

3.5 *Conclusion*

This chapter has shown the importance of the religious, social and political context of Paul's life and thought for an adequate study of his letters. More specifically, we have concluded first that Paul's Jewish matrix provided him with a worldview which shaped fundamentally his thought and praxis. Particularly, his strong belief in a creational monotheism gave him an understanding of the world as God's good creation in which God is present and active and in which God's people should be actively engaged towards its eschatological transformation.

Second, based on insights from the various social-scientific approaches to Paul, we have concluded that the message of the NT is intrinsically related to the complex social realities of everyday life, and that the social dimension is an integral part of the meaning of the text. We have further pointed to the need to resist the temptation of understanding the NT and Christianity as limited to an 'inner-spiritual dimension' or to 'an objective-cognitive system', and see it within the complex of social, cultural, political, economic, and religious contexts in which it initially developed. Equally significantly, we have seen that regarding the relation to the outside world Paul encourages a positive engagement. While Christians should maintain their different and specific identity, this should not cause them to separate or be indifferent towards the outside world, but rather to be engaged in its renewal and transformation.

We have seen that the gospel Paul preached had a significant political dimension, which cannot be ignored in a proper interpretation of Paul. It could not have been otherwise, since in the first century religion and politics were closely intertwined and it was not possible to think or comprehend one without the other. The cult of the emperor illustrated well this point. We have also noted that Paul's missionary endeavours brought him up against the imperial ideology which he challenged. However, we concluded that Paul's relation to the wider political world cannot be properly described as simply confrontational. In his engagement with the wider world Paul both partially affirmed and critiqued the dominant culture. Paul's political terms are a clear and strong support for the suggestion that his message is not restricted to the 'spiritual' dimension but addresses the entire domain of human existence.

Finally, this chapter has in various ways shown that an analysis of the social

---

46. *Paul and the Rhetoric of Reconciliation*. See also Robert Grant, *Paul in the Roman World*.

significance of reconciliation is both plausible and necessary, and that this larger religious, social, and political context provides an adequate framework of reference for our understanding of Paul's social meaning of reconciliation.

4

IDENTITY, OTHERNESS AND RECONCILIATION:
PAUL'S VISION OF RECONCILIATION

4.1 *Introduction*

As we have pointed out in our previous chapters, it is possible to argue that Paul's life, mission and writings, indeed his theology, were informed and supported from beneath by a narrative framework, an integrated set of beliefs, a unifying worldview, by a particular vision of reality.[1] And it was this underlining narrative framework in which the story of Christ played a significant role, that determined his life and conduct and his particular way of doing theology in and for particular contexts.

In his book *Creed and Personal Identity*, D. B. Harned captures the complex net of relationships between story, identity, vision and praxis:

> Our conduct is shaped by the condition of our vision; we are free to choose or to struggle against only what we can see. Our vision, however, is determined by the most important images of the self from which we have fashioned our sense of identity. These furnish us with our perspective upon everything else; they finally legislate not only what we will and what we will not see, but the particular angle or point of view from which the whole of reality will be assessed. How we see ourselves, then, determines how we will conduct ourselves in relation to others, to the world, and even to God.[2]

Even if there are many instances when one's particular deeds are determined by a complex set of immediate circumstances and pressures of all sorts, and thus not always and at every moment by one's overall vision of life, Harned's point is well taken and worth exploring.[3]

Following Furnish and Beker, Gordon Zerbe points out that 'Paul's ethical vision

---

1. N. T. Wright, 'Putting Paul Together Again: Toward a Synthesis of Pauline Theology', in Bassler, Jouette M. (ed.), *Pauline Theology, Vol. I: Thessalonians, Philippians, Galatians, Philemon* (Minneapolis: Fortress, 1994), pp. 184–86 and 193–95.
2. D. B. Harned, *Creed and Personal Identity* (Edinburgh: Handsel, 1981), p. 120.
3. I will return to this later on when discussing Paul's sense of identity and his vision of reconciliation.

is fundamentally related to his redemptive vision',[4] and that fundamental to the gospel Paul proclaimed was a vision of final cosmic reconciliation and peace:

> At the core of Paul's gospel is his vision of cosmic restoration – the eschatological redemption of the entire created order . . . 'Peace' is one of the essential characteristics of this coming order of salvation. While the language of 'peace' in Paul sometimes refers to eschatological salvation as a whole, terms such as 'the reconciliation of the cosmos/all things' and 'the subjection of all things' to Christ and God also express the vision of cosmic peace . . . For Paul, then, 'peace' refers fundamentally to the eschatological salvation of the whole person, all humanity, and the entire universe. It refers to the normal state of all things – the *order* of God's creative and redeeming action versus the *disorder* of the chaotic powers of Satan.[5]

Zerbe takes Paul's vision of peace as a backdrop against which he then discusses Paul's ethic of nonretaliation and peace. And he argues convincingly, I believe, that Paul's 'nonretaliatory ethic of apocalyptically motivated restraint', and his 'reconciling ethic of love' as expressed in Rom. 12.14, 17–21, can both be properly understood and sustained in the light of Paul's vision of cosmic peace.[6]

I also suggest, and I will attempt to argue in this chapter, that the social dimension of reconciliation in Paul could be properly understood within his larger vision of reconciliation of all things in Christ. As we will see, there is in Paul an understanding of reconciliation that is linked to a vision of reality that is transcendent and which offers a different set of values from those of this world, and produces different results. This vision inspired him throughout his life and ministry and gave him the impetus to be permanently engaged in *reconciling practices* – between Jews and Gentiles, between various individuals and groups within the churches, between Christians and outsiders. It was the same vision worked out in Paul's life that offered an incentive for his congregations to think and act likewise and, indeed, it also inspires us to continue to build on that vision.

The argument put forward in this chapter is that, beginning with his own radical experience of reconciliation on the Damascus road, a particular vision of reality started to emerge for Paul. In addition to his reconciliation, that event meant also a paradigm shift in Paul's life due to a radically new understanding of reality brought about by the death and resurrection of Christ. Paul's vision of reconciliation is thus radically shaped by, and grounded on, the story of Christ: a world of new possibilities and radical innovations is opened up now 'in Christ', with serious implications for all those living within this new reality. It then became clear for Paul that the great vision of restoration and peace found in Isaiah was being fulfilled in his days. And so

---

    4.   Gordon Zerbe, 'Paul's Ethic of Nonretaliation and Peace', in Swartley, Millard M. (ed.), *The Love of Enemy and Nonretaliation in the New Testament* (Louisville, KY: Westminster/John Knox Press, 1992), p. 181.

    5.   Ibid.

    6.   Ibid., pp. 204–05.

it was there that Paul found important material elements which solidly substantiated his further understanding and vision of reconciliation – especially as Isaiah connects closely his understanding of peace with such concepts as restoration, and truth and justice, expressed in social and communal relations, which will be the characteristic of the new creation in the age to come. Paul lived now in the new eschatological time when the things prophesied by Isaiah were being fulfilled. However, to give expression to such a profound and complex phenomenon of reconciliation, Paul uses many symbols and concepts from his Hellenistic Graeco-Roman context, particularly καταλλάσσω/καταλλαγή, a term used in the Hellenistic context primarily for interpersonal relationships, in the sociological and political spheres of life. Given his own personal experience of reconciliation and the Isaianic vision of peace, Paul gives expression to a complex concept of reconciliation which has personal, social, political, and cosmological dimensions.

4.2 *Damascus road experience: the foundation of Paul's vision of reconciliation*

It is commonly accepted by students of the NT that in his mission as a persecutor of the early Christians, on the road to Damascus Paul experienced a powerful event that was to change fundamentally both his deepest convictions and the basic orientation and commitment of his life. The significance of his encounter with Christ for his subsequent theology is illustrated not only by his direct references to that event (Gal. 1.15–16; 1 Cor. 15.8–10; Phil. 3.4–11) or by his allusions to it (1 Cor. 9.1; 2 Cor. 4.4–6; 5.16; Eph. 3.2–11; Col. 1.23, 25). Rather, the implications of that encounter, the paradigm shift it affected, 'is present in all his letters both as a fundamental assumption and as a recurring theme'.[7] Indeed, some scholars go as far as to argue that the whole gospel that Paul proclaimed so fervently throughout his life originated in that complex experience on the Damascus road.[8] The experience on the Damascus road introduced a radically *new* element into Paul's symbolic universe: Jesus of Nazareth, crucified in Jerusalem, appears to Paul as alive, confronting Paul with a reality he could not deny – Jesus was raised by God and thus confirmed that he was the Messiah of Israel and the Saviour of the world. Paul was evidently convinced of

---

7.   Terence L. Donaldson, *Paul and the Gentiles: Remapping the Apostle's Convictional* (Minneapolis: Fortress, 1997), p. 293. See also the argument by J. G. Gager, that a study of Paul's conversion helps us have a better understanding of his theology and mission to Gentiles (J. G. Gager, 'Some Notes on Paul's Conversion', *NTS* 27 (1980), pp. 697–704.)

8.   Seyoon Kim, *The Origin of Paul's Gospel* (Tubingen: Mohr, 1981). There are, of course, several different interpretations of Paul's 'Damascus experience' and its implications for Paul's life and thought. Some use it to refer to a singular event which radically transformed Paul, while others take it in a symbolic way as a reference to Paul's (continuous) encounter with Christ. One should probably consider both these possibilities. And though this was a particular event in Paul's life, it is also true that he lived continually 'in Christ' or in his presence and Paul continued to develop his understanding of Christ, and definitely grew in his understanding of the implications of the gospel for everyday life.

this reality, on the one hand, against his will or desire – after all, he was persecuting those who held just those convictions; on the other hand, his own experience of the reconciling grace of God was also an overwhelming reality, one which Paul could not doubt or deny. Moreover, in his activity as a persecutor, Paul reflected upon and rejected very consciously the claims of the earliest Christians. But now, confronted with this undeniable reality and understanding that Jesus was the Messiah, the Christ, Paul was forced to re-examine his fundamental convictions and beliefs; indeed, his entire worldview had to be redefined in this new light and reality. I cannot go into a full examination of Paul's conversion experience, nor is it the purpose of this study.[9] Rather I will be highlighting the effect of this event on Paul's life – particularly on those elements that are somehow related to his understanding of reconciliation.

What happened to Paul on the Damascus road and thereafter could probably be described in terms of Thomas Kuhn's 'paradigm shift', as some authors have pointed out.[10] Indeed, Paul's reconfigurations of his own assumptions and basic worldview and his redefinitions of his beliefs caused by his conversion do seem to point to such a radical 'paradigm shift'. Kuhn's concept provides a helpful model for analysing Paul's experience of conversion as a paradigm shift as well as Paul's way of theologizing as a process by which he takes existing conceptual paradigms and transforms them. The model seems to enable a better understanding of both the continuity and the discontinuity of Paul's new position and his Jewish worldview, providing an excellent window into the complex dynamic behind Paul's theologizing. I will illustrate this later in the chapter by looking at Paul's concept of reconciliation and the 'paradigm shift' that he makes with the concept. It may be also relevant as an argument against one-sided interpretations which attempt to view Paul from an either Jewish or Hellenistic perspective. More importantly, the 'paradigm shift' model may help to illustrate that we need to account for new elements in Paul's thinking that are neither Jewish nor Hellenistic, and so to understand some of his concepts, it is not enough only to read them against a Jewish or Hellenistic backdrop.

Though Paul's conversion is important for an overall understanding of Paul's thought, in this chapter we will argue that it was also his own experience of reconciliation which fundamentally shaped his subsequent understanding and articulation

---

9.   For good and detailed discussions see especially Alan F. Segal *Paul the Convert: The Apostolate and Apostasy of Saul the Pharisee* (New Haven and London: Yale University Press, 1990); Richard V. Peace, *Conversion in the New Testament: Paul and the Twelve* (Grand Rapids: Eerdmans, 1999); Beverly Roberts Gaventa, *From Darkness to Light: Aspects of Conversion in the New Testament* (Philadelphia, PA: Fortress, 1986) and 'Paul's Conversion: A Critical Sifting of the Epistolary Evidence' (unpublished Ph.D. dissertation, Duke University, 1978). For an excellent collection of essays on the significant influence of Paul's conversion on his life and thought see Richard Longenecker (ed.) *The Road from Damascus: The Impact of Paul's Conversion on His Life, Thought and Ministry* (Grand Rapids: Eerdmans, 1997).

10.   Terrence Donaldson, in *Paul and the Gentiles*, uses Kuhn's model to analyse Paul's conversion, attempting a *'Remapping [of] the Apostle's Convictional World'* – as the subtitle of his book illustrates. He sees Paul 'as one who experienced a paradigm shift' (p. 304). He is particularly interested in applying the model in order to analyse Paul's presentation of the Gentiles.

of reconciliation. One should be careful not to react immediately to the idea of Paul being 'reconciled with God' since, as a Pharisee, Paul was not 'estranged' from God. And indeed, this is also what Paul had thought about himself just before the event! However, it was during his encounter with the risen Christ that Paul was shockingly confronted with another reality. Whatever he had 'considered' to be the case before, whether he knew it or not, did not count: he was now confronted, and he understood that he was in fact fighting against God, that he was an enemy of God's people, of Christ, and ultimately an enemy of God himself.

4.2.1 *2 Corinthians 5.11–21 and Paul's experience of reconciliation*

In the chapter on the 'Review of Literature' I referred to Seyoon Kim's proposal that Paul's doctrine of reconciliation originated with his Damascus experience. The veracity of that claim is not my concern here.[11] Rather, I want to pursue further and somewhat in a different direction an important argument that Kim has presented in his article, namely that in one of Paul's earliest and direct elaborations on the theme of reconciliation (that is, 2 Cor. 5.11–21), Paul makes several allusions to his Damascus experience of divine reconciliation and conversion.[12] I should note from the start that Kim does not use these 'allusions' of Paul to his Damascus experience to inquire further as to how this might have eventually affected Paul's understanding of the horizontal dimension of reconciliation. Not only is he not interested in this dimension of reconciliation in 2 Cor. 5, but he clearly states the contrary: 'in 2 Cor. 5 Paul speaks only of God's reconciliation of human beings to himself and not of a reconciliation between himself and the Corinthian church'.[13] His absolute focus on

11. As I have pointed out earlier, it may be too much to assume that the origin of any such complex concept in Paul can be deduced or 'reduced' to one particular event/experience or even to one of the three particular contexts within which one needs to consider Paul's life and thought (Jewish, Christian, Graeco-Roman). Having said this, however, I do believe that Kim is right in emphasizing the conversion experience as a crucial event not only for understanding reconciliation but also Paul and his thought in general. There is not doubt that the Damascus event represented the 'paradigm shift' in Paul's life which fundamentally redirected Paul's thought and mission, and as such, it should be given considerable attention when studying Paul's theology.

12. Kim was not the first to have observed such allusions in this text. In his book, *The Origin of Paul's Gospel*, where, in fact, Kim first proposed the thesis about the origin of Paul's metaphor of reconciliation on the Damascus road, he points to other commentators who noticed the allusions in 2 Cor. 5.11–21 to that event (particularly v. 16): Windisch, Lietzmann, Kümmel, Plummer, Hughes, Bruce, Stuhlmacher, Schlatter. See *The Origin of Paul's Gospel*, pp. 13–20. To these, we may add some more recent studies which make the same point: Jan Lambrecht, '"Reconcile Yourselves . . ."', pp. 363–68; Christian Wolff, 'True Apostolic Knowledge of Christ'; A. Wedderburn (ed.) *Paul and Jesus: Collected Essays* (Sheffield: Sheffield Academic), pp. 81–98.

13. Kim, '2 Cor. 5:11–21', p. 365 (italics mine). This is clearly a very limited understanding of the complex metaphor of reconciliation in Paul. Many commentators recognize the double dimension of reconciliation being present in this passage. Consider, for example, Lambrecht's opening statement of his suggestive article, '"Reconcile yourselves . . ."': 'Both dimensions of reconciliation, the horizontal as well as the vertical, are, we think, also prominent in 5, 11–21. Hence the choice of our open-ended title "Reconcile yourselves . . ."'.

the origin of the language in Paul has made him unable to see anything else beyond the reconciliation of human beings to God. But does Paul refer in this text to his Damascus-road experience? Are there clear allusions to the event?

Arguments for the allusions

The present passage in which Paul alludes to his experience of conversion is part of Paul's *apologia* of his apostolic credentials. Paul's apostleship came under attack at Corinth. Among other things there seem to have been two major issues that his critics brought against Paul, issues that are relevant for the present study: first, he did not have a 'recommendation letter' from the proper authorities in Jerusalem, but rather was a self-made apostle and based his gospel on a single vision of Christ; second, not only was Paul not a follower of Jesus with no association with the true apostles in Jerusalem, but worse, he was a violent persecutor of the church. So it is in the context of Paul's response to these kinds of accusation that he makes a clear allusion to his Damascus experience. Here, in a succinct form, are the main arguments which support this proposal.[14]

Verse 14 reads as follows: ἡ γὰρ ἀγάπη τοῦ Χριστοῦ συνέχει ἡμᾶς, κρίναντας τοῦτο, ὅτι εἷς ὑπὲρ πάντων ἀπέθανεν, ἄρα οἱ πάντες ἀπέθανον, 'For the love of Christ urges us on, because we are convinced that one has died for all; therefore all have died.' Here Paul is saying that he came to a new and correct 'conviction' or 'judgement' (κρίναντας) regarding the significance of the death of Christ. There is indeed no doubt that the occasion on which Paul was confronted with a different reality regarding Christ's death – which fundamentally changed his previously held conviction – was his Damascus experience.[15] It was also there that he realized the extent of God's love for him and for the world, a love which 'compelled' him (συνέχει) to live 'no longer' for himself but in the service of God and others (v. 15). In v. 15 we find a very interesting and important parallel to Gal. 2.20 ('it is no longer I who live, but it is Christ who lives in me. And the life I now live in the flesh I live by faith in the Son of God, who loved me and gave himself for me') to which I will return in due course.

Verse 16 is also significant: Ὥστε ἡμεῖς ἀπὸ τοῦ νῦν οὐδένα οἴδαμεν κατὰ σάρκα· εἰ καὶ ἐγνώκαμεν κατὰ σάρκα Χριστόν, ἀλλὰ νῦν οὐκέτι γινώσκομεν, 'From now on, therefore, we regard no one from a human point of view; even though we once knew Christ from a human point of view, we know him no longer in that way.' ἀπὸ τοῦ νῦν ('from now on') points again to a radical turning point in Paul's life, which came as a direct consequence (Ὥστε, 'therefore') of the new conviction regarding the significance of Christ's death (vv. 14–15). It is clear that this cannot mean 'from the

---

14. See Kim, '2 Cor. 5:11–21', particularly pp. 268–71.
15. Cf. Margaret Thrall, *1 & 2 Corinthians, Vol. 1* (Cambridge: CUP, 1965), p. 409; Alfred Plummer, *2 Corinthians* (Edinburgh: T&T Clark, 2000), p. 174.

present moment, the time of writing',[16] but refers to Paul's Damascus experience[17] when he realized that Christ was the Messiah and that he died for all. It is interesting to note that the phrase ἀπὸ τοῦ νῦν is extremely rare in the NT, being used elsewhere only by Luke (Luke 1.48; 5.10; 12.52; 22.18; 22.69; Acts 18.6). Furnish is probably right to direct our attention to Isaiah, particularly 48.6, 'the new things *from now on* (ἀπὸ τοῦ νῦν)', as the context for understanding Paul's reference.[18]

Verse 17 is another allusion to Paul's experience on the Damascus road. It reads: ὥστε εἴ τις ἐν Χριστῷ, καινὴ κτίσις· τὰ ἀρχαῖα παρῆλθεν, ἰδοὺ γέγονεν καινά, 'So if anyone is in Christ, there is a new creation: everything old has passed away; see, everything has become new!' Though the statement regarding the καινὴ κτίσις ('new creation') is a general and universal statement of the new eschatological reality brought about by the death and resurrection of Christ, the overall context of Paul's apostolic defence indicates that Paul is also referring to himself when he came to be 'in Christ', thus being made a 'new creature'.[19]

The parallel aorist participles in v. 18, καταλλάξαντος ἡμᾶς ('having reconciled us') and δόντος ἡμῖν ('having given to us') point clearly to Paul's personal experience of reconciliation, conversion, and call to God's service on the Damascus road.[20] Surely, Paul makes it clear in v. 19 that he derives his own experience from the universal event of God's reconciling the world to himself – which consists in μὴ λογιζόμενος αὐτοῖς τὰ παραπτώματα αὐτῶν, 'not holding anyone's faults against them' (*NJB*). But it was exactly this fact that he realized personally in the encounter with Christ: though he was a persecutor, an enemy of God, Paul astonishingly grasps the fact

16. As correctly pointed out by Plummer, *2 Cor.*, p. 176. Similarly, C. K. Barrett states that '*hence-forth*' refers 'not from the time of writing but "from the time at which he saw that One had died for all"', quoting Denney. (C. K. Barrett, *A Commentary on the Second Epistle to the Corinthians* (London: Adam & Charles Black, 1976), p. 170.)

17. This is almost generally accepted by commentators of Paul. See particularly Wolff, 'True Knowledge'; Philip Hughes, *Paul's Second Epistle to the Corinthians* (Grand Rapids: Eerdmans, 1962), pp. 197–201; and Jan Lambrecht, 'The Favorable Time: A Study of 2 Corinthians 6:2a in its Context', in R. Bieringer and J. Lambrecht (eds), *Studies on 2 Corinthians* (Leuven: University Press, 1994a), p. 96.

18. V. P. Furnish, *II Corinthians* (The Anchor Bible, vol. 32A; New York: Doubleday, 1984), p. 312.

19. Barrett, *2 Cor.*, p. 174. In v. 17b, as in vv. 15–16, Paul seems to allude to the contrast between 'the former things' and 'the new things' found in Isaiah 43.18–19: 'Do not remember the former things, or consider *the things of old* (τὰ ἀρχαῖα μὴ συλλογίζεσθε). I am about to do *a new thing* (ἰδοὺ ποιῶ καινα); now it springs forth, do you not perceive it?' (cf. also Isa. 42.9; 48.6; 65.17; 66.22). Further, Paul's triple phrases μηκέτι, οὐκέτι ('no longer') ἀπὸ τοῦ νῦν ('from now on') in vv. 15–16, may be an indication of his understanding of the transition from the old to the new age envisioned in Isaiah and already brought into existence by the death and resurrection of Christ; Paul has experienced personally this radical new-ness by his own experience of forgiveness, reconciliation, and call to apostleship on the Damascus road. Cf. Larry Kreitzer, *2 Corinthians* (Sheffield: Sheffield Academic, 1996), p. 109. F. Danker also points to Paul's understanding of his ministry as being within the eschatological vision of Isaiah: 'Paul's intensive missionary effort, ignited by God's gift of Jesus as the Messiah, is the living demonstration that Isaiah's vision of salvation has found fulfilment'. (F. W. Danker, *2 Corinthians* (Augsburg Commentary on the New Testament; Minneapolis: Augsburg, 1989).)

20. This point is correctly emphasized, by, among others, Wolff, 'True Knowledge', p. 93.

that God does not hold his sin against him but rather forgives him and reconciles him. The reality of his own reconciliation and 'the message of reconciliation' he was called to proclaim were intrinsically interwoven in one single event which was so overwhelming for Paul that it is *set* or *placed* in his heart, and 'has grasped his entire inward being'.[21] The aorist participle θέμενος ἐν ἡμῖν ('having placed in us') in v. 19c points indeed to 'a once for all, finished event, namely, as with the δόντος in v. 18, the apostle's call'.[22]

Kim and others point to the parallels and close correspondences that exist between 2 Cor. 5.18–19 and Gal. 1.13–16, which make Paul's allusions to his Damascus experience in the former appear in an even clearer light.[23] Moreover, Rom. 5.10a ('if while we were *enemies*, we *were reconciled* to God') may also be a conscious reflection of Paul's own experience. If this is correct, then the argument presented above is significantly strengthened.

If this important passage on reconciliation is a clear allusion to Paul's radical experience on the Damascus road, it means, first of all, that his own experience of reconciliation is a vital part of the concept he will later develop. It also means that for a more comprehensive understanding of the concept in Paul it is worth exploring more carefully some other motifs that appear in this passage that are related to Paul's experience and understanding of reconciliation.

Paul's experience of reconciliation

Traditionally Paul's conversion experience was studied more in terms of his experience of 'being justified by faith'. More recently, however, biblical scholars have offered new and different models for understanding Paul's Damascus-road experience as a conversion/call and link it in a much closer way with his theology. It is thus proposed that Paul's personal profound experience of God's grace and revelation significantly shaped his theology, life, and ministry.[24] In a stimulating article, Kraftchick has shown that 'a full appreciation of Paul's theological construction must consider his personal experience' because 'Paul's theology is shaped not only by his heritage,

21. Ibid., p. 94.

22. Ibid., p. 94. I believe Wolff is right to make the important distinction between 'God's universal work of reconciliation' (accomplished once and for all in the death and resurrection of Christ) and 'the apostolic message of reconciliation' (which is the realization of that reconciliation in the present through the preaching), a distinction made obvious, in fact, by Paul's change from the present participle of λογιζόμενος ('counting') to the aorist participle θέμενος ('having placed'); see ibid., pp. 93–4.

23. Kim, '2 Cor. 5:11–21', p. 368, follows and builds on Hofius' similar observations; he also points to de Oliveira. They observe the following: (1) v. 19c is parallel to Gal. 1.12, 1.15–16a (Paul's own statements about God's revelation of the gospel in his Damascus experience); (2) v. 18c is parallel to Gal. 1.16b (Paul's testimony of God's commissioning); (3) v. 18ab corresponds to Gal. 1.13–14 (Paul's persecuting activity and the implications of Paul's strong emphasis on God's grace in response).

24. In addition to Kim's *Origin of Paul's Gospel* see also R. Longenecker (ed.) *The Road from Damascus*; Dunn, *Theology of Paul*, p. 48; Segal, *Paul the Convert*, p. 183; J. M. Everts, 'Conversion and Call of Paul' in G. F. Hawthorne *et al.* (eds), *Dictionary of Paul and His Letters* (Logos Library, electronic edn; Downers Grove, IL: IVP, 1997) [henceforth *DPL*].

his religious convictions and his struggles with his congregations, but also by his experience of the human condition'.[25] Other scholars have also stressed the intrinsic link between Paul's thinking/theology and his experience, the fact that various aspects of Paul's theology emerged also as he reflected upon, and offered insights into, the meaning of his remarkable experiences.[26]

There are several crucial aspects related to Paul's Damascus event, the foremost of which is his own experience of reconciliation. It is important to remember that it was while he was persecuting the church – which meant being a persecutor of Christ and ultimately an 'enemy' of God – that Paul was confronted with a radical new reality. And while being confronted for the wrong he was doing, Paul, contrary to his expectations, was not rejected by God, but found himself reconciled. He experienced personally the profound and radical nature of the grace of God, who did not count Paul's sin against him but rather accepted and forgave him. This was to change radically the direction of Paul's life because not only was Paul reconciled to God but he was commissioned into God's service to proclaim that message of God's radical grace and forgiveness, the message of reconciliation. Wolff is right to the point when he states that 'this experience of reconciliation shaped Paul's apostolic existence'.[27]

Paul's experience of reconciliation, as reflected in this important text of 2 Cor. 5.14–6.10, is significant in several respects. First, probably one of the most fundamental truths regarding reconciliation that Paul understood in that event was that reconciliation is purely *God's gift of grace* offered to an estranged and rebellious humanity. Reconciliation has grace as its starting point. Paul's personal experience of forgiveness, grace and reconciliation revealed to him the radical nature of God's grace, of a God who reached out to his enemies. *The victim takes initiative.* This is what Schwöbel refers to as '*the asymmetry of reconciliation*':

> The asymmetrical character of divine reconciliation and of divine love defines the reconciling act in Christ as of identification and exchange. Since reconciliation with those who cannot initiate reconciliation by themselves because they are captive in separation from God can only be achieved through the identification of God in Christ with his enemies, so divine love is directed to those who cannot love God.[28]

---

25. Steven J. Kraftchick, 'Death's Parsing: Experience as a Mode of Theology in Paul', in Janice Capel Anderson, *et al.* (eds.), *Paul's Conversations in Context* (JSNTS, 221; Sheffield: Sheffield Academic, 2002), p. 145.

26. See particularly Calvin Roetzel, *Paul: The Man and The Myth* (Columbia: University of South Carolina Press, 1998).; Michael Oakeshott, *Experience and its Modes* (Cambridge: CUP, 1985); and Peter Hodgson, 'Constructive Theology and Biblical Words', in F. Segovia and M. A. Tolbert (eds.) *Teaching the Bible* (Maryknoll, NY: Orbis, 1998).

27. Wolff, 'True Knowledge', p. 93.

28. Christoph Schwöbel, 'Reconciliation: From Biblical Observations to Dogmatic Reconstruction', in Colin E. Gunton (ed.), *The Theology of Reconciliation* (London: T&T Clark, 2003), p. 25.

These elements, which build into Paul's vision of reconciliation, will become very important as Paul explicates the social dimension of reconciliation, especially in Romans 12–15.

Second, the fact that 'God has reconciled the world' is presented to Paul as an *objective reality*. Everything else that Paul says about reconciliation at personal, social and political levels, can be properly understood only in that light.[29] As we will see later in the work, this gives the possibility for present reconciliation. By referring to his experience of reconciliation, Paul does not limit the reconciliation of God simply to those who have such an experience. On the contrary, and more fundamentally, that very experience revealed to Paul the permanent nature, attitude and action of God towards an estranged and rebellious humanity. God has reconciled the world to himself once and for all! And God's gracious stance towards Paul is an illustration of his stand towards the whole hostile world. This is what Paul understood on the Damascus road. The appearance of the resurrected Christ to him as well as Paul's own experience simply confirmed the objective nature of reconciliation. Thus, a ministry of reconciliation in the world is not merely *analogous* to what God has done, but it *is* what God has done. Reconciliation on the horizontal plane is not doing the sort of thing God did with us but it is doing the very thing God did with us. It is an extending of that cosmic reconciliation. It is not an extending of our terms of reconciliation but extending God's reconciliation.

Third, it is through *Christ's death and resurrection* that the objective reconciliation is accomplished and so it is Christ, the reconciler, that Paul focuses his attention on; thus, it is around Christ that any thought of reconciliation should be based. One cannot separate the concept of reconciliation – especially in its political and social aspects – from Christ, in whom the reality of reconciliation 'can be found and realized'.[30] This represents indeed the very foundation of Paul's vision of reconciliation and it is expressed in several texts in his letters, one of which (Rom. 5.1–10) is examined in detail in the next chapter.

Fourth, by echoing his own conversion experience, Paul wants to direct the Corinthians towards their own radical experience of reconciliation by God's grace so that they will be able to relate differently to each other, and even to their enemies. This may be seen clearly in 2 Cor. 6.1–10, where Paul insists that the Corinthians should not make the grace of God in their lives to be *in vain* . . . Indeed, the whole point of 6.1–10 is to illustrate that 'the gospel message, to be the gospel message, must be embodied, not just spoken'.[31] There is thus an *intrinsic relationship* between *the message* of reconciliation and *the messenger's* own reconciliation and life.

Lastly, it is significant that for Paul *there is no reconciliation without a cost!* Reading through Paul's catalogues of afflictions and sufferings (2 Cor. 6.3–10) one

29. Gunton, *The Theology of Reconciliation*, p. 6.
30. Ibid., p. 174.
31. Kraftchick, 'Death's Parsing', p. 151.

gets a very strong sense of this aspect. Schwöbel captures well this dimension of reconciliation:

> in view of the message that has been entrusted to them Christians know that the reality of reconciliation can spread – but at a price. Reconciliation understood from this theological perspective is not based on mutual agreement that has to be established first, but on a one-sided step to break up the pattern of the mutuality of enmity. Reconciliation is based on a one-sided offer of peace where there was conflict. As such, it is costly: it requires withdrawing from all attempts at retribution. The one who offers reconciliation is the one who must pay the price for the renewal of the relationship in the sense that there can be no retribution for the past misdeeds.[32]

The above discussion has shown that Paul's experience of conversion and call, in all its complexity, had significant and enduring implications for his life and thought, particularly as his radical experience of reconciliation shaped a new understanding of the concept.

4.2.2 *Identity, otherness and reconciliation: correlations in 2 Corinthians 5.14–6.10 and elsewhere in Paul*

In addition to his reconciliation, however, a careful reading of this passage will highlight other important aspects of Paul's life and thought that were fundamentally shaped by his Damascus experience and which also contributed to his overall vision of reconciliation. Among them, several are very important and relevant for our study.

1) *A new way of understanding and constructing his identity.* In two important accounts of this new way of perceiving other people and himself, Paul states:

> From now on, therefore, we regard no one from a human point of view; even though we once knew Christ from a human point of view, we know him no longer in that way. So if anyone is in Christ, there is a new creation: everything old has passed away; see, everything has become new! (2 Cor. 5.16–17)

> Χριστῷ συνεσταύρωμαι· ζῶ δὲ οὐκέτι ἐγώ, ζῇ δὲ ἐν ἐμοὶ Χριστός· ὃ δὲ νῦν ζῶ ἐν σαρκί, ἐν πίστει ζῶ τῇ τοῦ υἱοῦ τοῦ θεοῦ τοῦ ἀγαπήσαντός με καὶ παραδόντος ἑαυτὸν ὑπὲρ ἐμοῦ, 'I have been crucified with Christ; and it is no longer I who live, but it is Christ who lives in me. And the life I now live in the flesh I live by faith in the Son of God, who loved me and gave himself for me'. (Gal. 2.19c–20)

It should come as no surprise that one's radical conversion implies automatically a dramatic change in one's personal identity. Malherbe is thus correct to point out that

---

32. Schwöbel, 'Reconciliation', pp. 35–36.

'the redefinition of personal identity' was one of the central features of conversion.[33] Indeed, when we generally talk of a 'conversion' we refer to '*a radical change* of thought, outlook, commitments, and practice, which involves either an overt or a subconscious *break with one's past identity*'.[34] We could probably say that before his encounter with Christ, Paul had a more rigid definition of his identity, particularly because of the specific non-negotiable markers of his Jewishness, which determined fundamentally the way in which he related to others. This should not be taken to mean that he did not have any interaction with those who were different, particularly the Gentiles. In fact, as Terence L. Donaldson has argued, Paul had been engaged in a Gentile mission and he shared, with some groups within the Judaism of the Second Temple period, a conviction that there was 'space for Gentiles within the scope of God's saving purposes, without compromising in any way Israel's own covenantal self-understanding'.[35] However, what we want to highlight at this point is that Paul's encounter with the risen Christ on the Damascus road had a dramatic impact on his life. Not only was his new identity irreversibly shaped by Christ, but he was also 'shaken' in his previous definitions and construction of identity. He now realizes that his own identity is not as rigid as he thought and is not as closed as he tried to keep it. Rather, he discovers that Christ lives in him; that he is, in fact, embraced by Christ (and so, he realizes that Christ was open and made space for Paul, his initial enemy); that Christ's opening made it possible for Paul to open himself for Christ and, at the same time, for others; that he is now, paradoxically, both sure of who he is in Christ, and, at the same time not so sure: that his new identity is constantly in negotiation and interaction with 'the other'; that there is a somewhat mysterious dimension of who he is and who others are which requires a good deal of faith (Gal. 2.20);[36] and that his new sense of identity has enabled him to relate differently to those around him, to value and appreciate people from a completely different perspective (2 Cor. 5.16). Because of Christ, Paul has now a different set of values through which to judge everything and everyone else and a new basis from which to perceive and relate to 'the other'. As we will see in the later chapters, Paul shares his new understanding of identity with the Christians in Rome, thus becoming, what Esler calls 'an entrepreneur of identity'.[37]

---

33. Malherbe, *Paul and the Thessalonians*, pp. 26ff.
34. R. Longenecker, 'Introduction', in *The Road from Damascus*, p. xiii (italics added).
35. Donaldson, *Paul and the Gentiles*, p. 25.
36. This point was first suggested to me by Professor Haddon Willmer in a private conversation.
37. Philip Esler, *Conflict and Identity in Romans: The Social Setting of Paul's Letter* (Minneapolis, Fortress, 2003), p. 109. Using a complex of social-scientific methods (social identity theory and self-categorization theory), Esler offers a reading of Romans arguing that Paul wants to bring peace and unity among various groups in Rome by reinforcing the fundamental common identity they share in Christ, yet without sacrificing the specific elements of each group's identity. Similarly, William Campbell argues in his book *Paul and the Creation of Christian Identity* (LNTS, 322; London and New York: T&T Clark Continuum, 2006), that it was never Paul's intention to create a Christian identity that would replace Jewish identity, and that in the new community of Jews and Gentiles 'in Christ', each will maintain their specific

2) Another significant correlation which results from Paul's encounter with Christ is *an intellectual reorientation, a new way of knowing, a new understanding of reality.* In the new age inaugurated by Christ, the true knowing surpasses the knowing of the old age (κατὰ σάρκα), with a knowledge 'in Christ'. And this is true not only for Paul but also for all those belonging to this community of new creation. When Paul and his converts accepted the revelation of God in Christ they have experienced

> an *intellectual reorientation* in which they had to *change their understanding* of *human nature* and *the obligations* flowing from their new relationship to God, as well as *a new view of the cosmic scheme of things* . . . In turning to God, they were required to change their understanding of the divine and service to him; they had to think anew of human nature, no longer in terms of human potentiality and virtue, but from a perspective of their relation to God and his will; they had to reconstruct their view of a cosmic order to one that is under God's judgment while they themselves had a hope of deliverance from that judgment. And running through all of this new understanding was the theme of their moral responsibility.[38]

The new way of knowing is not simply a spiritual, ecstatic, or mystical way of knowing available to a few, nor a knowing in abstraction or isolation from the other. On the contrary, as Martyn remarks, 'it is life in the midst of the new-creation community, in which to know by the power of the cross is precisely to know and to serve the neighbour who is in need'.[39] Everything is now known, defined and lived out in the light of Christ – his love, cross and resurrection. Martyn continues:

> For, as the second half of 2 Cor 5:16 and the first half of v. 17 show, the epistemology characteristic of this community is thoroughly and without remainder christological. That is to say, together with the community that is being formed in him, *Christ* defines the difference between the two ways of knowing, doing that precisely in his cross. The cross of Christ means that the marks of the new age are at present hidden in the old age (2 Cor 6:3–10). Thus, at the juncture of the ages the marks of the resurrection are hidden and revealed in the cross of the disciple's daily death, and only there.[40]

3) *A new way of relating to others, including the enemy.* We should not pass too quickly over the fact that prior to his encounter with the risen Christ, Paul was

---

ethnicity. For further elaborations see the excellent discussion on the early Christian identity edited by Bengt Holmberg, *Exploring Early Christian Identity* (WUNT, 266; Tubingen: Mohr Siebeck, 2008).

38. Abraham Malherbe, 'Conversion to Paul's Gospel', in A. J. Malherbe, Frederick W. Noris and James W. Thomson (eds). *The Early Church in its Context* (Supplements to Novum Testamentum, vol. 90; Leiden: Brill, 1998), pp. 237–38, 240 (italics added).

39. J. Louis Martyn, 'Epistemology at the Turn of the Ages: 2 Corinthians 5:16', in J. L. Martyn, *Theological Issues in the Letters of Paul* (Edinburgh: T&T Clark, 1997), p. 109.

40. Ibid., p., 110.

a persecutor of the church, which meant that he was persecuting Christ and that ultimately he was an enemy of God. And it was from that position that he found himself forgiven, embraced and reconciled by God! His own reconciliation with God has completely altered his perception of, and relation to, his enemies. Not only was he able to acquire a different understanding but he was reconciled with his former enemies. Those he once persecuted now embrace him and they are reconciled! Of course, this did not mean that Paul never had enemies after the Damascus road. On the contrary, in the very passage where he describes the process of reconciliation, Paul is in dialogue with some of his opponents, his enemies. What changed for good, however, after Damascus was his perception, understanding, and mode of dealing with his enemies. 'From now on, therefore, we regard no one from a human point of view' (2 Cor. 5.16). It is very relevant that Paul discusses his new perception of human beings in the context in which he addresses his opponents/enemies in Corinth.

We should state here that the role of the Spirit is extremely important for all the above points and in Paul's theology of reconciliation, even though it is not explicitly presented in this passage. There is a significant and vital divine empowering for the actual life of the believer in embodying reconciliation, which is more than God-like service based on an analogy of the cross; it is empowerment through the work of the cross and the presence of God's Spirit.[41]

4.3 *OT (Isaianic) background: the substance of Paul's vision*

The gospel Paul preached was not an innovation of his own. On the contrary, throughout his letters Paul states in various ways that the subject matter of his gospel – the son of God, Jesus Christ, the Lord – was promised by the God of Israel and was recorded in the Scriptures, as he most clearly writes in Rom. 1.1–4. In explicating his understanding of the gospel, as well as its implications for the everyday life of Christians in their particular contexts, the Jewish Scripture was foundational for Paul. Indeed, what God was and is still doing through his son, Jesus Christ, is nothing other than a culmination of God's deeds done in the past and promised to his people. To understand what God is doing now, and will be doing in the future, is to understand what he has begun to do already – and this was recorded in the sacred Scriptures.

Of particular importance for this study is Paul's use of Isaiah. This is a vast subject of investigation which has been explored in detail from various angles, and many scholars have highlighted the crucial role of the OT in the writings of the NT.[42] My

---

41. This essential element was thoroughly examined and established by Gordon Fee in *God's Empowering Presence: the Holy Spirit in the Letters of Paul* (Peabody, MA: Hendrickson, 1994), and *Paul, the Spirit and the People of God* (Peabody, MA: Hendrickson, 1996).

42. See, for example, Hays, *Echoes of Scripture*; Shiu-Lun Shum, *Paul's Use of Isaiah in Romans: A Comparative Study of Paul's Letter to the Romans and the Sybylline and Qumran Sectarian Texts* (Tubingen: Mohr Siebeck, 2002); C. D. Stanley, *Paul and the Language of Scripture* (Cambridge: CUP,

intention is limited to Paul's use of Isaiah in explaining his understanding of reconciliation and its implications for the everyday life of Christians in the midst of social and political realities. Thus, it will be argued that for Paul, Isaiah provided the underlying 'substructure' for his narrative of reconciliation which we find in his letters.

In order for Paul to make sense of his dramatic experience on the Damascus road, and to understand the new reality he was living in, he turned to the OT, particularly to Isaiah. There were the images and the grand vision of the reconciliation of Israel to their God, of the reconciliation between Jews and Gentiles, and of the final eschatological reconciliation of all creation, that helped Paul to understand what had happened to him and also to understand that what Christ had accomplished was exactly the fulfilment of those promises. The new creation had been inaugurated, he lived now in the time of reconciliation and so he understood he had to proclaim it. This section argues that Paul's citations/allusions to Isaiah, their evocative power and their function in the context of 2 Corinthians 5–7, show that the substance of Paul's vision of reconciliation is found in the Isaianic themes of restoration and new creation, and in his vision of eschatological peace.

4.3.1 *2 Corinthians 5.11–7.1 and the restoration story in Isaiah*
A careful reading of 2 Corinthians 5–7 identifies 'reconciliation' and 'new creation' as key words with great significance for the whole passage and recognizes the Isaianic themes of restoration and new creation. Indeed, as several verses in the passage clearly indicate (5.17; 5.20; 6.1–2; 6.17–18), Paul combines his reconciliation language with references to 'restoration' and 'new creation' found in Isaiah 40–66.[43] A brief presentation of the way in which Paul uses these Isaianic themes in the present passage will highlight the connection and show that the citations from Isaiah are not simply isolated verses but that they function as hermeneutical lenses which explicate the meaning of reconciliation. I hope to show that, by referring to Isaiah, Paul does not simply intend to 'prove' that these promises are being fulfilled in the present; rather, he evokes the themes of restoration and new creation, within their wider Isaianic background, to provide meaning for his presentation of reconciliation in all its complexity.

1992); T. H. Lim, *Holy Scripture in the Qumran Commentaries and Pauline Letters* (Oxford: Clarendon, 1997); Dodd, *According to the Scriptures.*

43. Several scholars have stressed the intimate connection between Paul's language of reconciliation and the Isaianic background of restoration and new creation. Among others, Otfried Hofius, for example, in 'Erwägungen zur Gestalt und Herkunft des paulinischen Versöhnungsgedankens', pp. 1–14 argues that the background of 2 Cor. 5.18–21 is Isaiah 52–53. Peter Stuhlmacher also suggests the following OT texts for the origin of the NT language of reconciliation: Isaiah: 2.2–4; 9.1ff.; 11.1ff.; 25.6ff.; 40.9–11; 43.1ff.; 52.13–53.12; 56.1ff.; 60–63; Jeremiah: 23.7ff.; 31.31ff.; Zechariah: 9–13 ('Das Evangelium von der Versöhnung in Christus', pp. 44–49). Finally, as we have seen in Chapter 2, G. K. Beale proposes that Isaiah 40–66 represents the background of reconciliation in 2 Cor. 5–7 ('OT Background of Reconciliation').

2 Corinthians 5.17 and Isaiah 43.15–21; 48.6–7; 65.17–18

One of Paul's purposes in this whole section of 2 Corinthians 5.1–7.4 is to make the Corinthian believers realize and understand the significance of the death and resurrection of Christ for their everyday life, and their participation in God's new creation, and to highlight for them the significance and the implications of their reconciliation with God. In order to do that, he draws from Isaiah's images of 'restoration' and 'new creation'.

2 Corinthians 5.17 expresses the radical newness of the situation brought about by the death and resurrection of Christ and, as a consequence, the benefits for whoever participates in this new reality 'in Christ'. This is so radically new that it can only be compared to the original creation of God: ὥστε εἴ τις ἐν Χριστῷ, καινὴ κτίσις· τὰ ἀρχαῖα παρῆλθεν, ἰδοὺ γέγονεν καινά 'So if anyone is in Christ, there is a new creation: everything old has passed away; see, everything has become new.' The parallels drawn between God's creation and his final act of redemption were familiar in Judaism.[44] The language of creation and redemption is abundant in Isaiah and the two ideas are closely interconnected with the motif of salvation. Isa. 42.5–6; 43.1; 43.15–21; 44.24; 46.3–4; 51.9–11 are clear examples. Most probably, what Paul has in mind in v. 17 is Isa. 43.15–21:[45]

> I am the LORD, your Holy One, the Creator of Israel, your King. Thus says the LORD, who makes a way in the sea, a path in the mighty waters, who brings out chariot and horse, army and warrior; they lie down, they cannot rise, they are extinguished, quenched like a wick: *Do not remember the former things, or consider the things of old. I am about to do a new thing; now it springs forth, do you not perceive it?* I will make a way in the wilderness and rivers in the desert. The wild animals will honor me, the jackals and the ostriches; for I give water in the wilderness, rivers in the desert, to give drink to my chosen people, the people whom I formed for myself so that they might declare my praise.

The people of Israel are away from their land, in the Babylonian exile, being judged by God for their sins. But Israel is God's chosen people, created by God for his glory (43.1, 7), Yahweh is their God (43.2–3), the only God that exists (43.11), and so he will not abandon them (43.2). Through the prophet, God promises them that one day they will be gathered again and restored in their land (43.5–6), that they will experience a new exodus (43.16–17). They will also be fully restored in their communion with God (43.10–11). This is the immediate context of vv. 18–19 in which Israel is

44. Barrett, *2 Cor.*, p. 173.
45. There are, no doubt, other texts in Isaiah from which Paul may have taken his 'new creation' and 'restoration' motif – 11.6–12; 42.9; 48.3–6; 65.17–18; 66.22, to mention just a few. In his detailed study on the new creation language in Paul, Hubbard considers also other texts as possible sources for Paul's allusion in v. 17 but states that 43.15–21 'offers the closest parallel to Paul's allusion in 2 Corinthians 5:17.14'. (M. V. Hubbard, *New Creation in Paul's Letters and Thought* (SNTSMS, 119; Cambridge: CUP, 2002), p. 14.

urged not to remember what was in the past (sin, judgement, exile) but to concentrate on the promise of the great new redemptive act that God will accomplish. Thus, if the creation of the people of Israel was connected with the great Exodus from Egypt, the new exodus is the great redemption and the 'new creation' of God's people. Israel's liberation and re-creation are reoccurring themes. Indeed, the contrast between the 'former things' and the 'new things' occurs throughout Isaiah 40–55. However, the new creation promised in Isaiah is of a totally different nature: it speaks of God's people as a transformed people and of God's world as a transformed universe. Isaiah 65.17, 25 and 66.22 are particularly relevant: in the midst of judgement, the promise of Israel's restoration is described in the language of new creation where the former things will not be remembered, and where a completely new set of relationships will be established. And this will affect not only God's people but the entire creation. A radically new world will come into being, one in which peace shall reign:

> For I am about to create new heavens and a new earth; the former things shall not be remembered or come to mind . . . The wolf and the lamb shall feed together, the lion shall eat straw like the ox; but the serpent – its food shall be dust! They shall not hurt or destroy on all my holy mountain, says the LORD.
>
> (Isa. 65.17, 25)

By alluding to these passages, Paul wants to impress on his readers that the 'new creation' that God promised in Isaiah for the new age has been launched by Christ's death and resurrection. One of the characteristics of the new creation that was predicted by Isaiah was peace: between God and humanity, among people, and between different antagonistic groups. The eschatological peace will bring harmony and a new set of relationships between alienated and divided entities.[46] Paul wants to show that the Corinthians are experiencing the fulfilment of that promise, since they have been, through Christ's work, restored/reconciled with God. Moreover, he wants to make them realize that their new status should affect their life and behaviour; their reconciliation with God means also reconciliation with others. The whole of ch. 6 in 2 Corinthians develops further and elaborates exactly this understanding and significance of reconciliation in their everyday life. This is how Beale puts it:

> Paul's point in 2 Corinthians 5.14–21 is that if the Corinthians are truly partakers of the new creation and of a reconciled relationship with God (vv. 14–19), then they should behave like reconciled people (v. 20) . . . There is to be a connection between their identity as reconciled people and their behaviour as such people.[47]

---

46. Barrett, *2 Cor.*, p. 174. See also Beale, 'The NT and New Creation' in Scott I. Hafemann (ed.), *Biblical Theology: Retrospect and Prospect* (Downers Grove, IL: IVP, 2002), pp. 167–68; and Paul Minear, 'New Starting Point: Church Renewal and Social Renewal', *Interpretation* 19 (1965), pp. 3–15.
47. Beale, 'OT Background', pp. 223–24.

2 Corinthians 5.20–6.2 and Isaiah 49.4, 6, 8; 53.6, 9, 12

If we compare 2 Cor. 5.20–21 and Isa. 53.5–12 we find a very clear and close parallel between the work of Christ and that of the Servant of Yahweh. The work of Christ in almost all its fundamental elements is described by Paul through the language and images of the Servant of Yahweh: the great suffering he had to endure, being despised, punished, wounded, crushed, and afflicted for others, and his sinless life, being made a sin offering. A significant aspect is that this was presented as God's work: 'For our sake *he made him* to be sin who knew no sin' (2 Cor. 5.21). It was God who reconciled the world, through Christ, 'it is all God's work' (5.18), just as the Servant's work was not his own but Yahweh's. The Servant was simply following obediently God's will: 'Yahweh brought the acts of rebellion of all of us to bear on him' (53.6); 'It was Yahweh's good pleasure to crush him with pain; . . . and through him Yahweh's good pleasure will be done' (53.10). Further, it may not be a simple coincidence that Paul's Damascus experience, to which he also alludes in this passage, meant that he had to give credence to the fact that the crucified Messiah was indeed God's new revelation. Paul, like most of the people in his time, could not in any possible way see the crucifixion and shameful death of Jesus as the revelation of God – how could he, since for him and for most of the contemporaries, Jesus was 'being counted as one of the rebellious' (Isa. 53.12). Indeed, 'which of his contemporaries was concerned . . .?' (53.8). It was only when the resurrected Jesus Christ appeared to Paul that his eyes were opened and he was enabled to 'see': the crucifixion and death of Christ was indeed the revelation of God; Christ was not being punished for his sins but was 'bearing the sins of many and interceding for the rebellious' (53.12), thus reconciling all to God. We cannot miss Paul's allusion to his 'revelation' on the Damascus road and the strong connection to the song of the Servant in Isaiah: 'Who has given credence to what we have heard? And who has seen in it a revelation of Yahweh's arm?' (53.1)

2 Corinthian 6.2 is another important reference to Isaianic themes, this time a direct quote from yet another of the songs of the Servant:

καιρῷ δεκτῷ ἐπήκουσά σου καὶ ἐν ἡμέρᾳ σωτηρίας ἐβοήθησά σοι. ἰδοὺ νῦν καιρὸς εὐπρόσδεκτος, ἰδοὺ νῦν ἡμέρα σωτηρίας (At an acceptable time I have listened to you, and on a day of salvation I have helped you). (2 Cor. 6.2)

καιρῷ δεκτῷ ἐπήκουσά σου καὶ ἐν ἡμέρᾳ σωτηρίας ἐβοήθησά σοι (In a time of favor I have answered you, on a day of salvation I have helped you). (Isa. 49.8a)

As the text shows, Paul gives a *verbatim* citation from the Septuagint. He gives, no doubt, a christological interpretation of that passage and, taken with the preceding verses, Paul emphasizes that 'the acceptable time' and the 'day of salvation' have been realized in the death and resurrection of Christ. Not only were these realized in Christ but they are currently actualized in the life of the believers: Paul adds after the citation, 'behold, *now* is the acceptable time . . . *now* is the day of salvation' (6.2).

The very introduction of this citation from Isaiah at this point in Paul's argument is somewhat puzzling for exegetes.[48] Though the γάρ with which Paul introduces the quote clearly shows that it has a causal function, the difficulty is to know precisely what that function is. If γάρ is connected to the first part of v. 1 ('as we work together with him'), the quotation may be intended to refer to the work of the Servant.[49] The servant passage in Isa. 49.1–8 starts with the calling of the servant (vv. 1–3) and continues with a complaint of the servant for the unsuccessful mission and a request to God to vindicate him (v. 4). God answers and assures the servant that he will be vindicated but not before his mission extends to the nations (v. 6). There is no doubt that Paul would understand this text as referring primarily to Christ. But in the context of his apologia in 2 Corinthians, Paul attempts to defend himself by implying also close associations between his work and that of the Servant, especially if we consider the continuation of the quotation in Isa. 49.8, 'I have kept you and given you as a covenant to the people . . .' However, Paul does not stop here. He is applying the Isaianic text to Corinthian Christians as well, and wants to reassure them: as Christ, the original servant, suffered and seemed to have worked in vain but was vindicated by God in resurrection, so the Corinthians, who now share in the suffering of Christ, will be vindicated.

If, on the other hand, γάρ is connected to the second part of v. 1 ('we urge you also not to accept the grace of God in vain'), then, by introducing the Isaianic quotation, Paul wants to emphasize the importance of a responsible living in the present 'day of salvation', in the light of new eschatological reality that the Christians are experiencing in Christ. It is very probable that Paul has in mind Isaiah's vision of the day of salvation, particularly the predictions of what that day entails:

Thus says Yahweh: Make *fair judgement* your concern, act with *justice*, for soon *my salvation will come* and my *saving justice* be manifest. Blessed is anyone who does this, anyone who clings to it . . . abstaining from every evil deed. (Isa. 56.1–2, *NJB*)

How beautiful upon the mountains are the feet of the messenger who announces *peace*, who brings *good news*, who announces *salvation*, who says to Zion, '*Your God reigns*'. (Isa. 52.7)

If the Corinthians are living today in the day of salvation, then 'justice', 'peace', and 'reconciliation' should be manifested in their midst. Otherwise, the grace of God they have experienced will be in vain. That is how we should probably take Paul's exhortations to the Corinthians that they should 'not accept the grace of God in vain'

---

48. Jan Lambrecht offers an excellent treatment of both the difficulties that this quotation causes and an appropriate interpretation of the citation in Paul's argument. I am following his 'The Favorable Time', in Bieringer and Lambrecht (eds.), *Studies on 2 Corinthians*, pp. 515–29.

49. See Anthony Tyrrell Hanson, *The Paradox of the Cross in the Thought of St Paul* (JSNTS, 17; Sheffield: Sheffield Academic, 1987), pp. 55–63.

(2 Cor. 6.1). Indeed, being themselves witnesses of the great act of reconciliation that God has done in Christ in their midst, the Corinthians should embody in their lives that message of reconciliation.

Συνεργοῦντες δὲ καὶ παρακαλοῦμεν μὴ εἰς κενὸν τὴν χάριν τοῦ θεοῦ δέξασθαι ὑμᾶς, 'As we work together with him, we urge you also not to accept the grace of God in vain' (6.1), is a clear indication that Paul continues here his thought from 5.20: Ὑπὲρ Χριστοῦ οὖν πρεσβεύομεν ὡς τοῦ θεοῦ παρακαλοῦντος δι' ἡμῶν· δεόμεθα ὑπὲρ Χριστοῦ, καταλλάγητε τῷ θεῷ, 'So we are ambassadors for Christ, since God is making his appeal through us; we entreat you on behalf of Christ, be reconciled to God.' Even if the language of reconciliation is not used in 6.1, Paul's exhortation 'not to receive the *grace of God* in vain', especially his use of 'grace', refers most probably to 'the ministry of reconciliation' (5.18) and 'the word of reconciliation' (5.19).[50] To be reconciled – to accept and experience the love and grace of God – entails a particular response, a new way of life (5.14–15). The ministry of reconciliation then (5.18–19) does not refer simply to the proclamation of God's grace but also intrinsically to the living out, the enactment of God's grace, of God's reconciliation. That is why Paul expresses here, as in 5.20, an actual invitation for the Corinthians to accept the grace of God; i.e., to embody it.[51]

It is thus essential that, when we read Paul's treatment of reconciliation in 2 Corinthians, we do not stop at 5.21 but continue with his discussion in ch. 6, where the inherent relationship between the acceptance of reconciliation and its enactment in everyday life situations is emphasized. If we read the entire passage of 2 Cor. 5.11–7.4 as being shaped by the story of restoration and new creation from Isaiah, and particularly by the story of the Servant of Yahweh, we may gain some fresh insights into Paul's comprehensive understanding and presentation of reconciliation. Taken in the broader context, Paul's appeal to the Corinthians is to live in conformity with the grace they have received from God, which 'must be interpreted as a renewal and deepening of the reconciliation already received'.[52] Indeed, by adding the double ἰδοὺ νῦν 'behold, now!' in v. 2b, Paul wants to underline the human task in the present and to emphasize that what happened in the past, the salvation of God, has an extreme importance *now*. The Corinthians should be continually open to the grace of God; that is, to God's reconciliation and reconciling practices.

4.3.2 *Peace and the restoration of creation:* The Vision *of Isaiah*

As we have seen, Paul's references to Isaiah in 2 Corinthians are not simply proof

---

50. Beale makes this point and argues persuasively for the connection of 5.17–21 with 6.1ff. 'OT Background', pp. 226–32. Lambrecht also notes: 'God's grace in this context certainly consists in humanity's reconciliation with God, but since Paul exhorts his readers thus in the concrete situation of tension, reconciliation between him and his readers may be included as well.' ('The Favorable Time', pp. 520–21.)

51. See ibid., pp. 521–22 and Beale, 'OT Background', p. 227.

52. Lambrecht, 'The Favorable Time', p. 526.

texts that Paul used in order to prove his theological points. Rather, his clear allusions to the theme of restoration and new creation in Isaiah function as a hermeneutical lens through which his message of reconciliation could be properly understood. Hubbard correctly stresses the importance of knowing both the literary-conceptual framework and the theological context of particular words and ideas for an appropriate understanding of Paul. He states:

> Without a specific literary-conceptual framework to provide definition and texture, words remain intangible and amorphous entities capable of any number of meanings. Understanding an idea in its native environment means becoming acquainted with a whole host of other ideas indigenous to that environment. It is this conceptual network which furnishes the definitional boundaries of an idea and, to a great extent, determines its content.[53]

If this is correct, we are justified in exploring the Isaianic theological context of restoration, new creation, and vision of peace, as the adequate matrix within which the social dimension of reconciliation will make more sense – especially if, as in Isaiah, the great promise of restoration, new creation and peace are closely related with social-political realities of everyday life. If Paul's understanding of reconciliation was inspired by Isaiah's vision of restoration and peace, then it is most likely that, like Isaiah, Paul also understood reconciliation to have a social and political dimension as well as a religious/spiritual one. A closer look at Isaiah's vision highlights indeed the political aspect of peace, justice, and well-being.

John Watts describes the nature of the book of Isaiah as 'a Vision that dramatically portrays God's view of history', and states that 'the core of the Vision's theological message . . . is that Yahweh is the Lord of History. He calls and dismisses the nations. He determines their destinies. He divides the ages and determines the eventual courses of mankind.'[54] In that vision of the age to come that Isaiah portrays, righteousness, justice, and peace are non-negotiable elements.

The concept of peace (shalom) is an extremely prominent concept in the OT. The word-group *shalom* designates primarily a state of well-being, peace, friendship, happiness, prosperity, wholeness or fulfilment, and salvation. In addition, some authors also point out that a basic meaning of the verb שלם, is 'retribute, repay, reward' and so the particular context in which the word is used should be carefully considered in order to determine the appropriate meaning.[55]

In his vision of the final restoration of Israel, Isaiah speaks of 'peace' as one of the most important characteristics of God's restoration: Yahweh will restore

---

53. Hubbard, *New Creation in Paul's Letters and Thought*, p. 77.

54. John Watts, *Isaiah 1–33* (WBC, 24a; Logos Library, electronic edn; Dallas: Word, 1998). As we shall see later, Paul's deep understanding of the lordship of Christ over history was fundamentally shaped by this Isaianic vision of Yahweh as the Lord of history. That is why the lordship of Christ will represent a fundamental presupposition for Paul's life, theology and ministry.

55. Philip J. Nel, 'שלום', *NIDOTTE*, Vol. 4, pp. 130–35.

his righteousness and justice and will bring back his order in the world and so the entire earth will experience an unparalleled state of peace. It is interesting to note that together with recompense/reward of good deeds, Yahweh's punishment of evil (both of Israel's sins and of the evil of Israel's enemies) is seen as part of God's restoration (Isa. 65.6; 59.18; 66.6). As is seen clearly in the eschatological vision of Isa. 56.9–57.21, the peace which Yahweh brings contains both comfort/healing for the repentant (57.19) and accusation/punishment for the wicked (57.21).[56] A very important aspect of peace in the OT is its association with truth and justice. Isa. 32.17, for example, reads that 'the fruit of righteousness will be peace; the effect of righteousness will be quietness and confidence forever' (NIV), thus emphasizing the fact that peace is not simply the absence of conflict but a 'deep commitment to the work of justice'.[57] Indeed, throughout Isaiah peace is very closely associated with justice. Many times, 'peace' and 'justice' are presented as one and the same, as for example in Isa. 9.5, where the 'Prince of Peace' is also the bringer of justice whose 'kingdom shall be established and sustained with justice and righteousness'.[58]

An important aspect of 'peace' in Isaiah is that it is articulated as a component of social and communal relations. *Shalom* is used to express a friendly alliance between various parties, in the relations between friends, groups and nations. When the tension/conflict is over, there is *shalom* (Isa. 59.8). Nel points out the special relation of *shalom* to *tsedaqah (righteousness)* in Isaiah, particularly the impossibility of having peace while continuing in sin and evil.[59]

Peace as political justice. In the ancient world the idea of peace was understood first of all as political peace. In the Bible also, the concept of peace includes a political meaning even though it is not totally comprehended by it. Thus, the biblical tradition of 'peace' goes beyond political negotiations and 'builds onto this image the larger truth of complete reconciliation, physical and emotional, between feuding parties. In the Bible genuine peace is always just and moral . . . peace is seeking the well-being of others and of oneself.'[60] The political dimension of peace is present within the overall vision of Isaiah. The most obvious examples include Isa. 11.1–16 and 65.17–25. In Isa. 11.1–16, one finds the picture of Jesse's shoot, who will bring about righteousness and justice on earth, the shalom.[61] As Shum points out, such a vision is echoed in Isaiah 32, where a glorious future of righteousness and justice is promised (32.1–8), which will have as effect a state of peace (32.15–20) with the coming of God's Spirit. For Isaiah, this state of peace does not refer to individual tranquillity

---

56. Ibid., pp. 130–31.

57. Joseph P. Healey, 'Peace, Old Testament', in David Noel Freedman (ed.), *ABD* (Logos Library, electronic edn; New York: Doubleday, 1997).

58. Ibid.

59. Nel, 'שׁלוֹם', pp. 131, 132.

60. Leland Ryken *et al.*, 'Peace', *Dictionary of Biblical Imagery* (Logos Library, electronic edn; Downers Grove, IL: IVP, 2000). [Henceforth *DBI*.]

61. This particular verse from Isa. 11.10 is quoted by Paul in Rom. 15.12 referring to the incorporation of Gentiles into God's people.

and happiness but 'to political stability and social prosperity. God's people will by then dwell securely in a peaceful city with wealth' (32:18).[62]

An interesting aspect of this political stability and social prosperity is Isaiah's insistence that such a state is reached only on the premise of a right relationship with God and only together with God. In other words, it is not possible to have one without the other: political stability and social prosperity are conditioned by a reconciled relationship between Yahweh and his people, by obedience to Yahweh's commandments (cf. Isa. 31.6–9; 32, and 48.17–18). The other side of the coin is clearly that one cannot experience God's peace and righteousness if this is not marked by political stability and social prosperity.

In Rom. 5.1ff Paul also makes a close connection between δικαιοσύνη and ἐιρήνη/καταλλαγή. Paul has been, most probably, inspired by the Isaianic tradition which makes such close connection between δικαιοσύνη and ἐιρήνη (Isa. 9.6–7; 11.1–16; 32.17; 48.18; 54.13–14; 60.17). More concretely, the obedience and vicarious death of the Servant of Yahweh in Isaiah (53.5, 11) who caused many to become righteous and have peace, might have also been in Paul's mind.[63]

Peace and the Spirit of Yahweh. Another important element of Isaiah's vision of Israel's eschatological restoration is the significant role that the Spirit of Yahweh plays in the restoration of Israel and of the entire world. This is illustrated in such texts as Isa. 11.2; 32.15; 42.1; 59.21 and 61.1. As we shall see, this Isaianic concept exercised a strong influence on Paul. The work of the Holy Spirit explicated in Romans 5 and 8 may be, again, influenced by the Isaianic tradition of the significant role of the Spirit in the eschatological restoration/blessing of God's people. 'Peace' is God's gift and the kingdom of God is 'righteousness and peace and joy in the Holy Spirit' (Rom. 14.7). The association of these themes from Isaiah are also present in Paul's ethics.

In the light of such clear political connotations of the idea of peace in Isaiah, especially in the prophecy of the lordship of Messiah found in Isaiah 11, Shum's position is really questionable – the position, namely, that when Paul applies Isa. 11.10 in Rom. 15.12, his 'concern was by no means politically oriented; rather, it was completely spiritual'.[64] Shum's argument is very weak and even contradictory: how can Paul's fundamental concern here be simply with 'a spiritual state of peace' when he is strongly urging Roman Christians both to accept and be reconciled with one another and to live out that peace in the midst of the social and political situation in Rome? Shum himself acknowledges in his concluding section of his book that 'Paul's notion of peace, heavily indebted to Isaiah (e.g., Isa. 32.17; 54.1–14; 60.8–17), has at least two dimensions: God-human, and human-human'.[65] If 'heavily indebted to Isaiah' (where peace meant also political justice) and having also a human-human

---

62. Shum, *Paul's Use of Isaiah in Romans*, p. 194.
63. Ibid., p. 193.
64. Ibid., p. 255.
65. Ibid., p. 268.

dimension, Paul's notion of peace/reconciliation could not have been simply religious and spiritual.

Peace and God's eschatological salvation. It is relevant to mention that whereas for Isaiah – and for Paul's contemporary Jewish interpreters – God's eschatological restoration of Israel, with all the implications of such an event, lies completely in an unknown future, for Paul it is already being implemented, even though its total fulfilment lies also in the future. Since Isaiah profoundly shaped Paul's conception of eschatological peace, it is evident that his view of God's dealing with the nations reflects both his indebtedness to Isaiah and his eschatological outlook.

Peace and its religious dimension. It is important to understand that while the notion of peace in Isaiah has very clear social and political connotations, it is not limited or restricted to these. Peace cannot be reduced to social/political life since this always has a religious aspect as well. It is God who gives peace and he is the foundation of peace. Peace is an essential part of God's plan of salvation. Indeed, there cannot be peace if one's relationship with God is distorted. Since *shalom* describes a state of well-being and happiness, it is clear that this cannot be realized without or apart from God, but rather in a renewed relationship with God.[66]

4.3.3 *The implications of Isaianic themes for Paul's reconciliation*

The first thing we should emphasize from the very beginning is that Paul did not simply take concepts from the OT and apply them 'literally' into his letters. The fact that he interprets everything in the light of the new great thing that God has done in the world in Christ, gives Paul the freedom to change, shift, and develop further many concepts that he finds in the OT, particularly in Isaiah. Having said that, however, we have to stress that those concepts from the OT greatly help Paul to base his new understandings and explorations, in a fundamental way, on the same story of God's dealing with humanity and the world. It is not a different story but the same, one in which God's righteousness and faithfulness is shown.

For Paul, reconciliation is nothing else but the great 'restoration' of God's people, of humanity, of creation itself, to the initial purposes of God. By alluding to the story in Isaiah, Paul wants to point beyond the story of Israel to the story of God and the world. To be sure, the fulfilment of the promise of 'the restoration of Israel' proves God's faithfulness to his covenant with Israel and to God's way of restoring the world – via restoring Israel. But for Paul, now it is the church as the 'restored Israel' that has the same mission, the restoration of creation and so a ministry of reconciliation. Indeed, one of the most important things Paul wants to get across is that the restoration of the world, the grand vision of peace from Isaiah (65.17–25), has already happened in Christ and that the Christians should enact that great restoration and reconciliation in their everyday life. This is very clearly explained by Paul's elaborations in 2 Corinthians 6. As the passage in Isaiah so powerfully illustrates (65.11–25), it is

---

66. See Philip J. Nel, 'שלום', p. 132.

clear for Paul that the 'new great thing' that God has done in Christ, the reconciliation of the world, is not something that affects only their relationship with God but also their living together, as reconciled people, in the midst of concrete historical circumstances. Thus, not only is the peace and reconciliation of the eschatological new creation as depicted in Isaiah inaugurated in Christ, but Paul also suggests that the believers' reconciliation with God has indispensable social implications for their everyday life. By evoking restoration, new creation, and peace passages from Isaiah – themes with strong social, economic, and political resonance – Paul wanted to impress on the minds of his readers that those elements or defining features of restoration and new creation in Isaiah are implied in the very process of reconciliation.

Paul wants also to show that, exactly as in the case of Israel, the church, the new creation of God, is not meant for its own end but also to be a light to the nations, to act as an agent of reconciliation. The ultimate focus of the ministry of reconciliation should not stop at the believers' reconciliation with God but should extend to incorporate the world – just as with Israel, whose restoration was ultimately meant to be a light to the nations, as these texts from Isaiah clearly highlight: Isa. 42.1, 6; 49.6; 66.19.

With these considerations in mind it might become clearer why Paul, who understood himself to continue the work of the servant, has become 'the apostle to the Gentiles' par excellence![67] It was his call to announce to the world the great restoration of creation – that God's intention for the world (peace, justice, harmony) is beginning to take shape, as it is already being experienced in the life of Christians who are now themselves called to embody or enact that reconciliation in all its social and political aspects. However, to give expression to such a profound and complex reality of reconciliation in a Graeco-Roman context, Paul turned to a concept used in the Hellenistic context primarily for interpersonal relationships, in the sociological and political spheres of life. And to this we now turn for a closer examination.

4.4 *Hellenistic, diplomatic background of* καταλλάσσω/ καταλλαγή *and Paul's paradigm shift*

In addition to the key theological themes of 'peace', 'restoration', and 'new creation' that are predominantly used in Isaiah and to which Paul turned, he also had to look elsewhere in order to properly explain and describe to a Hellenistic/Roman audience his own experience as well as his new radical understanding of what God has done in Christ's death and resurrection. Being very much aware of the social and political realities of his time, he found καταλλάσσω/καταλλαγή and he used them

---

67. The centrality of the idea of being 'a light to the nations' is best encapsulated in the work of The Servant of Yahweh – found in Isaiah in the four so-called 'Songs of the Servant' (42.1–4; 49.1–6; 50.4–9; 52.13–53.12) – which describe a perfect servant of God whose two most important tasks are: to re-gather God's people and to be a light of the nations.

to further explicate and give expression to the multifaceted concept and vision of reconciliation.

As we saw in the second chapter, καταλλάσσω/καταλλαγή is a Greek word group used in Hellenistic diplomacy, in the politico-military context for peace treaties, in commercial dealings as a monetary 'exchange', 'settlement', or 'payment'.[68] It refers also to the restoration of various group and interpersonal relationships after a period of enmity between warring and estranged groups, culminating in a relationship of friendship. We pointed to Breytenbach's strong argument for the significance of 'reconciliation' in ancient politics, which draws attention to the importance of Graeco-Roman political life and concepts for Paul's formulations of his gospel and theology in the urban environment of the Graeco-Roman world.[69] The significance of this fact cannot be overestimated, because one simply cannot adequately understand Paul's use of a particular concept unless one struggles to understand first the overall intellectual, cultural, and social context in which such concepts were commonly being used. It is thus surprising that in various studies dealing with reconciliation in Paul, there has been a systematic 'downplaying' of this essential principle and that no major attempt has been made to do a thorough systematic analysis of the social dimension of reconciliation in Paul. This is all the more striking since καταλλαγή had such strong interpersonal, social and political connotations.

To be sure, words do not have a fixed meaning or connotation. Rather, they have a fluid semantic field and they acquire meaning also within the literary contexts in which they are used, and within the very specific sentences in which they are found. Thus, a word might have a particular meaning in one occurrence but might not preserve it in a different context or sentence. Given this ability of words and concepts to change and be changed in different contexts, any particular meaning or connotation of a word/concept must be determined through a rigorous exegesis of each individual sentence and context. More specifically, I am not saying that the word 'καταλλαγη' should be read as always referring to a political act, or that the political connotation is always present whenever the word is being used. Each sentence should support (or not support) a specific connotation. As we will see later in the work, there are instances in Paul where he uses 'reconciliation' in a very strong, religious sense to refer to the reconciliation between people and God, thus bringing a new connotation to the Hellenistic usage of the word. By doing this, Paul is not the first to bring God into the picture. Some of the first such usages are found in the Septuagint, in 2 Macc. 1.5; 5.20; 7.33 and 8.29, as we discussed in more detail earlier (in Chapter 2). In those

---

68. Particularly important were the contributions of Breytenbach (*Versöhnung*), pp. 40–83 and S. Porter, Καταλλάσσω, pp. 39–76.

69. Breytenbach, *Versöhnung*. We should mention here some other NT scholars who have also emphasized the importance of ancient politics and philosophy for Paul's theology: Malherbe, *Paul and the Thessalonians: The Philosophic Tradition of Pastoral Care* (Philadelphia, PA: Fortress, 1987) and other works (see Bibliography); Troels Engberg-Pedersen, *Paul and the Stoics* (Louisville, KY: Westminster John Knox, 2000); Blumenfled, *The Political Paul*.

texts, we find various instances where, as a result of people's prayers and pleas to God subsequent to their falling in sin and apostasy, God is reconciled to his people. While we are exploring in this chapter the Hellenistic background of 'reconciliation', it has to be stressed that Paul does not renounce or neglect this Jewish, 'religious' aspect of reconciliation. On the contrary, this aspect is essential for Paul's overall vision of reconciliation. However, in his various usages of the word in his letters, Paul puts a twist into the previous Jewish usage and presents people as being reconciled to God and not vice versa. It is thus essential when determining the meaning or connotation of a word or concept to pay careful attention to the specific way in which the author uses it in each context.[70]

Particularly important for Paul is the fact that he does not simply adopt existing ideas and then woodenly use them; he also changes and modifies them to fit his own symbolic universe. In other words, Paul makes a 'paradigm shift' in his use of various concepts. A brief note on the concept of 'paradigm shift' as brought in by Thomas Kuhn is now in order as it will help us better appreciate the innovation that Paul brings to the traditional Hellenistic understanding of the concept of reconciliation.

4.4.1 *Thomas Kuhn and the notion of 'paradigm shift'*

It is probably not an exaggeration to state that Thomas Kuhn's book *The Structure of Scientific Revolutions*[71] has enjoyed a unique and privileged position of academic influence, perhaps more than has any other single book in recent decades. This book on the history and interpretation of science has become a major reference for interdisciplinary discourse, being responsible, in particular, for introducing the terminology of 'paradigm shift' into the academic vocabulary. There is neither the space here, nor is it our purpose to go into anything like an analysis and critique of Kuhn's work.[72] An ultra-simplification of Kuhn's main theses may be given in these four brief statements: (1) paradigms dominate normal science; (2) scientific

---

70. Having made these important points about the various ways in which a 'word' acquires a specific meaning, I would like to point out that my overall thesis does not depend either on a Hebrew/Jewish or a Hellenistic usage of the word group καταλλάσσω/καταλλαγή. In fact, an important thesis I put forward and which I substantiate with detailed exegesis in the subsequent chapters, is that the concept of reconciliation in Paul is much larger than the 'word' καταλλαγή and that Paul is using a very rich symbolism of reconciliation which includes also such words as 'peace', 'love', 'unity', 'harmony', and 'welcome'. Thus, I argue that for a proper exploration into the way in which Paul understood and used the theme of reconciliation in his writing, such words and concepts must also be included.

71. Thomas Kuhn, *The Structure of Scientific Revolutions* (2nd edn; Chicago: University of Chicago Press, 1970). (First edition published in 1962.)

72. There is vast literature of response to and interaction with Kuhn's theory. An excellent example of interaction with and applicability of Kuhn's theory is Gary Gutting (ed.) *Paradigms & Revolutions: Appraisals and Applications of Thomas Kuhn's Philosophy of Science* (Notre Dame/London: University of Notre Dame Press, 1980), which evaluates and applies Kuhn's model to philosophy, social sciences, humanities and history of science. For an assessment of the model's use in biblical studies see Robert Shedinger, 'Kuhnian Paradigms and Biblical Scholarship: Is Biblical Studies a Science?', *Journal of Biblical Studies* 119 (2000), pp. 453–71.

revolutions are paradigm shifts; (3) observations are paradigm-dependent; and (4) criteria are paradigm-dependent. Though I cannot offer here an account of each of these main theses, I should briefly say at least this much: Kuhn's main contribution is to offer a new account of science and scientific progress. The dominant view was that 'scientific development' happened through a logical and linear accumulation of data through observation and experimentation. Thus, science advances through a constant forward movement of discovery, innovation and accumulation of knowledge to an 'ever growing stockpile that constitutes scientific technique and knowledge'.[73] Against this view, Kuhn argues that progress consists of 'scientific revolutions' in which an entire worldview in a particular field of knowledge is replaced by another through a shift in basic convictions in the scientific world. Thus, science progresses not through 'development-by-accumulation' (within the same paradigm), but through 'paradigm shifts'. Significantly, however, when a paradigm shift happens, it does not mean that the elements of the old paradigm disappear completely. Rather, they are reinterpreted and redefined, appearing now in a completely new configuration. Kuhn's analysis provides a helpful model for analysing Paul's experience of conversion as a paradigm shift as well as Paul's way of theologizing as a process by which he takes existing conceptual paradigms and transforms them. Paul seems to make such a shift in relation to the Hellenistic concept of reconciliation.

4.4.2 *Paul's paradigm shift in the concept of reconciliation*
In an illuminating article, John Fitzgerald applies the paradigm-shift analysis to Paul's concept of reconciliation. Fitzgerald highlights the way in which the concept was used in the Hellenistic environment and the modifications Paul makes when he employs the terminology.[74]

The standard paradigm of reconciliation
Set out below, in a very schematic form, are the most important elements which represented the *presuppositions* and *logic* of the standard paradigm of reconciliation.[75]
- Presupposing a wrongdoing of one or more parties which created the conflict, the basic principle in the standard paradigm was that *those responsible for the conflict* were to take initiative in restoring the relationships and seek reconciliation, while the offended party had to willingly accept the offer of reconciliation.
- The guilty party's initiative in reconciliation took the form of an *appeal*, often accompanied by some gesture showing affection and concern for the wronged person.

73. Kuhn, *The Structure*, pp. 1–2.
74. John T. Fitzgerald, 'Paul and Paradigm Shifts: Reconciliation and Its Linkage Group', in Troels Engberg-Pedersen (ed.), *Paul Beyond the Judaism/Hellenism Divide* (Louisville, KY: Westminster John Knox Press, 2001), pp. 241–62. It what follows I summarize schematically his major findings.
75. Ibid., pp. 228–32.

- *Reparations* were necessary in order to pacify the estranged party and achieve reconciliation. This was a standard precondition for reconciliation between warring nations.
- There were both *benefits* and *responsibilities* involved in the fact of reconciliation: 'one of the benefits was the knowledge that one could fulfill one's tasks in the full confidence of a restored relationship'; as for the responsibilities, 'the reconciled were to live in light of their renewed concord with one another and henceforth to live irreproachably'.[76]

Paul's shifts in the reconciliation paradigm

As with other concepts, Paul draws on ideas associated with reconciliation in the Hellenistic context, but in a remarkable way. He re-conceives reconciliation and shifts the traditional paradigm, bringing some new elements into the picture.[77] There are several significant changes that Paul brings to the concept. The first thing to be noted is that Paul takes the term used in diplomacy and politics, applies it to the divine-human relationship (2 Cor. 5.18–20; Rom. 5.10–11), and shifts the paradigm so that *God, the offended party, is taking the initiative* in reconciliation. That God intervenes prior to and apart from human repentance is most clearly expressed by Paul in Rom. 5.8, 10 where Paul states that God has taken the initiative and reconciled human beings while they were still sinners and hostile to God. As Fitzgerald correctly remarks, this is 'of momentous import, for it suggests a radically new and unprecedented understanding of God'.[78]

The death of Christ could be understood as the 'reparations' payment necessary for effective reconciliation between God and humanity. The shift Paul makes here, however, is that it is not the offending humanity who makes the reparations but God, who 'reconciled us through the death of his Son' (Rom. 5.10). One last important note we would like to make here refers to one of several features that remain intact from the traditional paradigm, namely *the responsibility* of those being reconciled to live their lives in the light of their achieved reconciliation; i.e., to live irreproachably. Paul maintains this element as essential and shows that he has assumed that responsibility and lived appropriately to his reconciliation with God. He is thus 'offering proof of the reality of his own reconciliation' by pointing to the blamelessness of his ministry (2 Cor. 6.3), to the virtues he exhibits (6.4–7) and to the way in which he gives himself for the benefit and spiritual enrichment of the other (6.10).[79]

Such an analysis brings significant insights and advances substantially the discussion of reconciliation in Paul.[80] It shows that within the traditional paradigm, reconciliation dealt with interpersonal, societal, and political aspects of life. While

---

76. Ibid., pp. 231–32.
77. Ibid., pp. 232–36.
78. Ibid., p. 233.
79. Ibid., p. 237.
80. It is surprising that Fitzgerald leaves the question open and does not explain *why* Paul was able to

Paul maintains these elements, he also brings God into the picture, thus enlarging the political concept of reconciliation with a vital, religious dimension and integrating these two elements into one reality. In addition, Paul regards as important the element of responsibility for those being reconciled to live in accordance with their reconciliation. Furthermore, the analysis highlights the other shifts in the paradigm that Paul makes; most significantly, that the offended party takes the initiative for reconciliation.

Since Paul, therefore, is using a concept drawn from the commercial/social and political environment to describe his own experience with God and with the other, we could initially conclude that, for Paul, the concept *must* have had inherent social and political meaning and implications.[81] As we suggested earlier, Paul's understanding of the complex reality of reconciliation is not exhausted by the καταλλάσσω/καταλλαγή terminology, though these were important elements that gave form to Paul's vision. We find throughout his letters a rich variety of ways which seem to describe the reality of reconciliation, all of which must be considered for an adequate inquiry into Paul's understanding of reconciliation, particularly in its social dimension(s). This is the subject of the last section in this chapter.

4.5 *Reconciliation symbolism in Paul: the vision is given expression*

We have alluded previously to the fact that, for Paul, the events proclaimed by his gospel of Jesus Christ were so complex and multifaceted that he used a rich metaphorical language in order to express their significance. Similarly, the profound life-transforming reality of the new life 'in Christ' that the believers were experiencing required from Paul a variety of images, metaphors, and symbols in order to describe adequately such experiences. James Dunn is right to point out that

> the very different metaphors Paul drew upon were presumably attempts to express as fully as possible a reality which defied a simple or uniform or unifaceted description. There was something so rich and real in the various experiences of conversion which Paul's gospel brought about that Paul had to ransack the language available to him to find ways of describing them. The vitality of the experience made new metaphors necessary if the experience was to be expressed in words (as adequately as that is possible) and to be communicated to others.[82]

---

transform the old paradigm and bring such a radical innovation into the understanding of reconciliation. I hope that my previous section has addressed that question.

81. Fitzmyer reminded us quite a number of years ago that in our treatment of reconciliation we should always bear in mind that 'the notions of enmity, hostility, estrangement, and alienation, as well as their counterparts, reconciliation, atonement, friendship, and intimacy are derived from social intercourse of human persons or from the relations of ethnic and national groups, such as Jews and Greeks, Palestinians and Romans' (*Pauline Theology* (Englewood Cliffs, NJ: Prentice-Hall, 1967), p. 162).

82. Dunn, *Theology of Paul*, p. 332. He also points out the significance of metaphors for the believers' experience: 'metaphors bring out the *reality* of the experience of the new beginning for Paul. Evidently they all described something in the experience of his readers with which they could identify. Something

The significance of the metaphoric or symbolic language for Paul's soteriology has been distinctly established by Gerd Theissen in his important study 'Soteriological Symbolism in the Pauline Writings: A Structuralist Contribution'.[83] To describe the dramatic events of redemption, Paul is drawing on images he finds in everyday human life, such as liberation, justification, reconciliation, transformation, life, death, and union.[84] Concerning the reconciliation symbolism, Theissen makes several important contributions. His focus and intentions lying elsewhere, he does not develop the theme of reconciliation as such but the contours he draws around it are noteworthy and very relevant for the purposes of the present study. First, he shows that, in the way Paul uses it, the symbolism of reconciliation is larger than it is usually acknowledged, and its theme describes the 'antithesis between hostility and peace, hate and love, separation and community',[85] and includes such words as 'peace', 'love', 'welcome', 'unity', and 'harmony'.[86] In this light, Rom. 8.31–39; 12.1–8; 12.9–21; 15.1–6 and 15.7–13, for example, become important texts for a comprehensive study on reconciliation.

Second, reconciliation is definitely a symbol taken from the sphere of social interaction like the terms 'justification' and 'liberation'. But Theissen is quick to point out that while the last two express thinking in vertical categories,[87] reconciliation depicts images of relationship on a horizontal level. This is clearly seen in the fact that Paul illustrates 'the event of reconciliation through the example of dying for another person' (Rom. 5.6, 7, 8, 10) whereby the redeemer and redeemed are now not in a relationship of 'victor and vanquished' but rather in a relationship of 'reconciled enemies'.[88] This is relevant for our discussion of Romans 5, in which chapter Paul

had happened in their lives, something of major importance. Underlying all these metaphors was some tremendously significant event, a turning point of great moment' (ibid., p. 331).

83. In Gerd Theissen, *Social Reality and the Early Christians* (Edinburgh: T&T Clark, 1993a), pp. 159–86.

84. Theissen distinguishes two major sets of symbolism in Paul's overall field of soteriology with specific metaphors attributed to each set: (1) sociomorphic interaction symbolism – here the images are drawn from various social interactions and salvation is depicted as a change in personal relationships: liberation, justification and reconciliation; (2) physiomorphic transformation symbolism – based on images taken from the organic sector; here salvation is presented as a transformation of the qualities and characteristics of the redeemed and the union with the redeemer, the main symbols being: transformation, death and life, union. (Ibid.)

85. Ibid., p. 171.

86. What is a unique feature in Theissen's proposal is that he includes, for example, Rom. 8.31–39 as a key text among the classical texts on reconciliation, Romans 5 and 2 Corinthians 5, and that he makes several other references to other Pauline texts that are not usually studied under the rubric of 'reconciliation'.

87. Justification and liberation both operate within the categories of 'dominance and subjection, superordination and subordination' as is shown from Paul's use of a specific line of argumentation: 'the human being is "under" sin; Christ is "above" other powers; the judge and the sinner are on absolutely different levels'. (Theissen, *Social Reality*, p. 171.)

88. Theissen, 'Soteriological Symbolism in the Pauline Writings', in Theissen, *Social Reality*, p. 171.

makes this significant shift from vertical to horizontal categories, thus attributing an intrinsic social dimension to the theme of reconciliation.

The third essential observation Theissen makes is in regard to the close connection Paul seems to make between the death of Christ, love, and reconciliation. Theissen states: 'In the reconciliation symbolism, the death of Christ is presented not so much as an accursed, vicarious death, but rather as the surrender of love'.[89] Romans 5 offers an excellent example: 'But God shows his love for us in that while we were yet sinners Christ died for us . . . when we were God's enemies, we were reconciled to him through the death of his Son (5.8, 10).[90] When this surrender of love is expressed by Paul's insistence that Christ died 'for us', he wants to highlight Jesus Christ's personal participation in the drama of reconciliation, that 'Christ himself is the subject of surrender'.[91] This particular emphasis, argues Theissen, enables Paul to use the dying 'for us' formula 'as an appeal for deliberate action'.[92] Indeed, as I will show in more detail in the next chapter, this double emphasis on the surrender of love and the dying 'for us', comes to new light when we read reconciliation within the framework of the story of Christ. I hope to be able to show in this way, beyond Theissen, that the appeal for deliberate action is present throughout the letter and not only in the ethical sections.

The last noteworthy aspect in Theissen's study is the close link he observes between reconciliation and resurrection. Since reconciliation is meant to overcome a separation, it cannot be accomplished by a dead person. That is why Paul is emphasizing the resurrected life of Christ with whom believers *are* being reconciled. Reconciliation is not only something that Christ accomplished in the past by his death, but is also a continuous experience in his new life. The passages from Rom. 4.25 and 5.10 are relevant, and I will comment on them in due time. But there are more implications in this important link between reconciliation and resurrection than Theissen points out. For Paul the power of resurrection is available for the believers and enables them to embody in everyday life the reconciliation that they have experienced with God. The presence of the resurrected Christ, through the Spirit, makes possible the practice of reconciliation.

The significance of Theissen's study consists first of all in a proper description of the rich symbolism of reconciliation in Paul. This goes far beyond the traditional limited understanding of reconciliation as expressed simply by the καταλλάσσω/ καταλλαγή terminology. But his careful discussion of the complex and dynamic interplay of symbols, of the inner logic of the entire field of soteriological symbolism in Paul, is also very helpful – particularly his insistence that Paul's themes cannot

---

89. Ibid., p. 172.
90. Other texts also illustrate this close connection: 'The life I now live in the flesh I live by faith in the Son of God, who loved me and gave himself for me' (Gal. 2.20); 'For the love of Christ controls us, because we are convinced that one has died for all' (2 Cor. 5.14).
91. Theissen, 'Soteriological Symbolism', p. 172.
92. Ibid., p. 173.

be abstracted from their own context and that they should be understood as part of Paul's dynamic theologizing.

Johannes Louw and Eugene Nida also point out in their *Dictionary of Semantic Domains* the complex semantic domain of reconciliation. They state: 'Because of the variety and complexity of the components involved in reconciliation, it is often necessary to use an entire phrase in order to communicate satisfactorily the meanings of the terms in this subdomain'.[93]

Another significant word in the symbolism of reconciliation is 'friendship'. If one of the meanings of reconciliation is 'to re-establish proper friendly interpersonal relations after these have been disrupted or broken'[94] the concept of friendship should be included in the same linkage group with reconciliation. Indeed, Fitzgerald has shown that Paul's dealings with the Corinthians illustrate a good deal of the language of ancient understanding of friendship.[95]

In conclusion we can say that in order to give expression to his vision of reconciliation, Paul has used a very rich symbolism, and for a proper understanding of the concept in Paul this symbolism needs to be explored and analysed in detail.

4.6 *Summary and conclusion*

In this chapter we have argued that a proper study of the concept of reconciliation in Paul needs to pay attention to several essential factors: Paul's own experience of reconciliation on the Damascus road; the OT story (particularly the Isaianic tradition of restoration, peace and new creation); the traditional Hellenistic paradigm of reconciliation; the paradigm shift that Paul brings to the concept, and the rich symbolism through which Paul expresses this complex concept. More specifically, we have shown that beginning with Paul's own radical experience of reconciliation on the Damascus road, a new vision of reality started to emerge for Paul. In addition to his personal reconciliation, that event meant also a paradigm shift in Paul's life – a radical new understanding of reality brought by the death and resurrection of Christ. Paul's vision of reconciliation was thus radically shaped by his new understanding of the story of Christ: a world of new possibilities and radical innovations is opened up now 'in Christ', with serious implications for all those living within this new reality.

To give expression to such a profound and complex phenomenon of reconciliation, Paul used many concepts, metaphors and symbols from his Jewish as well as the Hellenistic context. Significantly, we found that the frequently used word-group καταλλάσσω/καταλλαγή was used in the Hellenistic context primarily for interpersonal relationships, in the social, diplomatic and political spheres of life.

93. Johannes P. Louw, and Eugene A. Nida (eds), 'Reconciliation, Forgiveness', in *Greek-English Lexicon of the New Testament based on Semantic Domains* (Logos Library, electronic edn; New York: United Bible Societies, 1989).
94. Ibid. See also Buchsel, ἀλλάσσω, pp. 251–58; Porter, Καταλλάσσω, p. 13.
95. Fitzgerald 'Paul and Paradigm Shifts', pp. 257–60.

We have seen that Thomas Kuhn's analysis of cognitive structures can provide a theoretical framework for a specific line of inquiry in Paul that offers clear advantages and new insights into some aspects of Paul's theology, and more specifically into his theologizing. Of course, for a full assessment and use of such a model for doing Pauline theology, much more work should be done than this short presentation allows. However, our hope is that even this tentative exploration into the subject has shown that this is a legitimate and beneficial line of inquiry in Pauline studies, and that it will stimulate further, more nuanced and comprehensive studies of the way Paul did his theology.

To be sure, Paul's symbolism of reconciliation is not exhausted by one word-group but is much richer and more diverse, including such concepts as 'peace', 'love', 'unity', 'acceptance', and 'welcome'. Therefore, all these must be considered for an adequate inquiry into Paul's understanding of reconciliation, particularly in its social dimension(s). To emphasize just one dimension of reconciliation is to misinterpret Paul's own understanding of the complex concept. In our textual analysis of Romans 5–8 and 12–15 in Chapters 5 and 6 below, we will consider all these terms as they come up in the passages in Romans.

Finally, I would like to conclude this chapter with an extended quote from Professor Haddon Willmer, who captures in an extraordinary way Paul's overall vision and understanding of God reconciling the world, emphasizing in a special way the practices of reconciliation.

As we will see, there is in Paul an understanding of reconciliation that is linked to a vision (of reality) that is transcendent (and so, in a sense, subversive to the whole complex of social and political realities of the Roman empire) and which offers a different set of values than this world, and produces different results. And even though Paul may have never tackled, in any detail, concrete social and political questions of his day, that should not make us ignore the crucial fact that he was permanently engaged in reconciling practices – between Jews and Gentiles, between various individuals and groups within the churches, between Christians and 'outsiders' (see Thessalonians). The vision he had (including, among other elements, a community made up of Jews and Gentiles living in harmony) inspired him throughout his life and ministry and, despite some failures at times, it offered a springboard/incentive for his congregations to think and act likewise – and it inspires us to continue to build on that vision. What Paul gives us is unique, at least in this respect: he presents us with a God who does not give, from the 'outside', a decree or a 'law' of reconciliation, but one who exists in the very process of reconciliation (see Romans 5, 2 Corinthians 5) – and this shapes fundamentally Paul's eschatological horizons, especially his view of this world and its final conclusion: God did not abandon this fallen and corrupted world but wants to redeem it by his very presence in the painful process of reconciliation. It is within this framework that Paul's vision and commitment for reconciliation took shape and developed. However, this vision needs to be worked out socially, in concrete life situations. But, ultimately, it is Paul himself who gives us the important framework within which to discuss the social dimension(s) of reconciliation. In his doctrine of reconciliation one finds God in motion – justifying the enemies, by grace

– a God who gives himself. Reconciliation is embodied in the movement of God. It is very obvious in Paul that the God who moves in Christ and in the Spirit, sets people in motion too. Paul himself is part of that movement. But God's movement sets everything in motion, including society at large. For Paul God is constantly moving in history, in the world. So, even though Paul's talk is primarily talk about God, it is in that very talk that we may hear a God who is concerned with the world, with the social and political realities. Thus, we can find/hear more in Paul in so far as we listen and look for this God.[96]

This is probably what Barth hinted at when he wrote that 'Paul knows of God what most of us do not know; and his Epistles enable us to know what he knew'.[97]

Building on all these insights, we will be able to conduct a proper investigation into the social meaning of reconciliation in Romans as we pay considerable attention also to those texts where the symbolism and practices of reconciliation appear. It is hoped that the result will be a more comprehensive and adequate understanding of the concept of reconciliation in Paul. We will argue that it is Paul's larger vision that offers the *framework* for the social dimension of reconciliation and, more significantly, *determines* a reconciling life in the world. And a narrative reading will most appropriately enable us to perceive these two aspects. We are now ready for a detailed analysis of Romans 5–8 and 12–15.

96. Haddon Willmer, 'Paul's Vision and Reconciliation', in a private correspondence. Quoted with permission.

97. Karl Barth, *The Epistle to the Romans* (translated from the sixth edition by Edwyn C. Hoskyns; Oxford: OUP, 1968), Preface, p. 11.

THE SOCIAL MEANING OF RECONCILIATION IN PAUL (I): THE
STORY OF CHRIST AND RECONCILIATION IN ROMANS 5–8

5.1 *Introduction*

At various points throughout the previous chapters we have hinted at several important
findings by different authors regarding reconciliation in Paul that would be relevant
for the present research. Thus, the ethical, transformational aspect of 'righteousness'
was pointed out; that 'peace' had a wider, relational sense (vs. spiritual sense) and
that 'reconciliation' was inseparable from 'justification'. Further, we hinted that Paul
used the reconciliation language to bring about unity and mutual acceptance among
the believers in Rome and that the rhetoric of reconciliation was important for the
entire argument of Romans. Finally, we have seen that the concept of reconciliation
was larger than the word and that Paul used a very rich symbolism taken primarily
from social interactions and from diplomatic and political discourse.

These various insights, however, were not sufficiently corroborated as to give a
comprehensive analysis of the complex concept of reconciliation as found in Paul.
Consequently, a different approach that addresses this gap is needed. Thus, I propose
that the various aspects of reconciliation come together much better if read in close
connection with the 'story of Christ'. We will see in this chapter that Paul's presentation of reconciliation contains an essential horizontal/social dimension. I argue that,
beginning with Rom. 5.1, Paul uses interchangeably different metaphors and symbols
of salvation such as 'justification' (vertical category) and 'peace', 'love', 'reconciliation' (horizontal, relational categories), in order to express the inseparability of the
two aspects of reconciliation. Paul does not think in two segments, i.e., a vertical
one followed by a horizontal one; rather he envisions one complex reality which
encompasses the two. He is thus trying to communicate that unity, harmony and
acceptance among the believers in Rome are an intrinsic part of the very gospel of
reconciliation they profess. Paul is accomplishing his purposes in several ways, one
of which is to use a very rich symbolism of reconciliation (peace, love, reconciliation,
unity, welcome) in connection with the story of Christ. Paul reminds the believers
that because of their new identity and existence 'in Christ' they share now in the same
story of Christ. Through chs 5–8, and subsequently chs 12–15, Paul highlights the
implications of such an understanding of reconciliation for their everyday life, in the
concrete circumstances at Rome.

Several other significant features of Romans 5–8 may point to the validity of such a narrative endeavour. (1) A simple reading through Romans reveals that Paul makes more than twice as many references to Jesus, Christ and/or Jesus Christ in chs 5–8 (25 times) as he does in chs 1–4 (only 10 times). This may be an indication that Paul did intend his readers to understand his argument in these chapters in close connection with the story of Christ and with their being in Christ.[1] (2) There is also a clear shift in the use of personal pronouns in these chapters, from a clearly rhetorical 'you' (chs 1–4) to 'we' and 'us' as he addresses the 'family' of those 'in Christ'. (3) While not discounting the theological aspect, many authors point to the important ethical dimension of chs 5–8. A narrative reading will enable us to keep an appropriate balance between theology and ethics, between indicative and imperative in Paul, as 'the story' of Christ has the capacity to account for both without playing one off against the other. (4) Paul may have had a greater concern in Romans with 'assurance' than with appropriation; that is, to encourage the believers to maintain their commitment and loyalty to Christ through difficult circumstances. If that is the case, then 'a narrative appeal to the life of Christ is both appropriate and empowering'.[2]

It is my hope that a narrative approach will highlight other aspects which are not traditionally explored when interpreting the theme of reconciliation in Paul. More specifically, by analysing carefully the special references to Jesus Christ that Paul makes in Romans in connection with the rich symbolism of reconciliation, I will try to show that the various aspects of the christological narrative to which Paul alludes in Romans are meant to make the Roman Christians understand that the story of Christ is constitutive of their own story. As such, they are incorporated into the same story in which they are now active participants. Such an approach will highlight the social, horizontal, and dynamic aspect of reconciliation. If Minear is right when he states that '5.1–5 is as other-directed as 14.4, 7–9'[3] then we are right in our attempt to understand the whole passage 5.1–11 and the subsequent chapters as an argument equally concerned with a horizontal, social dimension of the gospel – as it refers also to the dynamic of living together in peace, harmony, love, reconciliation and hope.

The structure of this chapter is simple. After giving a brief background of the context of Romans and placing Romans 5–8 within the argument of the letter, it will locate and identify various allusions to the story of Christ in these chapters and present the major narrative features of that story. The main part of the chapter will then proceed to a textual analysis of the theme of reconciliation alongside the story of Christ. The findings will be summarized in the conclusion of the chapter.

1.   N. T. Wright, 'Romans and the Theology of Paul', in David M. Hay and E. Elizabeth Johnson (eds), *Pauline Theology, Vol. III: Romans* (Minneapolis: Fortress, 1995), pp. 508–09.

2.   D. Campbell, 'Story of Jesus', p. 122.

3.   Paul S. Minear, *The Obedience of Faith: The Purposes of Paul in the Epistle to the Romans* (London: SCM, 1971), 60.

5.2 *The context of Romans*

If traditional scholarship on Romans treated the letter as an essentially non-historical, abstract, *Compendia* or *Summa* of Pauline theology – in Melanchthon's words, *christianae religionis compendium* – a new consensus reached in recent years takes Paul's letter to the Romans to be, as all his other letters, addressing a specific audience, within a particular historical context, and responding to concrete concerns and problems.[4] Romans remains, for all that, Paul's most comprehensive and important letter. Paul was an apostle, a mission theologian, and one of his main purposes in writing was always to help the new believers discern and live out the implications of the gospel. It is therefore important that when one tries to determine the meaning of a particular text within its historical context, one should always pay considerable attention to the inner logic of the gospel that has contributed substantially to the development of its argument.[5]

That Christianity in Rome developed around Jewish synagogues explains its initial Jewish pattern of thought and behaviour.[6] The increasing number of Christians from among the Jews gave rise to frequent disturbances and conflicts between Jewish Christians and the Jews, which contributed substantially to the expulsion of the Jews and Jewish Christians from Rome, through Claudius' edict, most probably around AD 49.[7] The church(es) in Rome were thus left with a predominant and growing Gentile component, which for the purpose of self-preservation eventually made conscious efforts to distance themselves from the Jews.[8] Indeed, as Peter Lampe has shown in his influential study on the social history of Christianity in Rome, by careful analysis of a great variety of epigraphic, archaeological, historical, theological, literary, legal, and economic documents, the various nascent groups of Christians in Rome were separating from Judaism as a consequence of Claudius' edict.[9]

When the Jewish Christians began to return to Rome around the mid-50s, they found a completely new situation, with the Gentile Christians in leadership positions

---

4. A. J. M. Wedderburn, *The Reasons for Romans*; Donfried (ed.) *The Romans Debate*; James C. Miller, 'The Romans Debate: 1991–2001', *CR* 9 (2001), pp. 306–49.

5. This point is made by Leander E. Keck, 'What Makes Romans Tick?'; N. T. Wright, 'Romans and the Theology of Paul' and Richard B. Hays 'Adam, Israel, Christ – The Question of Covenant in the Theology of Romans: A Response to Leander E. Keck and N. T. Wright'. All three articles in Hay and Johnson (eds.) *Pauline Theology, Vol. III: Romans*.

6. Wedderburn, *The Reasons for Romans*, pp. 50–52.

7. James D. G. Dunn, *Romans*, 'Introduction' (WBC, Vol. 38 a,b; Dallas: Word Books, 1988); Donfried, *The Romans Debate*.

8. James C. Walters, *Ethnic Issues in Paul's Letter to the Romans* (Valley Forge, PA: Trinity, 1993), pp. 59–62. Also Wedderburn, *The Reasons for Romans*.

9. Peter Lampe, *From Paul to Valentinus. Christians at Rome in the First Two Centuries* (Minneapolis: Fortress, 2003), pp. 11–16. Lampe concludes his discussion in very clear terms (pp. 15–16): 'by the time of its composition in the second half of the 50s at the latest, urban Roman Christianity can be seen as separated from the federation of Synagogues. In the 64 c.e., even the authorities distinguished between Jews and Christians (urban Roman persecution under Nero: Tacitus, *Ann.* 15.44).'

and a life marked by non-Jewish patterns of religious life as well as a diminished emphasis on key Jewish convictions and practices.[10] Walters shows that in this new situation there was an increased potential for conflict, since the returning Jewish Christians were not restored to their positions of leadership and the Jewish practices were strongly resisted.[11] In addition, the social, ethnic and cultural diversity of Rome, which resulted in a similar diversity in the house churches in Rome, led to different understandings and practices of the gospel, with different and even competing forms of leadership, and different stances vis-à-vis other believers and outsiders.[12]

It is commonly accepted that Romans was written around the mid-50s, most probably from Corinth,[13] and that it addresses a mixed audience of Jewish and Gentile believers in Rome,[14] as Paul's specific remarks for each of these groups indicates: Rom. 1.6 and 13; 2.25–29; 9–11; 11.13–32; 15.7–12. What is not agreed upon, however, is the precise nature of the occasion and purpose of the letter.[15] The fact that every single one of Paul's 'undisputed' letters is addressed to specific situations counts as a strong support for the assumption that Romans could legitimately be understood as written to deal with concrete problems in the life of Christians in Rome.[16] Thus, it is clear from the letter that one of the major problems confronting the Roman Christians had to do with their differences, dissensions, and even divisions among various groups (particularly – but not exclusively – among the Jewish and

---

10. Allen, *Reconciliation*, pp. 28–29.

11. Walters, *Ethnic Issues*, pp. 59–64. Dunn concurs and states that it was due to the vulnerability of the returning Jews that Paul had to warn his Gentile readers against their feeling of superiority and self-confidence. This will also help one better understand Paul's counsel in chs 14 and 15, adds Dunn ('Introduction', *Romans 1–8*).

12. The concrete issues that Paul addresses in Romans 14–15 are a clear indication that there were 'disputes over opinions' (14.1), 'passing judgements' on each other and 'despising' one another (14.10). See Calvin L. Porter, 'Paul as Theologian: Romans', *Encounter* 65(2) (2004), pp. 109–36 (122ff).

13. For a good discussion of these issues see James Dunn, *Romans* 'Introduction'.

14. Minear (*Obedience*, pp. 7–15), for example, argues for the presence of not fewer than five house congregations in Rome. Especially relevant here is Peter Lampe's discussion (*From Paul to Valentinus*), particularly pp. 69–79, where he makes a very detailed and documented argument about the dynamics of the changing ratio between Jewish and Gentile Christians in Rome. He argues that after the separation from the synagogues, the Gentile Christians (a great majority of which were former 'God-fearing' pagans) were a majority in the Roman churches though the Jewish Christians still continued to exercise a significant theological and pastoral influence through the leadership role of such people as Aquila and Priscilla, Andronicus and Junia.

15. This point is excellently illustrated by the collection of essays gathered by Karl Donfried in *The Romans Debate*.

16. Donfried, 'False Presuppositions in the Study of Romans', in idem (ed.), *The Romans Debate*, pp. 103–4. For a comprehensive list of authors holding this view, see Gregory J. Allen, *Reconciliation*, pp. 19–21. Paul himself indicates different reasons for writing the letter (1.8–15; 15.14–33). However, when one tries to relate those reasons to the lengthy arguments and discussions of the letter, different opinions are offered for the exact occasion and purpose of Romans. James Dunn is probably right when he states that Paul most likely had several reasons for writing the letter (missionary, apologetic and pastoral) and that 'most of the disagreements are a matter of different emphases between these several reasons' (*Romans*, 'Introduction: The Purpose of the Letter').

Gentile believers), vis-à-vis such issues as ethnicity, religious practice (observance of dietary rules, of days, and of Jewish laws), and relationships with others within and outside the Christian community. This background explains Paul's interest in reconciliation, peace, love, unity, welcome – as he attempts not simply to put an end to any conflict and reconcile different groups[17] but, especially, to articulate so forcefully the inner logic of the gospel as being incompatible with such behaviour. For Paul, these misunderstandings and the inappropriate conduct were not only a sign of the failure of the Christian community but a departure from, and a denial of, the very essence of the gospel. In order to address these issues thoroughly, as we will see shortly, Paul makes use throughout the letter of various narratives, symbols, and practices of reconciliation, by which he combines a sustained argument for the seriousness of the ethical implications that are intrinsic to the gospel and their life 'in Christ'.

There are clear indications in the letter that Paul was aware of actual conflicts[18] in the house churches in Rome and that he addressed them.[19] In Rom. 2.17–29 and 3.27, for example, Paul warns the Jews that the law and circumcision are not reasons for pride. Similarly, Rom. 11.17–24 is a warning to Gentile believers not to place themselves above the Jews, while in 12.3 Paul addresses both groups, strongly advising everyone among them not to think of themselves more highly than they ought to think. Furthermore, the argument in chs 14 and 15 illustrates also the conflict between the 'weak' and the 'strong' and Paul's strong position against intolerance, inconsideration, judgemental attitudes, and various disputes (ch. 14, vv. 1, 3, 4, 10, 13, 15 and 20). The real issue was not that people had, in good conscience, different opinions on some issues. The danger that Paul foresaw was represented by the totally inadequate attitude and behaviour of those holding different positions, a practice in contradiction to the nature of the gospel and the 'obedience of faith'. Each group wanted the other to adopt its stance; they wanted to make their own understanding and practice the norm for the entire community. Paul, however, saw in all these 'an implicit betrayal of the gospel . . . [a] misunderstanding of the nature of the kingdom of God, along with distorted conceptions of God's justice and mercy;'[20] and since it had bearings on the very essence of the gospel, Paul treated the situation in Rome

---

17. Wedderburn, *The Reasons for Romans*, pp. 64–65 and pp. 140–42.

18. Lampe shows that the first conflicts most probably arose between law-abiding Jewish and uncircumcised Gentile Christians when the latter group tried to implement eating the Lord's Supper together at common tables (*From Paul to Valentinus*, pp. 69–70).

19. Minear (*Obedience*) and Willi Marxen, *Introduction to the New Testament* (Philadelphia, PA: Fortress, 1968), are representative of those who propose that Romans deals with the conflict between 'weak and strong' (Minear) and/or Jewish and Gentile Christians (Marxen). Hans Hübner (*Law in Paul's Thought* (Edinburgh: T&T Clark, 1984)) considers it possible that the conflict was between Gentile Christians and proselytes. But cf. Robert J. Karris ('The Occasion of Romans: a Response to Professor Donfried', in Donfried (ed.), *The Romans Debate*), who questions not only the precise nature of the conflict situation in Rome but whether such a conflict even existed.

20. Minear, *Obedience*, pp. 32–33. C. E. B. Cranfield (*A Critical and Exegetical Commentary on the Epistle to the Romans* (ICC, 2 vols; Edinburgh: T&T Clark, 1979), pp. 821–22) agrees with Minear that 'the Christian community in Rome was made up of a number of churches' and that Paul's purpose

with utmost seriousness. For him, to live in unsolved and un-reconciled conflicts was at odds with the central axioms of the gospel of reconciliation. Paul could not be moved from his conviction that the reality of salvation/reconciliation must translate into the reality of the life of the church.

Here we should make an important point regarding the tensions present in Rome, namely that not all of them were necessarily due to ill-conceived disputes of leadership, positions or power. There were also genuine struggles to define and/or redefine the identity of the members of the new community vis-à-vis its Jewish roots. They were no doubt trying to answer the questions related to the essence that defined the new people of God, the nature of community gathered now around Christ. This struggle and desire to serve God genuinely is recognized and supported by Paul in his assertion that the Roman believers do everything not out of false pretence but rather out of, and for the 'honour of the Lord' (14.6–8). It is thus in response to their differing positions to these questions of self-definition and identity that a large portion of Paul's argument in Romans can be understood.[21] It is equally important to have in mind while interpreting Romans that Jew–Gentile relationships represented one of Paul's fundamental concerns throughout his life: namely, the dynamic between the ethnic Israel and the great new redefinition of God's people in the light of the story of Christ, in which a new community is formed by Jews and Gentiles together. This particular question is addressed in Romans 9–11 where Paul shows the working out of God's longstanding plan of bringing together the Jews and Gentiles in one family, in Christ, as a fulfilment of his promise of dealing with the world.

Clearly, Paul addresses in Rome a very complex situation; and no matter what we assume regarding his knowledge of it, whether he knew it in all details, or only in broad terms with some details, he tries to respond to it with all responsibility. In his response to the situation, Paul tried, on the one hand, to defuse the various existing tensions and to promote unity; on the other hand, he wanted to explain clearly what the implications of the gospel for everyday living are. To that end he made extensive use of the theme of reconciliation both by using the actual language of reconciliation and by referring to various narratives, symbols, and beliefs which he related to the concept of reconciliation; and through all these he wanted to inspire practices of reconciliation. As Paul himself made clear, the ultimate goal of the gospel, and therefore his own in writing Romans, was 'to bring about the obedience of faith' (1.5 and 16.26). This thesis has been well established by James Miller in his study, *The Obedience of Faith, the Eschatological People of God, and the Purpose of Romans*. There the author shows that the theme of 'obedience' plays a significant role in Paul's argument, as he uses it in connection with other key themes in the letter, and that by 'the obedience of faith' Paul meant 'specifically the obedience of

in writing was 'to contribute to the peace and unity of the Christian community in Rome'. However, his interpretation of Romans puts more emphasis on Paul's theology than on the historical context.

21. Walters' subtitle of *Ethnic Issues* is illustrative: 'Changing Self-Definitions in Earliest Roman Christianity'.

welcoming one another after the model of Christ to the glory of God (15.7)'.[22] He also finds that the term 'obedience' indicated the proper response to the hearing of the gospel of Christ and that the obedience Christ showed plays a crucial role within the argument of Romans as ground and model for the believers' obedient life as they embody their true identity 'in Christ'.[23] As Miller points out, this aspect comes most clearly in view in Romans 5–8 and 12–15 where 'Christ's obedience not only makes Christian obedience possible (8.3–4), it also serves as the model for that obedience (6.4–5, 11–14; 15.7).'[24]

5.3 *The argument of Romans 5–8*

The structure of Paul's argument in Romans is understood in different ways by the commentators of Paul.[25] What is generally accepted is that Paul's statement in 1.16–17 represents the thesis of his central concerns in the letter: the gospel, and its transforming power, revealing the righteousness of God. The letter is thus an explanation and elaboration of this thesis, with careful discussions of its implications for the life of the Christians in Rome. One of the important themes in the letter is that of reconciliation, which Paul develops both as an explication of the inner logic of the gospel of God's righteousness and as an appropriate response to the concrete situation in Rome. I agree with Michael Gorman, and I will show in what follows, that 'for Paul the gospel of God's impartial righteousness is the gospel of God's love for "enemies" and those who are reconciled to this God by responding to the gospel in faith must express love to all'.[26]

In Romans 1–4 Paul describes the stance of an idolatrous and hostile Gentile world towards its creator and the unfaithfulness of the very people of God. In response, and despite this desperate situation, the gospel announces the revelation of the justice of God manifested in the death and resurrection of Jesus Christ, the Messiah, by offering forgiveness of sins and salvation to all, and by bringing into existence a new community in which Jews and Gentiles are united, as a sign of the new eschatological age, of the new creation of God. Parallel to this argument runs the implicit argument that

22. Miller, *Obedience*, p. 21.

23. Ibid., pp. 51–54.

24. Ibid., p. 54. Similarly, Richard Hays in 'ΠΙΣΤΙΣ and the Pauline Christology: What is at Stake?', in E. Elizabeth Johnson and David Hay (eds), *Pauline Theology, Vol. IV: Looking Back, Pressing On* (Atlanta, GA: Scholars Press, 1997), p. 40.

25. Throughout the history of interpretation, different sections of Romans have been taken as the 'key' for interpreting the rest of the letter, but generally it has been acknowledged that Paul built his argument in four major parts, respectively chs 1–4, 5–8, 9–11 and 12–16.

26. Gorman, *Cruciformity*, p. 244. Similarly, Ralph Martin makes a valid point that in our efforts to interpret the implications of reconciliation in Paul, we should not overlook the larger context of the story of God's reconciliation of the world to himself by which he repaired the rift that existed between him and humankind. The estrangement was real and it was only by restoring a relationship of amity and friendship that God's redemptive purposes for the world were to be accomplished. (Martin, 'Reconciliation: Rom. 5:1–11', p. 37.)

the gospel of the cross and resurrection of Christ proclaims and embodies a different kind of justice, one which is accomplished in a totally different manner from that brought about by Caesar. By what Paul had said so far, he had prepared the way and was now ready to move to the next stage of his argument.

In trying to determine Paul's train of thought, one should not limit it to just one main theme or idea since, as we have seen, Paul has several different issues in mind when he writes. Thus, in Romans 5–8 we can identify a number of points that Paul makes. First, following on the previous argument, Paul continues to explicate the complex dynamic of Christian salvation in all its dimensions. He offers a fuller exposition of the Christian life, as a life 'according to the Spirit', with peace, reconciliation, suffering, love, freedom and hope as the essential features of the life of those 'in Christ', representing the true, restored humanity.[27] The salvation is, of course, the achievement of Christ, as his death and resurrection are the grounds for justification/ reconciliation in the past, for the present Christian life (peace, celebration, suffering, love, reconciliation, hope), and for a secured future. What is relevant here is the way in which Paul connects and holds inseparably together the past, present, and future dimensions of salvation in a complex dynamic. Referring to Romans 8, Campbell captures well and aptly articulates this aspect:

> The same dynamic construction that moves us beyond a sinful and enslaved past, enabling us to act rightly but independently of written Torah (8:1–13), *also* guarantees our future inheritance and glorification (8:14–39). That is, we move out of the complex of Death, where Flesh and Sin are also involved, into a present existence free from the past, and one also assured in relation to the future (where the continuation of that past state of Death would have issued in condemnation) – and this despite any present appearances to the contrary (see esp. 8:33–35).[28]

As we will see, all these aspects of the nature and dynamics of salvation are held together by placing the entire argument in the context of the story of Christ and its implications for the Christian life. From this perspective we will be able to see reconciliation as an intrinsic part of the gospel which cannot be separated from its other two aspects – justification and hope.

Another concern that Paul addresses in this section has to do with the role of the law in Christian life. Some believers in Rome may have been anxious about 'freedom' from the law and may have felt that they had lost their true basis for ethics. Paul reassures them that freedom from the law does not mean freedom from ethical obligation, but rather a new foundation for their life: their new life 'in Christ' and the grace in which they now stand (5.2), which is indeed apart from the law, 'is a new

---

27. Wright, 'The Messiah and the People of God: A Study in Pauline Theology with Particular Reference to the Argument of the Epistle to the Romans' (unpublished Doctor of Philosophy dissertation, University of Oxford, Trinity term, 1980), pp. 134ff.

28. D. Campbell, 'The Story of Jesus', p. 103.

and adequate basis for ethical living'.[29] Thus, in Romans 5 and 6 and indeed in the whole section of 5–8[30] Paul articulates the intrinsic relationship between grace and the seriousness of the ethical stance of the believers. And this grace is incompatible with sin:[31] 'they are to act rightly and, indeed, *can* act rightly'.[32] One such sin that Paul clearly has in mind, which he specifically addresses later on in chs 12–15, is disunity and conflict among the believers. The theme of reconciliation, solidly grounded in the work of Christ and presented as an essential aspect of the gospel, is therefore used by Paul to also address the particular situation in the church in Rome.

The train of thought that begins in Rom. 5.2 and ends in 8.30, with the repeated reference to the 'glory of God'[33], may suggest that the entire section of chs 5–8 could be said to be also about the assurance of salvation or the certainty of Christian hope.[34] Within this larger framework there are, of course, other themes that Paul addresses, by which he particularly emphasizes 'ways in which the Christian's present status and future hope determine life in the present'.[35] But the overall thrust of the section points clearly to the secure future that the believers have, assurance grounded in the unfailing love of God towards all, demonstrated in the death of Christ for his enemies. In the face of suffering and struggles, Paul wants to assure the believers of their sure hope for the future and that God's love does not fail. However, Paul knows that for any hope to be real, one must take into account the reality of evil, of suffering and pain. But he places everything in the larger eschatological perspective of the ultimate redemption of the entire creation (8.18–30).

This brief overview has indicated which issues one should bear in mind when attempting to understand and interpret Paul's argument in general and his presentation of reconciliation in particular. We are now ready to go into a detailed analysis of the christological statements and allusions to the story of Christ and their significance for the specific question of the present study.

---

29. Thomas H. Tobin, *Paul's Rhetoric in its Contexts: The Argument of Romans* (Peabody, MA: Hendrickson, 2004), p. 11.

30. This is indeed anticipated in 5.1–11 and summarized again at the end of ch 8.

31. See Tobin, *Paul's Rhetoric*, pp. 154–218 for a compelling argument that Romans 5–7 is about the intricate dynamic between grace, sin and ethics.

32. D. Campbell, 'The Story of Jesus', p. 102. Similarly, Stuhlmacher shows that Romans 6.1–8.39 is about the 'the righteousness of God as the ground and power of the new life' (*Paul's Letter to the Romans. A Commentary* (Louisville, KY: Westminster/John Knox Press, 1994), pp. 88–89).

33. Wright makes the point that 'glory' here could be a clear reference to the indwelling presence of God with the people of Israel in the wilderness tabernacle or in the Temple, and that, throughout, the argument from 5.2 to 8.20 'involves specifically the indwelling of God, by the Spirit. The whole passage thus emphasizes that what God did decisively in Jesus the Messiah is now to be implemented through the Spirit.' (*Romans*, 509–10.)

34. So, Wright, Schreiter, Moo and Fitzmyer, among others.

35. Wright, *Romans*, p. 510.

5.4 *The story of Christ in Romans 5–8: identifying allusions and narrative features*

A closer reading of Romans 5–8 reveals that Paul builds his argument with a constant reference to Christ as if that is somehow required by the nature of the arguments that Paul develops here. The commentators usually remark on the density of references to Christ, particularly in Romans 5–8. Wright, for example, remarks that while in chs 1–4 Jesus is 'hardly mentioned', in chs 5–8 he 'is everywhere'.[36] He further notes that Paul's larger argument in chs 5–8 opens with four paragraphs (5.1–11; 5.12–21; 6.1–11; 6.12–23), each ending with a christological formula that sums up the paragraph, and ends in ch. 8 with another emphatic christological summary.[37] Building on the initial christological statements in 3.24–26 and 4.24–25, in chs 5–8 Paul elucidates the narrative of salvation in all its dimensions with a constant reference to key christological features in 5.6–11; 5.15–21; 6.3–11; 7.4,; 8.3 and 8.31–39.[38] There is an overwhelming emphasis on grace and of the free gift within the process of salvation (5.2 and 5.12–21) while at the same time there is a concern for the serious ethical implications of this grace for the present, ongoing aspect of salvation.

One characteristic of Paul's writing is that when he summarizes the basic content of his gospel he is able to do it by referring to a narrative sequence of events concerning Jesus Christ – the story which describes God's redemptive intervention in history (cf. 1 Cor. 15.3–8). To discuss the story of Christ in his letters, however, is not necessarily a straightforward task because to put together all the separate christological statements that are spread throughout Paul's letters does not give us an adequate picture of Paul's thought about Christ. And this is so primarily because of the amount of knowledge about Christ shared already with the audience and which Paul does not feel a need to repeat, and also because of the contingent factors that determine particular formulations in different places. Therefore, one needs to analyse those statements as allusions to the larger narrative of Christ.[39]

The following christological statements will be analysed in this section: 4.24–25; 5.6–11; 5.15–21 (vv. 17, 19, 21); 6.3–11 (vv. 4, 7, 9); 7.4; 8.3; 8.31–39 (vv. 29, 32). The intention is to establish which particular elements of the story Paul emphasizes, why, and how this advances his argument about reconciliation. We will identify key narrative features which will point unambiguously to the larger story of Christ. Our key question, however, is not so much about the story itself as about the way Paul uses it in order to advance his argument. As I have mentioned in the methodology section in the first chapter, following Campbell's approach I will attempt to locate

36. Ibid., p. 508
37. Ibid., pp. 508–09.
38. These statements, as Wright points out, are not simply disconnected statements about Christ, but rather key christological summarizations intended to point further to the entire story of Christ which Paul unfolds in Romans. See Wright, *Romans*, p. 513.
39. Witherington, *Paul's Narrative*, p. 83.

various *narrative features*, the possession of a sufficient number of which allows us to recognize narrative elements, or even relatively complete stories, in the broader texture of Paul's thought . . . Among those features that suggest narrative is *a striking personal dimension* conveyed largely by the activity of *personal actors*, who usually undertake *actions*, often in relation to *one another*, and to whom *events* occur. These actions and events often then unfold to create *a plot*, the latter often also exhibiting a *problem-solution* structure. Hence stories are especially useful types of texts for giving an account of the *behavior, actions, history,* and/or *accomplishments, of people* (or, more strictly, of personal actors).[40]

Campbell rightly points out that these key narrative features will be identifiable in a variety of formulations and that 'once an element has been recognized, the rest of the story – or at least part of it – will be implicit in this recognition'.[41] However, he cautiously adds that the 'allusions to key narrative elements must be genuine, and the further implied elements plausible and relevant'.[42] In what follows I will look for such narrative features and comment briefly on the significance of the narrative motifs in the context.

5.4.1 *Paul's christological statements and narrative motifs*
In Rom. 4.24–25 Paul states: ἀλλὰ καὶ δι' ἡμᾶς, οἷς μέλλει λογίζεσθαι, τοῖς πιστεύουσιν ἐπὶ τὸν ἐγείραντα Ἰησοῦν τὸν κύριον ἡμῶν ἐκ νεκρῶν, ὃς παρεδόθη διὰ τὰ παραπτώματα ἡμῶν καὶ ἠγέρθη διὰ τὴν δικαίωσιν ἡμῶν, 'It will be reckoned to us who believe in him who raised Jesus our Lord from the dead, who was handed over to death for our trespasses and was raised for our justification.' The clear narrative features in this passage cannot be missed: there is indeed a 'striking personal dimension' given by the personal actors described by Paul – God, Jesus, and 'us'; there is 'action' undertaken here by God with reference to Jesus ('raised Jesus from the dead') in relation to 'others', i.e., 'us' – who are also somehow actively involved in this whole drama of God's action by 'believe[ing] in him'. The expression τὸν ἐγείραντα Ἰησοῦν τὸν κύριον ἡμῶν ἐκ νεκρῶν, 'him who raised Jesus from the dead,' in 4.24 was one of the central elements of the initial narrative about Jesus. James Dunn rightly remarks that the statement '"God raised him from the dead" was evidently one of the earliest creedal-type affirmations of the first Christians'.[43] By pointing unambiguously to God as the object of 'our' faith and as the one who raised Jesus, Paul includes the believers' righteousness and the work of Christ in the larger narrative of God's redemptive purposes for the world. This may also be a hint to the 'origin' of the story of Jesus in God.

Two other issues are to be mentioned about this passage. First, the resurrected

---

40. D. Campbell, 'The Story of Jesus', p. 99 (italics added).
41. Ibid., p. 100.
42. Ibid., p. 101.
43. Dunn, *Romans*. The following texts illustrate this point: Acts 3.15; 4.10; 13.30; Rom. 7.4; 8.11; 10.9; 1 Cor. 15.12 and 20; Gal. 1.1; Eph. 1.20; Col. 2.12; 1 Thess. 1.10; 1 Pet. 1.21.

Jesus is κύριον ἡμῶν ('our Lord'), thus pointing to the present lordship of Christ over each believer, over the church, and indeed over the entire creation, an essential aspect for the argument that Paul will develop throughout chs 5–8. Second, not only are the death and resurrection of Jesus inseparably connected, but also the emphasis ὃς παρεδόθη διὰ τὰ παραπτώματα ἡμῶν καὶ ἠγέρθη διὰ τὴν δικαίωσιν ἡμῶν ('handed over to death *for our* trespasses and was raised *for our* justification') in v. 25 is important as it points to Christ's work done on behalf of *others*. Paul mentions twice that whatever Jesus has accomplished, he did it 'for us'. He does not elaborate here either on the nature of his death or on the mechanism of justification but simply states that Jesus' death was 'for our trespasses' and that the result of his being raised is 'our justification'. The story of Christ and of the believer are bound closely together. The 'death for our trespasses' is no doubt a reference to the passion narrative.

Although some would take 5.6 as the next christological reference, one should not overlook too soon 5.1–2: Δικαιωθέντες οὖν ἐκ πίστεως εἰρήνην ἔχομεν πρὸς τὸν θεὸν διὰ τοῦ κυρίου ἡμῶν Ἰησοῦ Χριστοῦ δι' οὗ καὶ τὴν προσαγωγὴν ἐσχήκαμεν [τῇ πίστει] εἰς τὴν χάριν ταύτην ἐν ᾗ ἐστήκαμεν καὶ καυχώμεθα . . ., 'Therefore, since we are justified by faith, we have [or, 'let us have'] peace with God through our Lord Jesus Christ, through whom we have obtained access to this grace in which we stand . . .' It is again, 'our Lord' Jesus Christ who is placed at the very centre of God's plan to redeem humanity, since Jesus plays the instrumental role in 'our' relationship with God and also in the experience of everyday life (in 'hope', 'glory', 'suffering'). Particularly significant is the expression διὰ Ἰησοῦ Χριστοῦ ('through Jesus Christ') which plays an important role in the overall argument of ch. 5 (it also appears in the key christological summaries of vv. 11 and 21 of the same chapter). As James Dunn shows, the expression has here a very full sense of Jesus' *continuous* and *active* mediatorial role, in his resurrected existence.[44] As in the previous two verses, we have here also a closely interconnected dynamic between the story of Christ and that of the believers: whatever the believer *is* or *does*, it is only because of, and determined by, the Lord Jesus Christ who, in turn, *is* and *does* everything *for others*, the believers included.

When we come to Rom. 5.6–11, we find more explicit statements and narrative motifs of Christ and his work alongside the discussion of reconciliation. We learn now that it is υἱοῦ αὐτοῦ, 'his son' (v. 10) who ἡμῶν ἀπέθανεν, 'died for us' (v. 8) 'while we were ἀσθενῶν ('weak') . . . ἀσεβῶν ('ungodly') . . . ἁμαρτωλῶν ('sinners') . . . ἐχθροὶ ('enemies')' (vv. 6, 8, 10) and ἐν τῷ αἵματι αὐτοῦ, 'by his blood' (v. 9) he has achieved reconciliation (v. 10). At the heart of this passage is the remarkable character of God's love demonstrated by 'the death of his son' (v. 10) in reconciling his enemies, in accordance to God's own purposes.[45] Inconceivable from a human

---

44. See Dunn, *Romans*.

45. This point has been highlighted by Hurtado in his analysis of Paul's divine-sonship motifs in Rom. 5.1–11. He shows that Paul's various christological motifs are not arbitrary but rather 'subtly and yet eloquently meaningful' and that 'divine-sonship rhetoric is invoked here most obviously to connote

perspective (v. 7), the blood of Christ was shed not for a righteous person but for the ungodly, for enemies. God's initiative at the 'right time' (κατὰ καιρὸν) has disclosed the desperate condition of humanity! There is also in this passage a strong reference to the continuous life of Jesus (v. 10), which is a strong assurance for the future salvation of the believers, especially as he is 'our Lord Jesus Christ' (v. 11). One cannot miss Paul's emphasis on both the greatness of the *fact* of reconciliation and *the manner* in which it was realized: by a costly sacrifice, by an initiative of love, by an offer extended to enemies.

Romans 5.12–21 presents yet another clarification on the life/accomplishments of ἑνὸς ἀνθρώπου Ἰησοῦ Χριστοῦ, 'that one man Jesus Christ' (v. 15). In a meticulous contrast with the first Adam, through whom sin and death reigned in the world, Paul shows how much more abundant the 'grace of God' and 'the free gift' are in operation now because of Jesus Christ (vv. 5–16) and how those who received this grace reign themselves in life through Christ (v. 17). What is significant in this passage is a clear reference to the obedience of Christ not simply as a stark contrast to Adam's disobedience, but particularly as the means by which he accomplished the 'righteousness' for many: ιὰ τῆς ὑπακοῆς τοῦ ἑνὸς δίκαιοι κατασταθήσονται οἱ πολλοί, 'by the one man's obedience the many will be made righteous' (v. 19). The passage concludes on the same note of the superabundance of grace διὰ Ἰησοῦ Χριστοῦ τοῦ κυρίου ἡμῶν, 'through Jesus Christ our Lord' (v. 21).

Most of the references to Jesus in ch. 6 are in the context of Paul's discussion of baptism, of the incorporation of the believers 'in Christ', and the dynamic of the 'newness of life' that results from such a powerful symbolism of dying and rising with Christ: συνετάφημεν οὖν αὐτῷ διὰ τοῦ βαπτίσματος εἰς τὸν θάνατον, ἵνα ὥσπερ ἠγέρθη Χριστὸς ἐκ νεκρῶν διὰ τῆς δόξης τοῦ πατρός, οὕτως καὶ ἡμεῖς ἐν καινότητι ζωῆς περιπατήσωμεν, 'Therefore we have been buried with him by baptism into death, so that, just as Christ was raised from the dead by the glory of the Father, so we too might walk in newness of life' (6.4). We will discuss later, in detail, these important aspects of the Christian life; here I only notice how Paul describes the way in which the story of the believers becomes incorporated into the very story of Christ, and how this affects directly and crucially the way they live their lives now. A similar strong emphasis of this new life 'in Christ' is made in the context of Paul's discussion of the law: ὥστε, ἀδελφοί μου, καὶ ὑμεῖς ἐθανατώθητε τῷ νόμῳ διὰ τοῦ σώματος τοῦ Χριστοῦ, εἰς τὸ γενέσθαι ὑμᾶς ἑτέρῳ, τῷ ἐκ νεκρῶν ἐγερθέντι, ἵνα καρποφορήσωμεν τῷ θεῷ, 'In the same way, my friends, you have died to the law through the body of Christ, so that you may belong to another, to him who has been raised from the dead in order that we may bear fruit for God' (7.4).

The close link between the story of the believers and that of Christ is again

the connection between Jesus' death and the divine purpose which is so much the emphasis in this epistle.' (Larry W. Hurtado, 'Jesus' Divine Sonship in Paul's Epistle to the Romans', in Soderlund and Wright (eds), *Romans and the People of God*, p. 229.)

highlighted by Paul in Romans 8. The chapter begins and ends with a strong affirmation about the secure destiny of believers 'in Christ': Οὐδὲν ἄρα νῦν κατάκριμα τοῖς ἐν Χριστῷ Ἰησοῦ, 'there is therefore now no condemnation for those who are in Christ Jesus' (8.1) and . . . ὕτε τις κτίσις ἑτέρα δυνήσεται ἡμᾶς χωρίσαι ἀπὸ τῆς ἀγάπης τοῦ θεοῦ τῆς ἐν Χριστῷ Ἰησοῦ τῷ κυρίῳ ἡμῶν '. . . nor anything else in all creation, will be able to separate us from the love of God in Christ Jesus our Lord' (8.39). The narrative motifs are particularly clear in several verses, especially in vv. 3, 29 and 32. There we learn about the central role of Jesus Christ in God's redemptive plan; i.e., about the mission of God's Son who, by assuming sinful flesh, atoned for sin (v. 3), thus making possible that those whom God called are συμμόρφους τῆς εἰκόνος τοῦ υἱοῦ αὐτοῦ, 'conformed to the image of his Son' (v. 29), and proving in this way the resolute divine love for humanity in the fact that God 'did not withhold his own Son, but gave him up for all of us', ὅς γε τοῦ ἰδίου υἱοῦ οὐκ ἐφείσατο ἀλλὰ ὑπὲρ ἡμῶν πάντων παρέδωκεν αὐτόν (v. 32). That he did not spare his own Son but was ready to sacrifice him 'for us' is the strongest proof that God will continue to sustain the believers through the difficult present situation as well as in the unknown future (vv. 18–39). Furthermore, crucial for Paul's argument in Romans 8 is the role of 'the Spirit of life' who enables the believers to walk in the newness of life and peace in the present (vv. 5–6), gives them confidence for the future (v. 11), and confirms that they are 'sons of God' (vv. 14, 19) and 'children of God' (vv. 16, 21). Thus, we should note that Paul's story of Christ, as in the previous chapters but more clearly here, includes the Father (who sends the Son), and the Spirit who resurrects Jesus from the dead, and incorporates other people 'into Christ' and therefore into the same story.[46]

In sum, we have seen several crucial aspects that stand out in Paul's presentation of Christ in Romans 5–8. The most obvious and repeated emphasis is on the death of Christ as an expression both of God's *love* and of Christ's willing *self-giving* for humanity. The *reconciliation* he thus accomplished was a *grace*, a *free gift* offered to enemies. Further, the beginning and ending of this large section – with clear and very strong references to *the lordship of Christ* (5.1; 8.39) – show that this aspect is also crucial for Paul's argument.[47] Through the death and resurrection of Jesus Christ, God has unambiguously shown his *grace* and *love* and has proven his faithfulness/ righteousness. Now, because Jesus is Lord, the entirety of human life and of creation is under the sphere of God's declared love, and nothing can change that state of affairs. This assurance and confidence that the believer can have 'in Christ' is one of the main points Paul makes in this section. However, Paul highlights also the

46. Douglas Campbell makes this point forcefully. He emphasizes that we should keep in mind all the actors of the story. He states: 'in speaking of a story of Jesus in Paul's theology in Romans 8, it is imperative in my view not to limit the story to that specific actor, important as he is, but to grasp that any such story is simultaneously a story of God the Father, of the Spirit of God, and of the incorporation of people into that story. *To lose sight of any one of these aspects is to falsify our account of this story as Paul articulates it.*' ('Story of Jesus', p. 107 (italics in the original).)

47. Grieb, *Story of Romans*, p. 3.

implications of the lordship of Christ for the life of each individual believer and of the Christian community in the world: it is by showing their ultimate loyalty to the true Lord of the world, Jesus Christ, loyalty expressed 'not least by their unity across traditional ethnic and cultural lines', that the believers in Rome are able to extend the rule of Jesus.[48]

Another crucial aspect which Paul highlights about Christ is his *faithfulness and obedience*. In a careful study of all the references to 'Jesus' in Romans, Leander Keck set himself 'to distinguish the Christ assumed to be known in Rome from the "Jesus" Paul's argument requires',[49] and concludes that Paul assumed that the Roman readers already had a good knowledge of Jesus, some of it in narrative-type material; that there was a shared understanding, and therefore Paul 'presents himself not as a bearer of new information about "Jesus" but as the interpreter of the figure the readers already know about'.[50] What is distinctive about 'Jesus' in Romans, continues Keck, 'is the way in which Paul nuances and deepens this shared understanding'[51] but only to the extent to which it helps Paul to 'advance his argument and pursue his agenda'.[52] Thus, Keck finds only three passages – 3.21–26; 5.12–21 and 5.8 – which show Paul's distinctive emphasis in Romans about 'Jesus', and they combine to highlight Jesus as 'faithful and obedient to God'.[53] This is indeed very significant and, as we will see, supports our analysis of the story of Christ and of the incorporation of the believers in this story, even though, surprisingly enough, Keck does not capitalize on his main conclusion and states that 'Paul does not explain why he emphasizes the fidelity/ obedience of "Jesus", nor can we retrace his reasoning!'[54] However, Keck's study reveals at least two other important and relevant points about Paul's distinctive way of referring to 'Jesus' in Romans: (1) everything about Paul and about the believer's identity and hope revolves around the figure of Jesus, 'in' whom and 'through' whom God acts decisively in human history; and (2) assuming that the readers have already

48. Wright, 'Paul & Caesar', p. 181.

49. Leander E. Keck, '"Jesus" in Romans', *JBL* 108(3) (1989), pp. 443–60 (444).

50. Ibid., p. 452.

51. Ibid.

52. Ibid., p. 458.

53. Ibid.

54. Ibid., p. 459. To be sure, Keck offers an explanation of Paul's emphasis on the faithfulness and obedience of Jesus as the ground of salvation, as the 'inner, material grounding of freedom from sin in "Jesus"' (ibid.). One will agree, of course, with Keck's tendency to secure salvation as an absolute gift from God, accomplished totally and exclusively in Jesus, with no human contribution whatever. On the other hand, however, I think Keck is in danger of misinterpreting Paul's position vis-à-vis the believer's participation 'in Christ' as a way of overcoming sin, when he excludes that possibility from Paul's thought in Romans. He states: 'Paul does not say that we participate in Christ's sin-breaking obedience, nor does he urge us to imitate Christ's obedience, for that would make it a requirement, a law' (ibid., pp. 459–60). As I will show later, this is a deficient and dichotomist way of understanding the very complex relation-ship between indicative and imperative, between theology and ethics in Paul's thought. I believe, on the contrary, that the believer's obedience is very important for Paul and he does not understand it as the basis of salvation.

a narrative of Jesus, Paul can simply make an allusion or a particular reference to Christ and presume that the readers will grasp the significance of the allusion and be able to connect it to the larger narrative of Christ.[55]

Finally, there is a very close link in these chapters between *the gospel*, the theme of *peace and reconciliation*, and the believer's life *in Christ*. Richard Longenecker puts forward an attractive argument that the letter to the Romans, or its major thrust, could be understood as Paul's offer of a 'spiritual gift' (1.11) to the believers in Rome, with Paul's unique contribution found in Romans 5–8.[56] In other words, Paul wishes to strengthen the believers in Rome by sharing with them his understanding of the gospel – as he again makes plain in his doxology: 'to him who is able to strengthen you according to *my gospel* and the preaching of Jesus Christ' (16.25). Thus, the entire focus of the letter, contends Longenecker, is to be found in chs 5–8, which highlight the unique Pauline themes 'of "peace" and "reconciliation" with God, the antithesis of "death" and "life", and the relationships of being "in Christ" and "in the Spirit".'[57]

Both Keck and Longenecker show how Romans 5–8 represents Paul's unique contribution in terms of the story of Jesus Christ and of reconciliation. However, it is Douglas Campbell who offers a detailed and insightful analysis of the narrative motifs in Romans 8, and presents the key narrative of Christ, in this schematic form:

Trajectory One: Descent

(1) God the Father (2) sends, delivers up, and does not spare, (3) his own (4) Son, Jesus. (5) Jesus suffers (6) and dies, (7) in an act of identification. (8) This act also atones, or (in the most general terms) deals with humanity's problems, especially in relation to Sin. (9) This is also an act that speaks of the love of both the Father and the Son.

Trajectory Two: Ascent

(10) The Spirit of God and Christ, (11) also the Spirit of life, (12) resurrects Jesus, that is, creates new life in and for him, (13) and glorifies him, (14) to the right hand of the Father, (15) from which point he reigns, (16) and also intercedes. (17) This is a glorious inheritance. (18) He cries 'Abba, Father'. (19) As such he is 'the firstborn' (20) among many other 'brothers', (21) for whom he is also an 'image'.[58]

There are several key points about the story of Jesus in Romans which Campbell makes in his analysis of the story of Jesus in Romans 8 and to which I will come back in due time. However, my intention is neither to reconstruct the entire story of Christ in Romans nor to make a case for or against his particular shape of the story. Rather, building on the premise established by Hays, Campbell and others, namely that Paul's

---

55. Keck, '"Jesus"', pp. 449–52.

56. Richard N. Longenecker, 'The Focus of Romans: The Central Role of 5:1–8:39 in the Argument of the Letter', in Soderlund and Wright (eds), *Romans and the People of God*, pp. 49–69.

57. Ibid., p. 50.

58. D. Campbell, 'Story of Jesus', p. 108.

Christology had definitely a narrative structure, and further, that the readers in Rome were themselves aware of the basic narrative shape of the story of Christ, I would like to explore the way in which Paul *uses* the story of Christ (or particular features of the story) in his argument of Romans, and *why?* As we have already anticipated above, there are strong hints which suggest that Paul's intention is to show that the story of Christ is not something that simply happened then and there, but that, in fact, it is a continuing story of God in which the readers themselves play an important role: they continue to live out the story of Christ, with Christ alive among them. In other words, Paul is telling a 'new story', one in which the believers are included (henceforth the 'we' of ch. 5), a story which continually shapes their way of life. If Tobin is right that some believers in Rome were 'anxious' about losing the law as their only guide to ethics, then the story of Christ offers them a model (and a shape) which they could follow, and a complex dynamic in which they find themselves as the new people of God, 'in Christ', empowered for a new life.[59] By using the story of Christ, Paul is drawing the readers into this new story: not simply into what God has done in Christ, but into what he continues to do with all of those 'in Christ'.

If there is a narrative of Jesus in Romans which Paul nuances and to which he assigns a particular emphasis, and if chs 5–8 contain Paul's unique contribution to the formulation of the gospel – 'peace', 'reconciliation', 'in Christ', etc. – then it is appropriate to investigate more carefully the connections that exist between these characteristic features of Paul's letter to the Romans. We have seen the basic narrative feature which Paul intentionally emphasizes from the story of Christ in order to draw the believers' attention. Why does Paul feel the need to emphasize only those particular aspects of Jesus' story? If there is a relationship between Paul's key concepts in Romans 5–8 and the story of Christ, precisely what is the nature of that relationship? And, more specifically, how does the concept of reconciliation fit within such a narrative framework? Do we get any new insights on reconciliation if we read it alongside the story of Christ in Romans? These and similar questions will be addressed as we explore in detail Paul's understanding and presentation of reconciliation in Romans 5–8.

5.5 *Textual analysis: the story of Christ and reconciliation*

It is remarkable to see the way in which Paul blends in his argument various stories, particularly the story of Christ and that of believers in Rome (Paul's own story included), beginning with 5.1–2 and throughout chs 5–8 and 12–15. Paul does not simply write about how God's reconciliation is achieved in Christ, as something done from afar, and of which the believers are passive recipients. Paul includes the readers, their story, into the larger story of God's decisive reconciliation in Christ; they are themselves an *integral part* of this ongoing story of reconciliation. And this is a point

---

59. Tobin, *Paul's Rhetoric*, pp. 11 and 155–60.

that we can see throughout Romans, but particularly and forcefully in Romans 6, as Paul describes there the dynamic by which the believers are incorporated 'in Christ' and therefore into his story.

Paul seems to introduce the entire discussion of Romans 5–8 with the important christological summary of 4.24–25: 'It will be reckoned to us who believe in him who raised Jesus our Lord from the dead, who was handed over to death for our trespasses and was raised for our justification.' There are at least two strong arguments to support this close link between 4.24–25 and 5.1: first is the shift to 'us', 'we', 'ours' already in 4.24–25, pronouns which will dominate the entire next section in chs 5–8; second is the 'therefore' of 5.1 which is a clear inference from the previous conclusion in 4.24–25.[60] Thus, Paul places the entire next section under the overarching theme of the death and resurrection of Christ. In fact, as it will become clearer as the argument progresses, these are clear pointers to the entire narrative of Jesus Christ to which Paul constantly alludes throughout chs 5–8. But since the role of ch. 5 within the overall structure of Romans has been debated, we should discuss this aspect before we move on.

5.5.1 *Romans 5*
Romans 5 within the argument of Romans
The place of ch. 5 in the overall structure of Romans has been disputed. As a result of ch. 5's close linguistic and conceptual affinities with the preceding section (chs 1–4) and with the following section (chs 6–8), as well as because of the close parallelism between reconciliation and justification in 5.1–11, scholars have been divided into at least three major groups as to the exact place of ch. 5 in the structure of Romans. There are (1) those who take ch. 5 as a conclusion of the larger section of chs 1–5; (2) those who take ch. 5 as a bridge between the sections, with 5.1–11 belonging to chs 1–4 and 5.12–21 to chs 6–8; (3) those who take ch. 5 as an introduction to chs 5–8.[61]

The first group of scholars, considering the prominence of the theme of justification in chs 1–5, argue for a division of the two main sections at 6.1.[62] There is indeed a strong linguistic affinity between chs 1–4 and ch. 5: the strongest connection is probably the δικαιοσύνη/δικαιόω terminology, which is introduced in 1.17, is prominent in chs 3–4, and is also found in ch. 5 vv. 1, 9, 16–19, 21. But there are also other verbal connections: ἐν τῷ αἵματι αὐτοῦ, 'by his blood' (3.25 and 5.9); ὀργῇ, 'wrath' (2.5; 2.8; 3.5; 4.15 and 5.9); καυχᾶσθαι, 'boast, take pride' (2.17; 2.23 and 5.2; 5.3). Moreover, the contrast between Adam and Christ that Paul makes in 5.12–21 could

---

60. See further Paul J. Achtemeier, *Romans* (Atlanta: John Knox, 1985), pp. 89–91.

61. See S. Porter, Καταλλάσσω, pp. 145–52. After surveying the current proposals for the place of ch 5 in the argument of Romans, Porter argues that in fact ch 5 stands in its own as a central place of convergence of various themes in chs 1–8.

62. So Dunn, *Romans*; Bruce, *Romans*, pp. 64–65; Murray, *Romans*, pp. 158ff. It has been customary since the Reformation to explain Romans 1–8 within a dogmatic scheme as 'justification' (chs 1–4) and 'sanctification' (chs 5–8). See also Beker, *Paul the Apostle*, pp. 66ff.

also be taken as a response to the plight of adamic humanity described in 1.19–25. There is also a strong link between 4.23–25 and ch. 5.

In light of these clear parallels, Cranfield's point is noteworthy: 'a significant linguistic affinity between ch. 5 and chs 1–4 is not to be denied'.[63] However, as Porter notes, the lexical evidence between chs 1–4 and ch. 5 must not be overstated since, for example, δικαιοσύνη is even more present in chs 6ff than in chs 1–4.[64] Therefore, there is still need for more compelling evidence that ch. 5 should be included with the preceding section. That is why some other scholars take a middle position and describe ch. 5, especially 5.1–11, as a 'bridge' between the two major sections,[65] or a place of convergence for many themes of the book,[66] but these represent a minority view in scholarship.

Whatever the solution to the place of Romans 5 in the argument of Romans, we should exercise caution vis-à-vis the exact nature of the division between chs 4 and 5 and should neither impose an external, dogmatic structure on Paul's argument,[67] nor make too rigid a separation between the two sections.[68] Indeed, Porter is right to point out the risk of an imposed solution which does not pay adequate attention to the significance of ch. 5 in the argument of Romans.[69] However, while paying careful attention to avoid any artificial imposition over Paul's structure, we should also give credit to Paul's theological argumentations throughout his letters and look for the changing points and progress in his arguments.[70]

The most adequate proposal, held by the majority of interpreters today, takes ch. 5 to belong with the next section, chs 6–8, arguing primarily on the basis of contents.[71] A major argument for the unity of chs 5–8 is found in the logical sequence of contents,

---

63. Cranfield, *Romans*, p. 253.

64. S. Porter, Καταλλάσσω, p. 146.

65. So Patricia M. McDonald, 'Romans 5.1–11 as a Rhetorical Bridge', *JSNT* 40 (1990), pp. 81–96.

66. So, for example, B. N. Kaye, *The Thought Structure of Romans with Special Reference to Chapter 6* (Austin, TX: Scholars, 1979).

67. Beker is right to give a clear warning against such tendencies (*Paul*, pp. 66–69). See also Douglas Moo, *The Epistle to the Romans* (NICNT; Grand Rapids: Eerdmans, 1996), p. 291.

68. As Albert Schweitzer's famous argument for two 'craters' dividing very sharply the two sections in the 'justification' crater (chs 1–4) and the 'in Christ' or mysticism crater (chs 5–8). See Schweitzer, *The Mysticism of Paul the Apostle* (London, 1931).

69. S. Porter (Καταλλάσσω, p. 148) has shown the danger of marginalizing the significance of ch 5 by treating it either as a conclusion to the previous section or as an introduction to the next and so not paying adequate attention to the actual argument of ch 5.

70. Moo, *Romans*, p. 291.

71. The list could begin with Anders Nygren, *Commentary on Romans* (Philadelphia, PA: Fortress, 1974), pp. 187–89; Cranfield, *Romans*, pp. 253–54; Werner G. Kümmel, *Introduction to the New Testament* (Nashville: Abingdon, 1975), p. 306; and continue with Ernst Käsemann, *Commentary on Romans* (Geoffrey W. Bromiley (trans. and ed.), (Grand Rapids: Eerdmans, 1980), p. 131; Beker, *Paul*, pp. 83–86; Joseph Fitzmyer, *Romans: A New Translation With Introduction and Commentary* (The Anchor Bible Commentaries; New York: Doubleday, 1993), pp. 393ff; Brendan Byrne, *Romans* (Harrington, Daniel J. (ed.), Sacra Pagina Series, vol. 6; Collegeville: The Liturgical Press, 1996), pp. 162–64; Moo, *Romans*, pp. 290–95; Schreiner, *Romans*, pp. 245–49; Wright, *Romans*, pp. 405–06, and pp. 410–11.

with the first sub-section of each of the four chapters representing a basic statement about the meaning of justification for the life of the believer – as reconciliation, sanctification, freedom from the Law, and the indwelling of the Holy Spirit – followed in each case by the necessary clarifications. In addition to the argument from the structure of the content, Cranfield points out that the formula 'through our Lord Jesus Christ', or 'through Jesus Christ our Lord' and 'in Christ Jesus our Lord' which appear three times in ch. 5, is found at the end of each subsequent chs 6, 7 and 8, thus binding all these chapters together.[72] Similarly, the key words that appear in 5.1–11 such as ἀγάπη ('love'), δόξα ('glory'), ἐλπίς ('hope'), ὑπομονή ('endurance'), are found again in the last section of 8.18–39, thus showing the unity of chs 5–8.[73]

In addition to the above, Thomas Schreiner correctly points out the major break in the argument between ch. 4 and ch. 5 based on a thematic shift: if in the first four chapters Paul emphasizes the faithfulness of God to his promises and an equal-base entrance, by faith, into the family of Abraham for both Jews and Gentiles, in chs 5–8 he highlights the theme of hope that those in Christ now share and the sure confidence in the future inheritance.[74] Within this structure, the function of the δικαιοσύνη terminology in chs 5–8 is not to explicate the meaning of justification by faith, which was already done in chs 1–4, but rather to build on the consequences of that justification, which is primarily hope. In Schreiner's words, '[t]o be righteous by faith signals that the future blessings promised to Israel belong to the people of God. Those who are right with God can be assured that they will be delivered from God's wrath and experience future glory.'[75] But this is not a fully satisfactory understanding of Romans 5–8, on several counts.

Firstly, there are other major themes, besides hope, discussed by Paul in these chapters which are not given an appropriate place: the love of God expressed in Jesus' death; peace and reconciliation; suffering and endurance; the Adam–Christ reversal; baptism as dying and rising with Christ; freedom from sin, law and death; and the empowering presence of the Spirit.

Secondly, and most significantly, Schreiner understands being 'right with God' as the basis of hope and assurance of future glory in somewhat static, vertical soteriological terms. Even when he agrees that there is an ethical aspect of righteousness and that this involves a moral transformation of the believers,[76] one still gets the impression of a static reality whereby those 'who have the Holy Spirit have received the only transformation that they need'[77] and so they have a sure hope in the future. Complementary to this, my claim, for which I will argue in more detail in the section

---

72. Cranfield, *Romans*, p. 254.
73. Moo, *Romans*, pp. 292–94.
74. Schreiner, *Romans*, p. 246.
75. Ibid., p. 249.
76. Ibid. Moo makes also the same point when he remarks that justification occurrences in chs 5–8 'have a more "ethical" connotation as a description of Christian obligation (6.15–23)' (*Romans*, p. 292).
77. Schreiner, *Romans*, p. 248.

below regarding these chapters, is that in this section Paul is using interchangeably various metaphors, traditionally described in Pauline scholarship as 'vertical' and 'horizontal' categories, in order to express an unified/integrative and dynamic understanding of both God's redemptive work in Christ and the believers' participation 'in Christ'. It will be only as they actively share and participate in this new life in Christ, in the dying and rising of Christ, by the power of the Spirit, that they will be sure of their glorification with Christ. This is clearly stated by Paul in 8.16–17: 'The Spirit himself joins with our spirit to bear witness that we are children of God. And if we are children, then we are heirs, heirs of God and joint-heirs with Christ, *provided that we share his suffering, so as to share his glory*' (*NJB*). For Paul there seems to be not two sequences of 'vertical' and 'horizontal' movements, but one reality comprising the two: the new life the believer is now living in the world is an intrinsic part of his new experience and identity with God, in Christ. To this point we now turn for a closer examination.

Romans 5 and the interchange in metaphors and personal pronouns

It is significant that, beginning with ch. 5, Paul shifts his emphasis from δικαιοσύνη 'justification' terminology, which is predominant in Romans 1–4, to terms that are more personal-relational such as εἰρήνη ('peace', 5.1), ἀγάπη ('love', 5.5 and 5.8) and καταλλάσσω/καταλλαγή ('reconciliation', 5.10 and 5.11). Similarly, there is a significant shift in the use of personal pronouns in these chapters, from a clearly rhetorical 'you' (chs 1–4), to 'we' and 'us' not only in 5.1–11 but throughout chs 5–8,[78] as Paul addresses the family of those 'in Christ'.

The unavoidable question is: why did Paul consider it necessary to make such changes at this point in his argument? Why does he bring in terms that are more social, horizontal in character, and metaphors rooted in the everyday realities of life? And why does he switch from an argumentative to a more confessional tone in this section? Is it simply a matter of linguistic preferences, whereby Paul decides to make use of his rich vocabulary but not necessarily with a particular purpose in mind? This is unlikely, given the carefully structured grammatical and conceptual parallels between εἰρήνη and καταλαγή (vv. 1, 10a) and between δικαιοσύνη and καταλλαγή (vv. 1, 9, 10).[79] Is then reconciliation simply a consequence of justification or is it a larger, more comprehensive concept? Or perhaps Paul is using different metaphors interchangeably to express different dimensions of the same, multifaceted reality?

---

78. Moo (*Romans*, p. 592) points out that Paul uses the first plural verbs only 13 times in Romans 1–4, 'mainly editorially or as a stylistic device', but that in chs 5–8 he uses 48 such verbs.

79. Indeed, as several authors remark, Paul's 'dialogical thinking' have made him adopt a very deliberate literary style, a diatribe style of the period – a dialogical form with a moral purpose. See, for example, William S. Campbell, 'Romans III as a Key to the Structure and Thought of the Letter', in Donfried (ed.) *Romans Debate*, p. 258; Beker, *Paul*, p. 28; James L. Bailey, 'Genre Analysis', in Joel B. Green (ed.), *Hearing the New Testament. Strategies For Interpretation* (Grand Rapids: Eerdmans, 1995), pp. 207–09; Stanley K. Stowers, *The Diatribe and Paul's Letter to the Romans* (SBLDS, 57; Chico, CA: Scholars Press, 1981).

Several answers have been suggested. Thus, Porter argues that the different meta-phors that Paul is using in Romans 5 overlap semantically but that each individual metaphor highlights a different aspect of the same work of God.[80] Paul does that, he maintains, first by using synonymously εἰρήνην ἔχομεν[81] πρὸς τὸν θεὸν (v. 1a) and κατηλλάγημεν τῷ θεῷ (v. 10a), both having God as the common object. Secondly, the structure of vv. 9–10 reveals an overlapping meaning for δικαιοω and καταλλάσσω:

πολλῷ . . . μᾶλλον δικαιωθέντες . . . σωθησόμεθα (v. 9) and

πολλῷ μᾶλλον καταλλαγέντες σωθησόμεθα (v. 10)

Porter's point is significant because it explains the use of two different metaphors, one from the courtroom sphere (δικαιοσύνη) and the other from the personal relational sphere (εἰρήνη and καταλλαγή). When used together they express a multifaceted reality[82] and also show the inseparable link between the two metaphors in Paul. He concludes:

καταλλάσσω is used to denote the same event which is described by Paul on the one hand as an initiatory juridical event, justification, treated at some length in chaps. 3 and 4 . . . and on the other hand as the appropriation of attendant peaceful status, developed further in subsequent chapters in the letter.[83]

Porter makes an important contribution to the relationship between justification, peace and reconciliation in Romans. However, it is somewhat regrettable that he does not carry through the implications of his observations for the concept of reconciliation at the horizontal level in Romans, a concept that Paul introduces in ch. 5 and then develops in the remaining chapters of Romans. This is indeed a classical example of an interpretation of reconciliation in Paul that suffers from the limited association of

80. He states: 'justification and reconciliation or enjoying peace are to be seen as overlapping meta-phors, even verging on equation, each suggesting a different perspective on God's one work' (S. Porter, Καταλλασσω, p. 155). Other scholars who hold similar positions are Barrett, Romans, p. 108; Dunn, Romans; Martin, Reconciliation, p. 134; and Furnish, 'Ministry of Reconciliation', p. 212.

81. Against this common reading, Porter prefers the variant reading, ἔχωμεν, and argues for the hortatory subjective reading: 'let us enjoy peace'. He makes a very helpful clarification: 'In this context the exhortation to enjoy peace (v. 1), using the hortatory subjunctive, is not to be seen as exhorting move-ment to a subsequent stage, but as exhorting appropriation of circumstances attendant with justification. Therefore, the juridical and the personal categories of the two metaphors are linked inseparably, making an obvious and immediate association between justification and peace.' (S. Porter, Καταλλασσω, p. 155.)

82. C. K. Barrett captures well this interplay: 'Justification and reconciliation are different metaphors describing the same fact. The meaning of the verb "to reconcile" is determined by the noun "enemies"; it puts an end to enmity, just as "to justify" puts an end to legal contention. "Reconciliation" evokes the picture of men acting as rebels against God their king, and making war upon him; "justification" that of men who have offended against the law and are therefore arraigned before God their judge.' (Romans, p. 108.)

83. S. Porter, Καταλλασσω, p. 156.

the concept solely with the word-group καταλλάσσω/καταλλάγη. Thus, the difficult question still remains: why does Paul consider it necessary to make such an interplay in his metaphors at this place in his argument? Does this make any difference to the way in which we used to interpret Paul's presentation of reconciliation in Romans?

Another attempt to answer the question about Paul's important shift to reconciliation has been made by Gregory Allen, who offers a cogent and – at least in part – satisfactory answer to the issue.[84] Building on the work of Mitchell, he argues that Paul uses reconciliation language in Rom. 5.1–11 as a strategic attempt to bring about unity and mutual acceptance in a fractured community in Rome. He further shows that the rhetoric of reconciliation in 5.1–11 functions in three ways: (1) to create common ground between Jewish and Gentile Christians; (2) to strengthen the new, communal identity among the believers; and (3) to create the premise or the 'preparatory grammar' for the later exhortation of 15.7–13 for mutual acceptance among believers.[85]

Allen's reading of 5.1–11 is very helpful and advances the discussion of reconciliation in Romans. The significance of his study consists in the fact that he reads reconciliation in the light of the contingent circumstances of Christians in Rome and emphasizes correctly the believers' reconciliation with God as the basis for their mutual acceptance. It also points to the importance of reconciliation rhetoric in the whole argument of Romans and highlights Paul's effort to effect reconciliation in Rome. However, he seems to present a rather limited understanding of the complex and dynamic interplay of the metaphors that Paul is using (justification, peace and reconciliation). He writes:

> Reconciliation and peace are equivalent expressions for Paul that describe the believers' new relationship with God. Reconciliation and justification are different metaphors used by Paul to describe the same fact. Reconciliation is a relational metaphor while justification is a forensic and covenantal metaphor, yet both point to the believers' new standing before God.[86]

Not only is Allen unable to allow the various metaphors to express different aspects of the reality Paul is referring to, but he also limits their meaning to the vertical dimension of reconciliation with God. Thus, he does not answer adequately why Paul uses *different* metaphors. Furthermore, by limiting himself to the text of 5.1–11, he does not seem to take into account Paul's larger and richer symbolism of reconciliation which is found in other places in Romans as well, as we saw in Chapter 4 above.[87]

If, in the light of our previous discussion, the two metaphors 'righteousness' and 'reconciliation' denote different aspects of the same, multifaceted reality of salvation,

84. Allen, *Reconciliation*, pp. 52–69.
85. Ibid., pp. 55–69.
86. Ibid., pp. 69.
87. Patricia McDonald also notices the shift in Romans 5, particularly of the personal pronouns, and argues that Paul's purpose in his change was to emphasize his own unity with the believers in Rome. See her 'Romans 5.1–11'.

and if Paul uses them synonymously, I propose that by changing the emphasis towards metaphors of social interaction, Paul shows (1) that reconciliation is an essential aspect of salvation, and that it contains an intrinsic social, horizontal dimension; and (2) that the vertical reconciliation with God is inseparable from the horizontal aspect, as two dimensions of the same reality. Paul is thus trying to communicate that unity, reconciliation, harmony, and acceptance among the believers in Rome are an intrinsic part of the very gospel of reconciliation they profess. Through Romans 5–8 and particularly Romans 12–15, Paul highlights the implications of such an under-standing of reconciliation for their everyday life, in the concrete circumstances at Rome. Beginning with Romans 5.1–11, Paul presents the reality of the believers being reconciled with God and implicitly with one another through the death of Christ. Indeed, as McDonald observes, the 'dynamics of this pericope require that the readers admit that we believers (including Paul) are united with one another'.[88] If Paul's overall goal was 'to bring about the obedience of faith', he wanted to show that the gospel they have received has clear and concrete implications for the believer's everyday life. To be justified and reconciled with God is to be reconciled and at peace with your sister and brother, to be at peace with 'the other'. The believers in Rome seem to have 'forgotten' these aspects and so Paul sends them a 'reminder', as he himself puts it in 15.15: 'I have written to you quite boldly on some points, *as if to remind you of them again*, because of the grace God gave me' (*NIV*). From the variety of dissensions, mutual criticisms and contempt among the various groups of believers in Rome, Paul seems to have sensed a profound misunderstanding on their part regarding the implications of the gospel of reconciliation for their life. He writes to correct that. As we will see, Paul's understanding of the social dimension of reconciliation includes peace between Jews and Gentiles, between Christians and the surrounding world, and peace within different Christian groups.[89]

Furthermore, if we consider the intentional changes in Paul's argumentation in the light of the abundance of references to Jesus Christ throughout Romans 5–8 and of the importance of the ethical dimension permeating this section, I suggest that Paul intended his readers to understand his argument in these chapters in close connection with the story of Christ and with their new status and responsibilities resulting from their being 'in Christ'. Indeed, Paul's shift in the personal pronouns seems to support this proposal. By using the 'we' and 'us' pronouns in a context in which he is retelling the story of Jesus, Paul includes himself and the believers in Rome in the same story of Christ, and prompts them to live out the 'story of Christ' as active participants in the ongoing story of God's reconciliation of the world in Christ.[90] As we will see,

---

88. McDonald, 'Romans 5.1–11', p. 90.

89. These points are excellently developed by Klaus Haacker (*The Theology of Paul's Letter to the Romans* (Cambridge New Testament Theology Series; Cambridge: CUP, 2003), pp. 45–53) in his chapter 'Romans as the proclamation of peace with God and on earth'.

90. This proposal goes beyond several other proposals which suggest that the shift in the personal pronouns signifies Paul's continuation of the dialogue with Judaism in chs 5–8 (so Schreiner, *Romans*,

the story of Christ functions not only as the ground of their reconciliation with God but also as the model for their reconciliation with the other. We are now ready to substantiate our proposal and begin with a clarification note on the use of δικαιωσύνη and καταλλαγή in Romans 5–8.

Righteousness, reconciliation and the social ethical aspect

The theme of δικαιωσύνη ('righteousness'/'justification') is, beyond any doubt, a central theme of the entire letter to the Romans. The concept of 'righteousness' (δικ-words) is very much present in chs 1–4 (31 times) and in chs 5–8 (21 times). However, there is a thematic shift in the use of the word in the second section which is significant for our purposes. If in the first four chapters the emphasis is on the status of justification attained by faith in Jesus Christ, i.e., how God has fulfilled his OT promises in Christ, and that they are now available by faith to all, in the next chapters (5–8) there is a shift towards an ethical, transformational aspect of 'righteousness' for the life of the believers. Several authors point to this aspect.[91]

The beginning of the paragraph in 5.1, Δικαιωθέντες οὖν ἐκ πίστεως ('Therefore, since we have been justified through faith . . .'), shows that Paul presupposes the discussion on 'justification by faith' previously established in 3.21–4:25, and that now he builds on it and describes the consequences and implications of that justification.[92] This is clearly and immediately seen in 5.9 where the reality of past justification represents the assurance of future salvation. The same aspect is found in the subsequent uses of δικ-words, particularly in 5.12–19 and 8.10, 8.31 and 8.33. But just as important as this future dimension of righteousness are the present implications of righteousness described by such words as εἰρήνη ('peace'), καυχάομαι ('rejoicing'), θλίψις ('suffering'), ἐλπίς ('hope'), ἀγάπη ('love') and καταλλαγή ('reconciliation') throughout chs 5–8. There is now a new dynamic of relationships in the life of those 'justified': there is love and acceptance instead of enmity and rejection (5.5, 5.10). One has to be cautious again and state that this very intense and personal relationship of love between the 'justified' and God as well as between all those 'in Christ' is not simply a 'consequence' of justification but, as Wright correctly remarks, a

---

p. 247), or the continuation of the diatribe style in Romans 5 (so S. Porter, 'The argument of Romans 5: Can a Rhetorical Question Make a Difference?', *Journal of Biblical Literature* 110 (1991), pp. 655–77), or even a celebration of Paul's unity with the Roman believers (so P. McDonald, 'Romans 5.1–11').

91. See particularly Schreiner, *Romans*, pp. 246–49; Moo, *Romans*, p. 292; Tobin, *Paul's Rhetoric*, pp. 11 and 155–60.

92. Schreiner is thus partially correct to note that '[t]he primary function of the δικ-words in Rom. 5–8 is not to explicate righteousness by faith, but to build on that justification and show what flows from it' (*Romans*, p. 249). But while it is true that Paul's emphasis in these chapters is on the ethical aspect of righteousness, one has to be very careful how one states it so as to avoid the danger of a too rigid, two-step sequential explanation of Paul's understanding of 'righteousness', as if one could have first 'justification' and then think about the consequences of that justification. I would argue that for Paul the ethical aspect of the believer's life is in itself an 'explication' of the same 'justification by faith'; i.e., the present transformation of the believer's life is an essential and intrinsic part of the 'justification by faith'.

'necessary further dimension of the doctrine of justification by faith.'[93] The argument in Romans 6.1–8.17 (particularly 6.15–23) is a clear illustration that by 'righteousness' Paul does not understand simply a vertical, legal transaction between God and people, but rather a process which necessarily involves a moral transformation in the lives of the believers.[94]

If it is true that with regard to 'justification' Paul maintains both aspects together, i.e., the juridical and the relational, then we argue that he does the same with regard to 'reconciliation', i.e., holding together the vertical and the horizontal dimensions of reconciliation. In fact, to put it the other way around, the very careful, parallel structuring of vv. 1, 9 and 10 in ch 5 – with δικαιωσύνη, εἰρήνη, and καταλλαγή inseparably linked – points to the fact that this is exactly what Paul intended to argue: that the juridical and the personal, the vertical and the horizontal dimensions of salvation belong together, inseparably.[95] Thus, one can say that Paul uses justification/reconciliation in the following chapters to highlight not only the legal, vertical dimension of these concepts but also their communal, horizontal dimension. The language of reconciliation introduced in ch. 5 and continued for the rest of the letter, is thus not simply used to point out the stance of the individual with God (as it has traditionally been understood), but also to indicate the believers' responsibility to extend this reconciliation to 'the other' in their own community and outside it.

ROMANS 5.1–11

As we have pointed out, one of Paul's concerns in this larger section (chs 5–8) was to offer a basis for the ethical life of the new believers. Not only for the Jews but also for Jewish Christians, the law represented the sure guide for their ethical behaviour, a higher ethical code which gave them reasons to consider themselves morally superior to their pagan neighbours. Since Paul was renowned for preaching a law-free gospel, it is no wonder that some believers in Rome might have had great concerns as to the foundation of their everyday ethical behaviour. If not the law, what else could provide a solid basis for the various ethical issues they faced? Would not a unilateral emphasis on the 'righteousness by faith', without the details of the law, lead to a kind

---

93. Wright, *Romans*, p. 514.

94. Moo (*Romans*, p. 292) shows also that the ethical dimension of righteousness is emphasized in chs 5–8.

95. Analysing this complex dynamic between justification and reconciliation in Romans 5, Cranfield argues for the inseparability of the two concepts. He writes: 'What did Paul understand to be the relation between reconciliation and justification? The correct answer would seem to be neither that reconciliation is a consequence of justification, nor that "Justification and reconciliation are different metaphors describing the same fact" [C. K. Barrett], but that God's *justification involves reconciliation* because God is what He is. Where God's justification is concerned, *justification and reconciliation though distinguishable, are inseparable* ... Thus Δικαιωθέντες ... εἰρήνην ἔχομεν is not a mere collocation of two metaphors describing the same fact, nor does it mean that, having been justified, we were subsequently reconciled and now have peace with God; but its force is that the fact that we have been justified means that we have also been reconciled and have peace with God.' (*Romans*, vol. 1, p. 258 (italics added).)

of ethical chaos?[96] These are crucial questions with extremely important implications for the gospel Paul preached and so he tackles them with all thoughtfulness. Indeed, by a careful argumentation in which he brings together and contrasts such topics as righteousness, reconciliation, love, hope, grace, free gift, Spirit, obedience, sin and law, Paul argues for the seriousness of the ethical life the believers now are to live 'in Christ'. Being made righteous by faith/grace (5.1–2) is not devoid of serious ethical implications. On the contrary, as Paul devotes a whole section to it (5.12–21), he shows how 'this grace' is incompatible with sin.[97]

Thus, Rom. 5.1–5 could be understood as a short ethical exhortation with two main clauses in the first-person-plural subjunctive,[98] εἰρήνην ἔχομεν [ἔχωμεν] πρὸς τὸν θεόν, 'let us have peace with God'[99] (v. 1) and καυχώμεθα ἐπ' ἐλπίδι τῆς δόξης τοῦ θεοῦ, 'let us boast in our hope of sharing the glory of God' (v. 2), with the last clause being further expanded in vv. 3–5.[100] By connecting this with his previous argument in ch. 4, Paul states that those being justified by faith (like Abraham), (should) have peace with God and access 'to this grace'. The 'peace' is synonymous with 'reconciliation' and comprises both a restored relationship with God and a radically new life 'in Christ' – a theme Paul will develop explicitly in ch. 6. Peace/unity/welcome among the members of the new community is a crucially important aspect of this new life 'in Christ' – indeed, the distinctive mark of the new people living in the kingdom of God, as Paul will illustrate later on in chs 14–15, particularly 14.17 and 4.19.

The close association between righteousness and peace which Paul makes here is not a novel thing. We find in various places in the OT this combination, particularly as an eschatological characteristic of the age to come. Isa. 32.17, for example, describes this as follows: 'The effect of righteousness will be peace, and the result of righteousness, quietness and trust forever.' Isa. 54.10, too, points to God's faithfulness to his

96. Paul seems to respond to exactly this form of criticism in 3.8 where he rebukes those in Rome who 'slandered' him by claiming in Paul's name a position he did not endorse vis-à-vis the law: 'And why not say (as some people slander us by saying that we say), "Let us do evil so that good may come"? Their condemnation is deserved!'

97. See Tobin (*Paul's Rhetoric*, pp. 157–87), who argues for this position and entitles his exposition on these verses suggestively, 'The Incompatibility of This Grace and Sin'.

98. The reading ἔχομεν/ἔχωμεν in 5.1 is debated, with some commentators arguing for the subjunctive ἔχωμεν, while the majority of modern Pauline students take ἔχομεν in the indicative. However, the strong textual attestation of ἔχωμεν and the subjunctive understanding by the patristic writers should be grounds enough to consider the matter carefully. If we accept a subjunctive reading, this will also affect a similar reading of καυχώμεθα ('let us boast') in verse 2. A subjunctive reading not only makes good sense of the ethical nuance of the entire section of Romans 5–8 but also helps keep in a better balance both aspects of reconciliation as one comprehensive reality of the believers' reconciliation with God and with one another.

99. An excellent possible translation is offered by Fitzmyer: 'let us now give evidence of this justification by a life of peace with God' (*Romans*, p. 395). However, Fitzmyer does not agree with the subjunctive reading, noting that Paul's statement indicates a *de facto* situation the believers find themselves in; i.e., one of peace and reconciliation with God which come from his grace. As we will see, while this position is true, it is also only half of the point that Paul wants to communicate.

100. Tobin, *Paul's Rhetoric*, p. 158.

covenant, which is a covenant of peace. Similarly, Ezek. 34.25 and 37.26 read: 'I will make a covenant of peace with them.' In the Psalms we also find this association: 'Righteousness and peace will kiss each other' (Ps. 85.10) and 'In his days may righteousness flourish and peace abound' (Ps. 72.7). Paul, no doubt, has these instances in mind when he writes about the present possibility and actuality of peace for the believers, because, 'through our Lord Jesus Christ' they live already in that promised 'age to come'. The reference in v. 5 to the Holy Spirit (which was also understood as a sign of the last days) strengthens Paul's eschatological perspective.

Paul goes on in v. 2 to make another important point: not only that it is 'through our Lord Jesus Christ' that the 'peace' is defined, but it is also 'through him' that we have access into '*this* grace'. It is a specific grace, one that is apart from the observance of the Jewish law and redefined again 'through Christ'. Furthermore, *this grace* has serious ethical consequences. By using the perfect tense – εἰς τὴν χάριν ταύτην ἐν ᾗ ἑστήκαμεν', it is *this grace, in which we have taken our stand*' – Paul wants to indicate that to 'stand firm' in this grace is also a mature and continued commitment of those who entered into this grace, into this new community 'in Christ'.[101] It seems that Paul's closing argument at the end of ch. 5 (vv. 20–21) with a reiteration of the reign of grace 'through righteousness for eternal life through Jesus Christ our Lord' (5.21) lends support for an understanding of Paul's ethical concerns in Romans 5.[102]

We noticed a significant dynamic interplay of 'righteousness', 'faith', 'grace', 'hope' and 'love' in 5.1–5, motifs that appear elsewhere in Paul's letters in various ethical contexts (Gal. 5.2–5; 1 Thess. 1.3 and 5.8; 1 Cor. 13.13). Faith working through love, in the power of the Spirit, represents a key ethical principle for Paul. However, this is not simply a matter of theoretical principle but rather something which the believers make manifest in their everyday practice of patience, character and hope in the midst of suffering and difficulties.[103] By bringing together all these themes in Romans 5.1–5, Paul expresses his understanding of the intrinsic relationship that exists between justification by faith and a Christian life of peace/reconciliation and love – both fundamentally centred in, and shaped by, the faithfulness of Jesus Christ.

Thus, we could infer from the above argument that Paul does not refer simply to peace/reconciliation between the individual believer and God. Rather, this is being incorporated in the discussion of a particular life of the Christian community gathered 'in Christ'. To have 'peace with God' means to live out that peace with joy, hope and

---

101. This possible sense is noted in *BAGD*, ι"στημι ('stand firm'), II.2.c. See also Dunn, *Romans* 5.2.

102. Tobin, *Paul's Rhetoric*, pp. 158–59.

103. One cannot read these closely worked out connections between patience, character and suffering/afflictions and not be invited to think that Paul draws on his earlier reflection and writing on the issues: 1 Thess 1.3; 2 Cor 1.6; 2 Cor 6.4; 2 Cor 12.12 (references to patience); 2 Cor 2.9; 2 Cor 8.2; 2 Cor 9.13; 2 Cor 13.3; Phil 2.22 (references to character); 1 Thess 1.6; 1 Thess 3.3 and 7; 2 Cor 1.4 and 8; 2 Cor 2.4; 2 Cor 4.17; 2 Cor 6.4–10; 2 Cor 7.4; 2 Cor 8.2 and 13 (references to afflictions, with his own experience of it described particularly in 2 Cor 12.7–10).

love, whatever the circumstances. Particularly relevant for the community in Rome is that the peace/reconciliation with God is to be reflected by their own unity as a new community 'in Christ' as well as by a reconciling life towards the outsiders – as Paul will specify in more detail in Romans 12–15.

If in the first five verses Paul introduces the subject matter of his concern – i.e., the dynamic of salvation which includes righteousness, faith, peace/reconciliation, love and hope – it is in the rest of the chapter and in the subsequent chapter that he spells out more concretely the ethical implications of his gospel. He begins with the christological basis of reconciliation and its significance for believers (vv. 6–11). It was 'by the death of his Son' that God reconciled 'us' while 'we were still weak . . . ungodly . . . sinners . . . enemies'. Anticipating 8.3 and 32, Paul puts the entire discussion in the context of Christ's story and thus establishes a direct link/identity between Jesus and God whose reconciling love he reveals. Thus, it was God who sent his Son to die and reconcile the world, a task only God can do. The story of Christ is the story of God's extraordinary love demonstrated by his Son, the Messiah, who died for us while we were enemies. And because believers have experienced God's love through the Spirit, they can be absolutely sure of their future in Christ.

The close connection Paul seems to make between the death of Christ, love and reconciliation is significant: συνίστησιν δὲ τὴν ἑαυτοῦ ἀγάπην εἰς ἡμᾶς ὁ θεός, ὅτι ἔτι ἁμαρτωλῶν ὄντων ἡμῶν Χριστὸς ὑπὲρ ἡμῶν ἀπέθανεν . . . εἰ γὰρ ἐχθροὶ ὄντες κατηλλάγημεν τῷ θεῷ διὰ τοῦ θανάτου τοῦ υἱοῦ αὐτοῦ, 'But God shows his love for us in that while we were yet sinners Christ died for us . . . when we were God's enemies, we were reconciled to him through the death of his Son (5.8 and 5.10).[104] Indeed, as Theissen remarks, within the symbolism of reconciliation 'the death of Christ is presented not so much as an accursed, vicarious death, but rather as the surrender of love.'[105] When this surrender of love is expressed by Paul's insistence that Christ's died 'for us', Jesus Christ's personal participation in the drama of reconciliation, his willingness in the process of surrender, is highlighted. This particular emphasis, argues Theissen, enables Paul to use the dying 'for us' formula 'as an appeal for deliberate action'.[106] Indeed, this double emphasis on the surrender of love and the dying 'for us' comes to new light when we read reconciliation within the framework of the story of Christ.

Paul's 'dying formula'
Following Martin Hengel's significant study on atonement in Paul,[107] Jeffrey Gibson

---

104. Other Pauline texts also illustrates this close connection: 'The life I now live in the flesh I live by faith in the Son of God, who loved me and gave himself for me' (Gal. 2.20); 'For the love of Christ controls us, because we are convinced that one has died for all' (2 Cor. 5.14–15).

105. Theissen, 'Soteriological Symbolism', p. 172.

106. Ibid., p. 173.

107. Martin Hengel, *The Atonement: The Origins of the Doctrine in the New Testament* (London: SCM Press, 1981).

has shown[108] how the 'dying formula' (that 'Jesus died for us'), while being one of the most important confessional formulae in the letters of Paul, did not originate with him; that it was widely used before and in the time of Paul in the Graeco-Roman world, and that it was something which Paul's audiences would have been familiar with. Starting with a clear set of questions about its usages,[109] and followed by a thorough analysis of various secular Greek instances of the 'dying formula',[110] Gibson is able to show that Paul's employment of the formula is distinctive, in comparison with its extra-canonical usages.

There are several important conclusions drawn from Gibson's study which are relevant and significant for the present study. Firstly, in the formula's secular usage, in most of the cases the 'hero' or the 'noble character' would die for *'that which has fostered them'* – most often the welfare of the 'city' and their native land, even though some would also die for their lover, spouse, or a friend. What is most remarkable, continues Gibson, is that *'never* does the one to whom the dying formula is applied die for an adversary or an enemy. The death for others, especially the "noble death" is always undertaken in an attempt to rescue or defend *one's own'*.[111] When compared with how Paul applies the formula to Christ and his death, a clear and definite contrast is evident. Jesus Christ was not, in Paul's understanding, a 'hero' or simply a 'noble character'; he was the Son of God, 'in the very form of God' (Phil. 2.6), who died for *others* – who were sinners, rebellious, enemies. What is significant in Paul's use of the formula, is that he presents Jesus' death as a model of humility and servanthood for the believers.

Secondly, Gibson found that in virtually all of the instances where the 'dying formula' was used in secular writings, the result of dying, in addition to the 'salvation' of persons or things, always includes 'the eventual, if not immediate, defeat or destruction of the persons or the powers that have caused the death or which threatened that for which the deceased died'.[112] Again, the way Paul understands and presents the death of Christ is radically different: while there is a defeat, conquering and victory, even 'destruction' of the powers of evil (personified in Paul by Sin and Death) as a result of Christ's death and resurrection, Paul has a much more nuanced and complex view vis-à-vis the 'powers' as we will see in our analysis of Romans 13.

Thirdly, Gibson discovers that the secular use of the dying formula in the Graeco-Roman world was intended for the following purpose or effect:

108. Jeffrey B. Gibson, 'Paul's "Dying Formula": Prolegomena to an Understanding of Its Import and Significance', in Sheila E. McGinn (ed.), *Celebrating Romans: Template for Pauline Theology: Essays in Honor of Robert Jewett* (Grand Rapids: Eerdmans, 2004), p. 20–41.

109. Ibid., pp. 21–22.

110. Gibson points to over thirty-five uses of the dying formula in the works of contemporary authors such as Philo, Plutarch, Josephus, Epictetus, Dionysius of Halicarnassus, Cassius Dio, Polyaenus, and Pseudo Apollodorus, as well as in the works of Roman writers like Horace, Seneca, Caesar, Tacitus and Cicero – even though in his study he analyses only the Greek literature.

111. Gibson, 'Paul's "Dying Formula"', p. 25 (italics in the original).

112. Ibid.

to inculcate, confirm, or reinforce the values that stood at the very heart of Graeco-Roman, Imperial ideology – values that were accepted by Jews, Greeks, and by those whom Paul called 'the rulers of this age' as essential for maintaining 'peace and security' – namely, that the warrior is the ideal citizen; that war is 'glorious'; that violence is a constructive force in the building of civilization; and that 'salvation' from that which threatens to harm or destroy a valued way of life is ultimately achieved only through the use of brute force . . . that honor and peace and security ultimately come through readiness for war and the willingness to kill.[113]

When Paul wrote that 'Christ died for us/our sins' he did it to a totally different effect. His usage is in sharp distinction to the usage of his contemporaries; thus he strongly challenges the established values of honour, peace, life, and ultimately of salvation, and offers to the early Christian a powerful alternative – an alternative vision guided by the controlling and irresistible story of the nature, character, and life of Jesus,

who, though he was in the form of God, did not regard equality with God as something to be grasped, but emptied himself, taking the form of a slave, being born in human likeness. And being found in human form, he humbled himself and became obedient to the point of death – even death on a cross. (Phil. 2.6–8)

In a significant article on the significance of Jesus' death in the NT, Larry Hurtado brings solid evidence to show that this is presented not simply as redemptive but also as paradigmatic, as 'inspiring, exemplary, and descriptive of, and criterion for, Christian life'.[114]

There is another important aspect of the story of Christ and of the believers that Paul alludes to in v. 10 which deserves attention: the believers, who were reconciled to God, 'shall be saved in his *life*' (σωθησόμεθα ἐν τῇ ζωῇ αὐτοῦ). This is a clear reference to the resurrection of Christ and its significance within the dynamic of the life 'in Christ' in which the believers are able to 'walk in the newness of life' as Paul will write later (6.4).[115] The close link between reconciliation and resurrection is substantial.[116] This connection in 5.10 is not singular but rather a confirmation of a similar statement he made earlier in 4.25, 'who was handed over to death for our trespasses and was *raised* for our justification', a verse which, as we have mentioned, introduces Paul's entire argument in which the theme of reconciliation, peace and love are predominant. Since reconciliation is meant to overcome a separation, it cannot

---

113. Ibid., pp. 38–39.

114. Hurtado, 'Jesus' Death as Paradigmatic in the New Testament', *Scottish Journal of Theology* 57 (2004), pp. 413–33 (413). His contribution is important since most of the studies on this question have concentrated on the redemptive aspect of the death of Jesus.

115. Wright, *Romans* p. 520. See also Dunn, *Romans* 5.10, who remarks that 'salvation will be achieved not simply by the power of Christ's risen life but through the believer's identification with it: the process of salvation as a sharing both in Christ's death and in his resurrection'.

116. This point was made well by Theissen, 'Soteriological Symbolism', p. 173.

be accomplished by a dead person. That is why Paul is emphasizing the resurrected life of Christ with whom believers *are* being reconciled. Reconciliation is not only something that Christ has accomplished in the past by his death, but also a continuous experience in his new life. Indeed, the strong implication of this close link between reconciliation and resurrection is that, for Paul, the power of resurrection is available for the believers and enables them to embody in everyday life the reconciliation that they have experienced with God. The presence of the resurrected Christ, through the Spirit, makes the practice of reconciliation possible.

With Paul, we also have to keep in tension the various dimensions of the multifaceted reality and dynamic of salvation. Thus, while we should understand reconciliation as a theme that Paul chooses to address in response to concrete needs in Rome, for Paul reconciliation is also an integral part of the gospel of the crucified and risen Christ. That Christ, the Messiah, has died so that enemies are reconciled to God *is* the good news. The reconciliation thus accomplished is *from God*, totally based on *God's love* and proven in *Christ's death*. It is good news because it was *God's absolute grace* and initiative in response to the universal human predicament under sin (as Paul so vividly described in chs 1–4) and the need for forgiveness and restored relationships. God, in his freedom, chooses to reconcile his enemies. That 'reconciliation' became Paul's preferred way to formulate and communicate his gospel to the Gentiles may have some justification.[117] An adequate treatment of reconciliation in Romans will always maintain these two aspects together as it describes both the event of God's reconciliation of people to him through Christ, and the social embodiment of this reality in the everyday life of those who belong 'to Christ' – two inseparable dimensions of the reality of salvation.

It is therefore not accidental that Paul introduces a direct discussion of reconciliation right at this point in his argument when he begins to address the seriousness of the ethical implications of faith for the believers. As later chapters (14–15) show, Paul's intention is to address the situation of disunity and conflict in the Roman community. By the way in which he builds his argument of reconciliation on the story of Christ, he wants to make them aware that their reconciliation with God is very much connected with their peace and reconciliation with one another. Indeed, God's reconciling initiative by the death of Christ on the cross, as the result of his obedient life to God (5.19), becomes not only the very act and pronouncement of reconciliation of humanity with God but also the ground and model for reconciling relationships among people. This is precisely why Paul appeals to the story of Christ as a way to address both these aspects and hold them together. Christ's story is not only his own story but includes the story of the believers, of those who came to be 'in Christ'. And it is because the believers share the same story that they can live rightly. This is not simply about imitation, as if they have to do what Jesus did. Rather, the

---

117. As Ralph Martin has argued over the years in his various writings on the theology of reconciliation in Paul.

same story of Christ is being unfolded in their midst as they are 'in Christ' and so active participants/actors in the story. And the logic of the story requires/implies a particular way of living, a reconciling life. Indeed Paul is reminding them that, by the Spirit, they have now in their hearts the same love of God at work in their life to transform them towards the true humanity that God always intended from creation, one that they are able to enact 'in Christ' (as the Adam and Christ contrast in 5.12–21 illustrates).

ROMANS 5.12–21

Having addressed and established the essential fact of reconciliation in 5.1–11, in the next section, by his references to Adam, Paul addresses the condition of humanity as a whole, the consequences of the rejection of God, i.e. sin and death, and how God has dealt with this problem: again, it is through Christ that God acted decisively and provided the solution. What is particularly relevant for the present study is to look more closely into the contrast that Paul is drawing between Adam and Christ, respectively between those who are 'in Adam' and those who are 'in Christ'. On the one hand we have Adam, whose sin brought death which spread to all his descendants: Διὰ τοῦτο ὥσπερ δι' ἑνὸς ἀνθρώπου ἡ ἁμαρτία εἰς τὸν κόσμον εἰσῆλθεν καὶ διὰ τῆς ἁμαρτίας ὁ θάνατος, καὶ οὕτως εἰς πάντας ἀνθρώπους ὁ θάνατος διῆλθεν, ἐφ' ᾧ πάντες ἥμαρτο, 'sin came into the world through one man, and death came through sin, and so death spread to all because all have sinned' (5.12). The end result was that a solidarity in sin and death was established for all those who are 'in Adam',[118] solidarity which universalizes the disobedience of Adam: δι' ἑνὸς παραπτώματος εἰς πάντας ἀνθρώπους εἰς κατάκριμα, 'by one man's disobedience many were made sinners' (5.18, RSV). On the other hand, there is Christ by whose free gift of righteousness God's grace of life came to many (5.15) so that ἱ τὴν περισσείαν τῆς χάριτος καὶ τῆς δωρεᾶς τῆς δικαιοσύνης λαμβάνοντες ἐν ζωῇ βασιλεύσουσιν διὰ τοῦ ἑνὸς Ἰησοῦ Χριστοῦ, 'those who receive the abundance of grace and the free gift of righteousness reign in life through the one man Jesus Christ' (5.17b, RSV). There is now a different solidarity established, one unto righteousness and life for all those who are 'in Christ', solidarity that universalizes the obedience of Christ for many: 'by one man's obedience many will be made righteous . . . so that as sin reigned in death, grace also might reign through righteousness to eternal life through Jesus Christ our Lord' (5.19, 5.21). Even though the contrast is present throughout 5.12–21, it is in v. 18 that we find the most complete statement of the contrast between the legacies of Adam and Christ and the implications for those who share in their solidarity: Ἄρα οὖν ὡς δι' ἑνὸς παραπτώματος εἰς πάντας ἀνθρώπους εἰς κατάκριμα, οὕτως καὶ δι' ἑνὸς δικαιώματος εἰς πάντας ἀνθρώπους εἰς δικαίωσιν ζωῆς, 'Then, as one man's

---

118. I follow here Byrne's basic point that the solidarity of sin and death 'in Adam' is overcome by a more powerful solidarity in righteousness and life 'in Christ'. (Byrne, 'Living out the Righteousness of God: The Contribution of Rom 6:1–8:13 to an Understanding of Paul's Ethical Presuppositions', *The Catholic Biblical Quarterly* 43 (1981), pp. 557–81 (560–62).).

trespass led to condemnation for all men, so one man's act of righteousness leads to acquittal and life for all men' (5.18, RSV). Ultimately, however, even though Adam and Christ share in universal significance, what is perhaps the most important point for Paul in this argument is the incomparability and superiority of Christ's accomplishment in contrast with Adam's transgression:

'Ἀλλ' οὐχ ὡς τὸ παράπτωμα, οὕτως καὶ τὸ χάρισμα· εἰ γὰρ τῷ τοῦ ἑνὸς παραπτώματι οἱ πολλοὶ ἀπέθανον, πολλῷ μᾶλλον ἡ χάρις τοῦ θεοῦ καὶ ἡ δωρεὰ ἐν χάριτι τῇ τοῦ ἑνὸς ἀνθρώπου Ἰησοῦ Χριστοῦ εἰς τοὺς πολλοὺς ἐπερίσσευσεν,

There is no comparison between the free gift and the offence. If death came to many through the offence of one man, how much greater an effect the grace of God has had, coming to so many and so plentifully as a free gift through the one man Jesus Christ! (5.15, *NJB*)

And this 'much greater' effect of the solidarity of Christ is based totally on the overwhelming power of the grace of God revealed through the death and resurrection of Jesus Christ.

The obedience of Christ plays a very important role in Paul's argument in Romans 5–8. He has just argued in ch. 4, based on the example of Abraham, that Jews and Gentiles are made righteous by sharing in Abraham's righteousness and, as in his case, this is the gift of God. But Abraham was a prefiguration of the faithful Christ who died for enemies and brought God's gift of life to everyone. Particularly in 5.6–10 Paul shows what the faithfulness of Christ entailed, i.e., he gave himself for the weak, the ungodly – indeed, for enemies. In 5.12–21 he gives expression to the justifying obedience of Christ in stark contrast to the disobedience of Adam. Subsequently, in chs 6–8, Paul intends to show how Christians can be faithful by sharing in Christ's obedience and life due to their intimate relationship 'in Christ'. Obedience and righteousness are closely connected. Paul explains that as Adam's disobedience affected all, so Christ's obedience affects all (5.19) and in ch. 6 he describes just how Christians, by virtue of being in Christ, have been freed from the slavery of sin and death and can now become obedient (6.16–17). They are now free to choose to live a reconciled life, as a sign of their own transformation by the Spirit and of the new community of Jews and Gentiles living in peace and harmony in Christ.[119]

119. Stanley Stowers makes a good case for the importance of the concept of obedience for the argument of Romans 5–6, in his commentary, *A Rereading of Romans: Justice, Jews and Gentiles* (New Haven: Yale University Press, 1994), pp. 251ff. However, I believe he restricts unnecessarily, and ultimately misleadingly, Paul's rhetoric of obedience to the Gentile audience. Paul's point is precisely that 'in Christ' there is a transformed, alternative community, made up of Jews and Gentiles who are to be faithful and obedient to their lord, Jesus Christ. Paul's extensive argument of reconciliation is made exactly with the purpose of addressing the issues of disunity, of conflict between different factions of the church, including the divide over ethnic identities. To restrict Paul's argument in Romans 5–8 as addressing predominantly the Gentile audience is problematic not only because of the difficulty of pinpointing the exact configuration

5.5.2 *Romans 6*

In ch. 6 Paul describes explicitly the dynamic by which the believers are incorporated 'in Christ', through baptism,[120] and the implications of this new reality. Before their baptism the believers were under the power of sin and so unable to break out of its domain and influence. However, their baptism into Christ's death meant a 'death' to sin and, as a consequence, a breaking out from its power and jurisdiction (6.2). As a result of their being buried with Christ they share in the effects of his death to sin. They are now free to belong to another, to Jesus Christ.[121]

It is interesting to note that for Paul, since the death of Christ on the cross and the subsequent resurrection, death itself receives a new meaning: it is a gateway to life. By being baptized in Christ's death, the believers share in it and also in its liberating effects from the reign of sin and unto life – symbolized by their rising from the water. The resurrection was always a sign of the eschatological age to come. Christ's resurrection thus inaugurated this age to come and so Christ, as the new Adam, has displaced the old Adam. By their dying-and-rising with Christ, the believers have been transferred from the realm of sin ('in Adam') to the realm of the power of the eschatological new age. They are now 'in Christ'. It is here, in its clearest expression, that Paul explains the fact of being 'in Christ' as a transmutation from the dominion of sin to the reign of life under the power and lordship of Christ. To be 'in Christ' is to have been transferred into a new mode of existence, from sin to righteousness, from death to life – a life within the sphere of the power and lordship of Christ.[122] Paul describes the event of baptism – with immersion into water and the rising from it – as signifying a death 'with Christ' and a rising 'with Christ'. But, as Nygren pointed out, for Paul the significance of baptism cannot be limited to its symbolical representation.[123] It also points to something that *really happens*: 'we have been united' with

---

of the communities but, even more significantly, because it works with a limited understanding of Paul's concept of reconciliation as referring only to its vertical dimension.

120. A brief history of the interpretation of this chapter, particularly of the first fourteen verses, reveals the multifaceted and complex issues being raised vis-à-vis the theme of baptism as it relates to other important themes in Paul's theology. For an excellent presentation of the issues involved, see Hendrikus Boers, 'The Structure and Meaning of Romans 6:1–14', in *CBQ* 63 (2001), pp. 664–82; and Anders Petersen, 'Shedding New Light on Paul's Understanding of Baptism: a Ritual-Theoretical Approach to Romans 6', in *Studia Theologica* 52 (1998), pp. 3–28.

121. For a specific emphasis on the meaning of the death of Christ and the corporate dimension of being in Christ expressed through baptism in this passage, see Sorin Sabou, *Between Horror and Hope: Paul's Metaphorical Language of Death in Romans 6:1–11* (Milton Keynes: Paternoster, 2005). Based on several examples from the Septuagint and Josephus, Sabou argues that the metaphorical language about death and burial, in baptism, represents the union or the gathering of the one being buried with his/her family or dynasty. Accordingly, to be 'buried with Christ', in baptism, means to be incorporated into his family.

122. Commenting on the meaning of the expression 'in Christ' in Romans 6 and in Paul in general, John Ziesler equates this expression with 'in Spirit' and so 'being in the Spirit is in effect being in Christ, and *vice versa*' (*Paul's letter to the Romans* (London: Trinity, 1989), p. 163).

123. Nygren, *Romans*, pp. 233–34.

Christ 'in a death like his . . . and a resurrection like his' (6.5). Being united with Christ, in his body, whatever is true of him is true of those 'in Christ'.

In Rom. 6.1–11 Paul presents, both in a negative and in a positive way, two inherent implications of baptism into Christ's death, of this new reality of being 'in Christ'. First, because they are united with Christ in a death 'like his' and because through his death Jesus has conquered and has broken the power of sin, the believers have been taken out of the power of sin and have entered another dominion, that of Jesus Christ. Second, being buried with Christ into his death, their rising means a radically new way of life, a 'walk in newness of life' (6.4): the *mode* and *nature* of life in the new age inaugurated by Jesus' resurrection have been radically changed. Paul showed in the previous chapter that as humanity shared 'in Adam,' so now it shares or participates 'in Christ' in a real sense. And further, as God has made Christ the head of a new, true humanity, to participate 'in Christ' means to share in this new humanity, to live a life appropriate for the new age inaugurated by Christ's death and resurrection. Not being enslaved to sin any longer (6.6), they are free to act in accordance with their new master. Paul is resolute: οὕτως καὶ ὑμεῖς λογίζεσθε ἑαυτοὺς [εἶναι] νεκροὺς μὲν τῇ ἁμαρτίᾳ ζῶντας δὲ τῷ θεῷ ἐν Χριστῷ Ἰησοῦ, 'So you also must consider yourselves dead to sin and alive to God in Christ Jesus' (6.11). It is here that we can see most clearly that by retelling the story of Christ, Paul intends to show that those 'in Christ' share in the same story by the virtue of their union with Christ. The story of Christ is their own story in which they participate as ὑπηκούσατε δὲ ἐκ καρδίας, 'obedient from the heart' (6.17) and ἐδουλώθητε τῇ δικαιοσύνῃ, 'slaves of righteousness' (6.18). Christ is not only the basis for their new life but also the model.

The discussion on baptism in ch. 6 seems to play a crucial role in Paul's larger argument of the ethical seriousness of the Christian life under grace. Paul starts from the significance of baptism: it represents the dynamic of incorporation into Christ. For Paul, it is precisely the believer's participation 'in Christ' that represents the basis for Christian ethics –both as its possibility and necessity.[124] And, as Paul showed in Romans 5, this is all based on the continuing power of the grace of God, operating through Christ and the Spirit – grace which acts both to rescue people from their totally alienated situation of sin (5.1, 5.6–10) and also to guide and empower them to 'reign in life' (5.10, 5.17, 5.20–21). But it was this very abundance of grace, without the detailed specifications of the law for ethical living, which might

---

124. Such a thesis is put forward by Byrne ('Living Out', pp. 557–81), where he shows that there is an intrinsic link between righteousness and obtaining eternal life. Byrne states: 'The saving righteousness of God proclaimed in the letter (1:16–17) operates precisely in and through this link: through association with Christ by faith and baptism the Christian is drawn into the sphere of the righteousness of God; it is through living out or, rather, allowing Christ to live out this righteousness within oneself that eternal life is gained' (ibid., p. 558). Even though this position is very close to an 'ethical' view of righteousness, by pointing clearly to its christological substance and foundation Byrne is careful to avoid a sense of righteousness as a human accomplishment. But he is right to emphasize the crucial point Paul is making in Romans 6–8 concerning the living out of the righteousness of God, a dynamic participation of the believer in the life faith 'in Christ'.

have been troublesome to at least some of the members of the Roman Christian community. This we understand from Paul's rhetorical question at the beginning of ch. 6: 'What then are we to say? Should we continue in sin in order that grace may abound?' (6.1). So, Paul's argument in chs 6–8 is also responding to this possible 'ethical objection'[125] while building his case for the seriousness of ethical life for the believers and a complete break with a life of sin: 'How can we who died to sin go on living in it?' (6.2).

In a very important sense Paul's argument in ch. 6 is crucial not only for this section but also for the entire letter, because it is here that he describes in detail the very dynamic of the believer's incorporation 'in Christ' – which is at the heart of Paul's understanding of salvation and the new life. It is here that Paul shows how Christ's story is not his story alone but it is also the believers' story by the virtue of their being 'in Christ'. Their union and participation with Christ is expressed by Paul's characteristic use of 'συν-' references in ch. 6, vv. 4, 5, 6, 8. It is through baptism 'into Christ' that the believers were baptized 'into his death', were 'buried with him' (6.3, 6.4a), 'united with him in a death like his' (6.5), and the 'old self was crucified with him' (6.6). But also, through their participation in Christ's death, the believers share in the risen life of Christ (though it is not yet a total sharing, since there is still a future aspect to be played out, as vv. 5, 7 and 8 show). So now, through their union with Christ, they are able to live out their new existence 'in Christ': ἐν καινότητι ζωῆς περιπατήσωμεν, 'walk in the newness of life' (6.4c), μηκέτι δουλεύειν ἡμᾶς τῇ ἁμαρτίᾳ, 'no longer be enslaved to sin' (6.6), συζήσομεν αὐτῷ, 'live with him' (6.8). And this living with him is climactically described in vv. 10 and 11: as Christ 'lives to God' so the believers, who live 'in Christ', are to consider themselves 'dead to sin' and 'alive to God'. It is clear now that those who are 'in Christ' are becoming part of Christ's continuing life for God and so they are, in a sense, active participants in the same story of Christ, by their continuation into a similar life for God. It will be now also more clearly understood what this 'life for God' means for the believers since Paul's point about Christ's life to God in ch. 5 is fresh in their minds: it is a life of total submission and obedience to God, a life of self-giving for the other, a life of righteousness and reconciliation. A key feature of the life of Christ that Paul described in ch. 5 is his voluntary self-giving, in love, for others – a life that led to death on the cross, but was followed by resurrection, i.e., a new life given by God,

125. Ibid., p. 562. However, I believe Byrne is mistaken to see the entire section (6.1–8.13) as simply a 'long excursus' in which Paul addresses this question. Byrne is unable to see any other function of this section in the structure of chs 5–8 because he places everything within his designated theme for these chapters, namely 'the hope of salvation (eternal life)'. While the theme of hope is indeed vital for Paul's argument, it does not stand apart from other important themes that Paul deals with here, such as 'peace', 'reconciliation' and 'love'. A much better view which accommodates all these important topics, is that Paul addresses here the complex dynamic of salvation with its past, present and future dimensions, and the clear implications of the gospel for the new life 'in Christ' that the believers are now living. Rather than being an excursus, this is a key passage within the larger argument in which Paul is offering the dynamics of the believers incorporation 'in Christ' – without which his whole argument is groundless.

totally transforming the old existence into a new dimension. Through baptism, the believers are incorporated 'in Christ' and so in their new life they are animated by the same life of obedience to God manifested through a renunciation of their own desires and a concern for the needs of others.

And this is exactly what Paul is saying next: αραστήσατε ἑαυτοὺς τῷ θεῷ ὡσεὶ ἐκ νεκρῶν ζῶντας καὶ τὰ μέλη ὑμῶν ὅπλα δικαιοσύνης τῷ θεῷ, 'present yourselves to God as those who have been brought from death to life, and present your members to God as instruments of righteousness' (6.13b); χάρις δὲ τῷ θεῷ ὅτι . . . ὑπηκούσατε δὲ ἐκ καρδίας . . . ἐδουλώθητε τῇ δικαιοσύνῃ, 'But thanks be to God that you . . . have become obedient from the heart . . . and . . . slaves of righteousness' (6.17, 6.18). So, while the grace of God is the foundation for the new ethical life of the Christian (6.14), this does not mean a life devoid of ethical specifications. On the contrary, it is a life of obedience and righteousness – life which is totally defined and shaped by their union with Christ, in the power of the Spirit. Indeed, Paul concludes his argument, as one might expect, with the strong affirmation of the necessity and possibility of a new life of righteousness: ἁμαρτία γὰρ ὑμῶν οὐ κυριεύσει· οὐ γάρ ἐστε ὑπὸ νόμον ἀλλὰ ὑπὸ χάριν, 'For sin will have no dominion over you, since you are not under law but under grace' (6.14).

Another relevant point for our discussion is Paul's reference to the 'pattern of teaching' in v. 17: χάρις δὲ τῷ θεῷ ὅτι ἦτε δοῦλοι τῆς ἁμαρτίας ὑπηκούσατε δὲ ἐκ καρδίας εἰς ὃν παρεδόθητε τύπον διδαχῆς, 'Once you were slaves of sin, but thank God you have given whole-hearted obedience to the pattern of teaching to which you were introduced' (*NJB*). We remember that Paul sets the entire discussion of ch. 6, with its solid argument about baptism, in the context of death and resurrection of Christ (with his consequent enthronement in God's glory, as Lord). So the believer enters the new life in a pattern of dying and rising with Christ. Thus, it is very possible that the παρεδόθητε τύπον διδαχῆς, 'pattern of teaching' here refers to this pattern of dying and rising into which they were introduced and in which they live. Their life is now a life in accordance with this pattern of Christ and under his lordship: a dying to self, to sin, and a rising for life to God as 'slaves of righteousness' (6.18).

By thoroughly anchoring his argument in the work of Christ and the initiative of God, Paul is avoiding the danger of a 'self-righteous', human 'contribution' to the saving act of God. However, arguing from the perspective of the life 'in Christ' that the believers share in, Paul is able to show what this new life entails. Their 'obedience which leads to righteousness' (6.16) is a voluntary submission to Christ who, recalling 5.19, is defined by his obedience to God. As Christ's obedience made many righteous (5.19), so their obedience leads to righteousness (6.16). Not only are they freed from the necessity of sinning, but also it is the empowering presence of the Spirit that makes this new life possible and actual. Paul begins and ends the larger section of chs 5–8 with strong references to the indwelling of the Spirit – especially 8.9–11. Their 'walk in the newness of life' is simply a manifestation of their intimate union with Christ and of their participation 'in Christ' – a participation in the logical sequence of the same story of Christ, whereby the resurrected and living

Christ has 'drawn' the believers into his own story which they enact now for God, in the world.

5.5.3 *Romans 8*

We noticed earlier the narrative motifs in Romans 8, the close link made here between the story of the believers and that of Christ, and the strong emphasis on the role of the 'Spirit of life' in enabling the believers to be active participants in the story of redemption. In addition, we have pointed out that Paul is also engaged in a response to the dominant imperial ideology present in Rome and in the midst of which the new community of the believers have to live out their obedience to the gospel. We now look more closely at this chapter as we attempt to explore the way in which Paul interconnected some of his important themes in Romans.

The paragraph that begins ch. 8 is about Christian life 'in the Spirit'. Paul qualifies this 'life' in several ways. Negatively, it is contrasted with death and it is said that is something the law 'could not do' (v. 3). Positively, this is a gift from God, made possible through the life, death and resurrection of the Son of God who dealt with sin and death (vv. 3b–4). Finally, to be under God's life-giving and indwelling Spirit is to be free from sin and death (v. 2), and it is 'life' and 'peace' (v. 6), privileges beyond the reach of those 'in the flesh' (vv. 5–8) but enjoyed by those who are 'in Christ'/'in the Spirit' (vv. 9–11).[126]

At the centre of this new life is the work of God 'in Christ', specifically portrayed here as the condemnation of sin on the cross (v. 3) – a clear reference to the obedience of Christ in 5.12–21. One notes immediately the striking contrast that Paul makes here: the law could not give life because it was 'weakened by the flesh' while through the Spirit the believers are now able to live the new life. If there were questions among the Roman believers about the role of the law for their ethical life, and if some of them regarded it still as their guiding principle, Paul responds to that now in most categorical terms: not only is the law no longer a valid guide for the believers' life, but it never was able to give life! Those who are now 'in Christ' are under the influence of the Spirit and thus in a totally empowered position for an adequate life and free from the necessity of sinning.[127]

It is interesting that Paul should describe the believers' life 'in Christ' as an attitude – 'mind of the Spirit' – as meaning 'life and peace' (8.6). Indeed, when they were still 'in the flesh,' the result of their living was hostility to God (8.7) and ultimately death (8.6). 'Flesh' does not here refer to one's physical existence as something of a lower nature, but is a theological concept referring to the fallen human existence under the power of sin – resulting in a self-centred, self-sufficient, conflictual life.

---

126. Wright, *Romans*, pp. 573–90.

127. Byrne is thus right to summarize Paul's point in 8.1–11 as showing 'how the ethical "impossibility" under the Law, so graphically described in 7.14–25, is converted into an ethical "possibility" through the influence of the Spirit, attached by Paul to the Christ-event and ultimately traced back to the initiative of God' ('Living Out', p. 567).

The law could not offer much help and did not have the capacity to make possible a proper behaviour in term of relationships, as Paul has shown in 7.7–8.3. However, those who are 'in Christ', i.e., 'in the Spirit' (8.9), no longer live according to the flesh, and are enabled to fulfil 'the right requirement of the law' (8.4) and to live a life of peace according to the Spirit. This is all possible because of what Christ has done on their behalf, taking on sinful flesh – he has become sin so that they can become what he is and live the new life of righteousness.[128] We find this idea expressed in other places in Paul's letters. For instance, in 2 Cor. 5.21 we read: 'For our sake he made him to be sin who knew no sin, so that in him we might become the righteousness of God.' The continuing obedience that the believers are now able to live out is simply due to their incorporation and life 'in Christ', as Paul has just shown in 6.1–11. It is Christ's life manifesting his resurrected power, through the Spirit, in the life of the believers so that they are now able 'in Christ' to live 'for righteousness' (8.10), for a life of peace.

It is indeed ὅσοι γὰρ πνεύματι θεοῦ ἄγονται, 'all who are led by the Spirit of God' (8.14) – 'those who allow the Spirit to create in them a new righteousness'[129] – who are the οὗτοι υἱοὶ θεοῦ εἰσιν, 'sons of God' (8.14), τέκνα θεοῦ, 'children of God' (8.16) who will be κληρονόμοι μὲν θεοῦ, συγκληρονόμοι δὲ Χριστοῦ, 'heirs of God and fellow heirs with Christ' (8.17). And the 'inheritance' is now the entire new world of the redeemed creation. That Paul's understanding of being 'in Christ' and living 'by the Spirit' as 'sons of God' entails a full participation of the believers into a new life is confirmed by Paul's somewhat surprising ending in v. 17: εἴπερ συμπάσχομεν ἵνα καὶ συνδοξασθῶμεν, 'provided we suffer with him in order that we may also be glorified with him'.[130] While they are guaranteed a future divine glory in sharing with Christ over the entire creation, Paul stresses that the present life is a cruciform life, one of suffering in following the way of the cross, just as that of Jesus Christ was. Even though Paul does not present in one place all the characteristics of the cruciform life of Jesus, it is clear that if we look closely at all his allusions to Christ's story throughout the letter (3.24–25; 4.24–25; 5.1–11; 5.17–19; 6.3–5; 8.2–4; 8.32–39; 13.8–10; 14.7–20; 15.7) we gather that, for Paul, to live 'in Christ' is to follow in the same cruciform life, consisting of selflessness, suffering, and above all, self-giving love for others, all of which is ultimately motivated by a faithful obedience to God.

In the methodology section I referred to several authors who argue for the presence of a distinctive narrative of Christ throughout Paul's letter to the Romans, particularly

128. Morna D. Hooker, 'Interchange and Atonement', in *From Adam to Christ: Essays on Paul* (Cambridge: CUP, 1990), pp. 26–41.

129. Byrne, 'Living Out', p. 580.

130. The ultimate salvation is a total gift of God's grace and yet it is something that shapes or determines a radically different way of life. In his conclusion to his argument on the ethical nature of the 'righteousness' in Paul, Byrne notes that it is precisely Paul's insistence on the graciousness of God that makes him deal emphatically with the ethical seriousness of the Christian life. This should not be seen as something that the believers 'contribute' to their salvation, but as a gift of God into which they participate, 'in Christ' ('Living Out', p. 581).

to Douglas Campbell's insightful analysis of the narrative motifs in Romans 8. He argues that the structure of Romans 8 could be understood as a dynamic interplay of two complementary arguments describing the complex nature of Christian salvation: on the one hand, there is a movement from the past dominion of sin and death to a new, present reality in which the believers are enabled to act rightly, independently of Torah (8.1–13); on the other hand, it is the same dynamic construction which guarantees the believers' assured future inheritance and glorification (8.14–39).[131] The salvation 'in Christ' enables the believers to act rightly.

If in 5.1–11 Paul described the very costly way of how Christ has reconciled 'us', and in 6.1–11 he detailed the complex process by which we were taken from the power/dominion of sin to the dominion of Christ by our being incorporated 'into Christ', in ch. 8 Paul offers the implications of the same dynamic of salvation for the present life of the believer, in the midst of sufferings and difficulties – a life that Paul describes as a life 'in the Spirit'. It is significant to observe here that for Paul's argument the story of Christ, intermingled with the role of the Spirit, is crucial for the present life of the believers or for their own 'story'. In fact, we can even say that for Paul, Jesus' story is also the story of those who bear the image of the Son and so are his brothers (8.29). Indeed, this is another illuminating point that Campbell makes about Romans 8, namely that the Spirit incorporates Christians into the same story of Christ:

> Implicit throughout this argument – whether in its ethical emphasis or its concern with assurance – is the notion that the Spirit is creating Christians at the behest of the Father but using the template (literally 'image') of the Son (see 8:29). What the Son has done, and where he has been, is what Christians are currently being 'mapped onto' by the activity of the Spirit. This process is by no means complete; however, it is decisively inaugurated – it is this inauguration that delivers a greater ethical capacity, free from slavery to Sin and Flesh, and that also provides an unshakeable assurance concerning the future that is grounded ultimately in God's love.[132]

Not only are the new believers incorporated into the same story of Christ but they are implicitly active actors in this complex and developing story. Furthermore, this is also a story of the Father and of the Spirit.[133]

If we have in mind the powerful and dominating presence of the Roman imperial ideology, and the kind of impact such a rhetoric might have had on the believers, we may get a clue as to why Paul wants to emphasize that the story of Jesus (into which they are themselves incorporated) is part of the larger drama of God's own intervention in the world, meant to save and transform it. Indeed, the story within which the

---

131. See D. Campbell, 'The Story of Jesus', p. 103.
132. Ibid., p. 106.
133. Ibid., p. 107.

believers are now active actors is God's own story of identification and liberation; it is a story of a 'divine rescue mission', a story that challenges and overcomes the Roman ideology and its story of power, domination and idolatry. Writing on God's own involvement in this story, Campbell notes that 'at the heart of the story rests the claim *that God himself* is intimately involved in this transformation of the plight of humanity, in a benevolent and highly costly fashion . . . In this story the Father, his Spirit, and his Son are all involved in the transformation of humanity, from within a matrix of loving relationships'.[134] Paul wanted to encourage the believers to maintain their commitment and loyalty to Christ in the face of difficult circumstances as they live out their faith in the midst of a powerful and hostile empire. To that end, an appeal to the story of Christ – to his faithfulness and obedience in the face of suffering and death and, subsequently, to his vindication shown in his resurrection – would be exactly what would encourage and empower the believers as well as assure them of their own vindication and triumph over evil and death.

Even though we get a sense that it is with, or in, the Father that the 'origin' or the beginning of the story of Christ lies, it is clear that Paul's ultimate concern is not to speculate about this 'entry' point. Rather, Paul was much more interested in the significance of God's salvific intervention in the world in and through the person of Christ – particularly his cross and resurrection – and also in the critical importance that this aspect of the story of Christ has for the identity and life of the believers in the world. I think Campbell is right to point out that Paul's focus was on 'the *transformational* point, namely, the progress of Jesus through death to resurrection, since it is at this point that the Christian is reconstituted',[135] and that Paul would not insist on any aspect of the story of Christ, the beginning of the story included, that would 'distract the reader from the real object of that entry, which was transformational'.[136] That Paul's goal in using the story of Christ was transformational will become very clear when we consider his direct address in Romans 12–15, where he deals specifically with concrete issues of the everyday life of the believers in Rome.

5.6 *Summary and conclusion*

This chapter started with the observation that several significant features of Romans 5–8 (an abundance of references to Jesus Christ, a significant shift in metaphors and in personal pronouns, and serious ethical concerns) provide a reason strong enough to employ a narrative analysis of the text, with a focus on Paul's presentation of the story of Jesus and reconciliation, and within his overall purpose 'to bring about the obedience of faith'. The letter to the Romans was taken to represent both a mature presentation of the nature and implications of the gospel of Jesus Christ for Christian

134. Ibid., p. 119 (italics in the original).
135. Ibid., p. 118 (italics in the original).
136. Ibid., p. 119.

life, and a response to a specific historical situation in Rome. Thus, we concluded that the argument of Romans is to be understood, on the one hand, as an exposition of the inner logic of the gospel which contains both the decisive intervention of God to redeem the world, through the death and resurrection of Christ, and a distinctive way of life, a 'walk in the newness of life' for those who profess to be 'in Christ'. On the other hand, Paul's argument was determined by his response to a specific historical situation in the Roman Christian communities (such as differences, dissensions and even conflicts among various groups in respect of such issues as ethnicity, religious practices and relationships with both insiders and outsiders). I have shown that it was against such a complex backdrop that Paul's use of the rich symbolism of reconciliation in his letter to the Romans must be understood.

The analysis of the christological narrative motif revealed several significant features about the story of Christ that Paul emphasizes in Romans 5–8. We have seen that the most frequent reference is to the death of Christ on the cross as an expression both of God's love and faithfulness and of Christ's willing self-giving for humanity resulting in the reconciliation of the world. Paul goes to great lengths to emphasize both the greatness of the *fact* of reconciliation and *the manner* in which it was realized by Christ: by a costly sacrifice, by an initiative of love, by an offer extended to enemies. In this context we found that Paul particularly highlighted the faithfulness and obedience of Jesus. Further, Jesus' resurrection was crucial for Paul's argument, as he stressed Jesus' continuous and active mediatorial role in his resurrected existence as well as his lordship over the entire creation. We have seen that Paul's concern was also with the implications of the lordship of Christ for the life of each individual believer and of the Christian community in the world: he wanted the believers to understand that it was only by their faithful and obedient life in total allegiance to the true Lord of the world, Jesus Christ, that the lordship of Christ would be extended. Similarly, we have pointed out that this emphasis on the lordship of Christ was perceived as a counter-rhetoric to that of the Roman imperial ideology. Finally, we have seen that Paul's discussion of the complex dynamic of the incorporation of the believer 'in Christ', through baptism, signifies a real sharing and participation of the believers in the same story, as active participants. From this perspective, we concluded that Paul does not simply write about how God's reconciliation is achieved in Christ, as something done from afar, of which the believers are passive recipients. Rather, Paul includes the readers, their story, into the larger story of God's decisive reconciliation in Christ; they are themselves an *integral part* of this ongoing story of reconciliation.

The examination of the interchange of metaphors and personal pronouns beginning with Romans 5 has led to the conclusion that by these intentional moves Paul shows two things: (1) that reconciliation is an essential aspect of salvation, and that it contains an intrinsic social, horizontal dimension; and (2) that the vertical reconciliation with God is inseparable from the horizontal aspect, as two dimensions of the same reality. The message Paul wanted to get across was clear: the unity, reconciliation, harmony and acceptance among the believers in Rome was an intrinsic part of the very gospel of reconciliation they profess. Paul's intention was to show that the gospel they have received has clear and concrete implications for the believers' everyday life. To be justified and reconciled with God is to be reconciled and at peace with one's sister and brother, to be at peace with 'the other'. Furthermore, interpreting these changes in light of the abundance of references to Jesus Christ throughout Romans 5–8, and in light of the importance of the ethical dimension permeating this section, we concluded that Paul intended his readers to understand his argument in these chapters in close connection with the story of Christ and with their new status and responsibilities resulting from their being 'in Christ'. The reality of believers' reconciliation with God, the new identity they now share as reconciled people 'in Christ', is the basis for their sharing in, or living out, a reconciled life with the others – an engagement in reconciling practices of peace, unity, welcome and love. Christ's work of reconciliation is also the paradigm for their life. We have shown that Paul's shift in the personal pronouns supported that conclusion. By using the 'we' and 'us' pronouns in a context in which he is retelling the story of Jesus, Paul included himself and the believers in Rome in the same story of Christ, and prompted them to live out the 'story of Christ' as active actors in an ongoing story of God's reconciliation of the world in Christ.

Our textual analysis of Romans 5–8 revealed several important aspects of reconciliation. The peace/reconciliation that the believers have with God is a grace, a free gift they have received from God, via Christ's death, while they were enemies. But by placing the discussion from the very beginning in a context in which Paul makes the claim of living in a way appropriate with 'this grace' in which they have taken their stand (5.2), the emphasis is also on living out that peace with joy, hope and love whatever the circumstances. Particularly relevant for the community in Rome is that the peace/reconciliation with God is to be reflected by their own unity as a new community 'in Christ' as well as by a reconciling life towards others modelled on the faithfulness and obedience of Christ. We found this intention of Paul confirmed by the close and significant connection he makes between the death of Christ, love and reconciliation, whereby Jesus' personal participation in the drama of reconciliation in his death 'for us', understood as a surrender of love, was used by Paul as an appeal for deliberate action. Indeed, by sharing an intimate union with Christ and his story, believers are reminded that they continue to participate in the same story. To be sure, the practice of reconciliation is made possible and real through the continuous presence of the resurrected Christ, by the Spirit. We concluded that an adequate treatment of reconciliation in Romans will always maintain together the two inseparable dimensions of the reality of salvation: the event of God's reconciliation of people to him, through Christ, and the social embodiment of this reality in the everyday life of those who belong 'to Christ'.

Significantly, our study revealed that it was precisely Paul's appeal to the story of Christ that enabled him to address and hold together the two aspects of reconciliation: God's reconciling initiative by the death of Christ on the cross, as the result of his obedient life to God (5.19), becomes not only the very act and pronouncement of reconciliation of the humanity with God but also the ground and model for reconciling relationships among people. Christ's story is not only his own story but it includes the story of believers. By virtue of their participation in Christ, believers can live rightly and be active actors as the same story of Christ is being unfolded in their midst. Paul's description of the contrast with Adam (5.12–19) illustrated the new solidarity between believers and Christ, a solidarity unto righteousness and life for all those who are 'in Christ' and share now into his obedience. Indeed, the logic of the story requires a particular way of living, a 'walk in the newness of life' (6.4), meaning concretely a life of peace, love, welcome, reconciliation and hope in the midst of suffering and difficulties. Indeed, as Paul anticipates his discussion in the later chapters, such a stance is to be manifested both within the community of believers and towards outsiders, including the governing authorities of the Roman Empire.

The mechanism of this incorporation 'in Christ' with all its implications was explicitly described by Paul in ch. 6 under the rubric of baptism. By their dying-and-rising with Christ, believers have been transferred into a new eschatological reality 'in Christ' which is a real transfer into a new mode of existence, from sin to righteousness, from death to life – a life within the sphere of the power and lordship of Christ. Being buried with Christ into his death, their rising means that the *mode* and *nature* of their present life in the new age inaugurated by Jesus' resurrection have been radically changed. To participate 'in Christ' means to share in his new and true humanity, to live a life appropriate for the new age inaugurated by the resurrection of Christ. We concluded that Paul retold the story of Christ with the purpose of showing that those 'in Christ' share in his story, their new life being a manifestation of their intimate union with Christ. In Romans 8 Paul offered further elaborations on the transformational aspect of the story of Christ for the present life of believers in the midst of sufferings and difficulties – a life that Paul described as life 'in the Spirit'. Paul's appeal to the story of Christ – to his faithfulness and obedience in the face of suffering and death and, subsequently, to his vindication shown in his resurrection – would be exactly what would encourage and empower the believers, as well as assure them of their own vindication and triumph over evil and death.

Finally, we have shown that Paul understands reconciliation as one comprehensive reality encompassing reconciliation with God and with one another. For him, to be reconciled with God is to live out that reconciliation; to be 'in Christ' is to live the new life in the Spirit. The social, horizontal dimension of reconciliation is an intrinsic aspect of one's reconciliation with God.

6

THE SOCIAL MEANING OF RECONCILIATION IN PAUL (II):
PRACTICES OF RECONCILIATION IN ROMANS 12–15

6.1 *Introduction*

Throughout the previous chapter we highlighted the way in which some of the things Paul wrote were intended to prepare the readers for a more detailed discussion in the later chapters. He has anticipated most of the points he is now ready to treat more fully, as he has already prepared their theological/christological basis. This chapter argues that Paul's exhortations in chs 12–15 are concrete elaborations of the theme of reconciliation, which he has so thoroughly grounded in the story of Christ in Romans 5–8. It will show that the overwhelming emphasis on 'unity', 'acceptance', 'love', 'peace', and 'welcome' illustrates Paul's rich symbolism of reconciliation which is now given expression in the form of 'reconciling practices' which Paul urges his readers to live out – practices that are integral to the nature of the gospel and to their being 'in Christ'. Even though at first glance one does not see a close association between these practices and the story of Christ, such as we have seen in the previous section, I hope to show that the practices of reconciliation Paul presents are also anchored in and presuppose the story of Christ both as the ground and the paradigm for their reconciling way of life.

Further, it will be argued that reconciliation, as an integral part of the gospel, is something that Paul wants to see embodied in the everyday life of the believers. It will be only as the believers manifest such practices that the truth of the gospel, which Paul has presented in the argument of the letter so far, will receive the final confirmation. As a mission theologian, Paul has no doubt that to respond to the gospel of Jesus Christ is to acknowledge and accept the truth it proclaims *and* to live it out in everyday life. Thus, in Romans 12–15 Paul explicates in concrete ways what reconciliation with God means for the believers' everyday life within and outside their own community; in other words, what the social significance of reconciliation is. However, before we go to detailed analysis of that section of Romans, we will offer a short presentation of the main points of Romans 9–11 and highlight several features of this passage that are relevant to our overall argument.

6.2 *Jews, Gentiles and reconciliation: Romans 9–11*

The question of the relationship between Jews and Gentiles, between the ethnic Israel and the great new redefinition of God's people in the light of the story of Christ, represented one of Paul's fundamental concerns throughout his life and ministry and is evident in his dynamic theologizing in his letters. The very same question has become in recent decades a major theological concern for the contemporary Christian churches.

Owing to the fact that Romans 9–11 represents the most sustained consideration of this issue in the New Testament, the passage has received distinctive attention in recent scholarship, becoming the locus of significant enquiry and debate.[1] Its thematic unity within the letter have caused chs 9–11 to be considered not simply as an integral part of the letter but also a necessary element of Paul's overall argument in Romans[2] – not least because of the questions of self-definition and identity of the new community 'in Christ', and of 'reconciliation'. In this section, Paul shows the working out of God's longstanding plan of bringing together the Jews and Gentiles in one family, in Christ, as a fulfilment of his promise of dealing with the world. This reconciliation was to be embodied in the life of the redefined people of God, the new community of Jews-and-Gentiles family created 'in Christ', and, as such, carried out in the world as a proclamation and embodiment of the gospel.

Given the limitations of space and the expressed different focus of the present work on Romans 5–8 and 12–15, it is impossible for me to offer here a comprehensive exegesis of this complex passage.[3] However, because Paul's arguments in Romans

---

1.   See, for example, the entire issues of several significant journals devoted to this question: *Interpretation* 39(4) (1985), pp. 339–413; *Ex auditu* 4 (1988), pp. 1–123; *Princeton Seminary Bulletin* 11 Suppl. (1990), pp. 1–139. Also, some recent books and studies devoted to the question of Israel and the church, to the Jewish-Christian relations: Zvi Gitelman *et al.* (eds), *New Jewish identities: contemporary Europe and beyond* (Budapest/New York: Central European University Press, 2002); Michael A. Signer, (ed.), *Memory and History in Christianity and Judaism* (Notre Dame: University of Notre Dame Press, 2001); John K. Roth *et al.* (eds), *Remembering for the Future: the Holocaust in an Age of Genocide* (Hampshire, NY: Palgrave, 2001); Tikva S. Frymer-Kensky *et al.* (eds), *Christianity in Jewish Terms* (Boulder, CO: Westview, 2000); Graham N. Stanton and Gedaliahu Stroumsa (eds), *Tolerance and Intolerance in Early Judaism and Christianity* (New York: CUP, 1998); Hubert G. Locke and Marcia Sachs Littell (eds), *Holocaust and Church Struggle: Religion, Power and the Politics of Resistance* (Lanham: University Press of America, 1996); Marvin Perry and Frederick M. Schweitzer (eds), *Jewish-Christian Encounters over the Centuries: Symbiosis, Prejudice, Holocaust, Dialogue* (Frankfurt am Main: Peter Lang, 1994); Yehuda Bauer *et al.*, eds. *Remembering for the Future, Vol. 1: Jews & Christians During and After the Holocaust* (Oxford: Pergamon, 1989a); and *Remembering for the Future, Vol. 2: The Impact of the Holocaust on the Contemporary World* (Oxford: Pergamon, 1989b); Manfred Gorg *et al.*, *Christen und Juden im Gesprach: Bilanz nach 40 Jahren Staat* (Regensburg: Friedrich Pustet, 1989); John G. Gager, *The Origins of Anti-Semitism: Attitudes Towards Judaism in Pagan and Christian Antiquity* (New York: OUP, 1983); Calvin L. Porter, 'A New Paradigm for Reading Romans: Dialogue Between Christians and Jews', *Encounter* 39 (1978), pp. 257–72.

2.   Byrne, *Romans*, pp. 281–82ff.

3.   It is not my view that Romans 9–11 is less important in the overall argument of Romans. On the contrary, I believe, this section is an integral and vital part of Paul's overall argument in the letter,

9–11 regarding the inclusion of Israel and the reconciling nature of the gospel would enhance my case for the social and ethical implications of reconciliation, I will point out several important features found in this passage, especially as they have important implications for inter-religious as well as intra-religious relations in the contemporary world. Of course, for an exhaustive treatment of this theme, further work needs to be done on each of the features presented below.

PAUL'S REDEFINITION OF GOD'S PEOPLE AND THE REDEMPTION OF THE WORLD

Romans 9–11 is one of the most elaborate statements of Paul's redefinition of 'election', of the 'people of God', within the framework of the 'covenant', in the context of God's purposes for the redemption of the world. In the earlier chapter of Romans, Paul addresses the question of the election of Israel and has shown that, as a result of the unfaithfulness of Israel and the threat it meant for God's redemptive purposes, God had decisively acted in the Messiah and in this way had provided a solution to the problem of Israel while, at the same time, he had remained faithful to his covenant (Romans 3.1–9). Paul explained that Israel's election was not for its own sake but, ultimately, for the sake of the world,[4] i.e., that God will redeem the world through Israel. Israel's disobedience and unfaithfulness to God's plan did not invalidate either God's plan or his faithfulness. Rather, through the faith(fullness) of Christ, the Messiah, God has worked out and accomplished the redemption of the world, by forming a new community as God's people, made up of Jews and Gentiles who believe (Romans 3.21–26). It is exactly through this *good news*, the reaching of the gospel to both Jews and Gentiles, that God shows his righteousness.[5] Paul's long reference, in Romans 4, to Abraham as the father of all those who believe is his best way of affirming Israel's mission in relation to the world. For Paul it was crucially important to emphasize that this new community is not simply 'saved' but that they are called to be God's people *for* the world's redemption: they are a people in the midst of whom Christ lives and through whom he continues the story of God's reconciliation and redemption of the world. Here Paul makes a similar point to the one he makes in connection with reconciliation: it is not something one receives

---

as are the other sections of chs 1–4, 5–8 and 12–15. I take the view that none of these sections is more important than the other and that there are strong and direct links which Paul makes between these large parts of his coherent argument in Romans. In his important study on the use of Isaiah in Romans, Wagner demonstrates, for example, very clear links between Romans 9–11 and 14–15, thus strengthening the view on the coherence of Romans. See J. R. Wagner, *Heralds of Good News: Isaiah and Paul in Concert in the Letter to the Romans* (Leiden: Brill 2003).

4.   For a different, more nuanced, position regarding the election of Israel, see W. Campbell, *Paul and the Creation of Christian Identity* (pp. 144–46) who, following Harrink ('Paul and Israel: An Apocalyptic Reading'), argues that Israel was not brought into being for primarily a redemptive purpose.

5.   See Robert Jewett (*Romans: A Commentary* (Minneapolis: Fortress, 2007)), who entitles the section of Romans 9–11 as 'The Triumph of Divine Righteousness in the Gospel's Mission to Israel and the Gentiles', pp. 555ff.

from God *only* for one's own benefit (though it is also this), but in order to share and extend it to the wider world.

THE ALL-INCLUSIVE NATURE OF THE FAMILY OF GOD

The insistence on the inclusion of the Gentiles as full members of God's people, coupled with the rejection of the gospel by some Jews, and Paul's climax in ch. 8 on the glorious destiny of those 'in Christ', might have created the impression among the Gentile Christians that they were now in a better/superior position than are the Jews and so they might have been tempted to consider the Jews completely excluded from God's plan and from this wonderful destiny. That is why Paul now turns (Romans 9–11) to address specifically this question and to correct the misunderstanding. His position is clear: the gospel of reconciliation he has presented is 'inclusive' for all – not simply for the Gentiles – it is equally 'inclusive' with respect to the Jewish people. In other words, the gospel of reconciliation is open to all, and includes all peoples and nations. In fact, Paul's concern throughout chs 9–11 is not to show that the Christian community has *replaced* the Jewish community as the people of God, but rather to emphasize the *unity* of both Jews and Gentiles, their coming *together* into one family. Here lies Paul's emphasis.

Indeed, one of the most amazing things about this Jews-and-Gentiles community is that it expresses the greatest statement of inclusiveness of the one family of God made up of Jews and Gentiles without any distinction – in the sense that whatever their previous status, they have now both equal standing before God. The coming together of Jews and Gentiles, their reconciliation, is the greatest proof of the new creation of God, of the truthfulness of the gospel, and an undeniable sign of hope for the redemption of the world.[6] That is why Romans 9–11 is an essential part of Paul's overall argument in the letter, particularly relevant for our question on the social significance of reconciliation. What Paul is trying to accomplish in this section is to correct a false theological and ethical 'superiority' presumption that Gentile Christians had vis-à-vis Jewish Christians, in particular, and Jews in general. Certainly, reconciliation would be difficult if not impossible when a person or group claims any superiority or privilege based on their distinct identity. This was the mistake that the Jewish people had made, being proud and arrogant about their special status before God and their special privileges, thus limiting God's intended purposes for the wider world, for the entire world. God's redemption/reconciliation is inclusive and does not exclude anyone. This new family of God should not boast about the condition of the Jews and think that God has excluded Israel. The way Paul uses the remnant motif in ch. 11 illustrates well the fact that God has not rejected Israel (11.1–6) and points to the final salvation of Israel (11.7–16). This motif enables Paul in vv. 17–24 to maintain both the identity and priority of Israel while affirming the equal salvation for the Gentiles. However, as Wright correctly points out, what Paul is saying is not that the unbelieving Jews

---

6.   See Wright, *Fresh Perspective*, pp. 118ff.

are all right as they are, but rather that they are not hindered 'from coming back into the family, their own family, that has been renewed by the gospel, and from which they are currently separated because it is marked out solely by faith, and they are currently in "unbelief".'[7] Thus, the christocentric nature of Israel's salvation at the end of history (11.25–27) is essential to Paul's argument.[8] To be sure, the eventual acceptance of Jesus as Messiah by the Jews is not equivalent to their cultural and theological annihilation but involves, as Paul's argument in Romans 14–15 indicates, a preservation of 'distinctive features of racial, cultural, and theological self-identity within the context of mutual acceptance'.[9]

GOOD NEWS FOR *ALL*

It is important to notice another distinctive element highlighted in this section. Paul's emphasis is not on the small number of the elect but rather on the will of God for the salvation of '*all* Israel' and 'the *full number* of the Gentiles' (11.25–26), on God's mercy 'upon *all*' (11.32), on God's plan for 'the reconciliation of the *world*' (11.15). The only difference that Paul plays out between Israel and the church is the distinction between the first and the last to fulfil God's election – election to be shared by both Jews and Gentiles.[10]

Up to this point in the letter, Paul has described in detail the complex dynamic of reconciliation; i.e., how from a state of alienation and hopelessness in which both Gentiles and Jews shared, God has taken the initiative and addressed the situation, through Jesus Christ, and made possible a new kind of solidarity for all – one of grace, righteousness and reconciliation. All these privileges and promises of God which belonged initially only to Israel are now available also to Gentiles who are thus part of this new family of those who are 'in Christ'. What is somewhat surprising is that this fact is accomplished against expectations – not for the Jews first and then for the Gentiles, but the other way around, and only after a time of rejection for Israel. This was not a mistake, says Paul, but rather God's plan recorded in the Scriptures and that is why he is using the Scriptures extensively to prove his point about the inclusion of the Gentiles, about the initial rejection and subsequent inclusion of Israel. However, even though there is a great reversal as to the order of this fulfilment, and so the first is to be last and the last first, there is ultimately good news for all. After rendering both Jews and Gentiles as unbelieving and disobedient people, Paul stresses that God

---

7.   Ibid., p. 126. Wright makes another very important point, namely that, from this perspective, the very christocentric passage of Romans 10.1–13 is crucial for the entire argument of chs 9–11. Thus, when Paul says in 11.26 that 'all Israel shall be saved', it is a clear echo of 10.13 which reads: 'all who call on the name of the Lord shall be saved' – which is, in its turn, offered as the solution to Paul's prayer about the salvation of currently unbelieving Jews in 10.1. Indeed, Paul makes that explicit in 11.23 saying that they can be grafted in 'if they do not persist in their unbelief'.

8.   Dan G. Johnson, 'The Structure and Meaning of Romans 11' *CBQ* 46 (1984), pp. 91–103.

9.   Robert Jewett, 'The Law and the Coexistence of Jews and Gentiles in Romans', *Interpretation* 39(4) (1985), pp. 341–56 (354).

10.   Shirley C. Guthrie, 'Romans 11:25–32', *Interpretation* 38(3) (1984), pp. 286–91.

has done so in order to show his mercy toward 'all': 'Both the first and the last, the last and the first, live by the good news of the election of those who deserve rejection, the good news of the God who "justifies" the ungodly (4.5).'[11]

This is indeed relevant for the social dimension of reconciliation in that it shows how the message of the gospel is all-inclusive. Paul's anxious effort to show that both Gentiles and Jews are reconciled in one new people of God, is a clear indication of both the impartiality of God, and the need for a similar '"inclusive" pattern that ought to be reflected in ongoing Christian community life'[12] as Paul will show in detail in chs 12–15. Paul's vision of the eventual inclusion of Israel in a predominantly Gentile community in Rome enforces such a pattern of an inclusive, reconciling life.

A MESSAGE OF GRATITUDE AND HOPE

Paul's argument in chs 9–11 not only annihilates any motives of superiority on the side of the Gentile Christians against the Jews but, much more, encourages an attitude of gratitude both to the Jews, as salvation comes 'from the Jews', and to God, who remains faithful to the sinners and the disobedient, and who seeks to mend and reconcile rather than destroy and exclude. Further, a central aspect regarding the Jewish–Christian relationship in chs 9–11 is the message of hope that ultimately comes across in the passage. Not simply hope for Israel and the church as such but a larger hope, for the entire world: for the new creation of God, for the coming of his kingdom, for the true humanity of which the new community of Jews-and-Gentiles is already an undeniable sign. This comes somewhat naturally in Paul's argument if we think back to his great eschatological vision of the redemption of creation with which he finished ch. 8. It is within this larger vision of hope for the reconciliation of the world, and with the constant awareness of their own totally undeserved acceptance into the family of God, that Christians will be enabled to act for reconciliation towards the Jews, in particular, and towards all. And this is, indeed, the pattern that they are admonished to follow in their everyday lives, in their dealings with one another and with all. This is exactly what Paul is trying to accomplish in the last major section of his letter, chs 12–15 where he elaborates specifically what it means to live as a reconciled and reconciling community in the world. To this task we turn now in the following section as we engage in a closer analysis of the symbolism of reconciliation expressed by Paul in such words as 'unity', 'acceptance', 'love', 'peace', and 'welcome'.

---

11. Guthrie, 'Romans 11:25–32', p. 288. Karl Barth (*Church Dogmatics* II/2, pp. 195–96) captures well this truth of God's mercy extended to all: 'Everywhere we begin with human disobedience and end with divine mercy . . . everywhere for all . . . the election of the God whose majesty consists in the fact that he is merciful.'

12. Byrne, *Romans*, p. 283.

6.3 *The argument of Romans 12.1–15.13*

It is generally accepted that Rom. 12.1 marks the beginning of a larger, ethical section in which Paul draws out the implications of his previous theological presentation of the gospel. If in the past this section of the letter was somewhat neglected, recent scholarship on Romans regards it as crucial for the understanding of Paul's letter. It was particularly the argument of chs 14–15 that contributed the most to an understanding of the letter as being written to address a real situation in Rome. It is partially due to the contextual nature of the letter that the material in these chapters is not to be taken as a comprehensive and systematic exposition of Paul's ethical system or of Christian ethics in general.[13]

Traditionally, Romans 12–15 was understood to represent the ethical imperative that grows out of the gospel of grace, of the 'mercies of God' which Paul has presented in the first eleven chapters. The strong 'therefore' with which Paul begins ch. 12 has been taken as the link between the indicative of the gospel (chs 1–11) and the imperative of obedience prescribed (chs 12–15). Thus, the last part of the letter has been seen, more or less, as an 'appendix' of ethical instructions added to the central, 'theological' part which Paul developed in the previous chapters. However, such a strict distinction between indicative and imperative, between theology and ethics in Romans, and in Paul's letters in general, has been exposed as inadequate, beginning with Victor Furnish's influential study.[14] Furnish has proven that Paul did not operate with a dichotomist thinking and that ethics was integral to his theology and vice versa. The role of this section will be clearer if we recall the point we made earlier that there were various charges brought against Paul according to which his gospel of grace undermined ethical conduct. Paul is trying to respond to those allegations throughout the letter, beginning with 3.8 and then again in 6.1 and 6.15. The same is true of 8.1–8 and even 11.30–32.[15] Similarly, we know that there was some degree of disunity within and among the Christian communities in Rome as well as confusion vis-à-vis the believers' relationship to outsiders, including the governing authorities, who probably manifested retaliatory and anarchic tendencies. Paul clearly understood the situation as a betrayal of the gospel. Seen from this perspective, chs 12–15 represent Paul's attempt to correct possible misunderstandings and distortions of the gospel, and in his appeal for 'unity in the church, and stability in society',[16]

---

13. As we have seen, contemporary studies of Romans have emphasized the contextual nature of Paul's letter and have rejected the view that this is a systematic treatment of either Paul's theology or ethics. See especially Wedderburn, *The Reasons for Romans*; Donfried (ed.), *The Romans Debate*; James C. Miller, 'The Romans Debate: 1991–2001', pp. 306–49; Brendan Byrne, 'Interpreting Romans: the New Perspective and Beyond', *Interpretation* 58(3) (2004), pp. 241–52.

14. Furnish, *Theology and Ethics in Paul*.

15. Calvin J. Roetzel makes a good point about the 'juxtaposition of disobedience and grace in 11:30–32 which serves as the threshold over which the reader crosses into chapters 12–15', in 'Sacrifice in Romans 12–15', *Word & World* 6 (1986), pp. 410–19 (414).

16. Philip H. Towner, 'Romans 13:1–7 and Paul's Missiological Perspective: A Call to Political

he explicates the inherent implications of the gospel. Thus, Romans 12–15 is not an 'ethical appendix' to his theological argument but rather a further elaboration of the gospel Paul presented in the previous chapters. More specifically, this section represents a working out of the implications of being 'in Christ', which commits those who respond to the gospel to a transformed and renewed life in obedience to Christ. In other words, indicative and imperative are intrinsically related. Or, as Moo puts it, '"[i]ndicative" and "imperative" do not succeed each other as two distinct stages in Christian experience, but are two sides of the same coin'.[17]

Because Paul's ethic has a fundamental theological/christological basis,[18] the ethical responsibility to which he turns now is a constitutive and necessary element of his gospel.[19] As we pointed out earlier, God's intervention to redeem the world in the Christ-event not only represents the basis for justification and reconciliation, but it also gives a particular shape to the lives of those who have been reconciled. They are now 'in Christ' and so through their death and rising with Christ, at baptism, they now share in the reality of a new life. Christ, as their Lord, is their ultimate point of reference, to whom they give total allegiance in a new life of obedience and righteousness.[20] Indeed, as Paul established in Romans 5–6, he again makes clear in this larger ethical section that the love of God manifested in Christ is both the basis of one's reconciliation and the criterion for conduct for those who are 'in Christ' (12.5). Thus, Paul begins in 12.1–2 with an 'appeal . . . by the mercies of God' pointing back clearly to previous chapters where he described the love/grace/mercy of God manifested in God's act of redemption in Christ in all its complexity, the event of reconciliation included. He makes a thematic link with his previous discussion on the believers being gathered 'in Christ', both at the beginning of the section (12.5) and at the end where we find a strong sequence of references to Christ in 15.2–3, and vv. 7–13. With these strong allusions to Christ, which bracket this section, Paul intends that the readers will understand the specifics of Christian life in close correlation with Christ, from whom they constantly draw, as both source and form.[21] These chapters are therefore an integral part of the overall structure and argument of the letter. Through them Paul wants to communicate to the believers in Rome that the appropriate conduct he demands is rooted in God's mercy[22] and that his concrete

---

Quietism or Transformation?', in Soderlund and Wright (eds), *Romans and the People of God*, pp. 153–55.

   17. Moo, *Romans*, p. 745.

   18. Schrage, *The Ethics of the New Testament*, pp. 164–86.

   19. Furnish, *Theology*, p. 225. Wright also notes that 'Paul's theology is always ethical, and his ethics are always theological' (*Romans*, p. 702).

   20. Schrage, *Ethics*, p. 172.

   21. See ibid., p. 174.

   22. This, of course, must be understood within the larger framework of δικαιοσύνη θεοῦ which Paul defends throughout the letter, as Wilson correctly points out. (Walter T. Wilson, *Love without Pretence: Romans 12.9–21 and Hellenistic-Jewish Wisdom Literature* (WUNT, 2/46; Tubingen: Mohr Siebeck, 1991), p. 128.)

exhortations follow from and are closely interrelated with his previous argument of the story of Christ and the believers' incorporation into it.

There is a possible objection to the scenario just described, namely that in Romans 12–15 Paul does not highlight Christ or his work as there are no direct references in the first two chapters to either his death or resurrection. Furthermore, even though Paul's conclusion in 15.7–13 seems to point to the larger eschatological narrative referring to God's work, there are no concrete references to the various christological motifs that we found in the previous section. In response to this we should remember the point made earlier that for Paul chs 12–15 and 1–11 are not two separate sets of arguments but two parts of a single complex theological and ethical argument about the gospel, placed within a new eschatological framework. Indeed, a significant aspect of the general exhortations in Romans 12–13 is the eschatological dimension of the Christian life, framed by a specific introduction (12.1–2) and conclusion (13.11–14),[23] and preceded by Paul's appeal based on the presupposition of the believer's transfer from 'this age' of sin and its dominion to the 'new age' of salvation under the dominion of Christ – which Paul elaborated in detail in chs 5–8.[24] Paul's appeal to the believers in Rome is for them to live lives transformed by the gospel, in accordance with their new position 'in Christ', and with the good, acceptable and perfect will of God for humanity (12.2). And this is exactly what Paul asked them earlier, for example in 6.4, to 'walk in the newness of life' and to 'become slaves of righteousness' (6.18). Similarly, in 8.4 he stated boldly that Christ died 'so that the just requirement of the law might be fulfilled in us, who walk not according to the flesh but according to the Spirit'. Paul picks up the thought of 8.4 in the larger section of chs 12–15 and identifies the fulfilment of the law, of God's will, with loving one's neighbour.[25] For instance, we read in 13.8–10 that love is the fulfilling of the law. Actions having as motivation the love for the other, expressed in concrete and tangible manifestations, represent for Paul a life lived 'according to the Spirit', described explicitly in Romans 8 and again here, in various ways throughout 12.1–15.13. Further, the mutuality of service, welcome, and genuine love, for which Paul calls in this section, is solidly grounded in the lordship and servant-like example of Christ (ch. 14 vv. 9, 4, 6, 8, 10–12 and ch. 15 vv. 3–4, 7, 8; and 14.3). These examples illustrate the fact that Paul's appeal is based on the christological premise he established in chs 5–8; namely, on the newness of life that the believers experience with their transfer into the eschatological reality of being 'in Christ'. Thus, after he has presented all the crucial narrative elements of the gospel centred in Christ in the first part of the letter, he presupposes them in the second part. So, if in the first eleven chapters Paul has presented the dynamic process of salvation, in this part he focuses on the implications of the gospel. While he does not need to repeat himself, he definitely presupposes

---

23. Furnish, *Theology*, pp. 215–16.

24. Moo, *Romans*, p. 747.

25. Joseph Fitzmyer, *Spiritual Exercises Based on Paul's Epistle to the Romans* (Grand Rapids: Eerdmans, 2004), p. 197.

every single aspect of the previous argument,[26] as our analysis of specific texts will illustrate in more detail.

As for the structure of these last chapters, it is generally agreed that there are here two sets of exhortations, one more general in nature (chs 12–13), and the other referring to specific issues facing the churches in Rome (chs 14–15).[27]

6.4 *Practices of reconciliation in Romans 12–13*

In these chapters Paul addresses in more concrete terms the issues of how one should relate to fellow believers within the community (12.1–13) and to outsiders (12.14–13.7). On the one hand, Paul calls the believers to accept one another and express their love in mutual service as is appropriate for the members of 'one body in Christ' (12.3–8). On the other hand, they are to behave accordingly towards outsiders: to bless the persecutors, to resist vengeance, to live peaceably with all, and to overcome evil by doing good. Significantly, there is no double standard, one for behaviour within the community and one for life in the public arena; both dimensions of Christian living form an integral whole in Paul's mind.[28] He emphasizes a specific, transforming and loving attitude towards everyone, including enemies. Indeed, the tone of the whole chapter is given by Paul's summary statement, in the first two verses (12.1–2), about the nature of their new communal life: a life of self-giving love in service of others.[29] With these preliminary remarks we are now ready for a closer look at his argument.

6.4.1 *Romans 12*

Paul begins with an introductory assertion (vv. 1–2), and after a discussion of the identity of the Christian community as the body of Christ (vv. 3–8), he devotes most of the chapter to 'genuine love' as the essential moral imperative for conduct (vv. 9–21). Paul opens the discussion in ch. 12 with a foundational and programmatic statement:

Παρακαλῶ οὖν ὑμᾶς, ἀδελφοί, διὰ τῶν οἰκτιρμῶν τοῦ θεοῦ παραστῆσαι τὰ σώματα ὑμῶν θυσίαν ζῶσαν ἁγίαν εὐάρεστον τῷ θεῷ, τὴν λογικὴν λατρείαν ὑμῶν· καὶ μὴ συσχηματίζεσθε τῷ αἰῶνι τούτῳ, ἀλλὰ μεταμορφοῦσθε τῇ ἀνακαινώσει τοῦ νοὸς εἰς τὸ δοκιμάζειν ὑμᾶς τί τὸ θέλημα τοῦ θεοῦ, τὸ ἀγαθὸν καὶ εὐάρεστον καὶ τέλειον,

I appeal to you therefore, brothers and sisters, by the mercies of God, to present your bodies

---

26. Wright, *Romans*, 702.

27. So, for example, Fitzmyer, *Romans*, pp. 637ff.; Byrne, *Romans*, p. 362; Käsemann, *Romans*, p. 323; Moo, *Romans*, p. 747; Wright, *Romans*, p. 701.

28. Towner, 'Romans', pp. 153–54.

29. Commenting on the nature of the believers' new life, Ziesler writes: 'it is living as a perpetual sacrifice of oneself to God, being inwardly changed so as to belong to the new reality, and so as to exist solely for God and his will' (Ziesler, *Romans*, p. 290).

as a living sacrifice, holy and acceptable to God, which is your spiritual worship. Do not be conformed to this world, but be transformed by the renewing of your minds, so that you may discern what is the will of God – what is good and acceptable and perfect (Rom. 12.1–2).

The opening of vv. 1–2 offers a strong indication that Paul's appeal here is theologically and logically linked with the previous material. That the formal transitional particle oὖν, 'therefore', means indeed 'in the light of the whole preceding argument',[30] is supported by the immediate διὰ τῶν οἰκτιρμῶν τοῦ θεοῦ ('by the mercies of God') which represents the basis and urgency of the appeal.[31] That the references to the mercies/mercy of God appear both at the beginning and the end of the section (12.1; 15.9) shows that the entire section (chs 12–15) is in fact linked to what precedes it and not only to 12.1. While 'the mercies of God' points immediately and unmistakably to the conclusion of chs 9–11, where God is shown to 'have mercy on all' (11.30–32),[32] there are also indications that the expression points to the love, compassion, and grace of God shown in Jesus Christ, which Paul described throughout chs 1–11,[33] particularly in chs 5–8. In his study on the influence the example and teaching of Jesus has on Paul's understanding of Christian conduct expressed in Romans 12–15, Michael Thomson identifies significant vocabulary links between 12.1–2 (as representative of the entire section Romans 12–15) and the previous part of the letter, and establishes that 'Paul's admonitions find their basis and shape in a Christology in which the obedience of Jesus was central'.[34] He points specifically to the obvious link to Adamic theology (Romans 1; 3.23; 5.12–19; 7.7–11; 8.19–22) that Paul makes here, showing above all that it was the obedience of Jesus that led to righteousness and life, in total contrast with, and the great reversal of, the disobedience of the first Adam, which led to sin and death. In ch. 6 Paul argued similarly that incorporation 'in Christ' should lead believers to 'walk in the newness of life' (6.3) and to present themselves to God 'as those who have been brought from death to life . . . as instruments of righteousness' (6.13).[35] Now in 12.1–2 he summons those 'in Christ' to participate themselves in this great reversal and live their lives as daily sacrifices, in self-offering, just as Jesus did, for the sake of others. This will be their service, 'acceptable to God', their true worship in accordance with the will of God.[36] The reference to 'transformation' in 12.2 is yet another confirmation of the link to Christ, as it points back to 8.29

---

30. Ibid., p. 292.

31. Michael Thomson, *Clothed with Christ: The Example and Teaching of Jesus in Romans 12:1–15:13* (JSNT, 59; Sheffield: Sheffield Academic, 1991), pp. 78ff.

32. Dunn, *Romans* 12–15: Introduction.

33. So, for example, Cranfield, *Romans* Vol. 2, p. 596 and Barrett, *Romans*, 230–31.

34. Thomson, *Clothed with Christ*, p. 78.

35. Several other authors show the close relationship between Romans 12–15 and ch. 6. Yet, the last major section of the letter should be understood as building on the entire argument of the letter up to this point and not only on ch. 6. See, for example, Cranfield, *Romans* Vol. 2, pp. 295ff.; Grieb, *Story of Romans*, p. 115; Moo, *Romans*, p. 744.

36. Thomson, *Clothed with Christ*, p. 83.

where the Spirit enables the believers to be shaped in Christ's image. Thus, we can say that Paul's appeal is based on the entire argument he has developed so far[37] and that, more specifically, the readers are urged to follow the example of Christ. If that is correct, then we may detect throughout Romans 12–15 a stronger christological underpinning than is usually recognized and which is in continuity with the previous argument built around the story of Christ.

It is significant that Paul uses here the language of appeal, παρακαλῶ, which denotes an authority that is different from that of a command. If the authority of the command relies on the status of the one who makes the command (Paul 'as apostle'), and on the power to compel, the authority that comes from an appeal is inherent in the reality which it invokes, namely the status of the addressees ('brothers in Christ'), and it relies on the freedom of the addressee to consent. Thus, Paul's appeal is to a reality which contains in itself a moral imperative – to be 'in Christ' is to live a newness of life shaped according to the pattern of Christ and enabled by the Spirit.[38] In other words, life in Christ carries with it some intrinsic obligations, which result from the grace/mercies bestowed by God.

Paul places the entire discussion about Christian life in chs 12–15 under the rubric of θυσίαν ζῶσαν, 'living sacrifice' (12.1).[39] We recall that in the earlier part of the letter, Paul argues that the event of salvation was brought about by Jesus' death as a sacrifice (particularly in 3.25 and 5.6–10). Jesus' death on the cross was the natural consequence of his obedience and faithfulness to God (5.19) and had as its result the redemption of humanity. Further, we saw that the dynamic of salvation for the individual begins with one's participation in Christ's death and resurrection (in baptism, 6.1–11), and continues in a life of obedience to God, which is a life of death to sin and slavery to righteousness (6.12–23). Though the believers experience even now the benefits of Christ's resurrected power, their final share in his inheritance is conditioned by their sharing in his suffering (8.17), just as for Jesus himself the suffering of an obedient life and his death on the cross were the condition for God's vindication and heavenly enthronement (8.34). With Christ's death clearly anchored in the cultic

---

37. Katherine Grieb, for example, shows that Paul's condensed statement in 12.1–2 combines three major ideas which Paul developed earlier in the letter: (1) the cultic metaphor of sacrifice (3.21–26); (2) the believer's identification with Christ's death at baptism (6.1–11); and (3) the eschatological themes of cosmic holy war, the two ages and new creation (chs 5–8). Paul's purpose in bringing all these ideas was 'to show that the lordship of Christ over believers is inevitably demonstrated by their embodied actions' (Grieb, *Story of Romans*, p. 117).

38. This point is made by Bernd Wannenwetsch, '"Members of One Another": Charis, Ministry and Representation: A Politico-Ecclesial Reading of Romans 12', in Bartholomew *et al.* (eds) *A Royal Priesthood?*, p. 200. We should also mention here the work of Carl J. Bjerkelund (*Parakalô: Form, Funktion und Sinn der parakalô-Sätze in den paulinischen Briefen* (Oslo: Universitetsforlaget, 1967)) who devoted an entire monograph to the study of the concept of παρακαλω in Paul's letters – as referred to in Wedderburn's *The Reasons for Romans*, pp. 67ff.

39. For a solid argument on the importance of living sacrifice for Paul's argument see Jeffrey Peterson, 'Living Sacrifices: Walking in Accordance with the Spirit in Romans 12–15', *Christian Studies Journal* 20 (2004), pp. 33–41 and Roetzel 'Sacrifice'.

sacrificial tradition (3.23–25), in 12.1 Paul appropriates sacrificial imagery and uses it as a controlling idea for the entire section by extending its meaning and influence from the altar into daily life, describing it as the daily, sacrificial obedience of the believers.[40]

As in the case of the symbolism of reconciliation we saw in a previous chapter, so here, too, Paul makes a paradigm shift in his usage of the metaphor of sacrifice, preserving some elements from the old and, at the same time, bringing in new meanings and connotations. Thus, Paul urges the believers to consider their bodies as living sacrifices that are 'holy and acceptable to God' (12.1) (in the same way as the animal brought for sacrifice had to be pure and the worshipper in a state of ritual purity in order for his/her worship to be acceptable); this will be their λογικὴν λατρείαν, 'godly form of worship'.[41] However, in the redefinition and extended meaning Paul brings to the traditional metaphor, sacrifice now becomes 'living sacrifice'. That is, a daily life of sacrificial obedience to the will of God, modelled on the template of Christ's self-giving love for others, and consistent with, and integral to, the gospel of grace.

καὶ μὴ συσχηματίζεσθε τῷ αἰῶνι τούτῳ, 'do not be conformed to this world' (v. 2) is the second element of Paul's appeal calling for resistance to the constant pressures and temptations of conforming τῷ αἰῶνι τούτῳ ('to this age')[42] and for openness to the new eschatological reality in which 'new modes and standards of behaviour are not only possible but commanded'.[43] The pattern of thinking and the life of 'this age' were most probably known and clear to them. Paul is calling for a different, transformed way of thinking and living, emphasizing the capacity of the empowered and renewed mind of the believers to discern the will of God – thus overcoming their previous inability when because of sin they could not discern what was good and acceptable to God (1.28; 7.28; 8.5–8). τῇ ἀνακαινώσει τοῦ νοὸς ('the renewal of the mind') is an allusion to the work of the Spirit, making the eschatological new age already a reality in the everyday life of the believer.

The image of the Christian community as ἓν σῶμά ἐν Χριστῷ, 'one body in Christ' (vv. 3–8), following the discussion of appropriate worship to God, shows unmistakably that, for Paul, Christian life is a harmonious integration of private

40. Roetzel 'Sacrifice', p. 416. Käsemann also argues that here Paul replaces the cultic image of animal sacrifice with the daily obedient service of the believers in relation to the world – service which is an expression of both God's command resulting from justification and the confirmation of the membership in the new family 'in Christ'. (Käsemann, *Romans*, pp. 323–31.)

41. This is Roetzel's translation of λογικὴν λατρείαν. He argues that the 'spiritual worship' adopted by most translations is not satisfactory since this may lead to an unpauline idea of a separation between 'spiritual' and 'earthly' worship, between the sacred and profane realities. On the contrary, he insists, 'Paul's intent is not to separate "spiritual" worship from "earthly" or inner experience from outer. He aims to sacralize everyday conduct and thus to remove the barrier between worldly and "spiritual" behavior for those in Christ'. (Roetzel 'Sacrifice', p. 416.)

42. J. B. Philips highlights well this aspect by translating this verse with 'Don't let the world around you squeeze you into its own mould'.

43. Wright, *Romans*, p. 705.

spirituality and corporate or social responsibility, a spirituality manifested through a mutuality of service among interdependent members. The social identity of the new community 'in Christ' highlights that what unites them in their common new identity is no longer their ethnicity or national solidarity but their being 'one body in Christ'.[44] Given the fact that the imagery of 'the body' was well established in the political rhetoric of the time, it is possible to think that Paul might have envisaged the church (as 'the body of Christ') as a model for the wider society.[45]

Paul's major point here is to show that because the new community is a united body in Christ, with members possessing and exercising diverse and complementary gifts, each should renounce high-mindedness and high self-esteem, and learn to appreciate and exalt the other. They are to do that μέτρον πίστεως, 'according to the measure of faith' (v. 3c). Throughout the letter Paul emphasizes the importance of orthopraxy as one's 'faith' should determine one's appropriate conduct in the world.[46] Paul uses the expression ἐκ πίστεως, 'from faith' (1.17; 3.26; 3.30; 4.16; 5.1; 9.30; 9.32; 10.6; 12.3 and 14.23) in order 'to demonstrate to the Roman Christians that the life of faith is a life of commitment rather than of vacuous freedom, of obligation to Christ and to other humans'.[47] For Paul the 'right faith' was to be embodied in one's life, particularly in one's attitude and conduct towards others – as Paul clearly expresses in 14.17: 'the kingdom of God is . . . righteousness and peace and joy in the Holy Spirit'. Any attempt to impose one's 'norm of faith' on others will be equated by Paul with sin (14.23). Finally, if the new people of God are shaped by Christ, in this section Paul argues strongly that it is 'unity' and the building up of the community that should characterize their lives.

Ἡ ἀγάπη ἀνυπόκριτος, 'Let love be genuine' (v. 9), represents the heading statement for the entire passage of 12.9–21 where genuine love, as the fundamental norm of conduct, is given concrete meaning. It is here that Paul shows what it actually means 'to present their bodies as a living sacrifice' (12.1): it is the realisation of genuine love through a life of harmony, hospitality, peace, renunciation of vengeance, and overcoming evil with good. These are indeed concrete and explicit practices of reconciliation, 'the reality of embodied existence',[48] both within and outside the

---

44. Regarding Paul's use of the 'body' metaphor, Dunn notes: 'Paul's choice was no doubt deliberate: it would give his readers a sense of coherence and identity which could sustain them over against the larger body politic in which they lived and worked, without that depending on a sense of national or racial solidarity. At the same time he prevents its being assimilated to a too vague idea of world citizenship or a too narrow concept of civic politics: they are one body in Christ; only "in Christ" do they function as a body; the "in Christ" provides a counter model of social identity no longer reducible to merely ethnic or cultural categories'. (Dunn, *Romans*, 12.3–8).

45. See ibid.

46. Fitzmyer, *Romans*, pp. 637ff.; Cranfield, *Romans*, Vol. 2, pp. 612ff.

47. W. Campbell, 'The Rule of Faith in Romans 12:1–15:13. The Obligation of Humble Obedience to Christ as the Only Adequate Response to the Mercies of God', in Hay and Johnson (eds), *Pauline Theology*, p. 281.

48. Michael Barram, 'Romans 12: 9–21', *Interpretation* 57 (2003), pp. 423–26 (424).

Christian community, practices that would represent the adequate response to the gospel of God's grace. Further, in order for them 'not to be confirmed to this world' (12.2) the believers are to live in constant care and concern for 'the other' – not looking to their own interest, not suspicious, not expecting to receive love in return.[49] It will be, of course, as the believers experience that radical 'transformation and renewal of their mind' that they will be able to 'discern' the will of God and incarnate it in their daily conduct.

Ἡ ἀγάπη ἀνυπόκριτος. 'Let love be genuine' (v. 9). As seen in the Greek, the construction of the opening sentence does not have a connection particle, but in the sequence of participles and adjectives that follows, Paul qualifies what genuine love[50] means:

> hate what is evil, hold fast to what is good; love one another with mutual affection; outdo one another in showing honour. Do not lack in zeal, be ardent in spirit, serve the Lord. Rejoice in hope, be patient in suffering, persevere in prayer. Contribute to the needs of the saints; extend hospitality to strangers.' (12. 9b–13)

The believers are to understand that by affection, honouring the other, rejoicing, sharing with the needy, and hospitality, they 'serve the Lord' (τῷ κυρίῳ δουλεύοντες, v. 11). And these should apply to all people, inside and outside the community without any differentiations, and even towards persecutors: εὐλογεῖτε τοὺς διώκοντας [ὑμᾶς], εὐλογεῖτε καὶ μὴ καταρᾶσθε, 'bless those who persecute you; bless and do not curse them' (v. 14). In expounding 'genuine love', Paul emphasizes its implications for everyday life by highlighting that it brings about a specific conduct towards *all* people. It is exactly these practices of reconciliation that Paul wants to inspire and cultivate among the believers in Rome, practices that will give evidence of their new life in Christ and enable them to be a witness to the world for the lordship of Christ over all reality. Paul stresses again and again that this transformation of their lives and the renewal of their minds are not about an ethical theory or abstract principles, but are realities they have experienced and which they must embody in concrete manifestations of love, peace, reconciliation, harmony, tolerance, and consideration for the other.

> χαίρειν μετὰ χαιρόντων, κλαίειν μετὰ κλαιόντων. τὸ αὐτὸ εἰς ἀλλήλους φρονοῦντες ... τοῖς ταπεινοῖς συναπαγόμενοι,
>
> Rejoice with those who rejoice, weep with those who weep, live in harmony with one another ... associate with the lowly (vv. 15–16).

---

49. We could call these 'practices of exclusion'.

50. Even though no verb appears in Greek in the first sentence – it simply reads ἡ ἀγάπη ἀνυπόκριτος 'love-genuine' – grammatically the succession of participles and adjectives seem to modify this opening phrase. So, Wright, *Romans*, p. 711.

Paul is urging believers in Rome not to retreat from interactions with their unbelieving (and even hostile) neighbours but, instead, to look for ways to establish a common ground, to understand their condition, 'to live imaginatively into the situation of the other',[51] to make friends even with the lowly – thus discouraging any arrogant and superior attitude.[52] The apparent return to issues dealing with the internal affairs of the community in a context which addresses the relationship of the churches with the wider world is a strong indication that for Paul there is no double standard of behaviour: the same norm of love, as exemplified in the life of Jesus, applies to their integrated life both within and outside the church, towards 'insiders' and 'outsiders' alike, despite their differences, ethnicity, or social and economic status.

μηδενὶ κακὸν ἀντὶ κακοῦ ἀποδιδόντες, προνοούμενοι καλὰ ἐνώπιον πάντων ἀνθρώπων· εἰ δυνατὸν τὸ ἐξ ὑμῶν, μετὰ πάντων ἀνθρώπων εἰρηνεύοντες,

Do not repay anyone evil for evil, but take thought for what is noble in the sight of all. If it is possible, so far as it depends on you, live peaceably with all (vv. 17–18).

The appeal here is for believers 'to pursue a behaviour that will have a positive impact on "all people".'[53] With this Paul repeats one of the main points of the paragraph; that is, defining the relationship of the believer with outsiders: 'repay no one evil for evil'. And this should not be just sporadic, spontaneous reactions but rather a constant, thoughtfully cultivated attitude *'take thought* for what is noble in the sight of all'– as the prefix to the participle προνοούμενοι ('thinking beforehand') indicates.[54] This is indeed the clearest point Paul makes regarding the need to consider in advance, thoughtfully and explicitly, the social implications of the gospel for a particular context. To respond to the gospel is to commit oneself to a particular way of being *in* the world and *for* the world. This is further confirmed by the phrasing that they 'take thought for what is noble in the sight of all' (v. 17b) where we detect an acknowledgment from Paul of at least some acceptable moral considerations in the wider world,[55] thus discouraging a total negative view of the outside world or a withdrawal from it. To be sure, Paul had just asked them not to conform themselves to this world; that remains true in as much as there are cultural values that they should resist, since they come in opposition to a gospel of love and reconciliation. Yet, Paul's point here

51. Grieb, *Story of Romans*, p. 121.
52. It is possible that in these chapters Paul is also trying to respond to charges brought against him that his law-free gospel of grace and of the abundance of the Spirit leads to moral negligence, arrogance, immorality, even apostasy and that it encourages a stance of indifference and contempt for others and disengagement from the world at large. Paul's response cannot be stronger in his emphasis that a life lived in the Spirit of Christ is indeed a life of total freedom but this freedom cannot be exercised to the detriment of others and in a detachment from the outside world. See further Roetzel, 'Sacrifice', pp. 419–20.
53. Moo, *Romans*, p. 785.
54. Wright, *Romans*, p. 714.
55. So Dunn, *Romans*.

(v. 17) is that wherever there is good in a culture which is universally recognized, they should be committed to that good.

Having an adequate grasp of reality around him, Paul is aware that living with a 'renewed mind' 'according to the Spirit' will inevitably bring opposition and hostility from the world. And yet, he admonishes the believers to make every effort from their side to μετὰ πάντων ἀνθρώπων εἰρηνεύοντες, 'live peaceably with all' (v. 18b), as Paul sees this as one of the most important practical outworkings of the gospel of love and reconciliation.[56] The double qualification that Paul uses in v. 18a, εἰ δυνατὸν ('if it is possible') and τὸ ἐξ ὑμῶν ('so far as it depends on you'), does not limit the believers' pursuit of peace. On the contrary, they should do everything that depends on them to live peaceably. The qualifications may indicate the inevitability of the tension, even conflict caused by the nature and the message of the gospel of Jesus Christ as the Lord of the world to which Christians bear witness! However, it is clear from the context that Christians are themselves not only to refrain from *any* action that may cause, maintain, or intensify the conflict, but rather to bless when persecuted, to return good for evil, and to live peaceably with all.

μὴ ἑαυτοὺς ἐκδικοῦντες, ἀγαπητοί, ἀλλὰ δότε τόπον τῇ ὀργῇ, γέγραπται γάρ· ἐμοὶ ἐκδίκησις, ἐγὼ ἀνταποδώσω, λέγει κύριος. ἀλλὰ ἐὰν πεινᾷ ὁ ἐχθρός σου, ψώμιζε αὐτόν· ἐὰν διψᾷ, πότιζε αὐτόν· τοῦτο γὰρ ποιῶν ἄνθρακας πυρὸς σωρεύσεις ἐπὶ τὴν κεφαλὴν αὐτοῦ. μὴ νικῶ ὑπὸ τοῦ κακοῦ ἀλλὰ νίκα ἐν τῷ ἀγαθῷ τὸ κακόν,

Beloved, never avenge yourselves, but leave room for the wrath of God; for it is written, 'Vengeance is mine, I will repay, says the Lord'. No, 'if your enemies are hungry, feed them; if they are thirsty, give them something to drink; for by doing this you will heap burning coals on their heads (vv. 19–21).

There are here two very significant points for our understanding of the social meaning of reconciliation. First, the believers are to never avenge themselves, μὴ ἑαυτοὺς ἐκδικοῦντες (v. 19a), or try to bring their own justice. It is not that they should not be concerned with justice and its pursuit. Rather, Paul prohibits personal vengeance and emphasizes that they should δότε τόπον τῇ ὀργῇ, 'leave room for the wrath of God' (v. 19b), who will bring justice. This point has two practical implications: (1) it is a strong incentive to resist the natural impulse of revenge which is so easily and so often hidden under the disguise of 'justice', and (2) by leaving the issue of justice to God, there is a strong sense that 'justice will be done' rather then being left with

---

56. It is somewhat puzzling that Moo is wondering as to the reasons why Paul included this admonition here. He states 'we do not know whether there was any special need to exhort the Roman Christians to live at peace with their fellow-citizens!' (*Romans*, p. 785). However, he rightly insists that given the unavoidable conflict and tension that the Christians may find themselves in with the world, they should not use such situations 'as an excuse for behavior that needlessly exacerbates that conflict or for a resignation that leads us not even to bother to seek to maintain a positive witness' (ibid., p. 786).

a feeling of despair and hopelessness, especially in extremely difficult situations where there may not be an easy, concrete and foreseeable solution of justice at hand. In fact, as Paul will show in ch. 13, it is not that justice will need to wait until divine intervention, but that the government, as an instrument of God, is in the business of bringing justice by commending the good and punishing the wrong.

Second, Paul goes much further in suggesting a radically different way of action which should replace private vengeance. Not only are the believers to refrain from retaliating, but they should also actively look for the good of those who have harmed them: ἐὰν πεινᾷ ὁ ἐχθρός σου, ψώμιζε αὐτόν· ἐὰν διψᾷ, πότιζε αὐτόν, 'if your enemy is hungry, feed him; if he is thirsty, give him something to drink' (v. 20a). Moreover, as Cranfield remarks, 'to fail to do to our enemies the good they stand in need of, when it is in our power to do so, is a "kind of indirect retaliation".'[57] In a sense, this might well be a concrete application of the appeal Paul made a little earlier in v. 14: 'bless those who persecute you; bless and do not curse them'.[58] To feed your enemies, to be good to them, is indeed to overcome evil with good, as Paul concludes this subsection in v. 21.

Paul goes yet a step further and hints at something beyond a simple concern with the appropriate behaviour of the believer – a real care for the enemy. Thus he points out that the result of their totally surprising goodness towards their enemies will ποιῶν ἄνθρακας πυρὸς σωρεύσεις ἐπὶ τὴν κεφαλὴν αὐτοῦ 'heap burning coals on their heads' (v. 20b), which is 'almost certainly intended as the burning shame of remorse for having treated someone so badly'.[59] By their appropriate behaviour, by their love towards the enemy, the victims may cause repentance and reconciliation.[60]

μὴ νικῶ ὑπὸ τοῦ κακοῦ ἀλλὰ νίκα ἐν τῷ ἀγαθῷ τὸ κακόν, 'do not be overcome by evil, but overcome evil with good' (v. 21), concludes the entire section, reinforcing the thought that the believers are to respond to the evil in the world with the same love and goodness they have themselves been shown by God in Christ. But this verse

---

57. Cranfield, *Romans* Vol. 2, p. 648.

58. While we agree with Dunn's suggestion that Paul advocated a 'policy of prudence', being aware of how small, insignificant, and vulnerable churches in the Roman Empire were, we also think one should not limit the force of Paul's advice by arguing that his 'first concern [was] . . . to urge a policy of avoiding trouble by refuting retaliation'. Rather, we take the position that while Paul would indeed be the first one to advise the churches not to go into unnecessary and futile provocations, his appeal is fundamentally based on the very nature of his gospel of sacrificial love and peace manifested in everyday life, following the pattern of Jesus, whatever the actual historical, political and social circumstances. Thus, Paul's first priority was that the believers in Rome would embody the gospel in active, positive ways, particularly through acts of goodness, love, and peace.

59. Wright, *Romans*, p. 715.

60. Cranfield, *Romans* Vol. 2, pp. 648–50. It is almost certain that Paul is thinking back to ch. 5, to God's unilateral love, manifested in Christ's self-sacrifice which made it possible that 'while we were enemies we were reconciled to God' (5.10). Similarly, one may trace here impulses from the teaching and example of Jesus. Finally, this may also be a tacit allusion to Paul's personal experience in the encounter with Christ, when even while he was a persecutor of the church and an enemy of Christ he found himself embraced, forgiven, and reconciled to God (2 Cor. 5.11–21).

also points to the possibility that evil will prevail if believers give in to patterns of actions characteristic of 'this age', such as returning evil for evil or vengeance for persecution. The only way to overcome evil is by responding with good. In line with the possible positive effect one's goodness may have on the enemy in v. 20, here Paul expresses a fundamental conviction in the power of goodness and self-giving love to be effective in a world of violence and domination. It is a pointer to Christ, who has conquered evil not by fighting back or by responding in kind, but by showing love and goodness in his self-sacrifice. It is by resisting evil, by breaking the cycle of violence, that the believers actually embody the gospel of Christ and make it effective in the world. Doing otherwise means letting themselves be 'conformed' to this world and be changed by the evil of one's enemy,[61] a situation which is the opposite of being 'transformed' and renewed by the mercies of God in giving themselves as 'living sacrifices'.

6.4.2 *Romans 13*

> Let every person be subject to the governing authorities; for there is no authority except from God, and those authorities that exist have been instituted by God. Therefore whoever resists authority resists what God has appointed, and those who resist will incur judgement (Romans 13:1–2).

The difficulties and moral dilemmas these (and the next five) verses have raised throughout the centuries are well expressed by John O'Neill: 'These . . . verses have caused more unhappiness and misery in the Christian East and West than any other seven verses in the New Testament by the license they have given to tyrants, and the support for tyrants the Church has felt called on to offer as a result of the presence of Romans 13 in the canon'.[62]

It is thus not surprising that interpreters have proposed a great variety of solutions in their dealing with this text. Opinions range all the way from removing it from the canon[63] and treating it as an interpolation of non-pauline origin;[64] to assigning it extremely limited or no relevance for a theology of the state considering that it is a contextual piece of instruction addressed to a very specific situation in Rome;[65] and

---

61. Wright, *Romans*, p. 722; Cranfield, *Romans* Vol. 2, p. 650.

62. J. C. O'Neill, *Paul's Letter to the Romans* (Harmondsworth: Penguin, 1975), p. 209 as quoted by Horrell, 'The Peaceable', p. 85.

63. O'Neill, *Romans*.

64. J. Kallas, 'Romans XIII.1–7: An Interpolation', *New Testament Studies* 11 (1964–65), pp. 365–74; W. Munro, 'Romans 13:1–7. Apartheid's Last Biblical Refuge', *Biblical Theology Bulletin* 20 (1990), pp. 161–68, argues that the text should be interpreted as a second-century overall redaction, in connection with the Pastorals, when the legitimacy of the Roman Empire was taken for granted; Käsemann calls it 'an alien body in Paul's exhortation', though he stresses that there are neither external nor internal reasons to doubt the authenticity of the text (*Romans*, p. 351).

65. Among others, Elliott, 'Romans 13:1–7', pp. 184–204. Similarly, Anthony Guerra understands

to seeing it as a general statement that applies to all governments at all times as an expression of God's desire and the purpose of God for order in society.[66]

I cannot, of course, go into a detailed analysis of this passage and a critical inter-action with the rich history of its interpretation,[67] nor is it my purpose to attempt to solve its many puzzles. There are several entire monographs and numerous articles dedicated to this subject, not to mention the extended interpretations in the commen-taries on Romans.[68] My intention is rather to offer a possible line of interpretation of Romans 13 within the context of Romans 12–15, and indeed of Romans as a whole, with particular attention to its place and meaning in the context of Paul's emphasis on the practices of reconciliation as an integral part of the gospel. The fact that Paul places this text at the very heart of this passage (chs 12–15)[69] suggests that he regarded it as an essential part of his whole argument. Therefore, its meaning proceeds from its intended role in the larger context.

The first important observation we need to make is that, given the thematic and linguistic links with the surrounding context, and the lack of any solid internal or external evidence for its being a later addition to the text, it is clear that Romans 13 should not be treated as an interpolation but as an integral part of Paul's argument and thus must be interpreted in the context of Paul's larger argument in Romans 12–15. More specifically, the text in view should be interpreted in close association with the exhortation to love from 12.9–21, which, together with the similar exhortation from 13.8–10, brackets it. It is clear that Paul wants to show that the Christian commitment to love is not limited to individual relationships (within and outside the Christian

---

this passage as a clear piece of political apologetic in response to the specific 'Roman factor'. (Anthony J. Guerra, *Romans and the Apologetic Tradition: The Purpose, Genre and Audience of Paul's Letter* (Cambridge: CUP, 1995), p. 160–64.)

66. So, for example, W. Sunday and A. C. Headlam, *A Critical and Exegetical Commentary on the Epistle to the Romans* (5th edn; Edinburgh: T. &. T. Clark, 1902), pp. 369ff.

67. For excellent summaries of the history of interpretation see Moo, *Romans*, pp. 806–10 and Wright, *Romans*, pp. 716–17.

68. Jan Botha, *Subject to Whose Authority? Multiple Readings of Romans 13* (Emory Studies in Early Christianity; Atlanta: Scholars Press, 1994); Clinton D. Morrison, *The Powers that Be: Earthly Rulers and Demonic Powers in Romans 13.1–7* (London: SCM Press, 1960); Walter E. Pilgrim *Uneasy Neighbors: Church and State in the New Testament* (Minneapolis: Fortress, 1999). Some of the significant studies on Romans 13 are T. L. Carter, 'The Irony of Romans'; Gerrit de Kruijf, 'The Function of Romans 13 in Christian Ethics'; Neil Elliot, 'Romans 13:17 in the Context of Imperial Propaganda'; N. T. Wright, 'New Testament and the State'; Philip H. Towner, 'Romans 13:1–7 and Paul's Missiological Perspective: A Call to Political Quietism or Transformation?'; Greg Herrick, 'Paul and Civil Obedience in Romans 13:1–7'; Robert H. Stein, 'The Argument of Romans 13:1–7'; J. D. G. Dunn, 'Romans 13.1–7: A Charter for Political Quietism?'; Alexander Webster, 'St Paul's Political Advice to the Haughty Gentile Christians in Rome: An Exegesis of Romans 13:1–7'; S. Hutchinson, 'The Political Implications of Romans 13:1–7'; E. Käsemann, 'Principles of the Interpretation of Romans 13'; J. Kallas, 'Romans XIII. 1–7: An Interpolation'.

69. Dunn takes 13.1–7 as the centre of the chiastic structure evident in chs 12–15. Similarly, Horrell ('Peaceable', pp. 86–87) and Wright (*Romans*, 703) regard 13.1–7, and 12.14–13.7 respectively as the centre of a similar structure in chs 12–13.

community) but includes also the believers' living as responsible citizens in the society at large. The call to be a community which does 'what is noble in sight of all' and embodies the practices of reconciliation (12.9–21) means that the believers should behave responsibly also towards the governing authorities. Seen from this perspective, Paul's position vis-à-vis authorities may not appear as making 'absurdly positive comments'[70] but rather as offering 'a crucial test-case of the Christians' external relations, and thus as providing a key exemplar of the instructions surrounding it'.[71] One of the points that Paul stressed in 12.14–21 was that when the believers experience persecution or wrongdoing they are not to seek retaliation or private vengeance but are to leave the matter of justice to God – 'leave it to the wrath of God, for it is written, "vengeance is mine"' (12.19) – while the believers were to continue in their business of overcoming evil with good and living peaceably with all. It is in 13.1–7 that Paul spells out, at least to some extent, the way in which God does justice, even now, not only at the final judgement (1.32; 2.1–16; 14.10): it is through the governing authorities, as God's instruments, that a measure of justice is done and order is preserved.[72] Otherwise, chaos would rule and life would not be possible, a situation which would be against God's intention to maintain order in his creation, therefore in society. That is why the believers should not take matters in their own hands but rather submit to the authorities whose responsibility is to keep order and peace.

As for the structure of the argument in Romans 13.1–7, it could be schematically presented in this way:[73]

A general imperative: every person subject to authorities (v. 1a)

The grounds for the command (vv. 1b–4):

Theological ground: authority is God's ordination (vv. 1b and c)

Practical ground: authorities maintain order and distribute justice (vv. 3–4)

A summary exhortation: be subject because of God's wrath and conscience (v. 5)

The argument from practice: authorities promote the social well-being (v. 6)

A specific and concluding imperative: pay to all what is due them (v. 7)

The text begins with an imperative: Πᾶσα ψυχὴ ἐξουσίαις ὑπερεχούσαις ὑποτασσέσθω, 'Let every person be subject to the governing authorities' (v. 1a). It is generally

---

70. Elliott, 'Romans 13:1–7', p. 196.

71. Horrell, 'Peaceable', p. 87. Klaus Wengst (*Pax Romana and the Peace of Jesus Christ* (John Bowden (trans.); London: SCM, 1987), p. 81) holds a similar position: 'relations with people outside the community . . . are not to be different from those within the community, despite the aggression with which they meet. As a particular case of behaviour towards such people generally, Paul considers attitudes to those holding power in the state.'

72. This point is made by Wright, *Romans*, p. 718.

73. See Stein, 'The Argument of Romans 13', p. 343.

accepted that πᾶσα ψυχή, 'every soul/person', is a strong indication that this is a general command for submission, applying to all people, grounded in Paul's broad, creational theological argument. Similarly, it is commonly understood that ἐξουσίαις ('authorities', 'powers', 'rulers') refers here to the earthly rulers (since they, for example, are to collect taxes), even though the term in Paul usually designates both spiritual and earthly powers, sometimes simultaneously and without making a clear distinction between the two (as in 1 Cor. 2.6–8 and Col. 2.14–15).[74] What is still frequently debated among Pauline scholars is the precise meaning and extent of 'submission'[75] and the occasion of this imperative. From the specific issues facing the Christians in Rome to which we have referred, it is possible to understand the command to submission as Paul's pastoral attempt to deal with incipient tendencies of antinomianism among some Christians in Rome,[76] thus trying to minimize the risks the community faced as it was no longer protected by the same privileges the Jewish community had,[77] and also trying to reject a possible Zealot option of violent rebellion against authorities and refusal to pay taxes.[78] We know indeed that the Jewish diaspora benefited from a privileged treatment which ensured not only their distinctive identity as the unique people of God but also their protection. As long as the early Christians communities were identified with Judaism, or considered a branch within it, they also enjoyed that protection. However, as Dunn correctly points out, because Paul redefines the people of God in terms other than ethnic categories, the Christian communities in Rome

> could therefore no longer claim the political privileges accorded to ethnic minorities. Paul
> must have been very conscious that by redrawing the boundaries of the people of God in
> non-ethnic terms he was putting the political status of the new congregations at risk.[79]

74. Walter Wink (*Naming the Powers: The Language of Power in the New Testament* (Philadelphia, PA: Fortress, 1984), pp. 45–47) and Wright (*Romans*, pp. 720–21) draw a parallel between Romans 13 and Col. 1.16, while Dunn (*Romans* 13) states that Paul refers to earthly rulers. See also Gordon Fee, *The First Epistle to the Corinthians* (Grand Rapids: Eerdmans, 1987), pp. 103–04 and idem, *New Testament Exegesis* (Philadelphia, PA: John Knox Press, 1983), pp. 87–89.

75. As illustrated by the *NRV* translation, some authors point to the difference between 'submission/ being subject to' and 'blind obedience': Moo (*Romans*, pp. 797, 807–10); Cranfield (*Romans*, pp. 660–63); A. Webster ('St Paul's', pp. 269); Hutchinson ('Political Implications', pp. 53–55). Emil Brunner (*The Letter to the Romans* (H. A. Kennedy (trans.); London: Lutterworth, 1959), p. 108), on the other hand, is representative of those who understand Romans 13 as a plea for 'obedient submission'. In reaction to such a position, and at the other end of the spectrum, James Moulder ('Romans 13 and Conscientious Disobedience', *JTSA* 21 (1977), pp. 13–23) argues that Paul's reason for writing Romans, his political idealism and his insistence on the ethical implications of the gospel, not only undermine the thesis of absolute obedience to one's government, but, in fact, support a conscientious disobedience.

76. Moulder, 'Romans 13', pp. 13–23.

77. Dunn, *Romans*.

78. Wright, *Romans*, pp. 716ff.

79. Dunn, 'Romans 13:1–7'. An additional argument supporting the idea that Paul had a practical purpose in mind when he wrote this passage is offered by Thomas Coleman, 'Binding Obligations in Romans 13:7: A Semantic Field and Social Context', *Tyndale Bulletin* 48(2) (1997), pp. 307–27. After a detailed

Nevertheless, as Paul's theological ground for the appeal makes clear, the distinctive Christian identity did not alter the basic Jewish political view of living under the given political structures.

οὐ γὰρ ἔστιν ἐξουσία εἰ μὴ ὑπὸ θεοῦ, αἱ δὲ οὖσαι ὑπὸ θεοῦ τεταγμέναι εἰσίν,

for there is no authority except from God, and those authorities that exist have been instituted by God (v. 1b and c).

This statement seems to suggest a more general position that Paul had vis-à-vis the powers that be and so the text should be interpreted in that light.[80] It is significant to observe that the first theological reason Paul gives for submission is not christological (that Christ conquered the powers) or eschatological (that the end is near) but creational (God's order in creation), thus keeping in line with his Jewish theology of creation and order.[81] The ordering of society under government is God's intention and so the believers should accept that fact and be willing to actively live within such structures. Otherwise they will be resisting 'what God has appointed' (2a) and as a result *'will incur judgment'* (2b). In keeping with his Jewish political theology, Paul understands the authority as being God-given and consequently the government's task is to work for the good of their citizens having the judicial authority to maintain order in society by imposing a legal restraint on any form of anti-social behaviour or anarchy.[82] Indeed, Paul's command in Romans 13 is a call to reject any kind of anarchy and/or withdrawal from actual engagement with the concrete conditions of everyday life in society. It is probable that there were Christians who understood the lordship of Christ to mean a rejection of all human lordship and government authority. In response, Paul corrects this misunderstanding and offers the believers in Rome a framework for their Christian life in which the political powers are God's intention and therefore have divine legitimisation.[83]

---

study of the four specific terms Paul uses in Romans 13:7 ('tribute', 'tax', 'reverence' and 'honour'), in the context of the Graeco-Roman semantic field of political obligation, Coleman suggests that the passage should be read as Paul's exhortation to submission in the light of Nero's increased taxation as well as his introduction of penalties for those who did not show reverence and honour for those in authority.

80. Horrell, 'Peaceable', pp. 85ff, remarks that this text is relevant for constructing a broader theology of the state. This does not mean that what Paul said was not contextually relevant to the situation in Rome. However, the interpretation should not be limited strictly to that context. As Horrell correctly observes, since all the biblical documents are contextually bound, one should not choose arbitrarily which one has applicability for today; rather one should apply the same critical distancing and hermeneutical considerations to all biblical texts.

81. Several OT texts illustrate this understanding of God's privilege and freedom to invest rulers and authorities: Jer. 27.5; Prov. 8.15; Dan. 4.17. Josephus shows a similar understanding when he states that 'no ruler attains his office save by the will of God' (*Jewish Wars*, II, 140).

82. Moulder, 'Romans 13', pp. 13–23.

83. See Ziesler, *Romans*, pp. 308–09. Unfortunately, this apparently unqualified theological basis Paul gives has been grossly misused in order to legitimise and maintain abuses of power by governments over the centuries. Elliott (*Liberating Paul*, pp. 3–24) offers a serious critique of the ways in which this text

Having said that, however, we should point out that the statements Paul makes regarding authorities also carry several significant implications in terms of their claims, prerogatives, and responsibilities. By saying that rulers are 'instituted by God' (v. 1) who 'has appointed' them (v. 2a) and that they are θεοῦ διάκονός, 'God's servants' (v. 4), Paul clearly implies that they are accountable to God and will be judged by him for the way in which they do their duties.[84] If this is true, then Paul's statements in this passage appear to take away the prerogative of divinity from the emperor. One may thus agree with Wright that while an appeal to submit to the authorities, Romans 13 also 'constitutes a severe demotion of arrogant and self-divinizing rulers' and it can be understood as 'an undermining of totalitarianism, not a reinforcement of it'.[85] However, one should not place too much emphasis on this point, since Paul's most important objective was to persuade the believers in Rome that

> even though they are servants of the Messiah Jesus, the world's rightful Lord, this does not give them carte blanche to ignore the temporary subordinates whose appointed task, whether they know it or not, is to bring at least a measure of God's order and justice to the world.[86]

It is in fact in line with Paul's understanding of a ruler's appointed task that besides theological reasons, Paul also offers practical grounds for submission: rulers are God's instruments for judgement, for praising for those who do good and for punishing the wrongdoers (vv. 2b–5), as well as for promoting the well-being of social order (v. 6–7). And that is why God's public servants, authorities, must receive their due: ἀπόδοτε πᾶσιν τὰς ὀφειλάς, τῷ τὸν φόρον τὸν φόρον, τῷ τὸ τέλος τὸ τέλος, τῷ τὸν φόβον τὸν φόβον, τῷ τὴν τιμὴν τὴν τιμήν, 'pay to all what is due them – taxes

has been used throughout the history of the church to suppress any opposition to the established political powers. Wengst (*Pax Romana*, p. 84) also points out that by making such plain language statements that there is no actual power except from God and that those in authority are God's instruments, Paul unintentionally 'exposes himself to the danger of providing theological legitimisation for *de facto* power no matter how it may have come into being and how it may be used'.

84. This was a common Jewish understanding, as can be seen from the intertestamental literature, for example in *Wisdom* 6.1–3. This view is also maintained by Paul, a fact which could be seen in his understanding elsewhere that everyone will come before God's judgement, particularly his 'servants'. However, Paul does not make this point explicit here, probably because he did not intend to offer a comprehensive view on the subject; so we should be cautious not to draw too much from it in this context. See further Wright, *Romans*, p. 719.

85. Wright, *Romans*, p. 719. Similarly, de Kruijf ('Function of Romans 13', p. 233), takes this aspect as extremely relevant for the political life of the church because of its effect of 'relativizing the significance of the state in the light of God's history, and limiting its task . . . [thus giving] every reason for critical participation in political life and constant vigilance against totalitarian tendencies such as Caesar's'. As further support he quotes from J. Chaplin, 'Government', in D. J. Atkinson *et al.* (eds), *New Dictionary of Christian Ethics and Pastoral Theology* (Leicester: IVP, 1995), pp. 415–16: 'The effect of declaring before Roman ears that government is a mere "servant" is first to repudiate Roman claims to the deity of the Emperor, and secondly, by bringing government under the limits of divine law, to undermine the Roman concept of absolute political sovereignty' (de Kruijf, 'Function of Romans 13', p. 334).

86. Wright, *Romans*, p. 719.

to whom taxes are due, revenue to whom revenue is due, respect to whom respect is due, honor to whom honor is due' (v. 7). Since this is the only place in his letters where Paul brings up the subject of paying taxes, this could be a possible indication of the fact that there was a specific situation of abuse regarding taxes in Rome, which might have led to potentially dangerous and widespread social unrest. Paul would want to protect the Christian community from such a risk and asks the believers to pay the tax faithfully.[87]

One of the difficult questions one has to consider in respect of this text refers to the attitude Christians should have towards a corrupt, unjust, oppressive, and even evil government, which acts in ways that are against its own people. Indeed, what about the situation in which the authorities themselves become 'the persecutors'? And further still, how do we use Paul's advice in a totally different context today, where believers are both Christians and part of the government? Even though this text does not offer a direct guide to answer such questions, we may find hints regarding Paul's attitude and actions in texts such as Acts 16.19–40; 22.22–29; 23.1–5, and 25.6–2. Seen in the light of Paul's teaching in Romans, Philippians and 1 and 2 Thessalonians, these instances show that when Paul himself encountered persecution from authorities he submitted to their authority while at the same time he also reminded them of their duty. The church's mission, in light of God's redemptive purposes for the world, should be guided by a desire for peace, justice, order, and a continuous search to discern the will of God for every concrete situation. These concerns, present in Romans 13.1–7, should have primacy in shaping one's attitude to the government rather than a blind, unconditional, unqualified submission.[88]

Given Paul's experiences of hardships at the hands of Romans, his understanding of the lordship of Christ, and the widespread cult of the emperor, a further question arises from Romans 13.1–7: is Paul's perspective on the government simply positive, or are there qualifications and nuances to Paul's message of being subject to the governing authorities?[89] As we have mentioned, there is a tension in this text, and we may not resolve in a simple way the sense of 'enduring and intrinsic ambiguities of

87. Dunn, *Romans* 13.6–7.
88. Ronald W. Johnson, "The Christian and the State: Romans 13:1–7', *Review and Expositor* 97 (2000), pp. 91–95 (94).
89. I found it somewhat surprising that Horrell, for example, despite offering a cogent analysis of the entire section, is not able to see any reserve or qualification to Paul's advice to submit to the government. He states: 'it is striking that [Paul] can speak here without any hint of reserve or irony of the state as God's servant in rewarding good and punishing evil' ('Peaceable', p. 87). Other authors, however, understand and interpret Paul's position in a more nuanced way. Carter, for example, takes an opposite stance and argues that Paul is using irony and that beyond the surface meaning of the discourse the readers would have been able to detect a hidden message. Here is how Carter describes his proposal: 'the original audience of the letter shared with Paul a common experience of oppression at the hands of the authorities and were aware of the abuses that took place in the opening years of Nero's reign. The consequent implausibility of Paul's language would have alerted his readers to the presence of irony. They would have been able to set aside the surface meaning of the discourse and to recognise that Paul was using the established rhetorical technique of censuring with counterfeit praise. While the passage can be read as a straightforward injunction

this text . . . [whereby] the (Jewish) strategy Paul adopts *both* legitimates *and* limits the state's authority at one and the same time'.[90] Ernst Käsemann concludes in his study on Romans 13 that there is a limit of obedience to the government when it does not allow a Christian to carry on her task – which is to acknowledge and authenticate the lordship of Christ in one's being and doing. He writes:

> Is there any thing which might rightly be called a limit to the obedience here being demanded of the Christian and, if so, where is it to be drawn? In a nutshell my answer would be: 'Christian obedience comes to an end at the point where further service becomes impossible – and only there'. That happens incontrovertibly when the suggestion is made to the Christian that he should deny his existence as a Christian and abandon his particular Christian task.[91]

But while Käsemann indicates the central Christian concern in the world as that of pointing to the lordship of Christ, he also correctly emphasizes that his lordship is being manifested many times in hidden forms beyond our perception and even understanding. It is worth quoting him in full:

> What we have to do is to authenticate the Christ as the hidden Lord of the world in our doing and in our being. The outward form which corresponds to this content of the hidden Lord of the world may be the narrowing down and straitening of the Church's room for manoeuvre even into the compass of a prison cell or a grave. Sometimes the Lord of the world speaks more audibly out of prison cells and graves than out of the life of churches which congratulate themselves on their concordat with the State. The space his lordship occupies is not identical with our space, the fact that we are hemmed in does not annul the breadth of his word, nor does our death annul his possibilities. A place on earth for us and our institutions is not the ultimate criterion about which our deeds and omissions have to be orientated. The boundary of our service is the point at which we cease to acknowledge Christ as Lord of the world, not the point at which the hiddenness of this Lord as such is demonstrated and made sensible to us.[92]

Thus, any effort to interpret this passage properly should consider its complexity and the multilayered distinctions and nuances Paul makes, and must avoid a rigid labelling of Paul as '*either* a liberator or an oppressor, a radical critic *or* [a] conservative supporter of the *status quo*'.[93] In doing so, we will be able to detect Paul's more complex

---

to submit to the authorities, an ironic reading of the text results in a subversion of the very authorities it appears to commend' (Carter, 'The Irony of Romans 13', p. 209).

90. Horrell, 'Peaceable', p. 88. He further adds: 'Insofar as Paul . . . regards rulers as there because God has given them their position, he does add a certain divine legitimisation to Roman imperial rule. But equally, by insisting that it is God who has granted the rulers their role, Paul . . . relativizes their position: it is theirs not on the grounds of their own might or (pseudo-divine) status, but only because God has chosen to allow it to be so; and what God has granted God can equally take away' (ibid.).

91. Käsemann, 'Principles', p. 214.

92. Ibid., p. 215.

93. Horrell, 'Peaceable', p. 89.

understanding of the dynamic of the Christians' relationship with the powers that be, to recognise his position as one of critical engagement in the life of the city.[94] James Dunn correctly observes that Paul's use of Hellenistic administration language and categories in this chapter reveals his concern for the churches' existence and function within the everyday social and political realities of Rome.[95]

> Μηδενὶ μηδὲν ὀφείλετε εἰ μὴ τὸ ἀλλήλους ἀγαπᾶν· ὁ γὰρ ἀγαπῶν τὸν ἕτερον νόμον πεπλήρωκεν. τὸ γὰρ . . . καὶ εἴ τις ἑτέρα ἐντολή, ἐν τῷ λόγῳ τούτῳ ἀνακεφαλαιοῦται [ἐν τῷ]· ἀγαπήσεις τὸν πλησίον σου ὡς σεαυτόν,
>
> Owe no one anything, except to love one another; for the one who loves another has fulfilled the law. All these and any other commandment . . . are summed up in this word, 'Love your neighbour as yourself' (vv. 8–10).

Paul concludes his argument about Christians' relationships with the wider world by reaffirming love as the central element of an authentic Christian living. It is clear from the context that for Paul love, as a practice of reconciliation, is not limited to the community of believers but must extend also to 'the other' – who might be the enemy (ch. 12 vv. 14, 17, 21) or the governing authorities (13.1–7).

The last verses, 13.11–14, place Paul's discussion within an eschatological framework as he encourages the believers to live appropriately 'between the times', following Christ as the pattern of their Christian living. Paul was firmly convinced that with the death and resurrection of Jesus the new eschatological age has dawned, but it will only be completely established with Jesus' second coming. Therefore, Christians live 'between the times', and as such they have the responsibility to live 'honourably, as in the day' (v. 13). Paul assumes that the believers in Rome also 'know what hour it is' and so they should 'wake from sleep' (v. 11) and live up to the expectations of the new age – that is, to live fully in a manner that is appropriate to the new life that they share in Christ. This means to 'lay aside the works of darkness' (v. 12b)

---

94. Towner, 'Romans 13'.

95. Dunn, *Romans*. However, Dunn's opinion that Paul draws on the Jewish political wisdom accumulated and tested over years of oppression and dispersion, in order 'to counsel a policy of political quietism', may need to be further nuanced. Following Pheme Perkins (*Love Commands in the New Testament* (New York: Paulist: 1982), p. 98), Dunn points out that Paul's use of such language indicated to his readers 'that the Christian is willing to belong to the larger society, and that he/she is not out to subvert the social order'. But see the position of de Kruijf, who states that 'for Paul, participation in social life appears to be entirely on the edge of his mind, receiving minimal concentration. The contextual point is really the admonition to the community to join in the *Pax Romana* and not to invite persecution' (de Kruijf, 'Function of Romans 13', p. 233). Similarly, Neil Elliott ('Romans 13:1–7', pp. 187–88) believes that Paul's benevolent characterization of the ruling authorities is a 'contradiction of Paul's thought' and that 'we can hardly suppose that Paul regarded the civil authorities with a resigned sense of inevitability'. However, as we have seen in our argument so far, this position gives no credit to Paul's more balanced and nuanced position vis-à-vis the place and role of authorities as part of God's intention for creation and for society.

such as 'reviling and drunkenness', 'debauchery and licentiousness', 'quarrelling and jealousy' (v. 13) and 'gratifying the desires of the flesh' (v. 14b).[96] Instead, they should 'put on the armour of light' (v. 12c) and indeed, ἐνδύσασθε τὸν κύριον Ἰησοῦν Χριστόν, 'put on the Lord Jesus Christ' (v. 14b). It is significant that Paul includes the reference to the 'Lord Jesus Christ' in the context of his emphasis on appropriate conduct in the world. This shows clearly, pointing back to the dynamic of baptism and of the believer being incorporated 'in Christ' (ch. 6), that their lives, being radically defined by their union with Christ, must also be shaped by it. The lordship of Christ and his sovereignty over all creation, to which Paul points here by identifying Jesus as 'Lord', is the strongest ally in the fight against all kinds and forms of evil.[97]

The above discussion leads us to conclude that Paul presents an active and positive involvement of the church in the world, advocating practices that are conducive to a meaningful and peaceful life in the larger society. While we can detect in Paul's position hints to support a view that the governing authorities can be held accountable to their God-given task, his exhortations give primacy to practices of reconciliation as the appropriate Christian attitude to, and relationships with, the wider world, including the authorities. The entire discussion is placed in the framework of the lordship of Christ and of the believers as beings 'in Christ' thus carrying out the story of God's reconciliation of the world in Christ. And they will do that both by proclamation and by living out the reconciliation accomplished in Christ.

6.5 *Practices of reconciliation in Romans 14–15*

In Romans 14–15 Paul addresses a specific issue that arose in the Christian communities in Rome, namely the clash between 'the weak' and 'the strong' (most probably between various groups of believers of Jewish and Gentile provenance),[98] having to do with their respective different convictions and practices regarding particular foods and the keeping of special days.[99] As is clear from the letter, there were believers in Rome who had taken arrogant attitudes and had shown strong tendencies towards pride and high self-esteem, based on their different religious commitments, ethnic

96. This is a clear reference to the 'works of the flesh' which Paul lists in Gal. 5.19–21, but also to what he just said in Rom. 1.28–32 describing the state of humanity in rebellion against God.

97. Wright, *Paul: Fresh Perspectives*, p. 39.

98. Caution should be shown in defining the exact identity of the 'weak' and the 'strong'. This has been a matter of dispute, and none of the groups is to be easily classified as either 'Jewish' or 'Gentile'. It is interesting that in these two chapters Paul does not use the word 'Jew' or 'Gentile' until the conclusion in 15:7–13. Paul as a Jewish Christian identifies himself with 'the strong'.

99. Against Karris, for example, who sees Romans 14–15 addressed to a hypothetical situation, 'Romans 14:1–15:13 and the Occasion of Romans', in Donfried (ed.), *The Romans Debate*, pp. 65–84. For a similar position, see J. Paul Sampley, 'The Weak and the Strong: Paul's Careful and Crafty Rhetorical Strategy in Romans 14:1–15:13', in L. Michael White and O. Larry Yarbrough (eds), *The Social World of the First Christians: Studies in Honor of Wayne A. Meeks* (Minneapolis: Fortress, 1994), pp. 40–52. For Sampley, the categories of 'weak' and 'strong' have 'no objective referents in the Romans congregations'.

background, and cultural superiority. The problem Paul has with such behaviour does not have to do so much with the various differences between their convictions and practices, but rather with the negative alteration of the internal dynamic of the community in ways incompatible with the gospel. To judge or despise the other, or to be a stumbling block for others, are practices of exclusion which Paul describes as sinful because they destroy the relationships between the members of the community, which is the body of Christ. In his response Paul tries to promote a sense of solidarity and unity; and he does that not by imposing uniformity but rather by legitimising different ethical convictions and practices, thus enabling the believers to renounce criticism and judgement of one another. Identifying with 'the strong', and insisting that they should follow the example of Christ rather than please themselves (15.1–6), Paul's major concern is not to defend and/or reject the legitimacy of the arguments brought forth by the 'weak' and the 'strong', but rather to urge them to 'pursue what makes for peace and mutual upbuilding' (4.19). Peace and mutual acceptance expressed in a life of genuine love for others represent Paul's central concern in this last section of the letter.

The structure of the argument in Romans 14.1–15.13 is simple: Paul begins his exhortations with a plea for 'welcoming the weak' (14.1) and ends with a similar plea for mutual acceptance (15.7), with the material in between being divided into three main sections. The first section, 14.1–12, introduces the issue and deals with it by showing how the weak and the strong find themselves on common ground: they all are serving the same Lord and will all appear at God's judgement. The second passage, 14.13–23, describes the practical ways in which the groups should live together, in love, respecting one another's conscience, and with the common purpose to 'pursue what makes for peace and for mutual upbuilding' (v. 19). The last section, 15.1–17, is an appeal for mutual acceptance and welcome based on the example of Christ. This is a clear allusion and connection to the previous section of Romans 5–6, especially to 5.6–21. Rom. 15.7–13, as the conclusion of the section (and of the letter), repeats the call to mutual acceptance grounded on Christ's example and rejoices for the great coming together of Jews and Gentiles in one family under the lordship of Christ, just as it was foretold in the Scriptures.

6.5.1 *Romans 14*

The main point of the first paragraph of this chapter (vv. 1–12) is simply that expressed in v. 3a: ὁ ἐσθίων τὸν μὴ ἐσθίοντα μὴ ἐξουθενείτω, ὁ δὲ μὴ ἐσθίων τὸν ἐσθίοντα μὴ κρινέτω, 'those who eat must not despise those who abstain, and those who abstain must not pass judgement on those who eat'. This point is then repeated towards the end of the section, in v. 10a. These instructions are then offered a strong theological basis. Paul begins by giving the essential reason why passing judgement and despising are unacceptable – 'for God has welcomed them' (3b); and then he elaborates this basis further by pointing out that every believer is a servant of Christ, the Lord (vv. 4–9), and that each will give an account before God's judgement seat (vv. 10b–12).

That both sides have experienced God's 'welcome' was the basic message of 3.21–5.11, which would result in 'righteousness, 'grace', 'peace', 'joy', and 'hope' (5.1–5) to which Paul most probably alludes here. This is confirmed by Paul's concise description of the key characteristics of 'the kingdom of God' as 'righteousness and peace and joy in the Holy Spirit' in 14.17 'in terms that exactly summarize 5.1–5'.[100] If this is true for Paul, to despise and/or judge the other is not to live out the essence of the gospel which calls for a constant concern to honour and serve the Lord (vv. 6–9). What defines the Christian community is a life lived not 'to himself' but 'to the Lord' (vv. 7–8). By his death and resurrection Christ became the Lord of the whole world, and to honour and serve the Lord means to live in harmony and unity, differences notwithstanding. Indeed, there is place for diversity as long as everyone's conscience is pure (v. 5) and allows for various forms of expression of the Christian truth. To live according to the logic of the gospel and in the light of the life of Christ is to be community oriented. Everyone is to nurture and embody reconciling practices – harmony and solidarity, peace, love, and regard for others – which enhance and enrich life together. But at the same time, the community is to maintain and manifest a degree of difference among its members as the 'body' metaphor illustrates (12.4–8). In other words, we can say that Paul encourages the diversity of gifts and practices while he insists on the fundamental value of love and regard for the other; that he stresses the need for corporate solidarity while acknowledging the presence of differences and diversity.[101] In the concrete context of chs 14–15, their freedom should not be a licence to despise or judge the other. On the contrary, they should live out their differences in such a manner as to bring honour to the Lord and thanks to God (v. 6). The frequent references to Jesus Christ as Lord in a section so concerned with the unity of the church across traditional barriers might be an indication that Paul is also concerned with the Christian witness to the lordship of Christ in the wider world.[102] In Ephesians we found exactly this fact expressed about the nature and mission of the church: to declare to the principalities and powers that the coming together of Jews and Gentiles in one community is the great act of God's reconciliation of the world through the Lord Jesus Christ (Eph. 3.10). A possible division along ethnic or cultural lines within the churches in Rome would show that they are still conformed to the patterns of this world and have not been transformed by this gospel of reconciliation.

In the second part of the chapter (vv. 13–23) Paul goes a step further in his

---

100. Wright, *Romans*, p. 736.

101. Horrell dedicates an entire book, *Solidarity and Difference*, to highlighting the value of corporate solidarity and difference as fundamental to Paul's ethics. As he rightly points out, these aspects are crucial for any social or political ethics. Elsewhere he states: 'the central challenge to any ethical theory, at least from a Pauline perspective, is to show how it proposes to engender such human solidarity . . . how to nurture a sense of community while also ensuring that difference and diversity are not obliterated in a drive to conformity and sameness' (Horrell, 'Peaceable', pp. 92–93).

102. Wright, *Romans*, p. 739. He also points out that internal conflicts over the implications of the gospel could determine an even greater tension with the Jewish communities and so it will inevitably give ground for persecution from the authorities.

argument. Merely refraining from judgement is not enough; Christians are encouraged to 'never put a stumbling block or hindrance in the way of another' (v. 13). This would be an intentional decision on the part of the 'strong' to use their freedom in such a way as to avoid causing spiritual harm to the 'weak' (vv. 13b, 15ac, 20–21),[103] to let love determine their conduct (v. 15) while their highest concern should be to 'pursue what makes for peace and for mutual upbuilding' – τὰ τῆς εἰρήνης διώκωμεν καὶ τὰ τῆς οἰκοδομῆς τῆς εἰς ἀλλήλους (v. 19).

In v. 17 Paul states: οὐ γάρ ἐστιν ἡ βασιλεία τοῦ θεοῦ βρῶσις καὶ πόσις ἀλλὰ δικαιοσύνη καὶ εἰρήνη καὶ χαρὰ ἐν πνεύματι ἁγίῳ, 'for the kingdom of God is not food and drink but righteousness and peace and joy in the Holy Spirit'. Since usually he does not use the expression 'kingdom of God', its use here may indicate Paul's dependence on a tradition emphasizing Jesus' own teaching on the true nature of the kingdom.[104] Significant about this instance, however, is Paul's emphasis on the fact that the essential characteristics of the kingdom reflect an adequate dynamic of relationships among the believers, whereby 'righteousness' indicates a proper conduct towards the other and 'peace' similarly refers to the horizontal, social dimension, a fact clearly shown by the qualification in v. 19 (see also 12.18).[105] If this is indeed a summary of the passage in Rom. 5.1–5, as it seems to bring together all its major themes, then Paul provides here a crucial link between practices of reconciliation (unity and acceptance) and the most important theological topics he dealt with previously. This illustrates once again that theology and ethics, faith and praxis, belong inseparably together. 'The one who *thus* serves Christ is acceptable to God and has human approval', continues Paul in v. 18; i.e., those who embody 'righteousness, peace, and joy in the Holy Spirit' in their life together, are serving Christ in a manner acceptable to God. The imperative in v. 19, 'let us then pursue what makes for peace and for mutual upbuilding' is a further confirmation that the kingdom of God – that is, life 'in Christ' – is characterized by a constant concern for the other, for peace and mutual upbuilding. In other words, the criteria by which the believers should guide their lives are the central characteristics of the kingdom of God: righteousness, peace,

---

103. Kathy Ehrensperger argues in her book, *That We May Be Mutually Encouraged: Feminism and the New Perspective in Pauline Studies* (London: T&T Clark, 2004), that Paul's concern in dealing with the relationship between the 'weak' and the 'strong' was to protect the weaker partner. Interpreting Paul from within Judaism, Ehrensperger shows that Paul is more a relational thinker rather than an abstract, systematic one, and that he defends mutuality and diversity, by protecting the weak and yet not alienating 'the other'. It is an excellent study that proposes an interpretation of Paul that goes beyond the 'new perspective' and beyond traditional feminist approaches. She is probably right to emphasize the Jewish categories of thought that shaped Paul in a significant way. However, in her desire to refute an interpretation of Paul based on an Western post-Enlightenment rationality (which Ehrensperger sees rooted in Graeco-Roman philosophical categories), she probably sees a too stark contrast between the 'Jewish' and the 'Hellenistic' elements in Paul's thinking.

104. See Thompson, *Clothed with Christ*, pp. 200–07.

105. Moo, *Romans*, p. 857.

and joy in the Holy Spirit. Food and drink, and other 'non-essential' aspects should be used and practised in such a way as to contribute to peace and mutual upbuilding.

6.5.2 *Romans 15.1–13*

This passage contains two parts with a similar structure: a command to welcome one another which is based on what Christ has done – first expressed negatively, not to please themselves because Christ did not please himself (vv. 2–3), and the second positively, to accept one another because Christ has welcomed them (vv. 7); the appeal is further supported by Scripture, and finally leads to praise of God and hope. It is clear that Paul's point is about practical reconciliation, i.e., mutual welcome and acceptance beyond the differences they have in their practice and convictions, reconciliation that would be expressed in their united worship and glorification of God.

> Ὀφείλομεν δὲ ἡμεῖς οἱ δυνατοὶ τὰ ἀσθενήματα τῶν ἀδυνάτων βαστάζειν καὶ μὴ ἑαυτοῖς
> ἀρέσκειν. ἕκαστος ἡμῶν τῷ πλησίον ἀρεσκέτω εἰς τὸ ἀγαθὸν πρὸς οἰκοδομήν· καὶ γὰρ ὁ
> Χριστὸς οὐχ ἑαυτῷ ἤρεσεν,
>
> We who are strong ought to put up with the failings of the weak, and not to please ourselves.
> Each of us must please our neighbour for the good purpose of building up the neighbour. For
> Christ did not please himself (vv. 1–3a).

Paul's exhortation to the strong is to bear the weakness of the weak and not to please themselves in seeking their own benefits, but rather to consider the benefit of the neighbour and build up the community as a whole. This is another explanation of what love means at the level of community. But if in 14.13–18 the example of Christ was implicit, now Paul brings the story of Christ to the forefront explicitly and forcefully, with the declared intention that believers let their lives be shaped by it. The Roman Christians are to make the example of Jesus the paradigm for their life, seen practically in their self-denial, active love for their neighbour expressed as 'seeking their good', and as living in harmony. Just as 'Christ did not please himself' but rather took upon himself the burden of others, so they should renounce their own privileges for the sake of the other.[106] As beneficiaries of God's grace, shown in Christ selflessly giving himself for others, the believers should show the same grace as they 'live in harmony with one another, in accord with Christ Jesus' (v. 5b). It will be only in such unity that they would 'glorify the God and Father of our Lord Jesus Christ' (v. 6), which is also a great act of witness to the gospel they profess, a point Paul strengthens further in vv. 7–13. Meanwhile, going through the present circumstances of difficulty

---

106. Dunn (*Romans*) puts it well: 'The model is Christ: if he was willing to suffer misunderstanding and abuse to the extent of giving his own life, how could those who both gloried in their own strength and called Jesus Lord refuse the much less self-limitation of curbing the liberty of their conduct when it was causing their fellow Christians to fall? Greater strength means greater responsibility for others.'

and suffering, the believers need the patience and encouragement provided by the Scriptures, which also leads to true hope (v. 4).[107]

In vv. 7–13 Paul seems to draw together the entire argument of the letter into a fitting conclusion, in which he also enlarges his previous argument to point to a more comprehensive unity between Jews and Gentiles in God's eschatological plan. Once again, it is the story of Christ, found in the OT that provides the basis for his last appeal.

Διὸ προσλαμβάνεσθε ἀλλήλους, καθὼς καὶ ὁ Χριστὸς προσελάβετο ὑμᾶς εἰς δόξαν τοῦ θεοῦ, 'Welcome one another, therefore, just as Christ has welcomed you for the glory of God' (v. 7). While προσλαμβάνεσθε ('welcome') points to the very same verb in 14.1 indicating that chs 14–15 are particularly in view here, by the use of ἀλλήλους ('one another') Paul enlarges his appeal from 14.1 to become a general call to all for mutual acceptance among those who continue to maintain different views and practices. It would only be by their mutual acceptance (and not by exclusion due to their different understanding and practices of their faith) that their life would be 'according to Christ Jesus' (15.5). The very reference to the example of Christ (as in v. 3), suggests that Paul has a double intention: to address the particular issues of the 'weak' and 'strong' in Rome, and to make a theological statement about the reconciling nature of the new family of God constituted 'in Christ'. It is particularly here, in v. 7, that Paul makes explicit one of the most essential points he made throughout the previous chapters, namely that Christ's work of reconciliation, as he described it especially in ch. 5, is 'the crucial basis and model for what the church must now do'.[108] Just as Christ welcomed and reconciled them, so the believers should welcome and reconcile one another. The believers are to 'welcome one another' because Christ has welcomed them (v. 7b). He has also brought together in the same community Jews and Gentiles (vv. 8–9a), according to, and in fulfilment of, God's promises recorded in the Scriptures (vv. 9b–12). A special emphasis is communicated here – the conjunction καθὼς, '*just as*', which Paul uses, indicates some sort of comparison, thus highlighting not only the fact of Christ's welcome but also *the manner* in which he did it.[109] On the one hand, the readers would bear in mind Paul's exposition of God's reconciliation and of them being accepted; this was an act of pure grace in which Christ manifested his love towards them while they were weak, sinners, even enemies of God. *In the same manner* they should manifest their love towards the other, to

---

107. Wright makes the point that, for Paul, the Scriptures provided such help for the believers as they learned to read the great story of Israel reaching its climax in Jesus Christ. (*Romans*, p. 746.)

108. Ibid. To be sure, Paul's reference here cannot and should not be limited to the work of reconciliation; it refers in a more comprehensive sense to the multifaceted work of Christ, who manifested God's faithfulness by fulfilling the Jewish promises and by being a blessing for the entire world. Indeed, as the next verses clearly explicate, it was by fulfilling the story of Israel that Christ made it possible for the Gentiles to share in God's blessings (vv. 8–9), in line with God's intention to have mercy on all, as Paul made clear in Romans 4 where he shows that through Abraham the entire world will be blessed. God's blessings and favours were not meant for the ethnic Israel alone but for all nations.

109. Dunn, *Romans* 15.7.

show the same grace to others that they have been shown by God. On the other hand, Χριστὸς διάκονον γεγενῆσθα 'Christ has become *a servant*' (v. 8.a), thus showing God's mercy to all nations, via Israel (vv. 8–9) and has dismantled the barriers that existed between Jews and Gentiles, forming one new community in which both groups share an equal status. *In the same manner*, the believers should live in harmony and service to both Jews and Gentiles, and their welcoming of the other should not be restricted by ethnic lines. Furthermore, Paul advocates a general welcome that should extend also to those with diverse ethical practices.

λέγω γὰρ Χριστὸν διάκονον γεγενῆσθαι περιτομῆς ὑπὲρ ἀληθείας θεοῦ, εἰς τὸ βεβαιῶσαι τὰς ἐπαγγελίας τῶν πατέρων, τὰ δὲ ἔθνη ὑπὲρ ἐλέους δοξάσαι τὸν θεόν, καθὼς γέγραπται· διὰ τοῦτο ἐξομολογήσομαί σοι ἐν ἔθνεσιν καὶ τῷ ὀνόματί σου ψαλω,

For I tell you that Christ has become a servant of the circumcised on behalf of the truth of God in order that he might confirm the promises given to the patriarchs, and in order that the Gentiles might glorify God for his mercy. As it is written, 'Therefore I will confess you among the Gentiles, and sing praises to your name' (vv. 8–9).

The references here to the priority and the privileges Jews enjoyed, as well as to the acceptance of the Gentiles into God's new family, are an indication that Paul is bringing to a conclusion the main thrust of the entire letter.[110] It was exactly this great new eschatological community of Jews and Gentiles gathered together in one family that represented Jesus' accomplishment on the cross. And Paul stresses this point through a series of quotations from the OT where he finds expressed the unified purposes of God for the entire world and the reality of the nations coming to worship the God of Israel as the true God, the creator and redeemer. And it is exactly what happens now through the work of Christ, when the Gentiles joining the new eschatological community of God's people in Christ recognize and worship the true God of the whole world. Indeed, Paul concludes in vv. 12–13 with an intentional quotation from Isa. 11.10 which, in the larger context of Isa. 11.1–12.6, speaks about the ultimate purposes of God to renew the entire creation and to make a new community of Jews and Gentiles that will worship the true God. Wright correctly remarks that one should not overlook the reference in v. 12 ('The root of Jesse will appear, he who rises up to rule the nations') as a clear echo of 1.3–4, especially to the resurrection of Jesus – which 'constituted him as the Messiah and Lord of the whole world'.[111] Most significantly, one cannot, and probably should not, miss the strong political implications of the statement that Jesus is the Lord who 'rules the nations', a statement made in the very heart of the Roman Empire, whose Caesar had similar claims about himself. In giving their total allegiance to Christ as their Lord, they would offer the strongest testimony to the message and power of the gospel. In this

110. Ibid., 15:8–9.
111. Wright, *Romans*, p. 748.

light, Katherine Grieb's fine point is well taken when she says that Paul's argument here 'leads to a redefinition of the imitation of Christ when it is understood in terms of "witnesses".'[112]

Ὁ δὲ θεὸς τῆς ἐλπίδος πληρώσαι ὑμᾶς πάσης χαρᾶς καὶ εἰρήνης ἐν τῷ πιστεύειν, εἰς τὸ περισσεύειν ὑμᾶς ἐν τῇ ἐλπίδι ἐν δυνάμει πνεύματος ἁγίου,

May the God of hope fill you with all joy and peace in believing, so that you may abound in hope by the power of the Holy Spirit (v. 13).

It is significant that Paul chooses to conclude this section and indeed his letter (vv. 5, 6, 13, 18) by reiterating themes (endurance, encouragement, joy, peace, hope, and the Holy Spirit), which strongly echo Rom. 5.1–5.[113] In this way he again makes plain that the practices of reconciliation he is appealing for belong together as essential aspects of the gospel. If in chs 5–8 Paul has shown the way in which the believers are incorporated 'in Christ' and that they share in the story of Christ, in 15.1–13 he points further to concrete ways in which they are to follow the example of Christ and be conformed to his image. Paul's final emphasis on the theme of 'hope', which is mentioned no fewer than three times in the last two verses of the section, thus recalling its development in chs 5–8, provides a most proper conclusion to Paul's line of argument: it is the eschatological perspective of God's assured future that represents the best foundation for an appropriate life lived in the power of the Spirit and according to the example of Christ. It would only be within the larger horizon of God's reconciliation of the world in Christ, which gives assurance and hope, that Christians can go about their Christian life in the world with the same message of love and reconciliation. There is no doubt that Paul was able to practise and proclaim such a message of reconciliation at the social level because, as we saw in a previous chapter, he had a grand vision of reconciliation as the larger horizon within which he operated. And he is nowhere suggesting that this was something he could claim only for himself; rather, he believed that all those 'in Christ', who have experienced God's grace and reconciliation, could be assured of the same vision of final reconciliation of all things in Christ. But the most fundamental aspect of reconciliation that Paul wanted to get across was the definitive reconciliation of the world achieved already in Christ. It is only the atoning and reconciling work of Christ that gives a real possibility for human reconciliation, and without this, any attempt at reconciliation is groundless. This important point is made very well by John Webster, who states:

112. Grieb, *The Story of Romans*, p. 119.

113. Wright, *Romans*, p. 744. What Paul wanted to communicate, states Wright, is this: 'This is how to obtain in practice the great central blessings I outlined at the heart of the letter. Allow "justification by faith" to produce "fellowship by faith", and you will know the peace, patience, joy, and hope that the Spirit brings' (ibid.).

Because this act was done by this one, there and then, acts of reconciliation are more than an attempt to create reality by establishing imagined communities which offer a different sort of social space from that of the world's routine violence. Human acts of reconciliation are in accordance with the structure of reality which God in Christ creates and to the existence of which the gospel testifies; and therefore they are acts which tend towards the true end of creation that God's reconciling act establishes once and for all in Christ's reconciling person and work'.[114]

It is only within such a vision of reality, generating a sure and sound hope that a real possibility exists and an irresistible impetus is given to the ministry of reconciliation in the world, including the world of Caesar.

By bringing together the various narrative features of the story of Christ in his conclusion in 15:7–13, Paul reasserts his conviction that this story functions as both the ground and the model for the life of the believers in the world. This also offers an excellent window into Paul's theologizing, thus challenging us to understand Paul's thought and theology not in terms of 'doctrines' and 'principles', though he holds these as very important, but in terms of the grand story of God's dealing with the world, through Christ, a story which takes concrete forms and shapes in many other smaller stories to which Paul refers again and again in his writings, not least in the stories of the Christians to whom he writes.

6.6 *Summary and conclusion*

This chapter has argued that Paul's exhortations in Romans 12–15 are not an 'appendix' to his letter but represent a further elaboration of the gospel and are therefore integral to the overall argument of the letter. We have shown that this section of the letter offers concrete elaborations of the theme of reconciliation which Paul so thoroughly has grounded in the story of Christ in Romans 5–8. Thus, we have pointed out that the overwhelming emphasis on 'unity', 'acceptance', 'love', 'peace', and 'welcome' illustrates Paul's rich symbolism of reconciliation which he has given expression in the form of 'reconciling practices'. Paul urged his readers to live out these practices as an integral part of the gospel, an inherent aspect of their being 'in Christ'. Indeed, we have seen that Romans 12–15 could be understood as a working out of the implications of being 'in Christ', a position which commits those who respond to the gospel to a transformed and renewed life in obedience to Christ. The social meaning of reconciliation in Romans 12–15 is explicated by Paul in various forms: as a genuine love for one another and for enemies; as welcoming the weak and powerless; as affirming 'the other'; as blessing persecutors; as overcoming evil with

---

114. John Webster, 'The Ethics of Reconciliation', in Colin Gunton (ed.), *The Theology of Reconciliation* (London: T&T Clark/Continuum, 2003), p. 117. See also Karl Barth's strong emphasis on the reality and finality of God's reconciliation of the world in Christ (*Church Dogmatics*, IV.1, p. 76).

good; as living at peace with all. These practices of reconciliation are anchored in, and presuppose, the story of Christ both as the ground and the paradigm for a reconciling way of life. We have argued that, for Paul, to respond to the gospel is to acknowledge and accept the truth it proclaims, *and* to live according to the logic of the gospel, the logic of the kingdom of God, the logic of the vision of the new creation. Thus, the radical transformation and renewal of the self is *both* enabled *and* required by the gospel. However, to live according to the logic of the gospel and in the light of the life of Christ also means to be community oriented; and that is to create a community in which everyone is to nurture and embody reconciling practices that enhance and enrich the life together: harmony and solidarity, peace, love, and regard for others. Paul encourages a diversity of gifts and practices while insisting at the same time on the fundamental value of love and regard for 'the other'.

More specifically, we have seen that in Rom. 12.1–2, which sets the tone for the entire section, Paul appeals, on the basis of the new identity and status of the believers before God, for a renewed and transformed way of life, for a total commitment to the will of God, and for a radically new way of conceiving and relating to the world. Paul wants to gets across very forcefully to his readers that persecutions and suffering from the surrounding society should not determine conformity to its dominant values and way of life. Even more significantly, he urges that in the face of difficulties and hostility the believers are to manifest a reconciling way of life even towards those who provoke suffering, towards their enemies, as he stressed it several times throughout chs 12–15. What Paul emphasized was not simply an acknowledgment of these virtues but rather their actual embodiment in the everyday life of the believers – it was this aspect that made the difference with the outside world when it came to the things that they commonly acknowledged as 'good' (12.17; 12.21; 13.3–4). Indeed, as members fulfil and develop their own part within the body of Christ it is their harmonious living that becomes the model for the wider world (12.3–8). The actual reality of the relationships among the various groups of believers in Rome (criticisms, superiority, judgements, contempt and conflict), was against the gospel and so Paul argued that the practices of reconciliation were an integral part of the gospel they professed. This is clearly expressed in the summary statement describing the new reality of life in 'the kingdom of God', as 'righteousness and peace and joy in the Holy Spirit' (14.17). Living in a reconciling way, and pursuing things that make 'for peace and mutual upbuilding' is what Paul calls a service to Christ which is 'acceptable to God and approved by men' (14.18–19). Presenting their bodies as living sacrifices implies therefore an important dimension of love, peace, and reconciliation with 'the other'. And this 'other' is not restricted to the community of believers but clearly extends to outsiders, including enemies and persecutors, the government and authorities (13.1–7), in fact to 'all', as Paul makes plain in 12.14–21. The topic of reconciliation is thus important for the entire letter, and the way Paul developed and argued for it shows that he understood it to have significant implications for the life of the believers in Rome.

We have also seen that for Paul, to live by the gospel means to live grounded on, and modelled by, the example of Christ (15.3, 7). The life of 'sacrifice' that Paul urges his readers to live, their sacrificial obedience to Christ, is a willing surrender of one's prerogatives for the sake of 'the other' as modelled by Jesus Christ himself, who 'did not please himself' but suffered on behalf of others (15.3). The barriers between the insider and the outsider are broken down by Paul as he urges the believers in Rome, with utmost seriousness, to 'live peaceably with all' (12.8) and to manifest a 'genuine love' towards all. This will give evidence of their new life in Christ and enable them to be a witness to the world for the lordship of Christ. For Paul, living out the gospel of reconciliation is a witness to God's intervention and redemption of the world in Christ, a truth that must be proclaimed and made known to the ends of the earth. By drawing obvious inferences from the earlier parts of his argument, Paul shows that the believers' life 'in Christ' and 'in accordance with the Spirit' means a transformation of their lives and renewal of their minds, leading to daily sacrifices for others expressed in concrete manifestations of love, peace, reconciliation, harmony, tolerance, and consideration for 'the other'. Such behaviour would illustrate their obedience and devotion to the only and true Lord, Jesus Christ.

We have also argued that Romans 13.1–7 should be interpreted within its immediate context as being bracketed by two exhortations to love (12.9–21 and 13.8–10). Paul wanted to show that the Christian commitment to love is not limited to the individual relationships (within and outside the Christian community) but includes also the believers' living as responsible citizens in the society at large. While responding to a specific situation in Rome, Paul develops a larger view of the governing authorities in line with his Jewish theology – he presents the ordering of society under government as God's intention. With this in mind, believers should accept and be willing to live within such structures. Significantly, by presenting the 'authorities' as God's instruments and so making them answerable to God, Paul overrides their claim to being the ultimate and highest point of reference and their demand for total and unqualified obedience. It is thus Paul's strong theological basis that legitimizes and – at the same time – limits the authority of the government. We have concluded that a proper interpretation of Romans 13 would consider carefully Paul's complex understanding of the dynamic of the relationship of Christians to the powers that be, as well as his appeal for critical engagement in the life of the city, and would thus avoid a rigid categorization of Paul as either a radical criticizer or a blind supporter of the political powers.

Our analysis of Romans 14–15 has revealed that Paul regarded the attitude of exclusion and mutually passing judgement as incompatible with the gospel of reconciliation. Grounding his appeal on the pattern of Christ's self-giving love for 'the other', he exhorts his readers to renounce practices of exclusion and instead welcome and accept one another, respect and have a high regard for one another, live in peace and build up one another. While Paul does not impose uniformity on the believers' various ethical convictions and practices, he is absolutely clear that these practices of reconciliation are binding for all, since they represent the very essence of the gospel, of their new life 'in Christ'. We see once again Paul's intrinsic link between one's ethical/theological convictions and the embodiment of those beliefs in everyday life.

Paul's emphasis on welcoming *just as* Christ has welcomed them, with clear reference back to his argument in ch. 5, illustrates clearly that God's reconciliation in Christ became the basis and model for the believers' welcoming and reconciling life towards 'the other'. Just as Christ manifested his love while they were weak, sinners, even enemies, *in the same manner* they should manifest their love towards 'the other' and show the same grace to others that they have received from God. Just as Christ became a servant to all, showing God's mercy to all nations, thus dismantling the barriers that existed between Jews and Gentiles, *in the same manner* the believers should live in harmony with and service to all, overcoming any division of ethnicity, religion and social status. It was such a life, in total allegiance and obedience to Christ as Lord, that would offer the strongest testimony to the message and power of the gospel of reconciliation.

Finally, we saw that the story of Christ functions as both the ground and the model for the life of the believers in the world and that Paul was resolute in his effort to persuade the Roman Christians that they were themselves active participants in the same grand story of God's redeeming the world. The practices of reconciliation are placed by Paul within the larger horizon of God's reconciliation of the world in Christ, thus providing an unshakable foundation for the possibility and actuality of social reconciliation. The ultimate vision of reconciliation of all things in Christ gives assurance and hope, and an irresistible impetus for the ministry of reconciliation in all its forms and manifestations.

PAUL'S UNDERSTANDING OF THE SOCIAL SIGNIFICANCE
OF RECONCILIATION AND THE ROMANIAN CONTEXT

7.1 *Introduction*

It is often said that religion represents a factor of disunity and conflict rather than of unity and mutual respect within a society. We have to admit that in many instances in the modern world that holds true. This was even true to some extent for the believers in first-century Rome, who did not necessarily understand the meaning and implications of their faith for their everyday life. What we have learned from Paul, however, is that a true understanding of a reconciling faith in Christ is an obedient faith which commits people to a life in which there is place for difference and diversity, a life of love and self-giving modelled after the pattern of Christ. Indeed, it is their faith that should determine their everyday life; significantly, however, this is the faith of the crucified Christ who, in love, gave himself for others so that they could walk in love and peace with God and with others, a faith that eliminates any ground for social, cultural, economic, ethical, or religious arrogance or superiority.

The centrality of love for Christian ethics as well as its radical, revolutionary nature is another significant aspect of Paul's argument in Romans 5–8 and 12–15. As Paul explicated the meaning of a genuine love in concrete life situations for the believers in Rome, so we today have to reflect, work out and explicate the meaning of love and reconciliation for our own contexts, both at a personal level and at a community level, with the ultimate aim of embodying it in everyday life in the world. Wright captures well this point and rightly insists that: '[w]e urgently need moral reflection, at every level of church and society; on what exactly love is, what it means and does not mean, and more especially the steps of moral learning and effort required to attain it'.[1]

The purpose of this chapter is not (and could not be) to offer an in-depth analysis of the Romanian context and how the Pauline theme of reconciliation has been understood and applied by every Christian tradition. This in itself would have been a sufficiently large topic for an entire separate project. Rather, in a much more limited scope, the intention is to offer some cogent, exegetically based and informed

---

1.   Wright, *Romans*, p. 726.

reflection on the social significance of Paul's understanding of reconciliation and the contribution it could make to an ongoing dialogue on the role of churches in the public arena in the contemporary Romanian context. More could and should be said about the complexity of the social, political, religious, cultural and economic factors which determine and shape the relationships between religion and society in general, between the Christian gospel and culture, between church and state, and between faith and ethnicity. Undoubtedly, further studies on the subject will have to consider research data from these various fields of study.

This chapter begins with a brief but important note on the re-emergence of religious phenomena as an important element in the social arena with a focus on Romania. We will then look at two ways in which Pauline reconciliation is understood and practised by the Romanian Orthodox Church (ROC) and the evangelical churches (EC) and compare these with the findings from our study. Then we will consider a specific issue of ethnic minorities in Romania and see how a Pauline understanding of reconciliation might be relevant to the issue. We will end with a brief summary and conclusion.

7.2 *The return of religious phenomena to the social arena*

If the end of the nineteenth and beginning of the twentieth centuries were dominated by a view of general scepticism regarding the role and future place of religion in the social arena,[2] the end of the twentieth and beginning of the twenty-first centuries mark a spectacular and somewhat unexpected return of the religious phenomenon as an important factor in the public sphere. In recent decades the role of religion has been seen as particularly influential, as a potential factor for social stability/instability and as the motivation for individual conduct; indeed, as an 'absolute necessity for democracy'.[3] The results of a decade of empirical studies conducted by Emory University throughout the world on religious sources and dimensions of human rights and democracy have confirmed that religion is a vital dimension of any democracy,

---

2.   The influence of L. Feuerbach, followed by that of the three 'masters of suspicion', Marx, Nietzsche, and Freud, has been enormous for the attempt to limit the significance of the religious factor and, indeed, to eradicate it completely as a dimension of human existence. For Marx, religion was 'the *opium* of the people' and the future of the classless society and the realization of the *New Man* would see religion disappear altogether, while Nietzsche announced, a little later, the death of God and the birth of *der Übermensh*. Freud, in his turn, saw religion as mental infantilism, social illness and an obsessive neurosis which needs treatment. In his work *The Future of an Illusion* (1927) he pretended to have given a final blow to religion and 'prophesied' a total 'healing' of this disease and its complete disappearance. However, despite the great influence and legacy of this trend of thought in late modernity, even a cursory analysis of the last decades reveals a totally different picture, one in which religion is not only still present but very vigorous and in ascendancy. See further, Silviu Rogobete, 'Morality and Tradition in Post-communist Orthodox Lands: On the Universality of Human Rights. With Special Reference to Romania', *Religion, State and Society* 32(3) (2004), pp. 275–97.

3.   Christoph Von Schönborn, *Oamenii, Biserica, Tara: Crestinismul ca provocare sociala* (Bucuresti: Anastasia, 2000), p. 87.

as it offers the highest framework of reference and values, and gives content and coherence to the structure of human communities and cultures.[4] More specifically,

> Religion is an ineradicable condition of human persons and communities. Religion invariably provides universal sources and scales of values by which many persons and communities govern and measure themselves. Religion invariably provides the sources and scales of dignity and responsibility, shame and respect, restitution and reconciliation that democracy and human rights need to survive and to flourish. Religions must thus be seen as indispensable allies in the modern struggle for human rights and democratization. Their faith and works, their symbols and structures, must be adduced to give meaning and measure to the abstract claims of democratic and human-rights norms.[5]

The findings of the project, however, revealed a paradox regarding both the state of democracy and the actual contribution of religious groups:

> In the 1990s, the world seems to have entered something of a 'Dickensian era'. We have some of the best human-rights protection and democratic policies on the books but some of the worst humans-right abuses and autocratic policies on the ground. Religious groups – in all their theological, cultural, and ethnic diversity – have emerged as both leading villains and leading victims in this Dickensian drama.[6]

Similar conclusions are confirmed by surveys conducted in recent years on the religious attitudes in Western Europe and in Central and Eastern Europe. They have found that in Western Europe, on average 75 per cent of people are associated with a particular religion, and in Eastern Europe more than 80 per cent of people identify themselves as religious.[7] Romania ranks among the highest in Europe in religious adherence, with an astonishing 99.96 per cent of the population indicating they belong to a religious group. The largest proportion affiliated with the Orthodox Church (86.8 per cent), only 0.03 per cent atheists and 0.01 per cent indicating no religious affiliation.[8] The same survey reveals that the church leads among institutions in which Romanians place their trust, with 86 per cent, followed by the army with 69 per cent. However, the implications of this high religiosity for the everyday life of people

---

4. The findings of these projects were published in various journal publications and in a two-volume work entitled *Religious Human Rights in Global Perspective* (The Hague and London: Martinus Nijhoff, 1996).

5. John Witte Jr., 'Introduction: Pluralism, Proselytism, and Nationalism in Eastern Europe', *JES* 24 (1999), pp. 1–6 (1).

6. Ibid., p. 2.

7. *GfK Custom Research Worldwide* on behalf of *Wall Street Journal* Europe, Nuremberg/Frankfurt, 10 December 2004.

8. According to the National Census conducted by the Gallup Organization, Metromidia Transilvania, 2002 and 2004. The other religious groups include: Protestants (6.8%), Catholics (5.6%) and other, mostly Muslim (0.4%).

and its effect on the concrete social, cultural, political and economic realities of the country reveal a disturbing and contradictory reality. Romania, the country with the highest ranking for religiosity in Europe, is also among the leading countries in terms of corruption, poverty and lack of trust.[9] This is how a Romanian journalist described in 2003 some of the Romanian characteristics:

> Defining psychological characteristics of the Romanian people include, for instance, great intolerance to other minority or ethnic groups, significant religious intolerance, great conservatism, unwillingness to participate in civic/social life and movements (unless remuner-ated!), hesitant to embark upon new trajectories in socio-political life, afraid of taking risks and making mistakes, lack of belief in their own strength and capabilities, uncertain about the future, waiting to join the EU but not involving themselves in the process of integration. Romanian society is portrayed as a traditional, conservative society still affected by a deeply embedded communist-era mentality, and traditional, rural beliefs.[10]

The causes are many for such a state of affairs and for the lack of correlation between the predominant religiosity and the actual practice of life.[11] This discrepancy does not invalidate the thesis that religion has a potential for being a positive factor for

---

9.   Silviu Rogobete, 'Between Fundamentalism and Secularization: The Place and the Role of Religion in Post-Communist Orthodox Romania', in S. Devetak, O. Sirbu and S. Rogobete (eds), *Religion and Democracy in Moldova* (Maribor/Chisinau: ISCOMET/ASER, 2005), pp. 105–10. See also Tom Gallagher's impressive and detailed analysis of the complex causes and factors which undermined the development of a stable, independent, and autonomous democracy in Romania, *Theft of a Nation: Romania Since Communism* (London: Hurst, 2005).

10.   Diana Evantia Barca, 'Romanii, inamicii schimbarii', *Evenimentul Zilei* (2 November 2003). A similar negative perception by the outside world media was revealed by a study produced by the Institute for the Communication Studies in the early part of 2004, after four months of close monitoring of the international media (US, UK, Germany, Russia). The conclusion is sombre: 'Romania is a poor country where intolerance, corruption, abandoned children and drug trafficking rule . . . Other negative issues international media discuss when reporting on Romania are organized crime, drug trafficking, religious discrimination . . .' ('Study: Romania Reflected Largely Negatively in World Media'. Available online at: www.pressreview.ro (accessed 20.08.2004)). See also Tony Judt, 'Romania: Bottom of the Heap', *The New York Review of Books* (1 November 2001), translated into Romanian with various responses and reactions by Romanian analysts as Tony Judt, *Romania: la fundul gramezii. Polemici, controverse, pamflete* (Iasi: Polirom, 2002).

11.   Rogobete ('Between Fundamentalism and Secularization', p. 116) offers these causes for the discrepancy, in the conclusion of his study: '[the] juxtaposition of identities (religious-denominational and ethnic-national) combined with the hatred and suspicion cultivated among the various religious groups are possible explanations both for the impersonal/unreflective appropriation and practice of religious life today and for the reluctance to accept other perspectives than one's own. Such attitudes can only lead to an absence of any kind of honest, constructive dialogue between various religious groups.' Similarly, Ronald Inglehart and Wayne Baker have concluded from their study on Romania, using the empirical data generated by a decade of World Values Surveys regarding the values of trust, tolerance, well-being, and self-expression, that 'Orthodox religious heritage and a Communist historical heritage both show negative impact on these values . . . with the ex-Communist variable making the greatest contribution by itself' ('Modernization, Cultural Change, and the Persistence of Traditional Values', *American Sociological Review* 65 (2000), pp. 19–51 (22).)

social, economic, and political change.[12] It shows, however, at least two things: first, that the religious 'potential' is not automatically translatable into the social realities; and, second, that it is not just any kind of religiosity that could contribute effectively to human flourishing and well-being. As the recent histories of Rwanda, former Yugoslavia, Northern Ireland and the Middle East would seem to indicate, the religious factor is a predominant factor in the conflict and, unfortunately, the religious communities are, in many instances, accomplices in conflicts rather than agents of peace and dialogue.

As we have seen, religion, however one understands it, is deeply rooted in the Romanian consciousness. The religious factor cannot thus be ignored or dismissed since it plays a major role in the fabric of human society. In the words of sociologist Peter Berger, religion represents 'the sacred canopy', 'the symbolic universe' within which people live and which helps integrate the various aspects of life, thus providing a comprehensive understanding of reality and the meaning of life.[13] That is why one's faith and one's God represent for most religious people the ultimate reality to which they give total allegiance. Thus, faith and/or God for many people still remains the ultimate point of reference for one's life and no amount of external impositions or

---

12. A number of significant recent studies on reconciliation highlight the positive role that such a concept can have for the common social, political and economic well-being: Mark R. Amstutz, 'Human Rights and the Promise of Political Forgiveness', *RE* 104 (2007), pp. 553–77; Elazar Barkan, 'Historical Reconciliation: Redress, Rights And Politics', *Journal of International Affairs* 60(1) (2006), pp. 1–15; Bashir Bashir and Will Kymlicka (eds), *The Politics of Reconciliation in Multicultural Societies* (Oxford: OUP, 2008); Amy Benson Brown and Karen M. Poremski, eds., *Roads to Reconciliation: Conflict and Dialogue in the Twenty-First Century* (Armonk, NY: M. E. Sharpe, 2005); Arville and Sheila Earl, 'Committed to the Ministry of Reconciliation: Moving Beyond Conflict in the Balkans' *RE* 104 (2007), pp. 603–21; Corneliu Constantineanu, 'Reconciliation as a Missiological Category for Social Engagement: a Pauline Perspective from Romans 12.9–21', in Rollin G. Grams *et al.* (eds), *Bible and Mission: A Conversation Between Biblical Studies and Missiology* (Schwarzenfeld: Neufeld, 2008), pp. 132–59; Alberto Gasparini, 'Globalisation, Reconciliation and the Conditions for Conserving Peace', *Global Society* 22(1) (2008), pp. 27–55; Rafi Nets-Zehngut, 'Analyzing the Reconciliation Process', *International Journal on World Peace* 24(3) (2007), pp. 53–81; Padraic Kenney, 'Martyrs And Neighbors: Sources of Reconciliation in Central Europe', *Common Knowledge* 13(1) (2007), pp. 149–69; Hanna Hjort and Ann Frisen, 'Ethnic Identity and Reconciliation: Two Main Tasks for the Young in Bosnia-Herzegovina', *Adolescence* 41(161) (Spring 2006), pp. 141–63; Ross Langmead, 'Transformed Relationships: Reconciliation as the Central Model for Mission', *Mission Studies* 25 (2008) 5–20; Colleen Murphy, 'Political Reconciliation, the Rule of Law, and Genocide', *The European Legacy* 12(7) (2007), pp. 853–65; Martin Ramírez, 'Peace Through Dialogue, '*International Journal on World Peace* 24(1) (2007), pp. 65–81; David W. Shenk, 'The Gospel of Reconciliation Within the Wrath of Nations', *International Bulletin of Missionary Research* 32(1) (2008), pp. 2–9; Miklós Tomka, 'Religious Identity and the Gospel of Reconciliation', *Religion in Eastern Europe* 29(1) (2009), pp. 20–28; T. M. Tripp *et al.* 'A Vigilante Model of Justice: Revenge, Reconciliation, Forgiveness, and Avoidance', *Social Justice Research* 20(1) (March 2007), pp. 3–34; Scott Veitch, *Law and the Politics of Reconciliation* (Aldershot: Ashgate, 2007); Tania Wettach, 'Religion and Reconciliation in Bosnia and Herzegovina', *Religion in Eastern Europe* 28(4) (2008), pp. 1–15.

13. Peter L. Berger, *The Sacred Canopy: Elements of Sociological Theory of Religion* (New Garden City, NY: Doubleday, 1969); Peter Berger (ed.) *The Desecularisation of the World* (Grand Rapids: Eerdmans, 2000); Peter Berger and T. Luckman, *The Social Construction of Reality: A Treatise in the Sociology of Knowledge* (New York: Doubleday, 1967).

legislation will be able to shape fundamentally the worldview of a believer as his/her faith does. It is therefore mandatory that we find the appropriate resources within our own faith and traditions that will best enable us to live authentically with our fellow human beings.

The memorable and often quoted words of the Catholic theologian Hans Küng express an important truth: *No peace among the nations without peace among the religions. No peace among religions without dialogue between the religions. No dialogue between the religions without investigation of the foundation of the religions.* This illustrates that the basis for an authentic freedom of religion and for the appropriation of the positive potential of religion in our societies cannot be based on external criteria extrinsic to religion itself. It is important, of course, that democratic societies guarantee this fundamental aspect of human rights and provide the legal framework within which every human being is free to choose and practise freely and responsibly his or her religion. But ultimately, for an effective and beneficial practice of religion, and in order for its potential to bring about hope, compassion, reconciliation, and social healing, we must find resources within our own religious texts and traditions and explicate them in ways that are relevant to the concrete social and political realities of the communities.[14] We need to explore and articulate clearly and forcefully those aspects of our faith which teach us how to love our neighbours and our enemies, how to relate to 'the other', how to live together with our deepest differences; we need to emphasize those teachings that promote human dignity, justice, love, forgiveness, peace and reconciliation.[15] There is thus a need to uncover and nurture a religiosity that will be beneficial and conducive to human flourishing.

Our study on Paul, specifically his emphasis on reconciling practices, is a small but concrete step towards that end. As we have seen, Paul's ultimate concern is not simply with 'doctrine' or theology for its own sake, but with the life of people in concrete historical situations. To be sure, for Paul theology is essential, but it is never detached from life, from a specific way of life appropriate to its theological

---

14. The positive and determinant role that churches/religion could have for a healthy political culture is well expressed in these two studies: Violeta Barbu, 'Bisericile in Europa – un partner social?' in Radu Carp (ed.) *Un suflet pentru Europa: Dimensiunea religioasa a unui proiect politic* (Bucuresti: Anastasia, 2005), and Alina Mungiu-Pippidi, 'Biserica si politica: religia ca determinant al culturii politice', in *Politica dupa cumunism* (Bucuresti: Humanitas, 2002).

15. See particularly John Howard Yoder, *The Priestly Kingdom: Social Ethics as Gospel* (Notre Dame: University of Notre Dame Press, 1985) and *For the Nations: Essays Evangelical and Public* (Grand Rapids: Eerdmans, 1997); D Leslie Hollon, 'Reconciliation: Pastoral Reflections and Resources', *RE* 104 (2007), pp. 442–62; John D. Roth, 'Forgiveness and the Healing of Memories: An Anabaptist-Mennonite Perspective', *JES* 42(4) (2007), pp. 573–88; Curtiss Paul de Young, 'The Power of Reconciliation: From the Apostle Paul to Malcolm X', *Crosscurrents* (Summer 2007), pp. 203–08; Megan Shore, 'Christianity and Justice in the South African Truth and Reconciliation Commission: A Case Study in Religious Conflict Resolution', *Political Theology* 9(2) (2008), pp. 161–78; Ann Belford Ulanov, 'Practicing Reconciliation: Love and Work', *Anglican Theological Review* 89(2) (2007), pp. 227–46; Annelies Verdoolaege, *Reconciliation Discourse: The Case of the Truth and Reconciliation Commission* (Amsterdam: John Benjamins, 2008).

foundation. Theology and ethics belong together, faith and conduct are inseparable. We have found this complex dynamic in Paul, whereby one's beliefs determine a specific way of life and one's practices in the world have a strong theological basis. As we have seen, Paul is not simply telling Christians that they should behave in a reconciling way towards 'the other' but he also tells them *why*, thus offering the strongest possible ground for their practice of reconciliation – God's reconciling his enemies through Christ. Furthermore, and equally significant, Paul also shows Christians *how* to live in a reconciling way towards 'the other', thus offering them the model for their practice of reconciliation – Jesus Christ's self-giving love in his obedient life, death on a cross, and resurrection.

If, as we have argued, Pauline reconciliation has a horizontal, social dimension indissolubly united with the vertical dimension, then it is reasonable to explore the significance of the Pauline view by asking how it does or could work out in the churches and in the public social reality of Christianity in Romania. There are many different churches in Romania and, in the light of the above discussion, in order for churches to engage in reconciliation, each church must make, on its own terms, a contribution to this discussion, but in such a way as to respect and allow space for other partners in the dialogue – for other churches and for those outside churches.

By their nature and call, churches in Romania are committed in principle to reconciliation, though throughout history some have proved to be less reconciling than others. Churches have to decide responsibly, in each generation, how to embody their Christianity in the world in such a way as to be agents of peace and to promote a culture of trust, acceptance and reconciliation. An in-depth analysis of the various ways in which reconciliation has been understood and practised in Romania would lead us into a wide-ranging consideration of all aspects of the churches' being, history, theology, and culture, and that is a task far beyond the confines of this book. Only one aspect can be considered here. I will look at the Pauline shape of the Romanian Orthodox Church (ROC) as the largest church, comprising 87 per cent of the population, and of the younger evangelical churches, the so called 'neo-Protestant' (representing my own experience and belonging). I will briefly investigate the way in which their life and spirit, in the broadest sense, are shaped by significant relations with Paul's teaching and then ask how these churches understand and practise reconciliation, whether (and to what extent) there are Pauline echoes and resonances in their life and practice, and how these compare with our reading of Paul.

7.3 *The Orthodox church and Pauline reconciliation*

One particular element of Eastern Orthodox theology and tradition is its essentially mystical, contemplative dimension. On the one hand, this gives Orthodoxy its uniqueness and makes it attractive to the contemporary world, particularly in the aftermath of an era of totalitarian and atheistic indoctrination, as well as in the frantic search for new forms of spirituality in a materialistic world void of any spiritual meaning. On the other hand, a disproportionate emphasis on the mystical dimension of faith has led Christians to an attitude of disengagement from the realities of social and political life. And there are, indeed, Orthodox forms of reducing Christianity to the spiritual, mystical relationship between the believer and God. For them, as a Romanian author recently observed, 'the prevailing attitude towards religious life is still one deeply embedded in mysticism and blind ritualism'[16] leading to a drastic separation of religious life from the social realities of daily life. In this case the Pauline reconciliation is restricted to its vertical dimension, with no social or political implications.

This position, however, is not representative for the entire ROC. It was in order to balance such an understanding that Dumitru Staniloae, the foremost Romanian Orthodox theologian, while affirming the importance of the mystical dimension of faith, argued that such spirituality does not necessarily lead to an attitude of indifference and withdrawal from public life. On the contrary, he maintained, the authentic mystical experience will produce perceptible positive changes in one's life.[17] He based this affirmation on a relational definition of human identity grounded on the inter-personal love within the Trinity. Thus, an individual is not merely a rational, self-sufficient being, but rather a social being who can find fulfilment only in interactions with others.[18] There is great potential in such an argument, which leads to a more adequate understanding of religious identity and its influence on the social sphere. Similarly, another senior Orthodox theologian and priest, Dumitru Popescu, has argued that the double divine-human nature of Christ is the foundation for a close relationship between Christianity and culture and that the divine revelation in the person of Jesus Christ made possible the progress of civilization and culture in the world.[19] Further, if a person is a social being who can fulfil itself only in relation to others, how much more 'Christianity has a social horizon, because the salvation of the believer takes place in relation to our fellow human beings who form the society.'[20] Thus, according to the Ortodox teaching, the church has 'the duty to militate for an integral Christianity which maintains a proper balance between spiritual and social dimensions of Christian responsibility'.[21]

It was such an understanding that allowed the ROC to be not only a spiritual guide for the people, but also to play a significant role in the preservation of the cultural identity – of the language and traditions – of the Romanian people throughout history, and to make a significant contribution to the process of the formation of the modern

16. Rogobete, 'Morality and Tradition', p. 23.

17. Dumitru Staniloae, *Spiritualitatea ortodoxa: ascetica si mistica* (Bucuresti: Institutul Biblic si de Misiune a BOR, 1992b), pp. 24–29.

18. This is also the central argument of John Zizioulas' important work *Being as Communion* (New York: St. Vladimir's Seminary Press, 1985).

19. Dumitru Popescu, *Hristos, Biserica, Societate* (Bucuresti: Institutul Biblic si de Misiune al BOR, 1998), pp. 9–20.

20. Ibid., p. 24 (author's translation).

21. Ibid., p. 33 (author's translation).

Romanian state.[22] For the young Staniloae there was an almost indissoluble blending between Romanian ethnicity and its Orthodoxy. He states:

> The Romanian soul was moulded in the essence of Orthodoxy which, as the rhythm of the fullness of life, has shaped in our people certain characteristics which are now an integral part of its specific spirituality . . . The Orthodox dogma was so profoundly imprinted in the Romanian ethnicity that this cannot know and live its religiosity other than in the form of Orthodoxy . . . The religiosity of the Romanian people finds its concrete expression only as Orthodoxy. Romanian essence has Orthodox form [author's translation].[23]

On the one hand, such arguments highlight the positive aspect in which Christianity takes form in concrete historical contexts. It enables Christian faith to take shape in a rich variety of cultural expressions, in ways which affirm the specificity of each nation. Indeed, the social, cultural, and religious values embedded in the formation of the human personality emphasized by the Orthodox tradition give a strong foundation for an embodiment of Christianity in concrete social realities. From this perspective, the broad social implications of Pauline reconciliation are clearly present. God and people are brought together in Christ not in a narrow spiritual sense but in a way which takes form in concrete cultural, social, and political realities.

On the other hand, however, it was exactly this positive role played by the church that made it difficult to resist the temptation of an intimate association between the Orthodox faith and 'Romanian' identity, culminating with the juxtaposition of Orthodoxy and the Romanian; with the national identity expressed often as a 'national symphony between the Church and people',[24] whereby to be Romanian is to be Orthodox and vice versa. This tendency is seen very clearly in the insistence of the ROC on being 'the national church', defining itself as 'the church of a nation which, through historical continuity, represents the spiritual axis of the formation of nation-state' [author's translation].[25] In a very detailed study of the ideology of the ROC during communism, Olivier Gillet has shown the extent to which the Orthodox Church has fostered an organic link between religion and nationalism, with the negative consequence of a too close connection between ethnicity and faith,

---

22. Dumitru Staniloae, 'Rolul ortodoxiei in formarea si pastrarea fiintei poporului roman si a unitatii nationale', in *Ortodoxia* XXX (1978), pp. 584–603; Ioan Vasile Leb, 'Contributia preotimii ortodoxe romanesti la realizarea unirii din 1859', in *Biserica in actiune* (Cluj-Napoca: Limes, 2001), pp. 35–54; Ion Bria, *Ortodoxia in Europa: Locul spiritualitatii Romane* (Iasi: Mitropolia Moldovei si Bucovinei, 1995), pp. 25–28.

23. Dumitru Staniloae, *Ortodoxie si Romanism* (Sibiu: Editura Consiliului Arhiepiscopiei, 1936), pp. 18–19.

24. Ion Bria, 'Teologia fata in fata cu Biserica de azi', *Studii Teologice* XLVII (1990), pp. 3–6 (3). See also Rogobete, 'Morality and Tradition', pp. 19–20. For an analysis and a critique of the 'symphony' model of the relation between church and state see Paul Negrut, *Biserica si statul: O interogatie asupra modelului 'simfoniei' bizantine* (Oradea: Emanuel, 2000), in particular, pp. 19–43.

25. Radu Preda, *Biserica in Stat: O invitatie la dezbatere* (Bucuresti: Scripta, 1999), p. 56.

leading inevitably to a form of ethnic exclusion and an exacerbation of nationalistic tendencies.[26]

Modern forms of nationalism with its emphasis on the superiority of one particular group of people, culture, or religion leading in many cases to discrimination, conflict and violence against other communities and even to ethnic cleansing and genocide, is rightly considered to be a most dangerous phenomenon of our days.[27] As a result of their intimate bond with the cultural heritage, traditions and language of the people, most Orthodox churches find themselves on the border-line of nationalistic tendencies, as some of the prominent Orthodox theologians have shown and denounced.[28] They have also noticed with disapproval the tendency in some Orthodox quarters to promote a nationalistic ideology which gives ethnicity a religious dimension, reinforcing the national feeling of the people who thus maintain their close identification with Orthodoxy and are induced into a rigid compartmentalization between 'us' and 'them', the non-Orthodox, an attitude which is just a first step to defining 'the other' as 'enemies'.[29] And here lies the danger of this expression of social Christianity and of this form of horizontal reconciliation, namely that it comes with a costly national restriction thus missing one fundamental element of Pauline reconciliation.

The apostle Paul, as we have seen, refused to let horizontal reconciliation be worked out on the basis of any particular political or ethnic identity in a way which would exclude others. The great news of the gospel he proclaimed was exactly the reconciliation of Jews and Gentiles into one new family in which they maintained their differences and yet were both included, necessary, and equal. Paul was constantly and resolutely engaged in a process of reaching out in all directions, making himself

26. Olivier Gillet, *Religie si nationalism: Ideologia Bisericii Ortodoxe Române sub regimul communist* (Bucuresti: Compania, 2001), pp. 133–89.

27. Basilius J. Groen, 'Nationalism and Reconciliation: Orthodoxy in the Balkans', *RSS* 26(2) (1998), pp. 111–28 (114–15).

28. So, for example, Timothy Ware, *The Orthodox Church* (3rd edn; Harmondsworth: Penguin, 1993), pp. 77 and 174–85; John Meyendorff, *The Orthodox Church: Its Past and its Role in the World Today* (4th rev. edn; New York: Crestwood, 1996), pp. 73, 81 and 131–32; Alexander Schmemann, *The Historical Road of Eastern Orthodoxy* (London: Harvill Press, 1963), pp. 276–81. See also an excellent analysis from an outsider into the entire controversy of the 'national church' in Earl Pope's 'Ecumenism, Religious Freedom and the "National Church" Controversy in Romania', *JES* 36 (1999), pp. 184–201.

29. This particular point is made by the French Orthodox Francois Thual, a specialist in geopolitics, *Geopolitique de l'Orthodoxie* (2nd edn; Paris: Dunod, 1994), pp. 17–18 and 125–32. It is well known that one of the major weaknesses of contemporary Orthodoxy is the great 'discrepancy between the perfection of theology and the fragility of its historical presence in the world' (Dan Pavel, *Cine, ce si de ce? Interviuri despre politica si alte tabuuri* (Iasi: Polirom, 1998), p. 45). Such inconsistency is well illustrated in this respect by the official theological position of Orthodoxy vis-à-vis the position of Christianity and culture, expressed, for example, by Dumitru Popescu: 'A church which disregards the divinity of Jesus assumes *the risk to close herself in her own national culture and to become intransigent and fanatic towards the culture of other people.* In this way *the value of one's culture is triumphalistically exacerbated at the expense of other cultures* with two major consequences: spiritual poverty but also *aggressivity towards other cultures.*' (*Hristos, Biserica, Societate*, p. 33 (italics added)). Ironically, the Orthodox Church is not always avoiding that risk in the historical life of the churches.

all things to all men. His understanding of reconciliation, reflecting his understanding of God in Christ, made him always extend the practice of reconciliation beyond the confines of the 'insiders', firmly rejecting any suggestions of such limitations. For Paul, Christian communities must be effectively engaged in the wider society, but they have to renounce any kind of ethnic, social, cultural, and political divisions that exist in the wider world. Paul had no doubt that only a Christian community driven constantly by a desire for reconciliation towards all people would remain faithful to God and their mission. Compared with Pauline reconciliation, the practice of the ROC falls short.

Even though the link between Romanian Orthodoxy and nationalism would deserve a closer examination,[30] we conclude with the statement that in order to contribute as a significant dialogue partner in the social and political arena, the ROC has to resist the temptation of 'identifying God's purpose of salvation with one particular nation's well-being and political dominance'.[31] If the ROC is to be faithful to its call, it has to re-evaluate and resist its strongest temptation of identifying and limiting its Christian witness by ethnic and/or national considerations.

7.4 *The evangelical churches and Pauline reconciliation*

The term 'evangelical churches' (EC) refers to a group of churches comprising largely the Baptists, Pentecostals, Christians according to the Gospel (the Romanian designation for 'Brethren') and Seventh-day Adventists. In order to distinguish them from the mainline Protestant communities, the Romanian authorities referred to them as 'neo-Protestants' (a name adopted subsequently by these churches to identify and present themselves). Even though they first arrived in Romania only in the eighteenth, and mostly in the late nineteenth and early twentieth centuries, these churches

---

30. As one looks specifically into each situation and context, one will discover within Orthodoxy a more nuanced picture with at least three tendencies in respect of this question: from a close identification between church, nation and people, to an attempt to look objectively into the facts and come to some realistic solutions, to a sole emphasis on 'the inner way of the heart and the eternal spiritual dimension and to reject nationalism because of its exclusiveness' (Groen, 'Nationalism and Reconciliation', p. 124).

31. Dunn, *Romans* 13:1–7. We should point out that there is a younger generation of Orthodox theologians and intellectuals who are beginning to address seriously the challenges facing the ROC in the contemporary situation. The following studies make a great contribution in this direction: various writings by Teodor Baconski, including *Ispita binelui: Eseuri despre urbanitatea credintei* (Bucuresti: Anastasia, 1999) and *Puterea schismei: Un portret al crestinismului european* (Bucuresti: Anastasia, 2001); Virgil Nemoianu, *Jocurile divinitatii: Gandire, libertate si religie la sfarsitul de mileniu* (Iasi: Polirom, 2000); Ioan Ica jr. and Germano Marani (eds), *Gandirea social a bisericii: Fundamente-documente-analize-perspective* (Sibiu: Deisis, 2002); Miruna Tataru-Cazaban (ed.), *Teologie si politica: De la sfintii parinti la Europa Unita* (Bucuresti: Anastasia, 2004); Razvan Codrescu, *Cartea indreptarilor: o perspectiva crestina asupra politicului* (Bucuresti: Christiana, 2004); George Enache, *Ortodoxie si putere politica in Romania contemporana* (Bucuresti: Nemira, 2005); Ionel Ungureanu, 'Doctrina social ortodoxa: intre propunere reala si discurs ideologic', in Radu Carp (ed.), *Un suflet pentru Europa: Dimensiunea religioasa a unui proiect politic* (Bucuresti: Anastasia, 2005). Mention should also be made of the Metropolitan Nicolae Corneanu's *In pas cu vremea* (Timisoara: Mitropolia Banatului, 2002).

grew very quickly and became among the largest communities of neo-Protestants in Europe.[32] Among their most significant convictions is that the Bible, as the infallible Word of God, represents the ultimate authority for matters of faith and conduct. As such, it plays a major role both in community gatherings and in the individual lives of the believers. Similarly, they focus on a personal religious experience with God, emphasizing the importance of the subsequent visible transformation of one's life expressed in ethical terms, while at the same time maintaining a strong eschatological orientation.[33]

Due to their strong commitment to the Bible and the above-mentioned characteristics, as well as their mainstream Protestant roots and outlook, the EC are shaped by significant relations with Paul's thought. As a tradition, they tend to read Paul more directly and intensely than the Orthodox. Their understanding and practice of reconciliation thus has strong Pauline resonances. Indeed, the experience of reconciliation, in Christ, is for them a social here-and-now reality. It has a strong social dimension, but this is expressed locally, within the community of those gathered in Christ. As in Paul's case, their own experience of reconciliation with God is played out as a life-transforming reality affecting their perception and relation to 'the other'. Their intimate and intense relation to Christ shapes their everyday life and they are committed, in very strong Pauline terms, to a transcending of ethnic and social barriers. It is significant in this respect to see that a local Pentecostal congregation in a large city has among its members a significant number of Roma (gypsies) who are fully integrated and accepted in the community as full members and active worshippers. These churches have allowed a Pauline redefinition and reconstruction of identity around Christ, an identity more open and welcoming of 'the other' and in which ethnicity lost its enchantment.[34] Their reconciling faith in Christ is an obedient faith which commits them to a life where there is place for difference and diversity, a life of genuine love and self-giving modelled after the pattern of Christ. It is this refreshing

32. In the Romanian context, however, these churches together represent just 2% of the entire population, according to the 2002 official census.

33. Danut Manastireanu, 'Evangelical Denominations in Post-Communist Romania I & II' *East-West Church & Ministry Report* 6 (1998); Overseas Council International, World Missions, 'Preliminary Report: The State of the Evangelical Churches in Romania 2000' (Cluj Napoca: OCI, August 2000); Iosif Ton, 'The Evangelicals in Romania', *Exploits* 33 (Eastebourne: Slavic Gospel Association, 1993). See also by Ton 'Towards Reformation in Romania', *East-West Church & Ministry Report* 1 (1993b), pp. 1–3; 'Key Theological Themes Needing Attention in the Post-Communist Europe', Paper presented at the Consultation on Theological Education and Leadership Development in Post-Communist Europe, Oradea, Romania, 4–9 October 1994; *Confruntari* (Oradea: Cartea Crestina, 1999);

34. Earl Pope, 'Protestantism in Romania' in Sabrina Petra Ramet (ed.), *Protestantism and Politics in Eastern Europe and Russia: Communist and Post-Communist Era* (Durham, NC: Duke University Press, 1992), p. 174. Pope notes that one of the primal causes of the neo-Protestant movement as a whole was exactly this 'disenchantment with the inordinate focus on the ethnic communities and the search for an alternative, not only to Marxist-Leninist ideology but also to the destructive tensions of the past'. See also Jolanta Babiuch, 'The Eastern European Church After Communism: Seeking New Ways to Serve – or New Enemies to Fight', *East-West Church & Ministry Report* 5 (1997), pp. 5–6.

reality that represents the strongest appeal for people outside to come and join the community, thus making these new churches the fastest growing communities.[35] And yet there is still an important dimension of Pauline reconciliation that is missing in these otherwise 'Pauline churches'.

Most of the EC in Romania entered the country through foreign missionary agencies and, as a result, these communities have always been regarded with suspicion both by the communist authorities and by the ROC.[36] As tiny minority churches they saw themselves persecuted and pushed to the very margins, making it difficult for them to engage effectively in any way in the social or political life of the country. With no public role to play in society and backed by their own eschatological theology, the EC compensated by living in the spirit, in the heavenly, and their sense of what it is to be church was thus freed from the call to be reconciling in the world outside church.[37] They turned the Christian faith into a private religiosity with all the drawbacks that result from that. Berger is right when he states the loss of such a move:

> Such private religiosity, however 'real' it may be to the individuals who adopt it, cannot any longer fulfil the classical task of religion, that of constructing a common world within which all of social life receives ultimate meaning binding on everybody . . . the values pertaining to private religiosity are, typically, irrelevant to institutional contexts other than the private sphere.[38]

As we have seen, this privatization of religion was not a Pauline option. In a similar situation in Rome, where the Christians were a small minority faced with persecution and suffering, Paul's solution was not an 'escape' from the world into a closed community. Rather, the Christians facing difficulties and hostilities were to manifest a reconciling way of life towards all, including those who provoked suffering. They

35. Peter Kuzmic, 'Evangelical Witness In Eastern Europe' in Waldron Scott (ed.), *Serving our Generation: Evangelical Strategies for the Eighties* (Colorado: World Evangelical Fellowship, 1980), pp. 77–87 and 'Why Romania has become the Korea of Europe', *Global Church Growth Magazine* 20 (1983), p. 13. Kuzmic highlights the quality of life and the numeric growth across all the denominations as signs of an authentic spiritual renewal.

36. Sabrina Petra Ramet, 'Holy Intolerance: Romania's Orthodox Church' in S. P. Ramet (ed.), *Nihil Obstat: Religion, Politics and Social Change in East-Central Europe and Russia* (Durham, NC: Duke University Press, 1998), pp. 181–201.

37. As correctly perceived by Prof Haddon Willmer in a private conversation. See also Peter Kuzmic, 'The Communist Impact on the Church in Eastern Europe' *Evangelical Review of Theology* 20 (1996), pp. 60–76, and 'Problems and Possibilities in European Ministry Today' *East-West Church & Ministry Report* 1 (1993).

38. Berger, *The Sacred Canopy*, pp. 133–34. One reason that there have been few attempts to think through the social implication of theology was that religion in general has been pushed to the margins of society, to the 'private sector' of individuals, as having nothing to do with society as a whole, nothing to offer to the public realm. This phenomenon has been aptly described by Peter Berger, who shows that the main causes for *privatisation of religion* are social in nature and are secularisation and pluralism. The loss is that as a 'private' phenomenon, however, religion loses its function. (Ibid., pp. 127–53.)

were to 'bless those who persecute you, bless and do not curse them' (Rom. 12.14), to 'live peacefully with all' (12.18) and not to let themselves 'be overcome by evil, but overcome evil with good' (12.21). This shows clearly that a Pauline reconciliation is also outward looking and promotes a particular engagement with the outside world. The life of 'sacrifice' that Paul urges his readers to live, their sacrificial obedience to Christ, is a willing surrender of one's prerogatives for the sake of the other as modelled by Jesus Christ himself, who 'did not please himself' but suffered on behalf of others (15.3). The barriers between the insider and outsider are done away with by Paul as he urges the believers in Rome with utmost seriousness to 'live peaceably with all' (12.8) and to manifest a 'genuine love' towards all.

If the EC want to follow the teaching and example of Paul then they must promote a living-out of the gospel of reconciliation outside the church's walls and by doing so they will witness to the truth of God's intervention, redemption and reconciliation of the world in Christ. Admittedly, there are signs now that EC are becoming interested in serious reflection on the social dimension of their faith, as some of the recent studies of an emerging generation of evangelical theologians suggest.[39] If the EC are to serve the gospel and promote a spirituality that leads to the well-being and human flourishing of all in the Romanian context, they have to enlarge their view of reconciliation with the social dimension that we have explored in Paul. A proper eschatological understanding of reality should not hinder in any way their involvement in the world. On the contrary, far from suggesting a withdrawal from active social life, the eschatological outlook of Paul's Christianity, by placing Christian existence in a larger framework within which everything else makes sense and is placed in its proper dimension, allows for a serious engagement of the church with the wider political life of society while at the same time relativizing the ultimate claims of politics.

---

39. Among various efforts I would point to two very young Evangelical scholars who are pursuing such questions in their advanced theological studies. Vasile Marchis, for example, offers an excellent survey and assessment of the state of affairs and maps the broad directions for the EC in order to be effective in the public arena: 'Christian Faith and Public Life: A Critical Analysis of the Missiological Praxis of the Evangelical Neo-Protestants in the Romanian Context' (unpublished MTh thesis submitted to the Evangelical Theological Seminary, Osijek, Croatia, June, 2004). Similarly, Cristian Romocea suggests some concrete steps for churches in their efforts to be reconciling agents: 'Reconciliation in the Ethnic Conflict in Transylvania: Theological, Political and Social Aspect', *RSS* 32 (2004), pp. 159–76; 'The Place of Church-State Debates in Post-Communist Romania', in *Sfera Politicii* 108 (2004), pp. 42–46. Even though, as a result of their different focuses, these studies do not offer a solid theological or biblical basis for their proposals and are more programmatic in nature, they are indicative of the new generation of theologically trained Evangelical Christians in Romania who are very much concerned with the social dimension of faith and with the public role of the churches in the wider society.

7.5 *Other issues: Romanian-Hungarian relations in Transylvania*

In the previous sections we looked at the Paulinism of Romanian churches, particularly at the various forms reconciliation takes within their traditions and practices as well as their limitations compared with Paul. In what follows I would like to touch briefly on another important issue confronting the churches in the Romanian context and to which our reading of Paul is relevant. That is the question of ethnic minorities, especially Romanian-Hungarian relations in Transylvania.

Of a total of 23 million people in Romania, minorities constitute 11 per cent (1.6 million ethnic Hungarians; 400,000 Gypsies; 200,000 Germans and 30,000 Jews). Even at the time when Romania became a parliamentary democracy, ethnic minorities were a weak area in its social policy. The various minority groups have faced ethnic and religious intolerance throughout history. If, during the communist regime, the issue of ethnic minorities was suppressed, with the collapse of communism in 1989 and the newly found freedom of speech and expression, the question of minorities came forcefully on the scene – and in particular, the question of Transylvania and the Hungarian minority.

In March 1990 several thousand Hungarians in the city of Targu Mures celebrated Hungary's national holiday by draping Hungarian flags on city buildings, a fact perceived by the Romanians as deliberately provocative. Ethnic tensions were exacerbated and the violent confrontations that followed in the city and the neighbouring areas resulted in several deaths and injuries on both sides. This episode was a very clear indication that, indeed, the problem of 'Transylvania' and Romanian-Hungarian relationships has to be tackled with all attention.[40] Thus, for at least two crucial closely related reasons, the issue has become urgent. First is the direct question of peaceful and meaningful co-existence of the two peoples in a territory that has been common to them for centuries. Second is the way in which the complex history of Transylvania has been used and abused by nationalists on both sides. On the one hand, there are the Hungarian nationalists who in the name of an imminent 'ethnocide' of the Hungarian minority by the Romanian state, claim that Transylvania should be 'reintegrated' into Hungary. On the other hand, the Romanian nationalists react violently against such claims and in the name of a potential territorial loss and of an imminent conflict, are pursuing an ultra-nationalistic agenda.[41] Legitimate or not, these perspectives have

40. There were several other incidents and provocations which aggravated the ethnic tension, such as the aggressive actions against the Hungarian community by the local council members in Cluj-Napoca to evict some ethnic organizations and publications from their premises, and to ban the use of bilingual signs. Similarly, the new constitution adopted in 1991, which includes the statement that 'Romania is a unitary state', was perceived by the Hungarians as implied intolerance.

41. In his book, *Romania after Ceausescu: The Politics of Intolerance* (Edinburgh: Edinburgh University Press, 1995), Tom Gallagher does an excellent analysis of how nationalism was being used for political reasons in Romania after December 1989, especially on the question of the Hungarian minority.

continued to feed suspicions and build tensions between the two groups and endanger their relationships.

While a history of the long and multifaceted relationship between Romanians and Hungarians in Transylvania cannot be attempted here, a very brief historical context will help us understand better the issue at hand. Transylvania is a province of Romania with a very rich and complex history, where today a large Hungarian minority lives together with Romanians, as it has for centuries.[42] It would be simply impossible to give even a short outline of the history of Transylvania.[43] The major difficulty inherent in such an attempt, however, lies not so much in the 'intense' or 'condensed' history of the region, as in the fact that there are two historical accounts of Transylvania, or two 'readings' of its history. In an intentionally oversimplified and contrasted form they appear as follows.

The Romanian reading[44] affirms that Transylvania has always been a Romanian territory. Yes, it was under Hungarian influence and occupation for almost a thousand years, but the Romanian people had been there first, have always been there as a majority, and have at times suffered persecution and discrimination by the Hungarians. Despite numerous attempts, unification with Romania did not succeed until 1918, after which Transylvania was internationally recognized as part of Romania by the Treaty of Trianon in 1920. During World War II, by a flagrant violation of the international conventions, Transylvania was 'annexed' to Hungary by the Vienna 'Dictate', and from 1940–1944, during Hungarian occupation, the Romanians experienced unimaginable atrocities under the Hungarian army led by general Horty.

The Hungarian reading[45] in its turn, affirms that Transylvania has always been

---

42. The 1992 census showed the population of Romania as being 22,810,035 (89.5% Romanians, 7.1% Hungarians, 3.4% others); the population of Transylvania: 3,306,948 Romanians (72.2%), 1,095,173 Hungarians (23.9%), 177,444 other nationalities (3.9 %). (Nicolae Endroiu, *Maghiarii din Romania* (Cluj-Napoca: Centrul de Studii Transilvane, Fundatia Culturala Romana, 1995), pp. 27–28).

43. John Cadzow, *Transylvania: The Roots of Ethnic Conflict* (Kent, OH: Kent State University, 1983), pp. 10–36, needed 26 pages for only a simple list entitled 'A Chronology of Transylvanian History' and Gabor Barta, *History of Transylvania* (Budapest: Akademiai Kiado, 1994), pp. 745–62, needed 17 pages for the same purpose.

44. For a Romanian perspective on Transylvania, see Constantin Botoran, *Transylvania and the Romanian-Hungarian Relationships* (Bucuresti: Institute of Military History and Theory, 1993); Nicolae Endroiu, *Nostalgia for an Empire of Sad Memory: The Austro-Hungarian Monarchy* (Bucharest: Agerpress, 1987); Ioan Suta, *Transilvania: himera ungarismului iredentist* ('Transylvania: the Chimera of Hungarian Irredentism') (Bucuresti: Editura Academiei de Inalte Studii Militare, 1995); D. Prodan, *Transylvania and Again Transylvania* (Cluj-Napoca: Romanian Cultural Foundation, 1992); Constantin Giurescu, *Transylvania in the History of Romania: An Historical Outline* (London: Garnstone, [n.d.]); Stefan Pascu, *A History of Transylvania* (Detroit, MI: Wayne State University Press, 1982).

45. See, for example, the following books in English for a Hungarian perspective on Transylvania: C. Michael-Titus, *In Search of 'Cultural Genocide'* (Upminster: Panopticum, 1976) and *The Magyar File* (London: Panopticum, 1984); N. M. Goodchild, *Hungarian Realities in Romania: Documentaries* (London: Panopticum, 1980); Lajos Kazar, *Facts against Fiction: Transylvania-Walachiam/Romanian Homeland since 70 BC?* (Sydney: Forum of History, 1993); George Schopflin *Romania's Ethnic Hungarians* (London:

a Hungarian territory, either separated from or integrated into Hungary. When the Hungarians came into the region for the first time in the ninth century, the territory was more or less empty and there were no Romanians there. They started to 'immigrate' into Transylvania first in the twelfth and thirteenth centuries and then, at a more intense rate, in the seventeenth and eighteenth centuries, until they became a majority in Transylvania. In 1920 Transylvania was 'given' to Romania by the allies that defeated Hungary in 1918, based on an arbitrary international decision, which was more a 'punishment' for Hungary at the end of World War I. Becoming a minority under Romanian rule, a terrifying 'romanization' campaign started, and the Hungarians were discriminated against, persecuted, and denied most minority rights. Under communist rule, this 'cultural genocide' reached its climax.[46]

The most important observation we need to make at this point is not which of the readings is more 'objective' or closer to reality. Rather, it should be pointed out that, *whether true or false, it is these traditions that have fundamentally shaped the thinking, understanding, and political consciousness of the two peoples.* It is with these realities in mind that any discussion of the Romanian-Hungarian relationship should begin.

There are several significant developments on these issues which have to be mentioned. First, there are serious efforts on both sides to compare history books and thus to read together the history of Transylvania in a new way which emphasizes its cultural uniqueness and the contribution made to it by both groups, efforts to change mentalities and demythologize history.[47] There are also different models of constructing one's *identity* which emphasize partnership and trust across ethnic and cultural perimeters and deal appropriately with 'the other'; which explore the interdependence as an intrinsic reality that shapes both identities, and will assert the role of 'difference'. Such recent efforts are building on similar approaches done by

Minority Rights Group, 1990); Istvan Lazar, *Transylvania: A Short History* (Budapest: Corvina, 1997); Louis L. Lote, (ed.), *Transylvania and the Theory of Daco-Roman-Rumanian Continuity* (Rochester, NY: Committee of Transylvania Inc., 1980).

46. I have to repeat that this is a gross oversimplification of a complex history and that there are, of course, many other elements that compose the historical picture given by the two sides. However, for a realistic approach to the issue of Romanian-Hungarian relationships, it is the elements I have presented that ought to be re-considered (re-defined?) very carefully, since those are the most 'disputed' ones and it is these points to which permanent references are being made by the parties when defending their 'historical right' over Transylvania.

47. Significant studies in this direction include: Dorel Abraham, Ilie Badescu and Septimiu Chelcea, *Interethnic Relations in Romania: Sociological Diagnosis and Evaluation of Tendencies* (Cluj-Napoca: Editura Carpatica, 1995); Adrian Neculau and Gilles Ferréol (eds), *Minoritari, Marginali, Exclusi* (Iasi: Polirom, 1996); Gabriel Andreescu, *Ruleta: Ramani si maghiari, 1990–2000* (Iasi: Polirom, 2001); Lucian Nastasa and Levente Salat, *Relatii interetnice in Romania postcomunista* (Cluj-Napoca: Ethnocultural Diversity Resource Centre, 2000); Walter Kolarz, *Mituri si realitati in Europa de Est* (Iasi: Polirom, 2003); Victor Neuman, *Ideologie si fantasmagorie: Perspective comparative asupra istoriei gandirii politice in Europa Est-Centrala* (Iasi: Polirom, 2001).

some historians in the past. Al Zub points to the illuminating statements made by Nicolae Iorga in this regard about a century ago:

> In contrast to his contemporaries, . . . Iorga was making systematic allusions to analogies, in order to discover common characteristics, affinities, for 'nobody is completely foreign to you, and you cannot be completely foreign to anybody'. He felt solitary with that 'vast humanity spread everywhere'. . . . In each one of us watches 'another' ready to ask, search, and punish . . . 'the life of a people is uninterruptedly intermingled with the lives of the 'others'.[48]

The twin realities of *otherness* and *identity*, the way they are defined and re-defined in their complex interrelation, are of paramount importance. And this is so not only because by their very nature they are permanencies of our life, but also because in moments of crisis they become acute, obsessive, and pressing issues. We are always to be reminded that '[w]e discover ourselves through others, we live under the watching of *the other*'.[49]

Finally, it is important to note that despite several sporadic incidents over the past fifteen years the relationship between the two groups has not developed into open conflict and that, in general, both the Hungarians and Romanians in Transylvania have behaved relatively peacefully towards one another. However, as Mungiu-Pippidi correctly concludes in her study on *Subjective Transylvania*, the centuries of rivalry, oppression and conflict are continuously 'feeding a fundamental conflict determined by the necessity of two peoples to share the same territory and state',[50] conflict which could degenerate into violent confrontation. The risk is always present and is kept alive by the nationalist rhetoricians on both sides who are prone to exploit the ethnic agenda for their political gain. That is why we always have to make conscious efforts to understand each other better, to learn to live with our deepest differences, to find resources which will enable us to live peacefully and meaningfully together.

We have learned from Paul that the Gospel does not eliminate ethnic or cultural differences and yet the distinctions of class, nation, race, or sex lose their ultimate significance because they no longer occupy the crucial position in the definition of one's identity. These elements, while still a part of one's self, become relative to the reality of the new identity that is taking form in Christ – an identity open for the other, centred on love and regard for the other, and modelled by the example of Christ. The horizon of reconciliation as promised by the gospel is the ultimate reality, the framework within which one's life is lived in obedience to Christ and service to the world. Similarly, we have seen that while Paul has a solid and realistic understanding of the role and function of politics, he also relativizes their claims. Paul's theological basis both legitimizes and limits the authority of the government

---

48. Al Zub, 'About the study of alterity to Romanians', in Zub, *Identitate, alteritate, in spatiul cultural romanesc* (Iasi: Editura Universitatii 'Alexandru Ioan Cuza', 1996), pp. 403–06.

49. Ibid., p. 414.

50. Alina Mungiu-Pippidi, *Transilvania subiectiva* (Bucuresti: Humanitas, 1999), p. 220.

at the same time, thus offering a solid starting point for his appeal for the Christians to 'discern' what is good. Politics is an important and necessary human enterprise, but it is not the ultimate and highest point of reference for one's existence. Following this understanding, Christians should be better prepared and discern, unmask and expose any unhealthy nationalistic propaganda and not allow themselves to be caught by such rhetoric. It is probably right to say that this relativization of ethnic, national, cultural and political absolutes represents one of the most significant implications of Paul's message of reconciliation.

Finally, by following the example and teaching of Paul, churches in Romania could make a contribution to the dialogue in the social arena and become effective agents of peace and reconciliation. Religious communities have to reflect profoundly on issues of ethnicity, identity and otherness in such a way as to endorse a living together in harmony and peace. To that end I think it is essential that, as religious people, we find theological and biblical bases for practices of reconciliation and explicate the social dimensions of our faith in concrete terms. Such a 'preventative' approach will better prepare us for situations of crisis and would give us the necessary resources to cope with difference and to live lovingly and reconcilingly towards 'the other', indeed, towards the enemy. To that end, the churches together might help reconciliation by getting people in churches to read and hear Paul afresh, by training a new generation of leaders and teachers who have in their theological curricula courses offering a reading of Paul in the way we have been arguing for. Churches in Romania would be in a better position to promote social reconciliation if they were enabled to listen to Paul and see the prominence he gave to the value of human life in the world, to the idea of discerning and resisting any form of human totalitarianism and absolutism, and finally, to the vision of hope given by the fundamental reality of God's reconciliation of the world through Christ.

7.6 *Summary and conclusion*

We have argued in this chapter that within the larger phenomenon of the 'return of religion' to the social arena, and with Romania being one of the countries in Europe with the highest religiosity, churches find themselves as potentially important agents of renewal in the public domain. We have shown that a high degree of religiosity, however, is not translated or capitalized into an effective impact on the cultural, social, economic and political realities of the country. It was pointed out that it is not just any kind of religiosity that could contribute to human flourishing and well-being. Religious people tend to give a high (sometimes even their highest) allegiance to their basic religious convictions which, in turn, shape fundamentally their worldview. On this basis, we have argued that in order for religion to bring about hope, compassion, reconciliation and healing among people and at the societal levels, we must find resources within our own religious texts and traditions and explicate them in ways that are relevant to the concrete social and political realities of the communities. Specifically, we pointed to the need to explore and articulate clearly and forcefully those aspects of our faith which teach us how to love our neighbours and our enemies, how to relate to 'the other', and how to live together with our deepest differences; and to emphasize those teachings that promote human dignity, justice, love, forgiveness, peace and reconciliation. There is thus a need to uncover and nurture a religiosity that will be beneficial and conducive to human flourishing.

We proposed that our study on Paul, with his specific emphasis on reconciling practices, offers a strong starting point and basis for a particular way of being Christian in and for the world. It follows from Paul's own concern that an authentic Christian life goes beyond a preoccupation with a mere or blind defence of doctrine to a dynamic in which one's beliefs determine one's life; as theology and ethics belong together, so faith and conduct are inseparable. Doctrine is essential but it is never detached from a particular way of life that is appropriate to its theological foundation. The social significance of reconciliation we have found in Paul, modelled as it is by Jesus Christ's self-giving love for others, has provided a criterion by which we have then assessed the understanding and practice of reconciliation in the Romanian Orthodox Church and the evangelical churches.

We have found that the ROC is closely associated with the culture, the language, and the history of the people, and that it gives expression to a social Christianity that is embodied in concrete historical realities. But a juxtaposition of Orthodoxy with the national identity has fostered an organic link between religion and nationalism, between ethnicity and faith, leading inevitably to a form of ethnic exclusion and an exacerbation of nationalistic tendencies. Compared with the Pauline reconciliation revealed in our study, the practice of the ROC falls short, particularly in its limitation of reconciliation to the national element. For Paul, Christian communities must be effectively engaged in the wider society, but they have to recognize and show a reconciling attitude towards various divisions that exist in the wider world. His understanding of reconciliation made him always extend the practice of reconciliation beyond the confines of the insiders, and made him reject firmly any proposal for limitations on social, ethnic, political or any other ground. We concluded that if the ROC is to be faithful to its call and be a significant dialogue partner in the social and political arena, it has to resist the temptation of limiting its Christian witness by ethnic and/or national considerations.

Regarding the EC in Romania, we have seen that their life is shaped by significant relations with the Scripture (and Paul's teaching in particular); that their understanding and practice of reconciliation have strong Pauline resonances. The experience of reconciliation, in Christ, is for them a social reality manifested within the community, which enables them to transcend ethnic and social barriers. While this was a positive assessment in terms of Paul's teaching, the EC have also fallen short of the Pauline reconciliation by withdrawing from the wider world and thus limiting Paul's notion to insiders. Based on our findings, we have suggested that for the EC to serve the gospel and promote a spirituality that leads to the well-being and human flourishing of all in the Romanian context, they have to enlarge their view of reconciliation with the social dimension that we have explored in Paul.

On the issue of ethnic minorities, our analysis has indicated that this is an area in which churches could make a contribution by reflecting seriously and acting on the issues of ethnicity, identity, and otherness in such a way as to endorse and promote difference within harmonious living. The biblical basis for the practices of reconciliation and the explication of the social dimension of faith will play an essential role to that end. Churches can learn from and follow Paul in that, while he did not eliminate ethnic or cultural differences, he did relativize the significance of the distinctions of class, nation, race, and sex. Indeed, we have concluded that probably the most significant implications of Paul's message of reconciliation is the relativization of ethnic, national, cultural and political absolutes and their replacement with an eschatological horizon of God's reconciliation of the world, within which one's life is lived in obedience to Christ and service to the world.

It might be true that in a modern context of democracy, where an ascending theory of power ascribes an absolute role to the people, such texts as Romans 13 are simply rejected on the basis that it is 'countercultural vis-à-vis liberal democracies, . . . a political embarrassment with the stature of Holy Writ'.[51] The solution often proposed is to depoliticize Paul. But our study has shown that Paul has a realistic and solid understanding of Christian participation in the world, grounded in a theology of creation and in the redemption of the world in Christ, and that there are numerous insights in Paul which enable us in our social endeavours as we attempt to promote a meaningful life together in a pluralistic context.

Can churches, building on the Pauline understanding of reconciliation, make a contribution to the social reality of the Romanian context? Our answer is affirmative. They can offer and maintain a sense of fundamental values for human life in the world; they can discern, unmask and resist any form of totalitarianism and absolutism; they can offer a framework of hope and a vision of life that will enable people not simply to cope with 'otherness' and 'difference' but also to promote a culture of peace and harmony, of freedom and love; a culture of forgiveness and reconciliation; a culture of life.

In our continuous efforts to appropriate Paul for our own times, in a very different context from the one in which Paul wrote, it is inevitable that his teachings in Romans leave us with gaps to fill in and with dilemmas with which we still have to wrestle. While some aspects of Paul's theology and ethics are more obvious and directly translatable to a different context, there are also challenges and difficult questions which arise when attempting such an exercise.[52] Further studies in this area will need to undertake the task and explore in further detail such questions as: since the first century Christians were a tiny minority and could not see the possibility of being participants in the structures of the state – how do we envisage our relationship to the state as Christians and also as active members of its structures? Given that Paul's ethic

---

51. Wayne Boulton, 'Riddle of Romans 13', *Christian Century* 93 (1976), pp. 758–61.
52. As well pointed out by Horrell, 'Peaceable', pp. 94–95.

and theology were inextricably related to, and grounded and operative 'in Christ', how can they make a contribution to the shaping of reconciling communities that take full account of religious commitments in mutual appreciation? In what way does our understanding of reconciliation in Paul help us discern the boundaries of tolerable difference and diversity both within Christian communities and in society at large?

Our study of the social meaning of reconciliation in Paul has indeed shown that Paul's teaching does not necessarily offer a direct and detailed guide for our contemporary life in the world. Therefore, we need to be always looking for appropriate analogies and correlations to help us translate adequately Paul's message of reconciliation to our contemporary situations, both within and outside Christian communities. It is our hope, however, that our conversation with Paul on the social significance of reconciliation offered in the present study has provided valuable insights and resources which could guide us in our commitment to 'live peaceably with all' in a pluralistic world torn apart by violence and conflict. Most importantly, it has established that reconciliation with God is inextricably related to one's reconciliation with 'the other' and that the two cannot be separated. Equally significant, it has found that there is a strong biblical/theological basis for the social dimension of reconciliation on which the churches can build a solid theology and practice of reconciliation in the wider world. Finally, it has pointed to some concrete forms that the practices of reconciliation might take in specific social and political contexts.

8

CONCLUSION

The present research has enabled us to draw several important conclusions regarding the social significance of reconciliation in Paul's theology. First we have found that traditional exegetical scholarship which has treated Paul's presentation of reconciliation as referring to reconciliation between people and God, and has primarily focused its attention on key καταλλάσσω/καταλλαγή passages in the Pauline corpus, is limited and unsatisfactory on several counts: it does not give sufficient consideration to Paul's overall Jewish framework of reference; it ignores the social dimension of beliefs and the close link between religion and politics in the ancient Mediterranean world; and it works with a reductionist understanding of Paul's theology and does not fully appreciate the complex nature of Pauline theologizing.

Second, we have discovered that beginning with his encounter with Christ and his radical experience of reconciliation on the Damascus road, a particular vision of reality started to emerge for Paul. In addition to his reconciliation, that event meant also a paradigm shift in Paul's life, a radical new understanding of reality brought about by the death and resurrection of Christ. Paul's emerging vision of reconciliation was thus radically shaped by, and grounded on, the Christ event: a world of new possibilities and radical innovations is opened up now 'in Christ', with serious implications for all those living within this new reality. It then became clear for Paul that the great vision of restoration and peace found in Isaiah (chs 40–66) was being fulfilled in his day. And so it was there that Paul found important elements which solidly substantiated his further understanding and vision of reconciliation – especially as Isaiah connects closely his understanding of peace with such concepts as restoration, truth, and justice, expressed in social and communal relations, which will be the characteristic of the new creation of the age to come. Paul lived now in the new eschatological time when the things prophesied by Isaiah were being materialized. We have thus concluded that the social meaning of reconciliation in Paul's theology is to be understood within Paul's comprehensive vision of reconciliation: a vision grounded in the Christ event and Paul's own reconciliation experience, substantiated by the Isaianic vision of cosmic peace, and given form and expression in a rich symbolism of reconciliation. This vision was assessed in the light of the overall framework of the religious, social, and political contexts in which Paul lived and has led to the conclusion that an analysis of the social dimension of reconciliation in Paul's thought is not only *plausible* but also *necessary*. We have also found that Paul's overall vision not only offers the *framework* for the social dimension of reconciliation but also *determines* a reconciling life in the world.

Thirdly, we have shown that Paul gave expression to such a profound and complex understanding of reconciliation by using many symbols and concepts from his Hellenistic, Graeco-Roman context. It is thus not surprising that Paul employs the word-group καταλλάσσω/καταλλαγή used in the Hellenistic context primarily for interpersonal relationships, in the sociological and political spheres of life. To be sure, Paul's symbolism of reconciliation, as we have seen, is not exhausted by this terminology, but is much richer and more diverse, including also such concepts as 'peace', 'love', 'unity', 'acceptance', 'welcome', and 'friendship'. Therefore, all these must be considered for an adequate inquiry into Paul's understanding of reconciliation, particularly in its social dimension(s). Given his own personal experience of reconciliation and the Isaianic vision of peace, Paul gives expression to his understanding of reconciliation using language of the social, political, and religious context in which he lives. Therefore, for him reconciliation is a complex concept, which has personal, social, political, and cosmological dimensions. To emphasize just one dimension of reconciliation is to misinterpret Paul's own understanding of the complex concept.

Fourthly, our analysis of Romans 5–8, with special attention to the place and function of the story of Christ within Paul's argument, has shown the inseparability of the horizontal and vertical dimensions of reconciliation. Significantly, our study revealed that it was precisely Paul's appeals to the story of Christ that enabled him to address and hold together the two aspects of reconciliation: God's reconciling initiative by the death of Christ on the cross as the result of his obedient life to God (Rom. 5.19), becomes not only the very act and pronouncement of reconciliation of humanity with God, but also the ground and model for reconciling relationships among people. Indeed, we have seen that Paul goes to great lengths to emphasize both the greatness of the *fact* of reconciliation and *the manner* in which it was realized by Christ: by a costly sacrifice, by an initiative of love, by an offer extended to enemies. In this context we found that the faithfulness and obedience of Jesus were particularly highlighted by Paul as a model to be followed. Christ's story is not only his own story but includes the story of the believers. By virtue of their participation in Christ, believers can live rightly and be active actors, as the story of Christ is being unfolded in their midst. It is through a description of the complex dynamic of the incorporation of the believer 'in Christ', through baptism, that Paul signifies a real sharing of believers in the same story as active participants. From this perspective, we concluded that Paul does not simply write about how God's reconciliation is achieved in Christ, as something done from afar, of which believers are passive recipients. Rather, Paul includes the readers, their story, into the larger story of God's decisive reconciliation in Christ: they are themselves an *integral part* of this ongoing story of God's reconciling the world through Christ.

Fifthly, our examination of the interchange of metaphors and shift in the personal pronouns beginning with Romans 5 has led to the conclusion that by these intentional moves Paul shows two things: (1) that reconciliation is an essential aspect of salvation, and that it contains an intrinsic social, horizontal dimension; and (2) that the vertical reconciliation with God is inseparable from the horizontal aspect, as two dimensions of the same reality. Paul's intention was to show that the gospel the believers have received has clear and concrete implications for their everyday lives. To be justified and reconciled with God is to be reconciled and at peace with one's sister and brother, to be at peace with 'the other'. Furthermore, interpreting these changes in the light of the abundance of references to Jesus Christ throughout Romans 5–8 and in the light of the importance of the ethical dimension permeating this section, we concluded that Paul intended his readers to understand his argument in close connection with the story of Christ and with their responsibilities resulting from their being 'in Christ'. The reality of the believers' reconciliation with God, the new identity they now shared as reconciled people 'in Christ', is the basis for their sharing in, or living out, a reconciled life with others.

Sixthly, we have concluded that a narrative reading enables us to keep in proper tension both dimensions of reconciliation. For Paul to be reconciled with God is for him to live out that reconciliation, as to be righteous by faith means also to live out that righteousness, and to be 'in Christ' is to live the new life in the Spirit. While the classical readings keep these categories separate, a narrative reading brings them together in a real sense. Similarly, a narrative reading has highlighted aspects which are not traditionally explored when interpreting the theme of reconciliation in Paul, particularly the social, horizontal dimension of reconciliation.

Seventhly, our analysis of Romans 12–15 has found that Paul expresses the social dimension of reconciliation in various ways: as genuine love for one another and for enemies, as welcoming the weak and powerless, as affirming 'the other', as blessing one's persecutors, as overcoming evil with good, and as living at peace with all. These, we have concluded, are practices of reconciliation which are anchored in, and presuppose, the story of Christ as both the ground and paradigm for a reconciling way of life. We have shown that by placing these practices within the larger horizon of God's reconciliation of the world in Christ, Paul provides an unshakable foundation for both the possibility and the actuality of social reconciliation. So then, Paul's ultimate vision of the reconciliation of all things in Christ gives assurance and hope, and an irresistible impetus to the believer's ministry of reconciliation in all its forms and manifestations.

Eighthly, we have concluded that by bringing together the various narrative features of the story of Christ in Rom. 15.7–13, Paul reasserts his conviction that this story functions as both the ground and the model for the life of believers in the world. And this also offers an excellent window into Paul's theologizing, thus challenging us to understand Paul's thought and theology not in terms of 'doctrines' and 'principles' – though he holds these as very important – but in terms of the grand story of God's dealing with the world, through Christ, a story which takes concrete forms and shapes in many other, smaller stories to which Paul refers again and again in his writings, not least in the stories of the Christians to whom he writes.

Ninthly, we have shown that the churches in Romania can build on a Pauline understanding of reconciliation as presented in this research and could make a contribution to the public arena by offering and maintaining a sense of fundamental values for human life in the world, by discerning, unmasking and resisting any form of totalitarianism and absolutism, and by offering a framework of hope and a vision of life that will enable people not only to cope with 'otherness' and 'difference', but also to promote a culture of peace and justice, of freedom and love, of forgiveness and reconciliation – i.e., a culture of life.

Finally, we would like to point out that further research can be built on our findings in several areas. Thus, studies of the social dimension of reconciliation (and indeed any other major Pauline theme) can be carried out in any other of the Pauline letters using a similar methodology, particularly an in-depth exploration of the rich symbolism of reconciliation analogous to the one employed in this study. Similarly, further work could be done into Paul's theology using a narrative framework of reference with the prospect of significant new insights into the complex nature and dynamic of Paul's theologizing. Further research can also be built on the present work in social ethics: we have shown that the social dimension of reconciliation is solidly grounded in Paul's theology. Further work would need to explore more concretely the appropriate analogies and correlations which would translate adequately Paul's message of reconciliation to our contemporary situations.

BIBLIOGRAPHY

Abraham, Dorel, Ilie Badescu and Septimiu Chelcea, *Interethnic Relations in Romania: Sociological Diagnosis and Evaluation of Tendencies* (Cluj-Napoca: Editura Carpatica, 1995).

Achtemeier, Paul J., *Romans* (Atlanta: John Knox, 1985).

Adams, Edward, *Constructing the World: A Study in Paul's Cosmological Language* (Edinburgh: T&T Clark, 2000).

Aldrich, Willard M., 'The Objective Nature of Reconciliation', *BS* 118 (1961), pp. 18–21.

Alexander, Loveday (ed.), *Images of Empire* (*JSOTS*, 122; Sheffield: Sheffield Academic, 1991).

Allen, Gregory J., *Reconciliation in the Pauline Tradition: Its Occasions, Meanings, and Functions* (ThD dissertation presented to Boston University, School of Theology, 1995); (UMI: Ann Arbor, 1998).

Amjad-Ali, Charles, 'The Religious Dimension of Social Change', in Chiba, Shin, George R. Hunsberger and Lester Edwin J. Ruiz (eds), *Christian Ethics in Ecumenical Context: Theology, Culture and Politics in Dialogue* (Grand Rapids: Eerdmans, 1995).

Amstutz, Mark R., 'Is Reconciliation Possible After Genocide? The Case of Rwanda', *Journal of Church and State* 48(3) (2006), pp. 541–65.

—'Human Rights and the Promise of Political Forgiveness', *RE* 104 (2007), pp. 553–77.

Anderson, Janice Capel *et al.* (eds), *Paul's Conversations in Context: Essays in Honor of Calvin J. Roetzel* (*JSNTS*, 221; Sheffield: Sheffield Academic, 2002).

Andreescu, Gabriel, *Ruleta: Ramani si maghiari, 1990–2000* (Iasi: Polirom, 2001).

Appleby, R. Scott, *The Ambivalence of the Sacred: Religion, Violence and Reconciliation* (Lanham, MD: Rowman & Littlefield, 1998).

Arnold, Clinton E., *Powers of Darkness: Principalities and Powers in Paul's Letters* (Downers Grove, IL: IVP, 1992).

Augsburger, Myron, *The Robe of God: Reconciliation, the Believers Church Essential* (Scottdale: Herald Press, 2000).

Babiuch, Jolanta, 'The Eastern European Church After Communism: Seeking New Ways to Serve – or new enemies to fight', *East-West Church & Ministry Report* 5 (1997), pp. 5–6.

Baconski, Teodor. *Ispita Binelui: Eseuri despre urbanitatea credintei* (Bucuresti: Anastasia, 1999).

—*Puterea schismei: Un portret al crestinismului european* (Bucuresti: Anastasia, 2001).

Bailey, James L, 'Genre Analysis', in Joel B. Green (ed.), *Hearing the New Testament: Strategies For Interpretation* (Grand Rapids: Eerdmans, 1995).

Banks, Robert (ed.), *Reconciliation and Hope: New Testament Essays on Atonement and Eschatology Presented to L. L. Morris* (Exeter: Paternoster, 1974).

Banyai, Laszlo, *Destin comun, traditions fraternelles* (Bucuresti: Romanian Academy, 1972).

—*Studii de istoria nationalitatii maghiare si a infratirii cu Romania* (Bucuresti: Editura Politica, 1976).

Barbu, Violeta, 'Bisericile in Europa – un partner social?', in Carp, Radu (ed.), *Un suflet pentru Europa: Dimensiunea religioasa a unui proiect politic* (Bucuresti: Anastasia, 2005).

Barca, Diana Evantia, 'Romanii, inamicii schimbarii', *Evenimentul Zilei* (2 November 2003).

Barclay, John M. G., *The Jews in the Mediterranean Diaspora: From Alexander to Trajan* (Edinburgh: T&T Clark, 1996).

Barkan, Elazar, 'Historical Reconciliation: Redress, Rights And Politics', *Journal of International Affairs* 60(1) (2006), pp. 1–15.

Barram, Michael, 'Romans 12: 9–21', *Interpretation* 57 (2003), pp. 423–26.

Barrett, C. K., *A Commentary on the Epistle to the Romans* (New York: Harper & Row, 1957).

—*A Commentary on the Second Epistle to the Corinthians* (London: Adam & Charles Black, 1976).

Bar-Siman-Tov, Yaacov (ed.), *From conflict resolution to reconciliation* (Oxford: OUP, 2004).

Barta, Gabor, *History of Transylvania* (Budapest: Akademiai Kiado, 1994).

Barth, Karl, *Church Dogmatics* (Edinburgh: T&T Clark, 1956).

—*The Epistle to the Romans* (translated from the sixth edition by Edwyn C. Hoskyns; Oxford: OUP, 1968).

Bartholomew, Craig *et al.* (eds), *A Royal Priesthood? The Use of the Bible Ethically and Politically* (Carlisle: Paternoster Press, 2002).

Barton, Stephen C., 'Paul and the limits of tolerance', in Stanton, Graham N. and Guy G. Stroumsa (eds), *Tolerance and Intolerance in Early Judaism and Christianity* (Cambridge: CUP, 1998).

Bashir, Bashir and Will Kymlicka (eds), *The Politics of Reconciliation in Multicultural Societies* (Oxford: OUP, 2008).

Bassler, Jouette M., (ed.), *Pauline Theology Volume I: Thessalonians, Philippians, Galatians, Philemon* (Minneapolis: Fortress, 1991).

—'Paul's Theology: Whence and Whither?', in Hay, David M. (ed.), *Pauline Theology Volume II: 1& 2 Corinthians* (Minneapolis: Fortress, 1993).

Battle, Michael Jesse, *Reconciliation: The Ubuntu Theology of Desmond Tutu* (Cleveland, OH: Pilgrim, 1997).

Bauckham, Richard J., *The Bible in Politics: How to Read the Bible Politically* (London: SPCK, 1989).

Bauer, Yehuda *et al.* (eds), *Remembering for the Future, Vol. 1: Jews & Christians during and after the Holocaust* (Oxford: Pergamon, 1989a).

—*Remembering for the Future, Vol. 2: The impact of the Holocaust on the contemporary world* (Oxford: Pergamon, 1989b).

Baum, Gregory and Harold Wells (eds), *The Reconciliation of Peoples: Challenges to the Churches* (Geneva: WCC Publications, 1997).

Beale, G. K., 'The Old Testament Background of Reconciliation in 2 Corinthians 5–7 and its Bearing on the Literary Problem of 2 Corinthians 6:14–7:1', in Beale, G. K. (ed.), *The Right Doctrine from the Wrong Texts? Essays on the Use of the Old Testament in the New* (Grand Rapids: Baker, 1994).

—'The NT and New Creation', in Hafemann, Scott I. (ed.), *Biblical Theology: Retrospect and Prospect* (Downers Grove, IL: IVP, 2002).

Beker, J. Christiaan, *Paul the Apostle: The Triumph of God in Life and Thought* (Philadelphia, PA: Fortress, 1984).

Berger, Peter L., *The Sacred Canopy: Elements of Sociological Theory of Religion* (New Garden City, NY: Doubleday, 1969).

Berger, Peter (ed.), *The Desecularisation of the World* (Grand Rapids: Eerdmans, 2000).

Berger, P. and T. Luckman, *The Social Construction of Reality: A Treatise in the Sociology of Knowledge* (New York: Doubleday, 1967).

Betz, Otto, 'Fleischliche und "geistiche" Christuserkenntnis nach 2 Korinther 5:16', in Betz, O. (ed.), *Jesus – der Herr der Kirche* (Tubingen: Mohr-Siebeck, 1990).

Bieringer, Reimund, 'Paul's Understanding of Diakonia in 2 Corinthians 5,18', in Bieringer, R. and J. Lambrecht (eds) *Studies in 2 Corinthians* (Leuven: University Press, 1994).

Bieringer, R. and J. Lambrecht (eds), *Studies in 2 Corinthians* (Leuven: University Press, 1994).

Binder, Herman, 'Versohnung Als Die Grosse Wende', *Theologische Zeitschrift* 29 (1973), pp. 305–12.

Biro, Sndor, *The Nationalities Problem in Transylvania, 1867–1940* (Boulder, CO: Social Science Monograph, 1991).

Bjerkelund, Carl J., *Parakalô: Form, Funktion und Sinn derparakalô-Sätze in den paulinischen Briefen* (Oslo: Universitetsforlaget, 1967).

Blumenfeld, Bruno, *The Political Paul: Justice, Democracy and Kingship in a Hellenistic Framework* (*JSNTS*, 210; Sheffield: Sheffield Academic, 2001).

Boers, Hendrikus, 'The Structure and Meaning of Romans 6:1–14', *CBQ* 63 (2001), pp. 664–82.

Bond, Gilbert I., *Paul and the Religious Experience of Reconciliation: Diasporic Community and Creole Consciousness* (Louisville, KY: Westminster John Knox, 2005).

Borhkamm, Gunter, 'The Revelation of Christ to Paul on the Damascus Road and Paul's Doctrine of Justification and Reconciliation', in Robert Banks (ed.), *Reconciliation and Hope* (Exeter: Paternoster, 1974).

Botoran, Constantin, *Transylvania and the Romanian-Hungarian Relations* (Bucuresti: Institute of Military History and Theory, 1993).

Botha, Jan, *Subject to Whose Authority? Multiple Readings of Romans 13* (Emory Studies in Early Christianity; Atlanta: Scholars Press, 1994).

Boulton, Wayne, 'Riddle of Romans 13', *Christian Century* 93 (1976), pp. 758–61.

Boyarin, Daniel, *A Radical Jew: Paul and the Politics of Identity* (Barkley, CA: University of California Press, 1994).

Brett, Mark G., *Biblical Criticism in Crisis* (Cambridge: CUP, 1991).

Brett, Mark G. (ed.), *Ethnicity and the Bible* (Leiden: Brill, 1996).

Breytenbach, Cilliers, 'Reconciliation – Shifts in Christian Soteriology', in Forster, W. S. (ed.), *Reconciliation and Construction: Creative Options for a Rapidly Changing South Africa*. (Pretoria: Unisa, 1986).

—*Versöhnung: Eine Studie zur paulinischen Soteriologie* (WMANT, 60; Neukirchen-Vluyn: Neukirchener, 1989).

—'On Reconciliation: An Exegetical Response', *Journal of Theology for South Africa* 70 (1990), pp. 64–68.

Bria, Ion, 'Teologia fata in fata cu Biserica de azi', *Studii Teologice* XLVII (1990), pp. 3–6.

—*Ortodoxia in Europa: Locul spiritualitatii Romane* (Iasi: Mitropolia Moldovei si Bucovinei, 1995).

—'Evangelism, Proselytism and Religious Freedom in Romania: an Orthodox Point of View', *Journal of Ecumenical Studies* 36 (1999):163–83.

Bria, Ion, *et al. Ecumenical Pilgrims: Profiles of Pioneers in Christian Reconciliation* (Geneva: WCC Publications, 1997).

Brown, Alexandra, 'Response to Sylvia Keesmaat and Richard Hays', *Horizons in Biblical Theology* 26 (2004), pp. 115–22.

Brown, Amy Benson and Karen M. Poremski (eds), *Roads to Reconciliation: Conflict and Dialogue in the Twenty-First Century* (Armonk, NY: M. E. Sharpe, 2005).

Bruce, F. F., 'Christ as Conqueror and Reconciler', *BS* 141/564 (1984), pp. 291–302.

—*The Letter of Paul to the Romans: An Introduction and Commentary* (Grand Rapids: Eerdmans, 1985).

Brummer, Vincent, 'Atonement and Reconciliation', *Religious Studies* 28 (1992), pp. 435–52.

Brunner, Emil, *The Letter to the Romans* (H. A. Kennedy (trans.); London: Lutterworth, 1959).

Brunt, P. A., '*Laus Imperii*', in Horsley, Richard A. (ed.), *Paul and Empire: Religion and Power in Roman Imperial Society* (Harrisburg, PA: Trinity, 1997).

Buchsel, Friedrich, 'ἀλλάσσώ κτλ', in Kittel, Gerhard (ed.), *TDNT*, Vol. 1. (Geoffrey Bromiley (trans.); Grand Rapids: Eerdmans, 1964).

Bultmann, Rudolf, 'The Problem of Ethics in Paul', in Rosner, Brian S. (ed.),

Understanding Paul's Ethics: Twentieth Century Approaches (Grand Rapids: Eerdmans, 1995).

Burdon, C. J., 'Paul and the Crucified Church', *Expository Times* 95 (1984), pp. 137–41.

Byrne, Brendan, 'Living out the Righteousness of God: The Contribution of Rom 6:1–8:13 to an Understanding of Paul's Ethical Presuppositions', *CBQ* 43 (1981), pp. 557–81.

—*Romans* (Harrington, Daniel J. (ed.), Sacra Pagina Series, vol. 6; Collegeville: The Liturgical Press, 1996).

—'Interpreting Romans: the New Perspective and Beyond', *Interpretation* 58(3) (2004), pp. 241–52.

Cadzow, John F., (ed.), *Transylvania: The Roots of Ethnic Conflict* (Kent, OH: Kent State University, 1983).

Cahill, Lisa Sowle, 'The New Testament and Ethics: Communities of Social Change', *Interpretation* 44 (1990), pp. 383–95.

Campbell, Douglas A, 'The Story of Jesus in Romans and Galatians', in Longenecker, Bruce W. (ed.), *Narrative Dynamics in Paul: A Critical Assessment* (Louisville, KY: Westminster John Knox, 2002).

Campbell, William S., 'Romans III as a Key to the Structure and Thought of the Letter', in Donfried, Karl P. (ed.), *The Romans Debate* (rev. and expand. edn; Peabody, MA: Hendrickson, 1991).

—*Paul's Gospel in an Intercultural Context* (Berlin: Peter Lang, 1992).

—'The Rule of Faith in Romans 12:1–15:13. The Obligation of Humble Obedience to Christ as the Only Adequate Response to the Mercies of God', in Hay, David M. and E. Elisabeth Johnson (eds), *Pauline Theology Volume III: Romans* (Minneapolis: Fortress, 1995).

—*Paul and the Creation of Christian Identity* (LNTS, 322; London and New York: T&T Clark Continuum, 2006).

—'Unity and Diversity in the Church: Transformed Identities and the Peace of Christ in Ephesians', *Transformation* 24(1) (2008), pp. 15–31.

Carp, Radu (ed.), *Un suflet pentru Europa: Dimensiunea religioasa a unui proiect politic* (Bucuresti: Anastasia, 2005).

Carter, T. L., 'The Irony of Romans 13', *NovT* 46 (2004), pp. 209–28.

Casalis, Georges, 'Reconciliation Through Christ as Basis for Living with Others and Living for Others', *Communio Viatorum* 2 (1961), pp. 103–16.

Catherwood, Christopher, 'Nationalism, Ethnicity and Tolerance: some Historical, Political and Biblical Perspectives', *Transformation* 14 (1997), pp. 10–16.

Chaplin, J., 'Government', in Atkinson, D. J. *et al.* (eds), *New Dictionary of Christian Ethics and Pastoral Theology* (Leicester: IVP, 1995).

Chvala-Smith, Anthony J., 'The Politics of Reconciliation in 2 Corinthians 5', *Proceedings* (Eastern Great Lakes Biblical Society) 11 (1981), pp. 210–21.

Codrescu, Razvan, *Cartea indreptarilor: o perspectiva crestina asupra politicului* (Bucuresti: Christiana, 2004).

Coleman, Thomas M., 'Binding Obligations in Romans 13:7: A Semantic Field and Social Context', *TB* 48(2) (1997), pp. 307–27.

Constantineanu, Corneliu, 'Reconciliation as a Missiological Category for Social Engagement: a Pauline Perspective from Romans 12.9–21', in Grams, Rollin G., I. Howard Marshall, Peter Penner and Robin Routledge (eds), *Bible and Mission: A Conversation Between Biblical Studies and Missiology* (Schwarzenfeld: Neufeld, 2008).

Corneanu, Nicolae, Metropolitan. *In pas cu vremea* (Timisoara: Mitropolia Banatului, 2002).

Cousar, Charles B., 'II Corinthians 5:17–21', *Interpretation* 35 (1981), pp. 180–83.

Cranfield, C. E. B., *A Critical and Exegetical Commentary on the Epistle to the Romans (International Critical Commentary*, 2 vols; Edinburgh: T&T Clark, 1979).

Daly, Erin and Jeremy Sarkin, *Reconciliation in Divided Societies: Finding Common Ground* (Philadelphia, PA: University of Pennsylvania Press, 2007).

Danker, Frederick W., *2 Corinthians* (Augsburg Commentary on the New Testament; Minneapolis: Augsburg, 1989).

Davies, W. D., *Paul and Rabbinic Judaism* (London: SPCK, 1948).

De Gruchy, John, 'The Struggle for Justice and Ministry of Reconciliation', *JTSA* 62 (1988), pp. 43–52.

De Kruijf, Gerrit, 'The Function of Romans 13 in Christian Ethics', in Bartholomew, Craig *et al.* (eds), *A Royal Priesthood? The use of tile Bible Ethically and Politically: A Dialogue with Oliver O'Donovan* (Grand Rapids: Zondervan, 2002).

De Oliveira, A., *Die Diakonie der Gerechtigkeit und der Versöhnung in der Apologie des 2. Korintherbriefes* (Münster: Aschendorff, 1990).

deSilva, D. A., 'Ruler Cult', in Craig A. Evans and Stanley E. Porter (eds), *Dictionary of New Testament Background* (Downers Grove: InterVarsity Press, 2000): (CD-ROM, electronic edn; Libronix Digital Library, 2000).

De Young, Curtiss Paul, 'The Power of Reconciliation. From the Apostle Paul to Malcolm X', *Crosscurrents* (Summer 2007), pp. 203–08.

Denney, James, *The Christian Doctrine of Reconciliation* (London: Hodder & Stoughton, 1919).

Dennison, William D., 'Indicative and Imperative: The Basic Structure of Pauline Ethics', *Calvin Theological Journal* 14(1) (1979), pp. 55–78.

Desjardins, Michel, *Peace, Violence and the New Testament* (Sheffield: Sheffield Academic, 1997).

Deyoung, Curtiss Paul, *Reconciliation: Our Greatest Challenge – Our Only Hope* (Valley Forge, PA: Judson, 1997).

Dimancescu, Dan (ed.), *Romania Redux: A View from Harvard* (Bucuresti: Humanitas, 2004).

Dodd, C. H., *According to the Scriptures: The Substructure of NT Theology* (London: Fontana, 1965).

Domeris, W. R., 'Biblical Perspectives on Reconciliation', *JTSA* 60 (1987), pp. 77–80.

Donaldson, Terence L., *Paul and the Gentiles: Remapping the Apostle's Convictional World* (Minneapolis: Fortress, 1997).

Donfried, K. P., 'False Presuppositions in the Study of Romans', in Donfried, K. P. (ed.), *The Romans Debate* (rev. and exp. edn; Peabody, MA: Hendrickson, 1991).

Donfried, Karl P. (ed.), *The Romans Debate*. Rev. and exp. ed. Peabody, MA: Hendrickson, 1991).

Du Bois, François and Antje du Bois-Pedain (eds), *Justice and Reconciliation in Post-Apartheid South Africa* (Cambridge: CUP, 2008).

Dunn, James D. G., 'Romans 13.1–7: A Charter for Political Quietism?', *Ex Auditu* 2 (1986), pp. 55–68.

—*Romans* (*WBC*, Vol. 38 a,b; Dallas: Word Books, 1988); (CD-ROM, electronic edn; Libronix Digital Library, 2002).

—*The Theology of Paul the Apostle* (Grand Rapids: Eerdmans, 1998).

—'The Narrative Approach to Paul: Whose Story?', in Longenecker, Bruce W. (ed.), *Narrative Dynamics in Paul: A Critical Assessment* (Louisville, KY: Westminster John Knox, 2002).

Earl, Arville and Sheila Earl, 'Committed to the Ministry of Reconciliation: Moving Beyond Conflict in the Balkans', *RE* 104 (2007), pp. 603–21.

Ehrensperger, K. *That We May Be Mutually Encouraged: Feminism and the New Perspective in Pauline Studies* (London: T&T Clark, 2004).

Elliott, Neil, 'Romans 13:1–7 in the Context of Imperial Propaganda', in Horsley, Richard A. (ed.), *Paul and Empire: Religion and Power in Roman Imperial Society* (Harrisburg, PA: Trinity, 1997).

—*Liberating Paul: The Justice of God and the Politics of the Apostle* (Maryknoll, NY: Orbis, 1999).

Ellis, E. Earle, *Pauline Theology: Ministry and Society* (Grand Rapids: Eerdmans, 1989).

Enache, George, *Ortodoxie si putere politica in Romania contemporana* (Bucuresti: Nemira, 2005).

Endroiu, Nicolae. *Nostalgia for an Empire of Sad Memory: The Austro-Hungarian Monarchy* (Bucharest: Agerpress, 1987).

—*Maghiarii din Romania* (Cluj-Napoca: Centrul de Studii Transilvane, Fundatia Culturala Romana, 1995).

Engberg-Pedersen, Troels, *Paul and the Stoics* (Louisville, KY: Westminster John Knox, 2000).

Engberg-Pedersen, Troels (ed.), *Paul Beyond the Judaism/Hellenism Divide* (Louisville, KY: Westminster John Knox, 2001).

Esler, Philip F., *The First Christians in their Social World: Social-Scientific Approaches to New Testament Interpretation* (London: Routledge, 1994).

—*Conflict and Identity in Romans: The Social Setting of Paul's Letter* (Minneapolis: Fortress, 2003).

Esler, Philip F. (ed.), *Modelling Early Christianity: Social-scientific studies of the New Testament in its context* (London: Routledge, 1995).

Everts, J. M., 'Conversion and Call of Paul', in Hawthorne, G. F. *et al.* (eds), *DPL* (Logos Library, electronic edn; Downers Grove, IL: IVP, 1997, ©1993).

Favazza, Joseph A., 'Reconciliation: On the Border between Theological and Political Praxis', *Journal for the Study of Religion and Ideologies* 3 (2002), pp. 52–64.

Fee, Gordon, *New Testament Exegesis* (Philadelphia, PA: John Knox Press, 1983).

—*The First Epistle to the Corinthians* (Grand Rapids: Eerdmans, 1987).

—*God's Empowering Presence: the Holy Spirit in the Letters of Paul* (Peabody, MA: Hendrickson, 1994).

— *Paul, the Spirit and the People of God* (Peabody, MA: Hendrickson, 1996).

Fitzgerald, John T., 'Paul and Paradigm Shifts: Reconciliation and Its Linkage Group', in Engberg-Pedersen, Troels (ed.), *Paul Beyond the Judaism/Hellenism Divide* (Louisville, KY: Westminster John Knox Press, 2001).

Fitzmyer, Joseph, *Pauline Theology* (Englewood Cliffs, NJ: Prentice-Hall, 1967).

—'Reconciliation in Pauline Theology', in Flanagan, James and Anita Robinson (eds), *No Famine in the Land: Studies in Honor of John L McKenzie* (Missoula, MT: Scholars Press, 1975).

—*Romans: A New Translation With Introduction and Commentary* (The Anchor Bible Commentaries; New York: Doubleday, 1993).

—*Spiritual Exercises Based on Paul's Epistle to the Romans* (Grand Rapids: Eerdmans, 2004).

Flanagan, James and Anita Robinson (eds), *No Famine in the Land: Studies in Honor of John L McKenzie* (Missoula, MT: Scholars Press, 1975).

Fong, Bruce W., 'Addressing the Issue of Racial Reconciliation According to the Principles of Eph 2: 11–22', *JETS* 38 (1995), pp. 565–80.

Forster, F., '"Reconcile," 2 Cor. 5:18–20', *CTM* 21 (1950), pp. 296–98.

Fowl, Stephen E., *The Story of Jesus in the Letters of Paul* (*JSNTS*, 36; Sheffield: Sheffield Academic, 1990).

Fowl, Stephen E. and L. Gregory Jones, *Reading in Communion: Scripture and Ethics in Christian Life* (London: SPCK, 1991).

Franzmann, Martin H., 'Reconciliation and Justification', *CTM* 21 (1950), pp. 81–93.

Fryer, N. S. L., 'Reconciliation in Paul's Epistle to the Romans', *Neotestamentica* 15 (1981), pp. 34–68.

Frymer-Kensky, Tikva S. *et al.* (eds), *Christianity in Jewish terms* (Boulder, CO: Westview, 2000).

Furnish, Victor Paul, *Theology and Ethics in Paul* (Nashville: Abingdon, 1968).

—*The Love Command in the New Testament* (Nashville, TN: Abingdon, 1972).

—'The Ministry of Reconciliation', *Currents in Theology and Mission* 4(4) (1977), pp. 204–18.

—*II Corinthians* (The Anchor Bible, vol. 32A; New York: Doubleday, 1984).

Gager, John G., 'Some Notes on Paul's Conversion', *NTS* 27 (1980), pp. 697–704.

—*The Origins of Anti-Semitism: Attitudes Towards Judaism in Pagan and Christian Antiquity* (New York: OUP, 1983).

Gallagher, Tom, *Romania after Ceausescu: The Politics of Intolerance* (Edinburgh: Edinburgh University Press, 1995).

—*Furtul unei natiuni: Romania de la comunism incoace* (Mihai Elin, Delia Razdolescu and Horia Barna (trans.); Bucuresti: Humanitas, 2004).

—*Theft of a Nation: Romania Since Communism* (London: Hurst, 2005).

Gasparini, Alberto, 'Globalisation, Reconciliation and the Conditions for Conserving Peace', *Global Society* 22(1) (2008), pp. 27–55.

Gaventa, Beverly Roberts, *From Darkness to Light: Aspects of Conversion in the New Testament* (Philadelphia, PA: Fortress, 1986).

—'Paul's Conversion: A Critical Sifting of the Epistolary Evidence' (unpublished Ph.D. dissertation, Duke University, 1978).

Gibson, Jeffrey B., 'Paul's "Dying Formula": Prolegomena to an Understanding of Its Import and Significance', in McGinn, Sheila E. (ed.), *Celebrating Romans: Template for Pauline Theology. Essays in Honor of Robert Jewett* (Grand Rapids: Eerdmans, 2004).

Gill, D. W. J., 'Roman Political System', in Evans, Craig A. and Stanley E. Porter (eds), *DNTB* (Logos Library, electronic edn; Downers Grove, IL: IVP, 2000).

Gill, Robin (ed.), *Theology and Sociology: A Reader* (London: Cassell, 1996).

Gillet, Olivier, *Religie si nationalism: Ideologia Bisericii Ortodoxe Române sub regimul communist* (Bucuresti: Compania, 2001).

Gitelman, Zvi *et al.* (eds), *New Jewish Identities: Contemporary Europe and Beyond* (Budapest/New York: Central European University Press, 2002).

Giurescu, Constantin, *Transylvania in the History of Romania: An Historical Outline* (London: Garnstone, [no date displayed]).

Gloer, William Hullit, *An Exegetical and Theological Study of Paul's Understanding of New Creation and Reconciliation in 2 Cor. 5:14–21* (Lewiston: The Edwin Mellen Press, 1996).

—'2 Corinthians 5,14–21', in *RE*, 86 (1989), pp. 397–405.

—'Ambassadors of Reconciliation: Paul's Genius In Applying the Gospel in a Multi-Cultural World: 2 Corinthians 5:14–21', *RE* 104 (2007), pp. 589–604.

Goodchild, N. M., *Hungarian Realities in Romania: Documentaries* (London: Panopticum, 1980).

Gorg, Manfred *et al. Christen und Juden im Gesprach: Bilanz nach 40 Jahren Staat* (Regensburg: Friedrich Pustet, 1989).

Gorman, Michael J., *Cruciformity: Paul's Narrative Spirituality of the Cross* (Grand Rapids: Eerdmans, 2001).

Gorringe, Tim, 'Political Reading of Scripture', in Barton, John (ed.), *The Cambridge Companion to Biblical Interpretation* (Cambridge: CUP, 1998).

Gort, Jerald D., Henry Jansen and Hendrik M. Vroom (eds), *Religion, Conflict and Reconciliation: Multifaiths Ideals and Realities* (Amsterdam: Rodopi, 2002).

Grams, Rollin, 'Gospel and Mission in Paul's Ethics' (unpublished Ph.D. dissertation, Duke University, 1989. Printed by University Microfilms International, Ann Arbor, MI, 1990).

—'Paul and Missions: The Narrative of Israel and the Mission of the Church' (unpublished paper presented at OCMS Lectures, Oxford, 1 August 2000).

—'Exploring Mission as Transformation in Paul's Letter to the Romans' (unpublished paper presented at OCMS Lectures, Oxford, 12 June, 2005).

Grant, Robert M., *Paul in the Roman World: The Conflict at Corinth* (Louisville, KY: Westminster John Knox Press, 2001).

Green, Joel B. (ed.), *Hearing the New Testament: Strategies for Interpretation* (Grand Rapids: Eerdmans, 1995).

Green, Joel B. and Max Turner (eds), *Between Two Horizons: Spanning NTS and Systematic Theology* (Grand Rapids: Eerdmans, 2000).

Grieb, A. Katherine, *The Story of Romans: A Narrative Defense of God's Righteousness* (Louisville, KY: Westminster John Knox Press, 2002).

Groen, Basilius J., 'Nationalism and Reconciliation: Orthodoxy in the Balkans', *RSS* 26(2) (1998), pp. 111–28.

Guelich, Robert (ed.), *Unity and Diversity in New Testament Theology* (Grand Rapids: Eerdmans, 1978).

Guerra, Anthony J., *Romans and the Apologetic Tradition: The Purpose, Genre and Audience of Paul's Letter* (Cambridge: CUP, 1995).

Gunton, Colin E. (ed.), *The Theology of Reconciliation* (London: T&T Clark, 2003).

Guthrie, Shirley C., 'Romans 11:25–32', *Interpretation* 38(3) (1984), pp. 286–91.

Gutting, Gary (ed.), *Paradigms & Revolutions: Appraisals and Applications of Thomas Kuhn's Philosophy of Science* (Notre Dame/London: University of Notre Dame Press, 1980).

Haacker, Klaus. *The Theology of Paul's Letter to the Romans* (Cambridge New Testament Theology Series; Cambridge: CUP, 2003).

Hafemann, Scott J., 'Paul's Use of the Old Testament in 2 Corinthians', *Interpretation* 52 (1998), pp. 246–57.

—'Roman Triumph', in Evans, Craig A. and Stanley E. Porter (eds), *DNTB* (Logos Library, electronic edn; Downers Grove, IL: IVP, 2000).

Hanson, Anthony Tyrrell, *The Paradox of the Cross in the Thought of St Paul* (*JSNTS*, 17; Sheffield: Sheffield Academic, 1987).

Harink, D, "Paul and Israel: An Apocalyptic Reading', *Pro Ecclesia* 16 (2007): 359–80.

Harned, D. B., *Creed and Personal Identity* (Edinburgh: Handsel, 1981).

Hasdeu, B. P., *Istoria tolerantei religioase in Romania* (Bucuresti: Editura 'Saeculum', 1992).

Hauerwas, Stanley, *Vision and Virtue* (Notre Dame: Fides, 1974).

—*Character and Christian Life* (San Antonio: Trinity University Press, 1975).

—*A Community of Character: Toward a Constructive Christian Social Ethic*
(Notre Dame: University of Notre Dame Press, 1981).

Hawthorne, G. F. *et al.* (eds), *DPL* (Logos Library, electronic edn; Downers Grove,
IL: IVP, 1997, 1993).

Hay, David M. and E. Elisabeth Johnson (eds), *Pauline Theology, Vol. III: Romans*
(Minneapolis: Fortress, 1995).

Hays, Richard B. *The Faith of Jesus Christ: An Investigation of the Narrative
Substructure of Galatians 3:1–4:11* (Chico, CA: Scholars Press, 1983).

—*Echoes of Scriptures in the Letters of Paul* (New Haven: Yale University Press,
1989).

—'Adam, Israel, Christ –The Question of Covenant in the Theology of Romans:
A Response to Leander E. Keck and N. T. Wright', in Hay, David M. and E.
Elizabeth Johnson (eds), *Pauline Theology, Vol. III: Romans* (Minneapolis:
Fortress, 1995).

—'ΠΙΣΤΙΣ and the Pauline Christology: What is at Stake?', in Johnson, E.
Elizabeth and David Hay (eds), *Pauline Theology, Vol. IV: Looking Back,
Pressing On* (Atlanta, GA: Scholars Press, 1997).

—'Is Paul's Gospel Narratable?', *JSNT* 7 (2004a), pp. 217–39.

—'Christ Died for the Ungodly: Narrative Soteriology in Paul?', *Horizons in
Biblical Theology* 26 (2004b), pp. 48–68.

—*The Conversion of the Imagination: Paul as Interpreter of Israel's Scripture*
(Grand Rapids: Eerdmans, 2005).

Hedquist, Paul Michael, 'The Pauline Understanding of Reconciliation in
Romans 5 and II Corinthians 5: An Exegetical and Religio-Historical Study'
(unpublished Th.D. dissertation, Union Theological Seminary, Virginia,
1979).

Healey, Joseph P., 'Peace, Old Testament', in Freedman, David Noel (ed.), *ABD*
(Logos Library, electronic edn; New York: Doubleday, 1997).

Hengel, Martin, *The Atonement: The Origins of the Doctrine in the New Testament*
(London: SCM Press, 1981).

Herrick, Greg, 'Paul and Civil Obedience in Romans 13:1–7' (Biblical Studies
Press). Available onine at: http://www.bible.org (accessed 28 October 2005).

Hjort, Hanna and Ann Frisen, 'Ethnic Identity and Reconciliation: Two Main
Tasks for the Young in Bosnia-Herzegovina', *Adolescence* 41(161) (Spring
2006), pp. 141–63.

Hodgson, Peter, 'Constructive Theology and Biblical Words', in Segovia, F. and
M. A. Tolbert (eds), *Teaching the Bible* (Maryknoll, NY: Orbis, 1998).

Hofius, Otfried, '"Gott hat unter uns aufgerichtet das Wort von der Versöhnung"
(2 Kor. 5:19)', *ZNW* 71 (1980), pp. 3–20.

—'Erwägungen zur Gestalt und Herkunft des paulinischen Versöhnungdgedankes',
in Hofius, O. (ed.), *Paulusstudien* (Tubingen: J. C. B. Mohr-Siebeck, 1989).

Hollon, D. Leslie, 'Reconciliation: Pastoral Reflections and Resources', *RE* 104
(2007), pp. 442–62.

Hollon, Ryan, 'Moving Beyond Boundaries: Restorative Justice and Reconciliation as Complementary Paths in Peacemaking', *RE* 104 (2007), pp. 579–87.

Holmberg, Bengt (ed.), *Exploring Early Christian Identity* (WUNT, 226; Tubingen: Mohr Siebeck, 2008).

Hooker, Morna D., *From Adam to Christ: Essays on Paul* (Cambridge: CUP, 1990).

Horrell, David G., 'Paul's Narrative or Narrative Substructure? The Significance of "Paul's Story"', in Longenecker, Bruce W. (ed.), *Narrative Dynamics in Paul: A Critical Assessment* (Louisville, KY: Westminster John Knox, 2002).

—"The Peaceable, Tolerant Community and the Legitimate Role of the State: Ethics and Ethical Dilemmas in Romans 12:1–15:13." *Review and Expositor* 100:1 (2003): 81–95.

—*Solidarity and Difference: A Contemporary Reading of Paul's Ethics* (London: T&T Clark, 2005).

Horsley, Richard (ed.), *Paul and Empire: Religion and Power in Roman Imperial Society*. (Harrisburg, PA: Trinity, 1997).

—*Paul and Politics: Ekklesia, Israel, Imperium, Interpretation* (Harrisburg, PA: Trinity, 2000).

—*Paul and the Roman Imperial Order* (Harrisburg/London: Trinity, 2004).

Horsley, Richard A. and M. A. Silberman, *The Message and the Kingdom: How Jesus and Paul Ignited a Revolution and Transformed the Ancient World* (Minneapolis: Fortress, 1997).

Hubbard, Moyer V., *New Creation in Paul's Letters and Thought* (SNTSMS, 119; Cambridge: CUP, 2002).

Hübner, Hans, *Law in Paul's Thought* (Edinburgh: T&T Clark, 1984).

Hughes, Philip E., *Paul's Second Epistle to the Corinthians* (Grand Rapids: Eerdmans, 1962).

Hurtado, Larry W., 'Jesus' Divine Sonship in Paul's Epistle to the Romans', in Soderlund, Sven K. and N. T. Wright (eds), *Romans and the People of God: Essays in Honor of Gordon Fee on the Occasion of his 65th Birthday* (Grand Rapids: Eerdmans, 1999).

—*Lord Jesus Christ: Devotion to Jesus in Earliest Christianity* (Grand Rapids: Eerdmans, 2003).

—'Jesus' Death as Paradigmatic in the New Testament', *Scottish Journal of Theology* 57 (2004), pp. 413–33.

Hutchinson, S., 'The Political Implications of Romans 13:1–7', *Biblical Theology* 21 (1971), pp. 49–59.

Hyde, Clark, 'The Ministry of Reconciliation', *St Luke's Journal of Theology* 31 (1988), pp. 111–25.

Ica, Ioan and Germano Marani (eds), *Gandirea sociala a bisericii: Fundamente-documente-analize-perspective* (Sibiu: Deisis, 2002).

Iorga, Nicolae, *Against Hatred between Nations: Romanians and Hungarians* (Iasi: Romanian Cultural Foundation, 1994).

Inglehart, Ronald and Wayne E. Baker, 'Modernization, Cultural Change, and the Persistence of Traditional Values', *American Sociological Review* 65 (2000), pp. 19–51.

Jervis, L. Ann and Peter Richardson (eds), *Gospel in Paul: Studies on Corinthians, Galatians and Romans for Richard N. Longenecker* (*JSNTS*, 108; Sheffield: Sheffield Academic, 1994).

Jewett, Robert, *Christian Tolerance: Paul's Message to the Modern Church* (Philadelphia, PA: Westminster, 1982).

—'The Law and the Coexistence of Jews and Gentiles in Romans', *Interpretation* 39(4) (1985), pp. 341–56.

—*Romans: A Commentary* (Minneapolis: Fortress, 2007).

Johnson, Dan G., 'The Structure and Meaning of Romans 11', *CBQ* 46 (1984), pp. 91–103.

Johnson, Ronald W., 'The Christian and the State: Romans 13:1–7', *RE* 97 (2000), pp. 91–95.

Johnston, Douglas and Cynthia Sampson (eds), *Religion, the Missing Dimension of Statecraft* (Oxford: OUP, 1994).

Jones, Gregory, *Embodying Forgiveness: A Theological Analysis* (Grand Rapids: Eerdmans, 1995).

Judt, Tony, *Romania la fundul gramezii: Polemici, contreverse, pamflete* (Iasi: Polirom, 2002). (A translation into Romanian with various responses and reactions by Romanian analysts to Judt's article 'Romania: Bottom of the Heap', *The New York Review of Books*, 1 November 2001.)

Kallas, J., 'Romans XIII.1–7: An Interpolation', *NTS* 11 (1964–65), pp. 365–74.

Karris, Robert J., 'The Occasion of Romans: a Response to Professor Donfried', in Donfried, Karl P. (ed.), *The Romans Debate* (rev. and exp. edn; Peabody, MA: Hendrickson, 1991a).

—'Romans 14:1–15:13 and the Occasion of Romans', in Donfried, Karl P. (ed.), *The Romans Debate* (rev. and exp. edn; Peabody, MA: Hendrickson, 1991b).

Käsemann Ernst, 'Some Thoughts on the Theme "The Doctrine of Reconciliation in the New Testament"', in Robinson James M. (ed.), *The Future of our Religious Past: Essays in Honour of Rudolf Bultmann* (Charles E. Carlston and Robert Scharlemaann (trans.); London: SCM Press, 1964).

—*New Testament Questions of Today* (W. J. Montague (trans); Philadelphia, PA: Fortress, 1969a).

—'Principles of the Interpretation of Romans 13', in *New Testament Questions of Today*. Translated by W. J. Montague (Philadelphia, PA: Fortress, 1969b).

—*Commentary on Romans* (Geoffrey W. Bromiley (trans. and ed.); (Grand Rapids: Eerdmans, 1980).

Kaye, B. N., *The Thought Structure of Romans with Special Reference to Chapter 6* (Austin, TX: Scholars, 1979).

Kazar, Lajos, *Facts against Fiction: Transylvania-Walachiam/Romanian Homeland since 70 BC?* (Sydney: Forum of History, 1993).

Keck, Leander E., '"Jesus" in Romans', *JBL* 108(3) (1989), pp. 443–60.
—'What Makes Romans Tick?', in Hay, David M. and E. Elizabeth Johnson (eds),
    Pauline Theology, Vol. III: Romans (Minneapolis: Fortress, 1995).
Keesmaat, Sylvia C., *Paul and his Story (Re)Interpretation of Exodus Tradition*
    (*JSNTS*, 181; Sheffield: Sheffield Academic, 1999).
Kenney, Padraic, 'Martyrs And Neighbors: Sources of Reconciliation in Central
    Europe', *Common Knowledge* 13(1) (2007), pp. 149–69.
Kim, Sebastian, Pauline Kollontai and Greg Hoyland (eds), *Peace and
    Reconciliation: In Search of Shared Identity* (Aldershot: Ashgate, 2006).
Kim, Seyoon, *The Origin of Paul's Gospel* (Tubingen: Mohr, 1981).
—'2 Cor. 5:11–21 and the Origin of Paul's Concept of "Reconciliation"', *NovT* 34
    (1997), pp. 360–84.
Klöpper, A., *Kommentar über das zwite Sendschreiben des Apostles Paulus und
    die Gemeinde zu Korinth* (Berlin: Reimer, 1874).
Kocur, Miroslav, *National and Religious Identity: A Study in Galatians 3,23–29
    and Romans 10,12–21* (Frankfurt: Peter Lang, 2003).
Koeberle, Adolf, 'Reconciliation and Justification', *CTM* 21 (1950), pp. 641–58.
Kolarz, Walter, *Mituri si realitati in Europa de Est* (Iasi: Polirom, 2003).
Koppandi, Sandor, *Nationalitatea maghiara din Romania* (Bucuresti: Editura
    Kriterion, 1981).
Kraftchick, Steven J., 'Death's Parsing: Experience as a Mode of Theology in
    Paul', in Anderson, Janice Capel *et al.* (eds), *Paul's Conversations in Context:
    Essays in Honor of Calvin J. Roetzel* (*JSNTS*, 221; Sheffield: Sheffield
    Academic, 2002).
Kreitzer, Larry, *2 Corinthians* (Sheffield: Sheffield Academic, 1996).
Kuhn, Thomas, *The Structure of Scientific Revolutions* (2nd edn; Chicago: Chicago
    University Press, 1970).
Kümmel, Werner Georg, *Perspectives on Paul* (London: SCM, 1971).
—*Introduction to the New Testament* (Nashville: Abingdon, 1975).
Kuzmič, Peter, 'Evangelical Witness in Eastern Europe', in Scott, Waldron (ed.),
    Serving our Generation: Evangelical Strategies for the Eighties (Colorado:
    World Evangelical Fellowship, 1980).
—'Why Romania has become the Korea of Europe', *Global Church Growth
    Magazine* 20 (1983), pp. 13.
—'Problems and Possibilities in European Ministry Today', *East-West Church &
    Ministry Report* 1 (1993). Available online at: http://www4.samford.edu/groups/
    (accessed 3 October 2003).
—'The Communist Impact on the Church in Eastern Europe', *ERT* 20 (1996),
    pp. 60–76.
—'Twelve Theses on Kingdom Servanthood for Post-Communist Europe', in
    Transformation 16(1) (1999), pp. 34–39.
Lakatos, Peter, 'Denominational and Cultural Models and a Possible Ecumenical
    Strategy from a Romanian Context I & II', *Religion in Eastern Europe* 18

(1998). Available online at: http://www.georgefox.edu/academics/undergrad/
departments/soc-swk/ree/art_list99.html (accessed 10 December 2003).

Lambrecht, Jan, 'The Favorable Time: A Study of 2 Corinthians 6:2a in its
Context', in Bieringer, R. and J. Lambrecht (eds), *Studies on 2 Corinthians*
(Leuven: University Press, 1994a).

—'"Reconcile Yourselves . . .", A Reading of 2 Corinthians 5, 11–21', in
Bieringer, R. and J. Lambrecht (eds), *Studies on 2 Corinthians* (Leuven:
University Press, 1994b).

—*Second Corinthians* (Sacra Pagina Series, vol. 8; Collegeville: The Liturgical
Press, 1999).

Lampe, Peter, *From Paul to Valentinus: Christian at Rome in the First Two
Centuries* (Minneapolis: Fortress, 2003).

Langmead, Ross, 'Transformed Relationships: Reconciliation as the Central Model
for Mission', *Mission Studies* 25 (2008), pp. 5–20.

Lazar, Istvan, *Transylvania: A Short History* (Budapest: Corvina, 1997).

Leb, Ioan Vasile, *Biserica in actiune* (Cluj-Napoca: Limes, 2001).

—'The Orthodox Church and the Minority Cults in Inter-War Romania
(1918–1940)', *Journal for the Study of Religion and Ideologies* 3 (2002),
pp. 131–41.

Lederach, John P., *Building Peace: Sustainable Reconciliation in Divided Societies*
(Washington, DC: United States Institute of Peace Press, 1997).

—*The Journey Toward Reconciliation* (Scottdale, PA: Herald Press, 1999).

Lewis, Jack P., *Interpreting 2 Corinthians 5:14–21. An Exercise in Hermeneutics*
(Studies in the Bible and Early Christianity, 17; Lewiston, NY: The Edwin
Mellen Press, 1989).

Lim, T. H., *Holy Scripture in the Qumran Commentaries and Pauline Letters*
(Oxford: Clarendon, 1997).

Livingstone, E. A. (ed.), *Studia Biblica 1978: III. Papers on Paul and Other New
Testament Papers* (Sheffield: Sheffield University Press, 1980).

Locke, Hubert G. and Marcia Sachs Littell (eds), *Holocaust and Church Struggle:
Religion, Power and the Politics of Resistance* (Lanham: University Press of
America, 1996).

Longenecker, Bruce W., 'Narrative Interest in the Study of Paul: Retrospective and
Prospective', in Longenecker, Bruce W. (ed.), *Narrative Dynamics in Paul: a
Critical Assessment* (Louisville, KY: Westminster John Knox Press, 2002a).

—'The Narrative Approach to Paul: An Early Retrospective', *Currents in Biblical
Research* 1(1) (2002b), pp. 88–111.

Longenecker, Bruce W. (ed.), *Narrative Dynamics in Paul: A Critical Assessment*
(Louisville, KY: Westminster John Knox, 2002).

Longenecker, Richard N., 'The Focus of Romans: The Central Role of 5:1–8:39
in the Argument of the Letter', in Soderlund, Sven K. and N. T. Wright (eds),
*Romans and the People of God: Essays in Honor of Gordon Fee on the Occasion
of his 65th Birthday* (Grand Rapids: Eerdmans, 1999).

Longenecker, Richard N. (ed.), *The Road from Damascus: The Impact of Paul's Conversion on His Life, Thought and Ministry* (Grand Rapids: Eerdmans, 1997).

Lote, Louis L. (ed.), *Transylvania and the Theory of Daco-Roman-Rumanian Continuity* (Rochester, NY: Committee of Transylvania Inc., 1980).

Louw, J. P. and E. A. Nida (eds), *Greek-English Lexicon of the New Testament Based on Semantic Domains* (2 vols; New York: United Bible Societies, 1988).

Lovering, Eugene H. and Jerry L. Sumney (eds), *Theology and Ethics in Paul and his Interpreters. Essays in Honour of Victor Paul Furnish* (Nashville, TN: Abindgon, 1996).

MacIntyre, Alistair, *After Virtue* (2nd edn; Notre Dame: University of Notre Dame Press, 1984).

Malherbe, Abraham J., *Social Aspects of Early Christianity* (Philadelphia, PA: Fortress, 1983).

—*Paul and the Thessalonians: The Philosophic Tradition of Pastoral Care* (Philadelphia, PA: Fortress, 1987).

—'Conversion to Paul's Gospel', in Malherbe, Abraham J., Frederick W. Noris and James W. Thomson (eds). *The Early Church in its Context: Essays in Honor of Everett Ferguson* (Supplements to *NovT*, vol. 90; Leiden: Brill, 1998).

Manastireanu, Danut, 'Evangelical Denominations in Post-Communist Romania I & II', *East-West Church & Ministry Report* 6 (1998). Available online at: http://www4.samford.edu/groups/ (accessed 10 April 2004).

—'The Wall's Long Shadow', *Christianity Today* 43 (15 November 1999), pp. 30.

Marchis, Vasile, 'Christian Faith and Public Life: A Critical Analysis of the Missiological Praxis of the Evangelical Neo-Protestants in the Romanian Context' (unpublished M.Th. dissertation, Evangelical Theological Seminary, Osijek, Croatia, June 2004).

Marshall, Christopher D., *Beyond Retribution: A New Testament Vision for Justice, Crime and Punishment* (Grand Rapids: Eerdmans, 2001).

Marshall, I. Howard, 'The Meaning of "Reconciliation"', in Guelich, Robert (ed.), *Unity and Diversity in New Testament Theology* (Grand Rapids: Eerdmans, 1978).

—*New Testament Theology* (Downers Grove, IL: IVP, 2004).

Martin, Ralph P., 'Reconciliation and Forgiveness in the Letter to the Colossians', in Banks, Robert (ed.), *Reconciliation and Hope* (Exeter: Paternoster, 1974).

—'New Testament Theology: Impasse and Exit', *Expository Times*, 91 (1980a), pp. 264–69.

—'New Testament Theology: A Proposal. The Theme of Reconciliation', *Expository Times* 91 (1980b), pp. 364–68.

—*2 Corinthians* (*WBC*, Vol. 40; Waco, TX: Word, 1986).

—*Reconciliation: A Study of Paul's Theology* (rev. edn; Grand Rapids: Zondervan, 1989).

—'Center of Paul's theology', in Hawthorne, Gerald F., Ralph Martin and Daniel G. Reid (eds), *DPL* (Leicester: IVP, 1993).

—'Reconciliation: Romans 5:1–11', in Soderlund, Sven K. and N. T. Wright (eds), *Romans and the People of God: Essays in Honor of Gordon Fee on the Occasion of his 65th Birthday* (Grand Rapids: Eerdmans, 1999).

Martyn, J. Louis, 'Epistemology at the Turn of the Ages: 2 Corinthians 5:16', in Martyn, J. L., *Theological Issues in the Letters of Paul* (Edinburgh: T&T Clark, 1997).

Marxen, Willi, *Introduction to the New Testament* (Philadelphia, PA: Fortress, 1968).

—*New Testament Foundation for Christian Ethics* (O. C. Dean (trans.); Edinburgh: T&T Clark, 1993).

May, John D'Arcy, 'Reconciliation in Religion and Society: A Conference in Honor of Irish Ecumenist Michael Hurley SJ', *Mid-Stream* 33 (1994), pp. 346–49.

McDonald, J. I. H., 'Paul and the Preaching Ministry. A Reconsideration of 2 Cor. 2:14–17 in its Context', *JSNT* 17 (1983), pp. 35–50.

McDonald, Patricia M., 'Romans 5.1–11 as a Rhetorical Bridge', *JSNT* 40 (1990), pp. 81–96.

McFadyen, Alistair I. *The Call to Personhood: A Christian Theory of the Individual in Social Relationships* (Cambridge: CUP, 1990).

McFadyen, Alistair I. and Marcel Sarot (eds), *Forgiveness and Truth* (Edinburgh: T&T Clark, 2001).

McGinn, Sheila E. (ed.), *Celebrating Romans: Template for Pauline Theology. Essays in Honor of Robert Jewett* (Grand Rapids: Eerdmans, 2004).

McGrane, Bernard. *Beyond Anthropology: Society and the Other* (New York: Columbia University Press, 1989).

McIntosh, Mary E. *et al.*, 'Minority Rights and Majority Rule: Ethnic Tolerance in Romania and Bulgaria', *Social Forces* 73 (1995), pp. 939–67.

Meeks, Wayne A, 'The Social Context of Pauline Theology', *Interpretation* 36 (1982), pp. 266–77.

—*The First Urban Christians: The Social World of the Apostle Paul* (New Haven and London: Yale University Press, 1983).

—'A Hermeneutics of Social Embodiment', *Harvard Theological Review* 79 (1986), pp. 176–85.

—*The Origin of Christian Morality: The First Two Centuries* (New Haven: Yale University Press, 1993).

Meierhenrich, Jens, 'Varieties of Reconciliation', *Law & Social Inquiry* 33(1) (Winter 2008), pp. 195–231.

Menzies, A., *The Second Epistle of the Apostle Paul to the Corinthians* (London: Macmillan, 1912).

Merdjanova, Ina, 'In Search of Identity: Nationalism and Religion in Eastern Europe', *RSS* 28 (2000), pp. 233–62.

Merrick, James R. A., 'Justice, Forgiveness, and Reconciliation: The Reconciliatory Cross as Forgiving Justice. A Response to Don McLellan', *ERT* 30(3) (2006), pp. 292–308.

Bibliography

Mertus, Julie and Kathryn Myniard Frost, 'Faith and (In)Tolerance of Minority Religions: A Comparative Analysis of Romania, Ukraine and Poland', *JES* 36 (1999), pp. 65–79.

Meyendorff, John, *The Orthodox Church: Its Past and its Role in the World Today* (4th rev. edn; New York: Crestwood, 1996).

Meyer, Ben F. *Critical Realism and the New Testament* (Pennsylvania: Pickwick, 1989).

Meyer, Marvin W., 'Mystery Religions', in Freedman, D. N. (ed.), *ABD* (electronic edn; New York: Doubleday, 1996).

Michael-Titus, C. *In Search of 'Cultural Genocide'* (Upminster: Panopticum, 1976).

—*Looking Forward: Aspects of Hungarian Realities in Romania* (London: Panopticum, 1978).

—*The Magyar File* (London: Panopticum, 1984).

Michaelis, W., *Versöhnung des Alls: Die frühe Botschaft von der Gnade Gotter* (Gunlingen: Siloah, 1950).

Miller, James C., *The Obedience of Faith, the Eschatological People of God, and the Purpose of Romans* (SBL Dissertation Series, 177; Atlanta: SBL, 2000).

—'The Romans Debate: 1991–2001', *CR* 9 (2001), pp. 306–49.

Minear, Paul S., 'New Starting Point: Church Renewal and Social Renewal', *Interpretation* 19 (1965), pp. 3–15.

—*The Obedience of Faith: The Purposes of Paul in the Epistle to the Romans* (London: SCM, 1971).

Mitchell, Margaret M., *Paul and the Rhetoric of Reconciliation: An Exegetical Investigation of the Language and Composition of 1 Corinthians* (Tubingen: Mohr, 1991).

—'Rhetorical Shorthand in Pauline Argumentation: the Functions of "the Gospel" in the Corinthian Correspondence', in Jervis, L. Ann and Peter Richardson (eds), *Gospel in Paul: Studies on Corinthians, Galatians and Romans for Richard N. Longenecker* (*JSNTS*, 108; Sheffield: Sheffield Academic, 1994).

Moellendorf, Darrel, 'Reconciliation as a Political Value', *Journal of Social Philosophy* 38(2) (2007), pp. 205–21.

Moo, Douglas, *The Epistle to the Romans* (NICNT; Grand Rapids: Eerdmans, 1996).

Moon, Claire, *Narrating Political Reconciliation: South Africa's Truth and Reconciliation* (Maryland: Lexington Books/Rowman and Littlefield, 2008).

Morris, Leon, 'Reconciliation', *Christianity Today* 13(8) (1969), pp. 331–32.

Morrison, Clinton D., *The Powers that Be: Earthly Rulers and Demonic Powers in Rowans 13.1–7* (London: SCM Press, 1960).

Mosala, Itumeleng J., 'The Meaning of Reconciliation: A Black Perspective', *JTSA* 59 (1987), pp. 19–25.

Mott, Stephen Charles, *Biblical Ethics and Social Change* (New York/Oxford: OUP, 1982).

—'The Use of Bible in Social Ethics: The Use of the New Testament',
Transformation 1 (1984), pp. 21–26.

Moulder, James, 'Romans 13 and conscientious disobedience', *JTSA* 21 (1977),
pp. 13–23.

Moule, C. F. D., *Forgiveness and Reconciliation and Other New Testament
Themes* (London: SPCK, 1998).

Müller, David L., *Foundations of Karl Barth's Doctrine of Reconciliation: Jesus
Christ Crucified and Risen* (Mampeter: Mellen, 1990).

Mungiu-Pippidi, Alina, *Transilvania subiectiva* (Bucuresti: Humanitas, 1999).

—*Politica dupa cumunism* (Bucuresti: Humanitas, 2002).

Munro, W., 'Romans 13:1–7. Apartheid's Last Biblical Refuge', *BTB* 20 (1990),
pp. 161–68.

Murphy, Colleen, 'Political Reconciliation, the Rule of Law, and Genocide', *The
European Legacy* 12(7) (2007), pp. 853–65.

Murray, John, 'The Reconciliation', *The Westminster Theological Journal* 29
(1966), pp. 1–23.

—*The Epistle to the Romans*, New International Commentary on the New
Testament (Grand Rapids: Eerdmans, 1968).

Nastasa, Lucian and Levente Salat, *Relatii interetnice in Romania postcomunista*
(Cluj-Napoca: Ethnocultural Diversity Resource Centre, 2000).

Neculau, Adrian and Gilles Ferréol (eds), *Minoritari, Marginali, Exclusi* (Iasi:
Polirom, 1996).

Negrut, Paul, 'Church and Mission: An Eastern European Perspective',
Transformation 16 (1999), pp. 17–20.

—*Biserica si statul: O interogatie asupra modelului 'simfoniei' bizantine* (Oradea:
Emanuel, 2000).

Nel, Philip J, 'סלם', *NIDOTTE, Vol. 4* (VanGemeren, Willem A. (gen. ed.); Grand
Rapids: Zondervan, 1997).

Nemoianu, Virgil, *Jocurile divinitatii: Gandire, libertate si religie la sfarsitul de
mileniu* (Iasi: Polirom, 2000).

Nets-Zehngut, Rafi, 'Analyzing the Reconciliation Process', *International Journal
on World Peace* 24(3) (2007), pp. 53–81.

Neuman, Victor, *Tentatia lui Homo Europaeus: Geneza ideilor mederne in Europa
centrala si de sud-est* (Bucuresti: All, 1997).

—*Ideologie si fantasmagorie: Perspective comparative asupra istoriei gandirii
politice in Europa Est-Centrala* (Iasi: Polirom, 2001).

Neyrey, J., *Paul In Other Words: A Cultural Reading of His Letters* (Louisville,
KY: Westminster/John Knox, 1990).

Ng, Kam-weng, 'From Christ to Social Practice: Christological Foundations for
the Social Practice in the Theologies of Albrecht Ritschl, Karl Barth, and Jurgen
Molmnann' (unpublished Ph.D. dissertaion; Cambridge University, 1989)
(Alliance Bible Seminary, 1996).

Nygren, Anders, *Commentary on Romans* (Philadelphia, PA: Fortress, 1974).

Oakeshott, Michael. *Experience and its Modes* (Cambridge: CUP, 1985).
O'Brien, P. T., 'Col. 1:20 and the Reconciliation of all Things', *The Reformed Theological Review* 33(1) (1974), pp. 45–53.
—*Gospel and Mission in the Writings of Paul: An Exegetical and Theological Analysis* (Grand Rapids: Baker, 1995).
O'Donovan, Oliver, *Resurrection and Moral Order: An Outline for Evangelical Ethics* (Grand Rapids: Eerdmans, 1986).
O'Neill, J. C., *Paul's Letter to the Romans* (Harmondsworth: Penguin, 1975).
Okure, Teresa, 'The Ministry of Reconciliation (2 Cor 5:14–21): Paul's Key to the Problem of "The Other" in Corinth', *Mission Studies* 23(1) (2006), pp. 105–21.
Overseas Council International's World Missions, 'Preliminary Report: The State of the Evangelical Churches in Romania 2000' (Cluj Napoca: OCI, August 2000).
Paleologu, Al, *Mostenirea Crestina a Europei* (Cluj-Napoca: Eikon, 2003).
Parsons, Michael, 'Being Precedes Act: Indicative and Imperative in Paul's Writing', in Rosner, Brian S. (ed.), *Understanding Paul's Ethics: Twentieth Century Approaches* (Grand Rapids: Eerdmans, 1995).
Pascu, Stefan, *A History of Transylvania* (Detroit, MI: Wayne State University Press, 1982).
Pavel, Dan, *Cine, ce si de ce? Interviuri despre politica si alte tabuuri* (Iasi: Polirom, 1998).
Pavel, Pavel, *Transylvania and Danubian Peace* (London: New Europe Publishing, 1943).
Peace, Richard V., *Conversion in the New Testament: Paul and the Twelve* (Grand Rapids: Eerdmans, 1999).
Pelican, Jaroslav, 'Unity and Reconciliation: The Historical Dialectic', *Mid-Stream* 31(2) (1992), pp. 123–28.
Perkins, Pheme, *Love Commands in the New Testament* (New York: Paulist, 1982).
Perry, Marvin and Frederick M. Schweitzer (eds), *Jewish-Christian Encounters over the Centuries: Symbiosis, Prejudice, Holocaust, Dialogue* (Frankfurt am Main: Peter Lang, 1994).
Pesch, Rudolf, 'Reconciliation: New Testament', in Bauer, Johannes (ed.), *Bauer Encyclopaedia of Biblical Theology, Vol. 2* (3rd edn; London: Sheed and Ward, 1970).
Petersen, Anders Klostergaard, 'Shedding New Light on Paul's Understanding of Baptism: a Ritual-Theoretical Approach to Romans 6', *Studia Theologica* 52 (1998), pp. 3–28.
Petersen, Norman, *Rediscovering Paul: Philemon and the Sociology of Paul's Narrative World* (Philadelphia, PA: Fortress, 1985).
Peterson, Jeffrey, 'Living Sacrifices: Walking in Accordance with the Spirit in Romans 12–15', *Christian Studies Journal* 20 (2004), pp. 33–41.
Philo of Alexandria, *Embassy to Gaius* (Logos Library Systems, electronic edn; Nashville, TN: Thomas Nelson, 1997).

Pilgrim, Walter E., *Uneasy Neighbors: Church and State in the New Testament*
(Minneapolis: Fortress, 1999).

Plummer, Alfred, *2 Corinthians* (Edinburgh: T&T Clark, 2000).

Pop, Ioan-Aurel, *Romanians and Hungarians from the 9th to the 14th Century:*
The Genesis of the Transylvania Medieval State (Cluj-Napoca: Centrul de Studii
Transilvane, Fundatia Culturala Romana, 1996).

Pope, Earl A., 'Protestantism in Romania', in Ramet, Sabrina Petra (ed.),
Protestantism and Politics in Eastern Europe and Russia: Communist and Post-
Communist Era (Durham, NC: Duke University Press, 1992).

—'Ecumenism, Religious Freedom and the "National Church" Controversy in
Romania', *JES*, 36 (1999), pp. 184–201.

Popescu, Dumitru. *Hristos, Biserica, Societate* (Bucuresti: Institutul Biblic si de
Misiune al BOR, 1998).

Porter, Calvin L., 'A New Paradigm for Reading Romans: Dialogue Between
Christians and Jews', *Encounter* 39 (1978), pp. 257–72.

—'Paul as Theologian: Romans', *Encounter* 65(2) (2004), pp. 109–36.

Porter, Stanley E., 'The Argument of Romans 5: Can a Rhetorical Question Make a
Difference?', *JBL* 110 (1991), pp. 655–77.

—'Peace, Reconciliation', in Hawthorne, Gerald F. *et al.* (eds), *DPL*. Leicester:
IVP, 1993).

—Καταλλάσσω *in Ancient Greek Literature with Reference to the Pauline Writings*
(Cordoba: Ediciones El Amendro, 1994).

Preda, Radu, *Biserica in Stat: O invitatie la dezbatere* (Bucuresti: Scripta, 1999).

Price, S. R. F., 'Rituals and Powers', in Horsley, Richard A. (ed.), *Paul and*
Empire: Religion and Power in Roman Imperial Society (Harrisburg, PA:
Trinity, 1997).

Prodan, D., *Transylvania and Again Transylvania* (Cluj-Napoca: Romanian
Cultural Foundation, 1992).

Rader, W., *The Church and Racial Hostility: A History of Interpretation of*
Ephesians 2:11–22 (Tubingen: Mohr, 1978).

Ramet, Sabrina Petra, 'Holy Intolerance: Romania's Orthodox Church', in Ramet,
S. P. (ed.), *Nihil Obstat: Religion, Politics and Social Change in East-Central*
Europe and Russia (Durham, NC: Duke University Press, 1998).

Ramet, Sabrina Petra (ed.), *Protestantism and Politics in Eastern Europe and*
Russia: Communist and Post-Communist Era (Durham, NC: Duke University
Press, 1992).

Ramírez, J. Martin, 'Peace Through Dialogue', *International Journal on World*
Peace 24(1) (2007), pp. 65–81.

Reasoner, Mark, 'The Theology of Romans 12:1–15:13', in Hay, David M. and E.
Elisabeth Johnson (eds), *Pauline Theology Volume III: Romans* (Minneapolis:
Fortress, 1995).

—*The Strong and the Weak: Romans 14.1–15.13 in Context* (SNTSM, 103;
Cambridge: CUP, 1999).

—*Romans in Full Circle: A History of Interpretation* (Louisville, KY: Westminster John Knox Press, 2005).

Ridderbos, Herman, *Paul: An Outline of His Theology* (John Richard De Witt (trans.); Grand Rapids: Eerdmans, 1975).

—'The Biblical Message of Reconciliation', in Ridderbos, H. *Studies in Scripture and Its Authority* (Grand Rapids: Eerdmans, 1978).

Ritschl, Albrecht, *The Christian Doctrine of Justification and Reconciliation: The Positive Development of the Doctrine* (Clifton, NJ: Reference Book Publishers, 1966).

Roberts, J. H., 'Some Biblical Foundations for a Mission of Reconciliation', *Missionalia* 7 (1979), pp. 3–17.

Robotin, Monica and Levente Salat, *A New Balance: Democracy and Minorities in Post-Communist Europe* (Budapest: Open Society Institute, 2003).

Roetzel, Calvin J., 'Sacrifice in Romans 12–15', *W&W* 6 (1986), pp. 410–19.

—*Paul: The Man and the Myth* (Columbia: University of South Carolina Press, 1998).

Rogobete, Silviu, *O ontologie a iubirii: Subiect si realitate personala suprema in gândirea lui Dumitru Staniloae* (Iasi: Polirom, 2001).

—'Morality and Tradition in Post-communist Orthodox Lands: On the Universality of Human Rights. With Special Reference to Romania', *RSS* 32(3) (2004), pp. 275–97.

—'Between Fundamentalism and Secularization: The Place and the Role of Religion in Post-Communist Orthodox Romania', in Devetak, S., O. Sirbu and S. Rogobete (eds), *Religion and Democracy in Moldova* (Maribor/Chisinau: ISCOMET/ASER, 2005).

Romocea, Cristian, 'Reconciliation in the Ethnic Conflict in Transylvania: Theological, Political and Social Aspect', *RSS* 32 (2004a), pp. 159–76.

—'The Place of Church-State Debates in Post-Communist Romania', *Sfera Politicii* 108 (2004b), pp. 42–46.

Romsics, Ignac (ed.), *Geopolitics in the Danube Region: Hungarian Reconciliation Efforts, 1848–1998* (Atlantic Studies on Society in Change, 97; Budapest: CEU Press, 1998).

Rosner, Brian S., *Understanding Paul's Ethics: Twentieth Century Approaches* (Grand Rapids: Eerdmans, 1995).

Roth, John D., 'Forgiveness and the Healing of Memories: An Anabaptist-Mennonite Perspective', *Journal of Ecumenical Studies* 42(4) (2007), pp. 573–88.

Roth, John K. *et al.* (eds), *Remembering for the Future: the Holocaust in an Age of Genocide* (Hampshire, NY: Palgrave, 2001).

Rowland, Christopher and Mark Corner, *Liberating Exegesis: The Challenge of Liberation Theology to Biblical Studies* (Louisville, KY: Westminster/John Knox Press, 1989).

Runyon, Theodore (ed.), *Theology, Politics and Peace* (Maryknoll, NY: Orbis, 1989).

Rutgers, Leonard V., *The Jews in Late Ancient Rome: Evidence of Cultural Interaction in the Roman Diaspora* (Leiden: Koninklijke Brill, 2000).

Ryken, Leland, James C. Wilhoit and Tremper Longman III (eds), 'Peace', *DBI* (Logos Library, electronic edn; Downers Grove, IL: IVP, 2000).

Sabou, Sorin, *Between Horror and Hope: Paul's Metaphorical Language of Death in Romans 6:1–11* (Milton Keynes: Paternoster, 2005).

Sampley, J. Paul, 'The Weak and the Strong: Paul's Careful and Crafty Rhetorical Strategy in Romans 14:1–15:13', in White, L. Michael and O. Larry Yarbrough (eds), *The Social World of the First Christians: Studies in Honor of Wayne A. Meeks* (Minneapolis: Fortress, 1994).

Sampley, J. Paul (ed.), *Paul in the Greco-Roman World: A Handbook* (Harrisburg, PA: Trinity, 2003).

Sanders, E. P., *Paul and Palestinian Judaism* (London: SCM Press, 1977).

Sanday, W. and A. C. Headlam, *A Critical and Exegetical Commentary on the Epistle to the Romans* (5th edn; Edinburgh: T. &. T. Clark, 1902)

Schaap, Andrew, *Political Reconciliation*. Abingdon: Routledge, 2005).

Schmemann, Alexander, *The Historical Road of Eastern Orthodoxy* (London: Harvill Press, 1963).

Schmiechen, Peter, *Christ the Reconciler: A Theology for Opposites, Differences, and Enemies* (Grand Rapids: Eerdmans, 1996).

Schnackenburg, Rudolf, *New Testament Theology Today* (David Askew (trans.); London: Geoffrey Chapman, 1963).

Schopflin, George, *Romanian's Ethnic Hungarians* (London: Minority Rights Group, 1990).

Schrage, Wolfgang, *The Ethics of the New Testament* (David E. Green (trans.); Edinburgh: T&T Clark, 1988).

Schreiner, Thomas R., *Romans* (Baker Exegetical Commentary of the New Testament; Grand Rapids: Baker, 1998).

Schreiter, Robert J., *Reconciliation: Mission & Ministry in a Changing Social Order* (Maryknoll, NY: Orbis, 1992).

—*The Ministry of Reconciliation: Spirituality & Strategies* (Maryknoll: Orbis, 1998).

—'Reconciliation and Healing as Paradigm for Mission', *International Review of Mission* 94 (2005), pp. 74–83.

Schutz, John H., 'Introduction', in Theissen, Gerd (ed.), *The Social Setting of Pauline Christianity* (Edinburgh: T&T Clark, 1982).

Schweitzer, A., *The Mysticism of Paul the Apostle* (London, 1931).

Schwöbel, Christoph, 'Reconciliation: From Biblical Observations to Dogmatic Reconstruction', in Gunton, Colin E. (ed.), *The Theology of Reconciliation* (London: T&T Clark, 2003).

Scroggs, Robin, 'The Sociological Interpretation of the New Testament: The Present State of Research', in Gill, Robin (ed.), *Theology and Sociology: A Reader* (London: Cassell, 1996).

Segal, Alan F., *Paul the Convert: The Apostolate and Apostasy of Saul the Pharisee* (New Haven and London: Yale University Press, 1990).

Segovia, Fernando F. and M. A. Tolbert (eds), *Teaching the Bible* (Maryknoll, NY: Orbis, 1998).

Seifrid, M. A., 'In Christ', in Hawthorne, Gerald F. *et al.* (eds), *DPL.* (Logos Library, electronic edn; Downers Grove, IL: IVP, 1998).

Shedinger, Robert F., 'Kuhnian Paradigms and Biblical Scholarship: Is Biblical Studies a Science?', *Journal of Biblical Studies* 119 (2000), pp. 453–71.

Shenk, David W., *Justice, Reconciliation & Peace in Africa* (rev. edn; Nairobi: Uzima, 1997).

—'The Gospel of Reconciliation Within the Wrath of Nations', *International Bulletin of Missionary Research* 32(1) (2008), pp. 2–9.

Shore, Megan, 'Christianity and Justice in the South African Truth and Reconciliation Commission: A Case Study in Religious Conflict Resolution', *Political Theology* 9(2) (2008), pp. 161–78.

Shriver, Donald W., *An Ethic for Enemies: Forgiveness in Politics* (New York: OUP, 1995).

Shum, Shiu-Lun, *Paul's Use of Isaiah in Romans: A Comparative Study of Paul's Letter to the Romans and the Sybylline and Qumran Sectarian Texts* (Tubingen: Mohr Siebeck, 2002).

Sider, Ronald J., *Christ and Violence* (Scottdale: Herald Press, 1979).

—'Toward a Biblical Perspective on Equality: Steps in the Way Towards Christian Political Engagement', *Interpretation* 43 (1989), pp. 156–69.

Signer, Michael A. (ed.), *Memory and History in Christianity and Judaism* (Notre Dame: University of Notre Dame Press, 2001).

Sinclair, Victor, 'The Sovereignty of God in Reconciliation, with Karl Barth as a Guide', *Irish Biblical Studies* 18 (1996), pp. 156–69.

Smit, Dirkie J., 'The Truth and Reconciliation Commission – Tentative Religious and Theological Perspectives', *JTSA* 90 (1995), pp. 3–16.

Soderlund, Sven and N. T. Wright (eds), *Romans and the People of God: Essay in Honor of Gordon D. Fee on the Occasion of his 65th Birthday* (Grand Rapids: Eerdmans, 1999).

Stagg, F. *New Testament Theology* (Nashville, TN: Broadman, 1962).

Staniloae, Dumitru, *Ortodoxie si Romanism* (Sibiu: Editura Consiliului Arhiepiscopiei, 1936).

—'Rolul ortodoxiei in formarea si pastrarea fiintei poporului roman si a unitatii nationale', *Ortodoxia* XXX (1978), pp. 584–603.

—*Reflexii despre spiritualitatea poporului roman* (Craiova: Scrisul Romanesc, 1992a).

—*Spiritualitatea ortodoxa: ascetica si mistica* (Bucuresti: Institutul Biblic si de Misiune a BOR, 1992b).

—*Teologie dogmatica ortodoxa, Vol. 3* (Editia a doua; Bucuresti: Institutul Biblic si de Misiune a BOR, 1997).

Stanley, C. D., *Paul and the Language of Scripture: Citation Technique in the Pauline Epistles and Contemporary Literature* (Cambridge: CUP, 1992).

—'"Neither Jew Nor Greek": Ethnic Conflict in Graeco-Roman Society', *JSNT* 64 (1996), pp. 101–24.

Stanton, Graham N. and Gedaliahu Stroumsa (eds), *Tolerance and Intolerance in Early Judaism and Christianity* (New York: CUP, 1998).

Stegner, W. R., 'Jew, Paul the', in Hawthorne, G. F. *et al.* (eds), *DPL* (Logos Library, electronic edn; Downers Grove, IL: IVP, 1997, ©1993).

Stein, Robert H., 'The Argument of Romans 13:1–7', *NovT* 31 (1989), pp. 325–43.

Stendahl, Krister, 'Hate, Nonretaliation, and Love: Coals of Fire', in Stassen, G. *et al.* (eds), *Meanings: The Bible as Documents and as Guide* (Philadelphia, PA: Fortress, 1984).

Stenschke, Christoph, 'The Death of Jesus and the New Testament Doctrine of Reconciliation in Recent Discussion', *The European Journal of Theology* 9 (2000), pp. 131–58.

Stott, John, *Involvement: Being a Responsible Christian in a Non-Christian Society* (Old Tappan, NJ: Flemming H. Revell Company, 1984).

Stowers, K. Stanley, *The Diatribe and Paul's Letter to the Romans* (SBLDS, 57; Chico, CA: Scholars Press, 1981).

—*A Rereading of Romans: Justice, Jews and Gentiles* (New Haven: Yale University Press, 1994).

Strom, Mark, *Reframing Paul: Conversations in Grace & Community* (Downers Grove, IL: IVP, 2000).

Stuhlmacher, Peter, *Historical Criticism and the Theological Interpretation of the New Testament.* (Roy Harrisville (trans.); Philadelphia, PA: Fortress, 1977).

—'Das Evangelium von der Versöhnung in Christus', in Stuhlmacher, Peter and Helmut Class (eds), *Das Evangelium von der Versohnung in Christus* (Stuttgart: Calwer Verlag, 1979).

—'The Gospel of Reconciliation in Christ: Basic Features and Issues of a Biblical Theology of the New Testament', *Horizons in Biblical Theology* 1 (1979), pp. 161–90.

—*Paul's Letter to the Romans: A Commentary* (Louisville, KY: Westminster/John Knox Press, 1994).

Susin, Luiz Carlos and Maria Pilar Aquino (eds), *Reconciliation in a World of Conflict* (London: SCM, 2003).

Suta, Ioan, *Transilvania: himera ungarismului iredentist* (Bucuresti: Editura Academiei de Inalte Studii Militare, 1995).

Swartley, Willard M. (ed.), *The Love of Enemy and Nonretaliation in the New Testament* (Louisville, KY: Westminster, 1992).

Talbott, Thomas, 'The New Testament and Universal Reconciliation', *Christian Scholar's Review* 21(4) (1992), pp. 376–94.

Tamez, Elsa, *The Amnesty of Grace: Justification by Faith from a Latin American Perspective* (Nashville, TN: Abingdon, 1993).

Tanner, R. G., 'St. Paul's View of Militia and Contemporary Social Values', in
    Livingstone, E. A. (ed.), *Studia Biblica 1978: III. Papers on Paul and Other New
    Testament Papers* (Sheffield: Sheffield University Press, 1980).
Tataru-Cazaban, Miruna (ed.), *Teologie si politica: De la sfintii parinti la Europa
    Unita* (Bucuresti: Anastasia, 2004).
Tavuchis, Nicholas, *Mea Culpa: A Sociology of Apology and Reconciliation*
    (Stanford, CA: Stanford University Press, 1991).
Taylor, Nicholas H., 'The Social Nature of Conversion in the Early Christian
    World', in Esler, Philip F. (ed.), *Modelling Early Christianity: Social-scientific
    Studies of the New Testament in its Context* (London: Routledge, 1995).
Taylor, Vincent, *Forgiveness and Reconciliation: A Study in New Testament
    Theology* (2nd edn; London: Macmillan, 1946).
Theissen, Gerd, *The Social Setting of Pauline Christianity* (Philadelphia, PA:
    Fortress, 1982).
—*Social Reality and the Early Christians: Theology, Ethics, and the World of the
    New Testament* (Edinburgh: T&T Clark, 1993a).
—'Soteriological Symbolism in the Pauline Writings', in Theissen, G., *Social
    Reality and the Early Christians: Theology, Ethics, and the World of the New
    Testament* (Edinburgh: T&T Clark, 1993b).
—'Social Integration and Sacramental Activity: An Analysis of 1 Cor 11:17–34',
    in Horrell, D. G. (ed.), *Social-Scientific Approaches to New Testament
    Interpretation* (Edinburgh: T&T Clark, 1999).
Thomson, Michael, *Clothed with Christ: The Example and Teaching of Jesus in
    Romans 12:1–15:13* (JSNT, 59; Sheffield: Sheffield Academic, 1991).
Thrall, Margaret E., *1 & 2 Corinthians* (Cambridge: CUP, 1965).
—'Salvation Proclaimed, 2 Corinthians 5:18–21: Reconciliation with God',
    Expository Times 93 (1981), pp. 227–32.
—*A Critical and Exegetical Commentary on the Second Epistle to the Corinthians,
    Vol. 1* (Edinburgh: T&T Clark, 1994).
Thual, Francois, *Géopolitique de l'Orthodoxie* (2nd edn; Paris: Dunod, 1994).
Thuren, Lauri, 'Romans 7 Derhetorized', in Porter, Stanley E. and Dennis L.
    Stamps (eds), *Rhetorical Criticism and the Bible* (*JSNTS*, 195; Sheffield:
    Sheffield Academic, 2002).
Tidball, Derek, *The Social Context of the New Testament* (Carlisle: Paternoster
    Press, 1997a).
—'Social Setting of Mission Churches', in Hawthorne, G. F. *et al.* (eds), *DPL*
    (Logos Library, electronic edn; Downers Grove, IL: IVP, 1997b, ©1993).
Tobin, Thomas H., *Paul's Rhetoric in its Contexts: The Argument of Romans*
    (Peabody, MA: Hendrickson, 2004).
Tolbert, M, 'Theology & Ministry: 2 Cor. 5:11–21', *Faith and Mission* 1 (1983),
    pp. 63–70.
Tombs, David and Joseph Liechty (eds), *Explorations in reconciliation: new
    directions in theology.* (Aldershot: Ashgate, 2006).

Tomka, Miklós, 'Religious Identity and the Gospel of Reconciliation', *Religion in Eastern Europe* 29(1) (2009), pp. 20–28.

Ton, Iosif, 'The Evangelicals in Romania,' *Exploits 33* (Eastebourne: Slavic Gospel Association, 1993a).

—'Towards Reformation in Romania', *East-West Church & Ministry Report* 1 (1993b), pp. 1–3.

—'Key Theological Themes Needing Attention in the Post-Communist Europe', Paper presented at the Consultation on Theological Education and Leadership Development in Post-Communist Europe, Oradea, Romania, 4–9 October 1994.

—*Confruntari* (Oradea: Cartea Crestina, 1999).

Towner, Philip H., 'Romans 13:1–7 and Paul's Missiological Perspective: A Call to Political Quietism or Transformation?', in Soderlund, Sven and N. T. Wright (eds), *Romans and the People of God* (Grand Rapids: Eerdmans, 1999).

Tripp, T. M., J. B. Robert and K. Aquino, 'A Vigilante Model of Justice: Revenge, Reconciliation, Forgiveness, and Avoidance', *Social Justice Research* 20(1) (March 2007), pp. 3–34.

Turner, David L., 'Paul and the Ministry of Reconciliation in 2 Cor. 5:11–6:2', *Criswell Theological Review* 4(1) (1989), pp. 77–95.

Turner, Max, 'Human Reconciliation in the New Testament with Special Reference to Philemon, Colossians and Ephesians', *European Journal of Theology* 16(1) (2006), pp. 37–47.

Ulanov, Ann Belford, 'Practicing Reconciliation: Love and Work', *Anglican Theological Review* 89(2) (2007), pp. 227–46.

Ungureanu, Ionel, 'Doctrina sociala ortodoxa: intre propunere reala si discurs ideologic', in Carp, Radu (ed.), *Un suflet pentru Europa: Dimensiunea religioasa a unui proiect politic* (Bucuresti: Anastasia, 2005).

Vanhoozer, Kevin J. *Biblical Narrative in the Philosophy of Paul Ricoeur: A Study in Hermeneutics and Theology* (Cambridge: CUP, 1990).

Vegge, Ivar, *2 Corinthians: A Letter about Reconciliation* (WUNT, 239; Tubingen: Mohr Siebeck, 2008).

Veitch, Scott, *Law and the Politics of Reconciliation* (Aldershot: Ashgate, 2007).

Verdoolaege, Annelies, *Reconciliation Discourse: The Case of the Truth and Reconciliation Commission* (Amsterdam: John Benjamins, 2008).

Verhey, A. *The Great Reversal: Ethics and the New Testament* (Grand Rapids: Eerdmans, 1984).

Volf, Miroslav, 'When the Unclean Spirit Leaves. Tasks of the Eastern European Churches after the 1989 Revolution', *European Journal of Theology* 1 (1992a), pp. 13–24.

—'Exclusion and Embrace: Theological Reflections in the Wake of "Ethnic Cleansing"', *JES* 29 (1992b), pp. 230–48.

—'A Vision of Embrace: Theological Perspectives in Cultural Identity and Conflict', *Ecumenical Review* 47 (1995a), pp. 195–205.

—'Fishing in the Neighbor's Pond: Mission and Proselytism in Eastern Europe',
    International Bulletin of Missionary Research 20:1 (1995b), pp. 26–31.
—*Exclusion and Embrace: A Theological Exploration of Identity, Otherness and
    Reconciliation* (Nashville, TN: Abingdon, 1996).
—'A Theology of Embrace in an Age of Exclusion', *The 1997 Washington Forum*
    (World Vision, 1997).
—'When Gospel and Culture Intersect: Notes on the Nature of Christian
    Difference', *ERT* 22(3) (1998a), pp. 196–207.
—'The Trinity is our Social Program: The Doctrine of the Trinity and the Shape of
    Social Engagement', *MT* 14(3) (1998b), pp. 403–24.
—'The Social Meaning of Reconciliation', *Transformation* 16(1) (1999), pp. 7–12.
—'Forgiveness, Reconciliation, and Justice: A Theological Contribution to a More
    Peaceful Social Environment', *Millennium: Journal of International Studies*
    29(3) (2000a), pp. 861–77.
—'Love Your Heavenly Enemy: How are we Going to Live Eternally with Those
    We Can't Stand Now?' *Christianity Today* (23 October 2000b).
—'The Final Reconciliation: Reflections on a Social Dimension of the
    Eschatological Transition', *MT* 16(1) (2000), pp. 91–113.
—*Free of Charge: Giving and Forgiving in a Culture Stripped of Grace* (Grand
    Rapids: Zondervan, 2005).
—*The End of Memory: Remembering Rightly in a Violent World* (Grand Rapids:
    Eerdmans, 2006).
Von Schönborn, Christoph, *Oamenii, Biserica, Tara: Crestinismul ca provocare
    sociala* (Bucuresti: Anastasia, 2000).
Vorlander, H. and C. Brown, 'Reconciliation', in Brown, Colin (ed.), *NIDNTT,
    Vol. 3* (Exeter: Paternoster, 1978).
Vorster, Nico, 'Preventing Genocide: the Role of the Church', *Scottish Journal of
    Theology* 59(4) (2006), pp. 375–94.
Wagner, J. R., *Heralds of Good News: Isaiah and Paul in Concert in the Letter to
    the Romans* (Leiden: Brill 2003).
Walters, James C., *Ethnic Issues in Paul's Letter to the Romans: Changing Self-
    Definitions in Earliest Roman Christianity* (Valley Forge, PA: Trinity, 1993).
Walvoord, John F., 'Reconciliation', *BS* 120 (1963), pp. 3–12.
Wannenwetsch, Bernd, '"Members of One Another": Charis, Ministry and
    Representation: A Politico-Ecclesial Reading of Romans 12', in Bartholomew,
    Craig *et al.* (eds), *A Royal Priesthood? The Use of the Bible Ethically and
    Politically: A Dialogue with Oliver O'Donovan* (Grand Rapids: Zondervan,
    2002).
Ware, Timothy, *The Orthodox Church* (3rd edn; Harmondsworth: Penguin, 1993).
Watson, Francis, *Paul, Judaism and the Gentiles: A Sociological Approach*
    (Cambridge: CUP, 1986).
—*Text, Church, and World: Biblical Interpretation in Theological Perspective*
    (Edinburgh: T&T Clark, 1994).

—'Is There a Story in These Texts?', in Longenecker, Bruce W. (ed.), *Narrative Dynamics in Paul: A Critical Assessment* (Louisville, KY: Westminster John Knox, 2002).

—*Paul and the Hermeneutics of Faith* (London: T&T Clark International, 2004).

Watson, Francis (ed.), *The Open Text: New Directions for Biblical Studies?* (London: SCM Press, 1993).

Watts, John D. W., *Isaiah 1–33* (*WBC*, 24; Logos Library, electronic edn; Dallas, TX: Word Books, 1998).

Weathers, Robert, 'Reconciliation: The Work of Ralph Martin and Its Implications for Psychotherapeutic Practice', *Journal of Psychology & Christianity* 14 (1995), pp. 365–73.

Webster, Alexander, 'St Paul's Political Advice to the Haughty Gentile Christians in Rome: an Exegesis of Romans 13:1–7', *St Vladimir's Theological Quarterly* 25 (1981), pp. 259–82.

Webster, John, 'Christology, Imitability and Ethics', *Scottish Journal of Theology* 39 (1986), pp. 309–26.

—*Barth's Ethics of Reconciliation* (Cambridge: CUP, 1995).

—'The Ethics of Reconciliation', in Gunton, Colin (ed.), *The Theology of Reconciliation* (London: T&T Clark/Coninuum, 2003).

Wedderburn, A. J. M., *The Reasons for Romans* (Edinburgh: T&T Clark, 1988).

Wedderburn, A. (ed.), *Paul and Jesus: Collected Essays* (Sheffield: Sheffield Academic, 1989).

Wengst, Klaus, *Pax Romana and the Peace of Jesus Christ* (John Bowden (trans.); London: SCM, 1987).

Wettach, Tania, 'Religion and Reconciliation in Bosnia and Herzegovina', *Religion in Eastern Europe* 28(4) (2008), pp. 1–15.

Willard, M. Aldrich, 'The Objective Nature of Reconciliation', *BS* 118 (1961), pp. 18–21.

Williams, David T., 'Reconciliation: God, Humanity, Society: A Christian Approach', *Theologia Evangelica* 25 (1992), pp. 32–43.

Williams, Stephen, *Revelation and Reconciliation* (Cambridge: CUP, 1995).

Willmer, Haddon, 'Weariness with Politics', *Theology* 78 (1975), pp. 310–18.

—'The Politics of Forgiveness – A New Dynamic', *The Furrow* (April 1979), pp. 207–18.

—'The Sociology of Forgiveness in Relation to Politics' (unpublished papers, November, 1987).

—'The Justification of the Godless: Heinrich Vogel and German Guilt', in Robbins, K. (ed.), *Protestant Evangelicalism* (Oxford: Blackwell, 1990).

—'Transforming Society – or Merely Making it?' (paper presented at the Society for the Study of Theology, Leeds, March, 1995).

—'Jesus Christ the Forgiven: Christology, Atonement and Forgiveness', in McFadyen, Alistair I. and Marcel Sarot (eds), *Forgiveness and Truth* (Edinburgh: T&T Clark, 2001).

—'"Vertical" and "Horizontal" in Paul's Theology of Reconciliation in the Letter to the Romans', *Transformation* 24(3 & 4) (2007), pp. 151–60.

Wilson, Walter T., *Love without Pretence: Romans 12.9–21 and Hellenistic-Jewish Wisdom Literature* (WUNT, 2/46; Tubingen: Mohr Siebeck, 1991).

Wink, Walter, *The Bible in Human Transformation: Toward a New Paradigm for Biblical Study* (Philadelphia, PA: Fortress, 1973).

—*Naming the Powers: The Language of Power in the New Testament* (Philadelphia, PA: Fortress, 1984).

—*Unmasking the Powers: The Invisible Forces That Determine Human Existence* (Philadelphia, PA: Fortress, 1986).

—*Engaging the Powers: Discernment and Resistance in a World of Domination* (Minneapolis: Fortress, 1992).

—*When the Powers Fall: Reconciliation in the Healing of the Nations* (Minneapolis: Fortress, 1998).

Winter, Bruce W., 'The Public Honouring of Christian Benefactors: Romans 13:3–4 and 1 Peter 2:14–15', *JSNT* 34 (1988), pp. 87–103.

—*Seek the Welfare of the City: Christians as Benefactors and Citizens* (Grand Rapids: Eerdmans, 1994).

Witherington III, Ben, *Paul's Narrative Thought World: The Tapestry of Tragedy and Triumph* (Louisville, KY: Westminster/John Knox Press, 1994).

—*The Paul Quest: The Renewed Search for the Jew of Tarsus* (Leicester: IVP, 1998).

—'Contemporary Perspectives on Paul', in Dunn, James (ed.), *Cambridge Companion to St. Paul* (Cambridge: CUP, 2003).

Witherington III, Ben with Darlene Hyatt, *Paul's Letter to the Romans. A Socio-Rhetorical Commentary* (Grand Rapids: Eerdmans, 2004).

Witte, John, 'Introduction: Pluralism, Proselitism, and Nationalism in Eastern Europe', *JES* 24 (1999), pp. 1–6.

Wolff, Christian, *Der zweite Brief des Paulus an die Korinther* (Berlin: Evangelische Verlagsanstalt, 1989).

—'True Apostolic Knowledge of Christ: Exegetical Reflections on 2 Cor. 5.14ff', in Wedderburn, A. J. M. (ed.), *Paul and Jesus: Collected Essays* (*JSNTS*, 37; Sheffield: Sheffield Academic, 1989).

Wright, N. T., 'The Messiah and the People of God: A Study in Pauline Theology with Particular Reference to the Argument of the Epistle to the Romans' (unpublished Doctor of Philosophy dissertation, University of Oxford, Trinity term, 1980).

—'New Testament and the State', *Themelios* 16 (1990), pp. 11–17.

—*The Climax of the Covenant: Christ and the Law in Pauline Theology* (Edinburgh: T&T Clark, 1991).

—*The New Testament and the People of God* (*NTPG*) (London: SPCK, 1992).

—'Putting Paul Together Again: Toward a Synthesis of Pauline Theology', in Bassler, Jouette M. (ed.), *Pauline Theology, Vol. I: Thessalonians, Philippians, Galatians, Philemon* (Minneapolis: Fortress, 1994).

—'Romans and the Theology of Paul', in Hay, David M. and E. Elizabeth Johnson (eds), *Pauline Theology, Vol. III: Romans* (Minneapolis: Fortress, 1995).

—'Paul, Arabia and Elijah (Galatians 1:17),' *JBL* 115(4) (1996), pp. 683–92.

—'New Exodus, New Inheritance: the Narrative Substructure of Romans 3–8', in Soderlund, Sven K. and N. T. Wright (eds), *Romans and the People of God: Essays in Honor of Gordon Fee on the Occasion of his 65th Birthday* (Grand Rapids: Eerdmans, 1999).

—'Paul's Gospel and Caesar's Empire', in Horsley, Richard A. (ed.), *Paul and Politics: Ekklesia, Israel, Imperium, Interpretatio* (Harrisburg, PA: Trinity, 2000).

—'Paul and Caesar: A New Reading of Romans', in Bartholomew, Craig *et al.* (eds), *A Royal Priesthood? The Use of the Bible Ethically and Politically* (Carlisle: Paternoster Press, 2002).

—*The Letter to the Romans: Introduction, Commentary and Reflection*, in Keck, Leander E. *et al.* (eds), *The New Interpreter's Bible, Vol. 10* (Nashville, TN: Abingdon, 2002).

—'God and Caesar: Then and Now', in Percy, Martyn and Stephen Lowe (eds) *The Character of Wisdom* (Festschrift Wesley Carr; Aldershot: Ashgate, 2004), pp. 157–72.

—*Paul: Fresh Perspectives* (London: SPCK, 2005).

Yee, T. L. N., *Jews, Gentiles, and Ethnic Reconciliation: Paul's Jewish Identity and Ephesians* (SNTSMS, 130; Cambridge: CUP, 2005).

Yoder, John Howard, *The Priestly Kingdom: Social Ethics as Gospel* (Notre Dame: University of Notre Dame Press, 1985).

—*For the Nations: Essays Evangelical and Public* (Grand Rapids: Eerdmans, 1997).

Young, Brad H., *Paul the Jewish Theologian: A Pharisee Among Christian, Jews, and Gentiles* (Peabody, PA: Hendrickson, 1997).

Zanker, Paul, 'The Power of Images', in Horsley, Richard A. (ed.), *Paul and Empire: Religion and Power in Roman Imperial Society* (Harrisburg, PA: Trinity, 1997).

Zerbe, Gordon, 'Paul's Ethic of Nonretaliation and Peace', in Swartley, Millard M. (ed.), *The Love of Enemy and Nonretaliation in the New Testament* (Louisville, KY: Westminster/John Knox Press, 1992).

Ziesler, John, *The Meaning of Righteousness in Paul: A Linguistic and Theological Inquiry* (Cambridge: CUP, 1972).

—*Paul's Letter to the Romans* (London: Trinity, 1989).

—*Pauline Christianity* (rev. edn; Oxford: OUP, 1990).

Zizioulas, John, *Being as Communion* (New York: St. Vladimir's Seminary Press, 1985).

Zub, Al (ed.), *Cultura si societate* (Studii privitoare la trecutul romanesc; Bucuresti: Editura Enciclopedica, 1991).

—*Identitate, alteritate, in spatiul cultural romanesc* (Iasi: Editura Universitatii 'Alexandru Ioan Cuza', 1996).

Modern Author Index